# SHELLEY

# LONGMAN CRITICAL READERS

*General Editors:*

RAMAN SELDEN, late Emeritus Professor of English,
Lancaster University, and late Professor of English,
University of Sunderland Polytechnic;

STAN SMITH, Professor of English, University of Dundee

*Published titles:*

K. M. NEWTON, *George Eliot*

MARY EAGLETON, *Feminist Literary Criticism*

GARY WALLER, *Shakespeare's Comedies*

JOHN DRAKAKIS, *Shakespearean Tragedy*

RICHARD WILSON AND RICHARD DUTTON, *New Historicism and Renaissance Drama*

PETER BROOKER, *Modernism/Postmodernism*

PETER WIDDOWSON, *D. H. Lawrence*

RACHEL BOWLBY, *Virginia Woolf*

FRANCIS MULHERN, *Contemporary Marxist Literary Criticism*

ANNABEL PATTERSON, *John Milton*

CYNTHIA CHASE, *Romanticism*

MICHAEL O'NEILL, *Shelley*

# SHELLEY

Edited and Introduced by

MICHAEL O'NEILL

LONGMAN
LONDON AND NEW YORK

**Longman Group UK Limited,**
Longman House, Burnt Mill,
Harlow, Essex CM20 2JE, England
*and Associated Companies throughout the world*

*Published in the United States of America
by Longman Publishing, New York*

First published 1993

ISBN 0 582 08668 X CSD
ISBN 0 582 08667 1 PPR

**British Library Cataloguing-in-Publication Data**

A catalogue record for this book is
available from the British Library

**Library of Congress Cataloging-in-Publication Data**

Shelley / edited and introduced by Michael O'Neill.
     p. cm. – (Longman critical readers)
   Includes bibliographical references and index.
    ISBN 0–582–08668–X. – ISBN 0–582–08667–1 (pbk.)
     1. Shelley, Percy Bysshe, 1792–1822 – Criticism and interpretation.
 I. O'Neill, Michael, 1953–. II. Series.
PR5438.S43 1993
821'.7 – dc20                             92–34202
                                           CIP

Set by 9K in 9/11½ pt Palatino
Produced by Longman Singapore Publishers (Pte) Ltd.
Printed in Singapore

# Contents

# General Editors' Preface

The outlines of contemporary critical theory are now often taught as a standard feature of a degree in literary studies. The development of particular theories has seen a thorough transformation of literary criticism. For example, Marxist and Foucauldian theories have revolutionised Shakespeare studies, and 'deconstruction' has led to a complete reassessment of Romantic poetry. Feminist criticism has left scarcely any period of literature unaffected by its searching critiques. Teachers of literary studies can no longer fall back on a standardised, received, methodology.

Lecturers and teachers are now urgently looking for guidance in a rapidly changing critical environment. They need help in understanding the latest revisions in literary theory, and especially in grasping the practical effects of the new theories in the form of theoretically sensitised new readings. A number of volumes in the series anthologise important essays on particular theories. However, in order to grasp the full implications and possible uses of particular theories it is essential to see them put to work. This series provides substantial volumes of new readings, presented in an accessible form and with a significant amount of editorial guidance.

Each volume includes a substantial introduction which explores the theoretical issues and conflicts embodied in the essays selected and locates areas of disagreement between positions. The pluralism of theories has to be put on the agenda of literary studies. We can no longer pretend that we all tacitly accept the same practices in literary studies. Neither is a *laissez-faire* attitude any longer tenable. Literature departments need to go beyond the mere toleration of theoretical differences: it is not enough merely to agree to differ; they need actually to 'stage' the differences openly. The volumes in this series all attempt to dramatise the differences, not necessarily with a view to resolving them but in order to foreground the choices presented by different theories or to argue for a particular route through the impasses the differences present.

The theory 'revolution' has had real effects. It has loosened the grip of traditional empiricist and romantic assumptions about language and literature. It is not always clear what is being proposed as the new agenda for literary studies, and indeed the very notion of 'literature' is questioned by the post-structuralist strain in theory. However, the uncertainties and obscurities of contemporary theories appear much less worrying when we see what the best critics have been able to do with them in practice. The series aims to disseminate the best of recent criticism and to show that it is possible to re-read the canonical texts of literature in new and challenging ways.

RAMAN SELDEN AND STAN SMITH

The Publishers and fellow Series Editor regret to record that Raman Selden died after a short illness in May 1991 at the age of fifty-three. Ray Selden was a fine scholar and a lovely man. All those he has worked with will remember him with much affection and respect.

# Acknowledgements

I should like to thank Stan Smith and the late Raman Selden, the General Editors of the Longman Critical Readers series, for their assistance and advice. I am grateful to Timothy Clark and Jerrold E. Hogle for sharing with me their knowledge and ideas.

The Editor and Publishers are grateful to the following for permission to reproduce copyright material:

Cornell University Press for an extract from *Dark Interpreter: The Discourse of Romanticism* (by Tilottama Rajan). Copyright © 1980 by Cornell University, and for the essay 'Shelley's *Mont Blanc*: What the Mountain Said' by Frances Ferguson in *Romanticism and Language* ed. Arden Reed. Copyright © 1984 by Cornell University; Harvard University Press for extracts from *Shelley's Major Verse: The Narrative and Dramatic Poetry* by Stuart M. Sperry, Cambridge, Mass. Copyright © 1988 by the President and Fellows of Harvard College; Harvester Wheatsheaf/Barnes & Noble Books for an extract from 'Shelley's Perplexity' by Isobel Armstrong in *Language as Living Form in Nineteenth-Century Poetry*, publ. Harvester Press, Sussex and in USA – Barnes & Noble Books, Totowa, N.J. 1982. Copyright Isobel Armstrong 1982; Leicester University Press for an extract from 'Shelley's Doubles: An Approach to *Julian and Maddalo*' by Kelvin Everest in *Shelley Revalued: Essays from the Gregynog Conference* ed. Kelvin Everest, 1983; The University of Nebraska Press for an extract from *Shelley and His Audiences* by Stephen C. Behrendt. Copyright © 1989 by the University of Nebraska Press; Oxford University Press for an extract from *Embodying Revolution: The Figure of the Poet in Shelley* by Timothy Clark. © Timothy Clark 1989; Oxford University Press Inc. for extracts from *Shelley's Process: Radical Transference and the Development of His Major Works* by Jerrold E. Hogle. Copyright © 1988 by Oxford University Press Inc; Princeton University Press for an extract from *Shelleyan Eros: The Rhetoric of Romantic Love* by William A. Ulmer. Copyright © Princeton University Press, 1990, and for an extract from *The Linguistic Moment: From Wordsworth to Stevens* by J. Hillis Miller. Copyright © Princeton University Press 1985; Routledge for an extract from *Shelley's Style* by William Keach, publ. Methuen, New York & London 1984; Managing Editor for an extract from the article 'Last Clouds: A Reading of "Adonais"' by Peter Sacks in *Studies in Romanticism* **23** (Fall 1984); University of Toronto Press for an extract from *The Poetry of Life: Shelley and Literary Form* by Ronald Tetreault. Copyright 1987 University of Toronto Press.

# 1 Introduction

To write this Introduction in 1992, the bicentenary of Shelley's birth, is to be aware of the resurgence of interest in his poetry over the last thirty years or so. The belated establishment of sound texts – or, on occasions, the clarification of how difficult it is to establish a reliable text for a work by Shelley – is both symptom and cause of this upturn in the poet's reputation. The high regard in which Shelley's poetry is held also reflects its responsiveness to theoretical approaches now in favour. But contemporary literary theory problematises even as it explains or vindicates Shelley's poetry. The editing referred to above has adhered to traditional scholarly norms, yet it has been put to unconventional use by some critics. For instance, in *The Supplement of Reading* (1990) Tilottama Rajan claims that the editorial production of a reading text of *The Triumph of Life* has only ever been achieved by choosing between alternatives left uncancelled in the manuscript, and contends that 'The manuscript . . . encourages us to read the poem as a palimpsest of traces, as the site of its own constant displacement.'[1] Again, attacks on the very notion of a 'canon' call into question the assumption that the poetry's 'greatness' has been established once and for all. It is probable that Shelley's work will continue to be the site of battles over value.

Such is a reasonable surmise, given the history of the poetry's reception. It is a striking fact that the most famous literary critics writing in English during and since Shelley's lifetime – William Hazlitt, Matthew Arnold, T.S. Eliot, and F.R. Leavis – have expressed strong reservations about the success and significance of his poetry. Hazlitt's review of Shelley's *Posthumous Poems* tilts at the poet's utopianism and his style, the latter said to be 'a fever of the soul, thirsting and craving after what it cannot have, indulging in love of power and novelty at the expense of truth and nature'. Hazlitt allows for the poet's right to a certain imaginative autonomy, but seeks, ultimately, to tether the imagination's creations to 'existing materials': 'Poetry, we grant, creates a world of its own; but it creates it out of existing materials.' Shelley transgresses this referential obligation since, for Hazlitt, 'Mr Shelley is the maker of his

1

own poetry – out of nothing.' A staunch liberal, Hazlitt would seem to be a natural ally of the politically radical Shelley, but, in fact, Hazlitt bore the poet a special grudge for bringing radical ideas into disrepute through the extremeness with which he espoused them. Hazlitt blames Shelley for giving 'great encouragement to those who believe in all received absurdities, and are wedded to all existing abuses', and he detects in the poetry a perversely heterodox rejection of 'the probable or the true': 'Epithets are applied, because they do not fit: subjects are chosen, because they are repulsive: the colours of his style, for their gaudy, changeful, startling effect, resemble the display of fire-works in the dark, and, like them, have neither durability, nor keeping, nor discriminate form.'

Subsequent accounts of the poetry can often be seen as taking Hazlitt's remarks as their point of departure, even if they come to different conclusions about the poetry's value. For example, post-structuralist criticism, with its view that meaning and the truth-claims of any thought-system are unstable, relishes the elusiveness which stings Hazlitt into asserting, 'Instead of giving a language to thought, or lending the heart a tongue, he utters dark sayings, and deals in allegories and riddles.'[2] For the critic influenced by Jacques Derrida, Hazlitt's approval of 'giving a language to thought' is an example of 'logocentrism', that tendency discerned by Derrida in Western thinking to seek a centre or ground on which to base meaning. Indeed, much contemporary criticism of Shelley has brought out the degree to which the poet is beforehand with his critics. Rajan argues that *A Defence of Poetry* 'contains the seeds of a deconstructive theory of language' as well as encouraging a reading which 'renews the originality of the text by liberating it from the tyranny of the original intention behind it'.[3] Questions which absorb the modern critic intrigued and often vexed the Romantic poet. What is the relationship between language and thought, author and text, text and reader, poet and society? What is the nature of personal identity? What is the relationship between the aesthetic and the political? What are the ideological implications of the pursuit of desire so frequently narrated by the poems? Moreover, it is wrong to think of 'contemporary literary theory' as springing into being out of nothing; much of the finest contemporary criticism of Shelley still engages in fruitful dialogue with criticism written before the 'theoretical revolution' which has overtaken literary studies in the last few decades. In what follows, therefore, I map briefly the critical response to Shelley in the 'pre-theory' part of the century, before going on to discuss more recent theoretical accounts of the poetry.

## New Criticism, T.S. Eliot, F.R. Leavis

First of all, however, a brief digression on the phrase, 'pre-theory', which
I have just used. In one sense, 'pre-theory' is a myth; as theorists never
tire of asserting, all critical responses betray or are enabled by theoretical
assumptions, unacknowledged or proclaimed. But in another sense, it
suggests that the relation between general notions about literature and
analysis of specific works has altered over the course of the century.
Empsonian 'ambiguity', for example, seems less a theory than a device, a
means of shedding light on the workings of particular poems. *Seven Types
of Ambiguity* (1930) is the work of a critic committed to the view that there
is such a thing as good poetry and that verbal analysis involves the
attempt to reason about effects created by poets using language in subtle
and complex ways. By contrast, the user of contemporary theory is often
dangerously tempted to regard the particular text as illustrating an all-
embracing idea (such as the concept that meanings are ultimately
indeterminate). One criterion I have employed in selecting pieces for the
present volume is that they should apply theory to Shelley's poems in a
flexible and discriminating spirit, and leave the reader with a sense of the
poetry's distinctiveness and richness.

Underpinning much current Shelleyan criticism is the view that the
poet suffered unfairly at the hands of ideologically conservative opinion-
formers in the period between the Great War and circa 1950; any
narrative of contemporary criticism of Shelley must address the slighting
treatment he received then, especially at the hands of T.S. Eliot, F.R.
Leavis, and the so-called New Critics. The New Critics developed a series
of implicit and explicit criteria for reading and evaluating poetry,
including the following: the proper matter for a critic of poetry is 'the
words on the page', somehow isolated from their historical context, their
emotional impact on the reader, and their author's intention; the
language and structure of achieved poems fuse opposing meanings into
unified wholes; coherence and complexity are equally hallmarks of a
successful poem; the meaning and form of a poem are inextricable; and,
therefore, although (or because) a poem orders its language to mean
uniquely what it means, this meaning cannot be paraphrased. Two
things about the criticism of Shelley produced by the New Critics and
their fellow-travellers strike the reader. The first is its disregard for the
range of Shelley's achievement. T.S. Eliot, admittedly, was one of the
early admirers of *The Triumph of Life*, praised for 'a precision of image and
an economy . . . that is new to Shelley'. Yet a note dismisses *The Witch of
Atlas* as 'a trifle', albeit one with 'charm', a judgement that ignores the
poem's sophistication and power. The second is the fact that Shelley's
language, though bearing the brunt of adverse comment, is never read
with the attention to nuance which characterises the best work of the

3

New Critics (and of Eliot and Leavis); rather, the reader is aware of a nitpicking hostility which does nothing for Shelley and little for the critics themselves. A sense of wasted opportunity hangs about the affair; Shelley's verbal art could have lent itself to the methods of these critics more easily than they allowed themselves to see.

But critics of the order of Eliot, Allen Tate, and Leavis inevitably raised significant points in writing about Shelley, even if their evaluative conclusions were narrow-minded. In *The Use of Poetry and the Use of Criticism* (1933), Eliot addresses an issue which remains of great importance: that is, is it possible to separate a poet's poetry from his beliefs? Eliot feels that it is not possible. Since he dislikes Shelley's ideas (which he does not trouble to define) he concludes that it is impossible for him to enjoy the poetry; the bad ideas infect the language, as is shown by 'the catchwords of creeds outworn, tyrants and priests, which Shelley employed with such reiteration'.[4] It is self-evident to Eliot that the use of such catchwords made for indifferent writing. Even though there have been excellent studies of the effects achieved by the use of recurrent words and images, Shelley's later champions have tended to bypass such criticism; the tendency has been less to pause over local effects in an evaluative spirit than to focus on larger contexts informing and led on to by particular textual moments.

Two demolition-jobs on Shelley's poetry were supplied by Allen Tate (in *Reason in Madness*, 1941) and F.R. Leavis (in *Revaluation*, 1936). Tate focused on the late lyric, 'When the lamp is shattered'; the nature of his criticisms can be gauged by looking at his account of the final stanza. Here Tate objects to the way the opening line supplies us with 'an abstraction that will relieve us of the trouble of examining the particular instances'.[5] Tate does not read the poem with care, but his muddling attempts to define muddle bear witness to a sense, shared by Shelley's admirers and detractors alike, that the poet's use of figurative language is idiosyncratically mobile. Frederick A. Pottle, whose essay 'The Case of Shelley' (1960) seeks to defend Shelley against the New Critical attack, points out that Tate's sense that there is 'confusion' in the final stanza of 'When the lamp was shattered' derives from an implicit rule 'that there shall never be any crossing-over of tenor into vehicle'; he goes on to concede that 'Shelley constantly flashes back and forth between tenor and vehicle', but says that 'such practice is not carelessness but a brilliant extension of poetic possibilities'.[6] (Pottle is making use of the distinction proposed by I.A. Richards between the 'tenor' of a metaphor, that is, the subject to which the metaphor is applied, and the 'vehicle' of a metaphor, that is, the figurative expression being applied.) Foreshadowed here is the post-structuralist's obsession with instability, though for Pottle Shelley's methods make possible a more intense poetic experience of meaning.

F.R. Leavis consigned Shelley to the B-team of literary history, arguing that the poetry's intensity was a cheap thrill, the product of the poet's 'surrendering to a kind of hypnotic rote of favourite images, associations, and words'. Leavis's case against Shelley grows out of his dislike of the affective workings of the poetry. This should not be confused with *a priori* anti-Romanticism. Wordsworth, on Leavis's account, 'seems always to be presenting an object (wherever this may belong) and the emotion seems to derive from what is being presented'. By contrast, 'Shelley . . . offers the emotion in itself, unattached, in the void.' He does this 'at his best and worst', but the hint of concession in 'best' is rhetorical. Shelley's procedures, for Leavis, are, for the most part, reprehensible. One uses the word advisedly since Leavis's assault on Shelley prides itself on involving 'moral judgements'; so the poet's fondness for certain words, such as 'corpse' and 'phantom', is illustrative of 'viciousness and corruption'. The whole performance still has power to provoke thought and simply to provoke. Undoubtedly Leavis is made queasy by the utopian aspirations of Shelley's poetry; the author of *Prometheus Unbound* may be 'unmistakably a distinguished poet', yet 'the elusive imagery, the high-pitched emotions, the tone and movement, the ardours, ecstasies, and despairs, are too much the same all through'. This has the unjust brilliance of a brutal caricature. For Leavis, Shelley's language delivers less than it seems to offer and fails to repay the attention its elusiveness demands, even as the rhythmic movement of the writing seeks to take our minds off 'any inconvenient degree of realization'. Leavis's account of Shelley's language is one which, as description, many of Shelley's post-structuralist admirers might, with some modification, be happy to share; where they differ is in not seeing Shelley's 'confused generations and perspectives'[7] as blameworthy.

## After New Criticism: Bloom, Wasserman, and others

Prior to discussing post-structuralist and other recent theoretical approaches to the poetry, I shall explore the work of a number of critics who sought to defend and clarify the nature and value of Shelley's writing. Drawing on Martin Buber's distinction between two primary words, 'I–Thou' and 'I–It', the former establishing an imaginative world of relation between human beings and reality, the latter evoking a world of experience and separation, and 'looting the work of the Frankforts [on mythic imagery] for [his] own purposes', Harold Bloom in *Shelley's Mythmaking* (1959) treats Shelley as a 'mythopoeic [mythmaking] poet'.[8] Bloom valuably insists on the visionary drama enacted in Shelley's poetry, and though he has been criticised for an over-dogmatic

5

application of Buber's ideas,[9] he answers New Critical objections to Shelley with vigour and force. Bloom has no time for the New Critical shibboleth that images should always be apprehensible by the senses; hence his analysis of the 'Life of Life' lyric in *Prometheus Unbound* demonstrates that the lines are not intent on 'sending [the reader] to the sketching board'. In his fine chapter on *The Witch of Atlas*, which he describes as 'the supreme example of mythmaking poetry in English', Bloom tackles the crucial issue of 'reality'. Whereas Leavis and others had alleged that Shelley evades the 'real', Bloom retorts that in Shelley's poetry the 'quest toward confrontation seeks a relationship at the cost of commonplace observation', and that the crucial question is '"whose reality?" and the answer is forever disputable'. At the same time, Bloom cannily points out that, even judged by central New Critical premises, Shelley comes off well; his poetry is often 'built on ironic foundations that can withstand contemporary criticism'. Moreover, Bloom appeals to the quintessentially New Critical notion of the 'achieved' poem. The presence invoked by Shelley in 'Ode to the West Wind' has a 'reality' which is 'in the poem' and 'achieved there'; therefore 'no faith need be asked of the most sceptical reader, if he will but read and not preconceive'. *Shelley's Mythmaking* goes some way towards fulfilling hints dropped in essays by Yeats as to how Shelley might be read; so Bloom declares that 'Yeats rightly characterized Shelley's morning star as being the "star of infinite desire"'.[10] Shelley emerges as a poet of infinite and necessarily defeated desire. Bloom's influential account sets up an implicit canon running from 'the 1816 Hymns' to *The Triumph of Life*, but missing out more discursive and politically explicit poems such as *Queen Mab*, *The Revolt of Islam*, *Peter Bell the Third*, and *Hellas*. His book depicts Shelley's poetry as artistically shaped and emotionally passionate, and reads the poems as something different from the versifying of other people's ideas (principally those of Plato); instead, disregarding contexts, whether biographical or political, Bloom focuses on the poetry with a humanist energy that makes his readings more than 'formalist' or 'aesthetic', though formal and aesthetic issues are never downgraded.

For Bloom, Shelley is a poet, not a philosopher. For Earl Wasserman, he is a poet who cannot but philosophise. Wasserman discusses three of Shelley's poems (*Mont Blanc*, *The Sensitive Plant* and *Adonais*) in *The Subtler Language* (1959); his answer to the 'Shelley Question' provoked by New Critics is to argue that the New Critics idly blame Shelley's poems for not being what the poems never attempt to be: that is, poems that shape themselves round a 'structure of images'.[11] Rather, the images are controlled by a larger structure of ideas. As with many subsequent accounts of the poet, Wasserman's book-length study, *Shelley: A Critical Reading* (1971), builds on the case made by C.E. Pulos in *The Deep Truth*

(1954) for viewing Shelley as a sceptical idealist. Pulos defines the poet's kind of romantic transcendentalism with precision: Shelley's thought 'exhibits the sincere idealism of the strict transcendentalist, but not his dogmatism; it possesses the sceptical awareness of the ironic transcendentalist, but not his deliberate irony'. The key, for Pulos, to Shelley's philosophical position is its 'fundamental relation' to the 'sceptical tradition, whence it derives not only its scepticism but also its "sceptical solution to doubt"'.[12] Pulos stresses Shelley's debt to William Drummond's *Academical Questions*, contending that the poet embraced a version of Drummond's 'intellectual system'. The 'intellectual system', or 'intellectual philosophy' as Shelley also calls it in the same essay, *On Life*, rejects materialism, and denies the distinction between 'ideas' and 'external objects'. It leads Shelley to doubt 'the existence of distinct individual minds similar to that which is employed in now questioning its own nature'; the 'intellectual philosophy', writes Shelley, situates us 'on that verge where words abandon us, and what wonder if we grow dizzy to look down the dark abyss of – how little we know'.[13]

That 'dark abyss' is one into which post-structuralist critics have been staring for a while now, and G. Kim Blank is right to claim that 'Pulos and Wasserman have in a way "prepared" Shelley for critical theory by having firmly placed him in the tradition of radical scepticism.'[14] *Shelley: A Critical Reading* is double in its perspectives and legacy. The book reads Shelley's poems in the light of the 'mental structure . . . formulated by the total body of his available works'. Yet Wasserman emphasises the sceptical basis of Shelley's thought, a scepticism that gives rise to faith, hope and desire; the 'ultimate function of Shelley's empirical skepticism . . . is to clear the ground for a probabilism based on imagination and belief'. For Wasserman, therefore, poem after poem is the scene of struggle between opposing yet related impulses: scepticism and faith, optimism and pessimism, the 'desire to reconcile [Shelley's] dedication to the possibility of a utopian world with his faith in immortality'. Because of the critic's own faith in the coherence of Shelley's 'poetic mind', these struggles are viewed as under the poet's governing control. 'Progressive revelation', the dynamic ascribed to poems such as *Epipsychidion* and *Adonais*, also defines the interpretative strategy of Wasserman's chapters. Wasserman's Shelley has an 'intellectual system' which the details of the poetry bear out; this 'system'cannot be aligned with that of any other philosopher, and its 'anchor of assurance' is 'the axiom that we can think of nothing we have not perceived and that therefore all thoughts must be perceptions, not fictions'. Here Shelley's mentalism is granted an immunity from doubt, but it is to Wasserman's credit that his readings of individual poems are alive to the presence in Shelley's writing of 'skeptical incertitude'. So in *Mont Blanc*, 'the apprehension of the eternal Power came about through an "imagining", a dream, or trance, that . . .

may be only illusory'. 'Imagining' in this sentence strays close to the 'fictions' outlawed earlier, and this potential contradiction in Wasserman's argument is at once its most valuable and vulnerable aspect. Wasserman writes out of a New Critical fascination with coherence and a phenomenologist's interest in the 'mental structure' or consciousness feeding into and emerging from textual structures; and yet it is arguable that his most critically productive bequest is his alertness to Shelley's sense (as embodied in *Julian and Maddalo*) that 'the human self is divided and contradictory, infinite but finite, free but limited'.[15]

Wasserman's influence on subsequent criticism of Shelley has been extensive, and his readings have almost canonical status; when critics wish to break new ground, they have to challenge the cogency of Wasserman's account of, say, the sceptical dialogue established between the perspectives of the Narrator and Visionary in *Alastor*. Occasionally the emphasis on Shelley as sceptic has grown formulaic. But in *Destroyer and Preserver* (1979), Lloyd Abbey looks ahead to deconstructive strategies in a series of analyses that present the poet's career as 'a demonstrative exercise in self-destruction or, at least, self-repudiation'.[16] What might be called the pre-deconstructive wave of Shelleyan criticism is marked by subtlety, good scholarship and good sense. One thinks of Stuart Curran's *Shelley's Annus Mirabilis* (1975), which stresses both the 'wholeness of Shelley's vision' and the fact that poems such as *The Mask of Anarchy* are not 'organic and self-contained, but contextual'.[17] Or of Kenneth Cameron's *Shelley: The Golden Years* (1974), which demonstrates that Shelley's poetry was concerned with political events and social movements of his time. Cameron edited the first four volumes of *Shelley and his Circle: 1773–1822*, a series which, along with diplomatic transcripts of manuscripts in the possession of the Pforzheimer Library, includes essays and commentaries that supply information about and meditate on the circumstances surrounding the published manuscripts. The push of the venture is anti-New Critical in its interest in context. Volumes five to eight were edited by Donald Reiman, and Reiman's essay, 'Keats and Shelley: Personal and Literary Relations' (V, pp. 399–427), typifies the series at its best. Reiman's is a mode of criticism which could be called traditional, yet whose grounding in historical detail means that critics who ignore it do so at their peril. Aware of Shelley's scepticism, he underlines, too, the poet's belief in 'the life of the imagination' as sowing 'the seeds of the values that could continually regenerate individual men and, at fortunate moments in human history, renovate entire societies'.[18] This declares a trust in Romantic literature eloquently articulated by M.H. Abrams in *Natural Supernaturalism* (1971). Abrams's book – much-challenged in recent years – focuses on attempts made by the Romantics to construct in their work secular versions of established theological plots. In *Prometheus Unbound*, for example, Shelley 'fused the pagan myth of a lost Golden Age with the Biblical design of a fall, redemption, and millennial return to a lost felicity'.[19] Abrams is alive to the work's own awareness of threats to the harmony it imagines, but his emphasis falls on the poem's imaginings of integration. *Natural Supernaturalism*, like Wasserman's *Shelley: A Critical Reading* which was published in the same year, marks the highpoint of critical faith in the possibility of poems imagining and attaining visions of unity; the tide has since been flowing in an opposite direction.

## Structuralism, deconstruction, post-structuralism

This section is divided into three sub-sections. The first sub-section concentrates on the way structuralist, deconstructive and post-structuralist (including Lacanian and feminist) approaches have shaped criticism of Shelley's texts; the next sub-section concentrates on their implications for the reader; and the third sub-section concentrates on critics who recognise the influence of, yet, in varying degrees, differentiate their work from, these approaches. 'Concentrates' is the operative word since there is considerable overlap between the three sub-sections, which, for the most part, highlight different emphases rather than radical oppositions. There is also considerable interplay between the approaches described in this section and the following section, which looks at political and contextual criticism of Shelley.

### i. The text

Shelley's poetry has proved fertile territory for critics influenced by deconstruction. This critical movement builds on yet swerves from Saussurean structuralism. The structuralist locates meaning in a code-governed system of signs, each of which signifies only in so far as it is different from other signs in the same signifying system. Aspects of structuralist thinking are evident in Isobel Armstrong's chapter on *Prometheus Unbound* (excerpted in this volume) in her *Language as Living Form in Nineteenth-Century Poetry* (1982). Armstrong is interested in how the language of Shelley's idealist poetry at once generates and abolishes dualisms, in its 'systematic dematerialising of the sensory into the *structure*, not the "feel", of immediate sensory experience'. In her awareness of how Shelley's text 'raises by its form the question of relationship itself', Armstrong instigates a *rapprochement*, which is always threatening to turn into a quarrel, between idealist and structuralist modes of thinking; in her awareness that Shelley strives to keep open the possibility of relationship between mind and language by means of images of reflection that can be endlessly repeated and recombined, she approaches a post-structuralist position: the Shelley of her essay writes out of the 'want' Demogorgon describes, 'But a voice / Is wanting, the deep truth is imageless' (II, iv, 115–16). Language occupies the site of some original 'want', some gap between words and meaning, which it forever seeks to complete. Yet it is in the act of acknowledging incompleteness that the possibility of some utopian 'deep truth' can be kept alive, validated by the fact that any approach to it must be means of 'the infinitely propagative power of "the human mind's imaginings"'.[20]

Here Armstrong respects the otherness of nineteenth-century idealist poetry, allowing for the way the poetry's concerns with freedom and relationship feed into, even as they are shaped by, historical forces. But at the same time she comes close to that aspect of deconstruction which celebrates, however guardedly, the play of indeterminacy in poetry. Deconstruction is a troubling and frequently troubled approach to literature, which spins with self-cancelling yet often productive ingenuity round a number of positions. Its pivot is the view that the structuralist model of a system of internal differences seeks an illicit stability; for Derrida, the structuralist's differences cannot resolve into determinate meaning since they are also forms of 'différance'; not only do they differ from each other, but they endlessly defer the possibility of meaning. There is nothing, according to Derrida, outside the text, no transcendental signified which will stabilise the play of signifiers. Like all types of sceptical thought, Derridean deconstruction is vulnerable to the charge that it exempts itself from the scepticism on which it is grounded. Above all, its attack on determinate meaning ignores the fact that it avails itself of the possibility (illusion?) of determinate meaning to communicate its attack. The usual retort is that deconstruction does not seek to replace the logocentric, but rather to expose the strategies on which it relies. Certainly the Shelley who in *On Life* questions the nature of the subject whilst continuing to use the word 'I', who in *A Defence of Poetry* both celebrates and betrays doubt about language's adequacy to thought, who in a note to *Hellas* couples confession of ignorance about the 'origin of evil' with conscious attachment to 'ideas which exalt and ennoble humanity'[21] has something in common with the deconstructive enterprise. But Shelley still clings to logocentric assumptions, such as the notion of authorial agency; if he employs deconstructive strategies to 'free us from "the misuse of words and signs"',[22] he does so in order to bring before us the possibility of human freedom.

Paul de Man's version of deconstruction is harrowed by the supposed impossibility of making sense or interpreting correctly. It is less a method than an attack on interpretative method. De Man regards Romanticism as primarily a rhetoric, a form of persuasion through tropes and figures that, in the cases of Rousseau and Wordsworth especially, often knows about its own 'rhetoricality'; where, for de Man, commentators have gone wrong is in uncritically believing that Romantic poetry enacts the achieved unity or presence it often seems to talk about. The symbol, which seeks to present itself as a linguistic embodiment of such unity, is toppled off its critical pedestal by de Man in favour of allegory, a mode which concedes the perpetual gap between word and meaning. De Man's 'Shelley Disfigured' appears in *Deconstruction and Criticism* (1979), a volume which was originally conceived as focusing entirely on Shelley. Geoffrey Hartman implies in the volume's Preface that deconstruction does not deny 'the importance – or *force* – of literature'; rather it refuses to identify this force with 'any concept of embodied meaning'.[23] 'Shelley Disfigured' is concerned with *The Triumph of Life*, a poem which, interrogating as it does the possibility of 'embodied meaning', is peculiarly suited to de Man's approach. The repeated forgettings and erasures, both at a thematic and figurative level, which occur in the poem are described by de Man as 'disfiguration'. The word denotes the way the poem continually covers the tracks of its attempts to 'impose meaning'; such 'positing power' is, in de Man's opinion, 'entirely arbitrary . . . and entirely inexorable'.[24] Language posits because it emerges out of the gap between consciousness and reality; it can never 'give a foundation to what it posits except as an intent of consciousness'.[25] The quest for meaning is, thus, inevitable and doomed.

De Man sees *The Triumph of Life* as an exemplary text in that it knows as much about itself and its procedures as even the most rigorous deconstructionist will ever know; so the poem is able in the passage describing the 'shape all light' (l. 352) to thematise the seductive allure of an 'illusion of meaning'. But he does not exempt such self-knowledge or 'negative knowledge' from his scrutiny; for him, consciousness of inauthenticity is not the same thing as being authentic. The poem may expose the arbitrariness of language's positing power, but it engages in such positing all the same. It may, in turn, warn readers of the inescapable drive to find meaning; but readers are the product not the origin of this drive, in de Man's view, and critics will continue to participate in the 'historical and aesthetic system of recuperation that repeats itself regardless of the exposure of its fallacy'.[26] De Man says many sharp things about the self-reflexive aspects of the poetry's figurative procedures, yet his larger arguments about textuality provoke resistance. As Stuart Curran notes wittily, 'the abyss does tend to yawn'[27]; and while de Man would be the first to concede that critical insight involves blindness, his own essay focuses myopically on the way the poem's rhetorical workings are thematised in and by the language; one begins to feel that because de Man knows in advance that it is the fate of texts to discover and evade knowledge of their own textuality, he inevitably finds the same double-bind at work in *The Triumph*. What one misses, for all the essay's originality, is any sense that a poem uses language to explore what Shelley calls 'the before unapprehended relations of things' (*PP*, p. 482). This is another way of agreeing with Colin Falck's spirited claim that 'the opposition of "referentiality" and "rhetoricality" is wholly illusory'[28] since the gap between the linguistic and extra-linguistic enables as much as it frustrates meaning. There is an intimidatory terrorism about de Man's essay, meant to warn the unwary reader of the dangers of 'the seductive grace of figuration'. And yet, paradoxically, de Man's insistence that *The Triumph of Life* 'warns us that nothing . . . ever happens in relation . . . to anything'[29] not only seeks to deal a body blow to historicising criticism but also betrays a strong, if repressed, response to the poem's aesthetic seductiveness.[30]

If, in de Man's words, the 'rigor exhibited by Shelley' in *The Triumph of Life* is 'exemplary',[31] does this mean that authorial control over a text has been readmitted into the deconstructive scheme of things? From structuralism onwards, the humanist notion of the author as the controller of textual meaning has been under attack. The self is not the source of meaning but a construct shaped by larger cultural discourses. However, structuralism resurrects the self in the form of the decentred subject who does not make meaning but through whom meaning moves; similarly, some deconstructive critics feel able to attribute to a text an at least partial awareness of its own activities.

The reintroduction of, or reluctance wholly to abandon, the idea that the poet is a subject involved in the drama of the text's pursuit of significance is evident in Tilottama Rajan's chapter on Shelley (excerpted here) in her book, *Dark Interpreter* (1980). Rajan takes a more sympathetic view of Romantic idealism than de Man allows himself. For one thing, poems like Keats's *The Fall of Hyperion* or Shelley's *The Triumph of Life* are engaged in 'questioning the aesthetic assumptions with which they begin', thereby releasing hitherto repressed or sublimated 'areas of experience'; for another, the practice of the Romantics 'raises legitimate questions about the productive role of illusion in life'.[32] Rajan begins with the end of Shelley's career, since, for her, *The Triumph of Life* questions his earlier idealism, subsuming and overcoming tensions evident in earlier poems such as *Alastor*. *Alastor* moves in 'contradictory directions' (p. 255), on Rajan's reading, but its 'troubled ambivalence' (p. 255) should not, *pace* Earl Wasserman, be read as ironic self-awareness, and whether 'a final deconstruction of [the poem's] idealism is intended by Shelley . . . is extraordinarily difficult to say' (p. 260). In *The Triumph of Life* – so Rajan implies – such deconstruction is intended, yet Shelley's encounter with Rousseau confronts the poet's previous, Promethean idealism in such a way that he will not succumb to 'the inevitable disillusion that follows the failure to attain the ideal' (p. 249). The poem's 'infernal vision' is not its 'final image' so much as 'something with which the dreamer must come to terms' (p. 250). The poem leaves us with an image of life as Janus-faced, yet this process of permanent deconstruction is, Rajan claims, 'part of the shape of truth' (p. 251). The more knowingly deconstructive the text, the more it is able, in Rajan's view, to resist the nihilism inextricable from deconstruction.

For J. Hillis Miller, the deconstructive critic, thinking to deconstruct, discovers in the act of reading that the text has already exposed to itself its illusions of unitary meaning. Miller subscribes to the de Manian view that interpretative error is necessarily involved in the construction of meaning. And like de Man he ascribes to poems an uncanny awareness of this necessity. Yet this awareness, so sombrely noticed by de Man, gives rise in Miller's prose to barely concealed excitement, the excitement of the deconstructive chase when the critic discovers that what he sought to outwit had outwitted him. The quarry turns on the hunter. 'Deconstruction', writes Miller, 'is not a dismantling of the structure of a text but a demonstration that it has already dismantled itself.'[33]

Miller's piece on *The Triumph of Life* (again) in *The Linguistic Moment* (1985), from which an extract is printed in this volume, wrestles with the issue of how much the text knows about itself. The linguistic moment is defined by Miller in his contribution to *Deconstruction and Criticism* as 'the moment in a work of literature when its own medium is put into question'.[34] The passive construction, there, dodges the issue of whether the putting into question is effected by a questioner. Such a putting into question occurs at the end of *Epipsychidion*; the longing for unity tries, according to Miller, to efface its status as language but 'Words are always there as remnant, "chains of lead" which forbid the flight to fiery union they invoke.' In this piece, Miller enquires, 'Who, however, is "Shelley"?', and emerges with the deconstructive conundrum that the word 'must name something without identifiable bounds'[35] since 'Shelley' is at once the host to and parasitic upon other writers, a relationship mirroring that of meaning and indeterminacy, text and interpretation.

In the extract printed here, Miller seems closer to claiming for *The Triumph of Life* some mastery over its self-undoings. For instance, following Harold Bloom's lead in a number of books (see Further Reading), Miller argues that Shelley's 'misreadings' of Wordsworth and Rousseau 'may be the distortion of a more genuine insight' (p. 223). However, Bloom's theory – that all strong poets develop their poetic identities by 'misreading' their predecessors – recasts Freud to stress a will to meaning that shapes expression; Miller's approach is resolutely textual. He concentrates on the poem's famously tricky images of light, which he sees as divorced from any 'central and abiding light source' (p. 225); instead, the poem offers 'the endless turning and substitution of one shape of light for another' (p. 225). Light can never be seen for what it is, but must be given a shape or assume a figure, and the poem both traces and enacts this process of substitution and re-presentation. The 'shape all light' represents the gap between 'pure seeing or pure theory, and that instant interpretation of the light that names it, gives it a shape, makes it a sign, a figure, or an allegorical person' (p. 231). Miller laments yet relishes the impulse to allegorise, part of the inescapable, never-concluded process of substitution which gives interpretation its chance yet ensures its necessary failure. His sense of the critic's duty or compulsion to re-enact and, therefore, distort the events of the poem finds affecting expression in the last words of the piece; Miller anticipates the concern of my next sub-section by turning on his own performance as a reader:

> As a reader of 'The Triumph of Life' I am the next in a chain of repetitions without beginning or end. I find myself again enfolded in a fold, asleep under a caverned mountain beside a brook, watching a sequence of shapes all light, projecting in my turn figures over those shapes, figures that fade even as they are traced, to be replaced by others, in an unending production of signs over signs. . . .
>
> (p. 239)

Here the critical essay is close, in its representation of the pathos of interpretation, to a prose poem, and reminds us that deconstruction has often denied, or put in question, the priority of the literary work over the critical commentary. If Miller's prose has sufficient power to evoke a version of the poem, it is a version which mutes the poem's historical and political implications. The rephrasing of the poem's 'Signs of thought's empire over thought' (l. 211) as 'signs over signs' is revealing. Shelley, or the Rousseau of the poem, is diagnosing the capacity of human 'thought' to set up symbols ('Signs') of authority over itself, engendering restrictive ideologies; Miller's reading is not incompatible with this idea, but it centres itself more on the process of erasure than on relatively stabilised moments of clarity and insight.

For all the excited tone mentioned above, Miller, like de Man, inclines towards a sorrowful, even tragic view of poetry, condemned forever to reflect upon its own inadequacy. Post-structuralism, however, is also the begetter of a ludic and would-be mischievous criticism – hence the presence in much recent critical writing of turgid word-play and punning, supposedly demonstrating the instability of the sign. Frances Ferguson's essay on *Mont Blanc* is more adroitly written than many post-structuralist analyses, and brings out how the poem refuses to settle for demystified 'irony' as 'it exhibits its own repeated failures to let Mont Blanc be merely a blank, merely a mass of stone' (p. 45). Ferguson plays a post-Derridean variation on Harold Bloom's argument in *Shelley's Mythmaking* that Shelley is pre-eminently a poet of relationship. It is as if post-structuralist suspicion of the extra-linguistic had sensitised her to the poem's almost inevitable pursuit of dialogue; 'difference', even 'différance', is bound up with relationship, and Ferguson finds in the poetry's language 'an elaborate schema of reciprocity' (p. 47). The poem is, for Ferguson, less the showpiece for Shelleyan metaphysics which Wasserman's reading makes of it than a revelation of 'the inevitability of any human's seeing things in terms of relationship' (p. 48). It becomes a kind of love poem, in which Shelley converts Burkean sublimity to his own ends; yet Ferguson does not reinstate human consciousness as the source of meaning so much as suggest that the poem's strategy is to attempt a reinstatement of this kind.

Post-structuralist readings of Shelley also include criticism influenced by the psychoanalytic revisionism of Jacques Lacan. Lacan revises Freud in post-structuralist terms; the self is a fictive unity constituted out of the discovery of lack, which creates desire, the wish to unite with something beyond the self which is perceived as completing the self. Such strategies are doomed only to exacerbate the condition they seek to heal. A tell-tale symptom of Lacan's influence is the use of the word 'specular' which alludes to the process of fictive unity achieved by seeing the self mirrored in something beyond itself. For Lacan the unconscious is structured like a language, and for the Lacanian texts can be read as though they were psyches, frequently engaged in repression. Peter Sacks's essay on *Adonais* (included in this volume) draws on Freud to explain the text's 'work of mourning' (p. 177), its attempt to accept 'Death's castrative power' (p. 181), and the operations of its 'narcissism' by which Shelley's ego splits into two, the 'weak' half identifying with Keats the victim, the 'strong' half projecting itself into the Adonais of the last third of the poem. Sacks brings in Lacan to suggest that Shelley's identification with Adonais is, at best, specular, a fantasy of wholeness, a 'coherent but fictional image of an idealized self' (p. 189). For Lacan, as for Derrida, there is no escape from the chain of discourse through which desire seeks to articulate itself; *Adonais*, however, behaves as if it wished to leave behind the mediations of language, the poet refusing to accept that the 'consolatory image' of Adonais 'exists only by virtue of his own material figurations' (p. 195).

The feminist implications of Lacanian thought – principally that it deconstructs the workings of (male) desire including the identification of woman with the Other – have been applied to Shelley's poems by a number of critics, most interestingly by William A. Ulmer in *Shelleyan Eros* (1990) and Jerrold E. Hogle in *Shelley's Process* (1988). Ulmer and Hogle come to different conclusions, however, Ulmer seeing Shelleyan eros as implicated in patriarchal structures, Hogle hearing in Shelley a warning against objectifying others. (See below for further discussion of these two critics.) Stuart M. Sperry also shows the influence of feminist analysis of gendered modes of perception in his account of, say, *The Revolt of Islam* in *Shelley's Major Verse* (1988; see below), ascribing to the Shelley of this poem an awareness of aggressiveness as a product of socially conditioned masculinity. Certainly the highly eroticised nature of Shelleyan desire, whether personal or political, can be expected to receive further exploration from critics influenced by feminism. The uncomplicated view, put forward by Nathaniel Brown (see Further Reading), that Shelley was a fully paid-up feminist is likely to fall under more intense scrutiny in years to come, as critics explore, in the light of feminist thought, contradictions, tensions and insights evidenced by the poetry.

Barbara Charlesworth Gelpi's *Shelley's Goddess* (1992) promises to be an important feminist study in the light of her essay 'The Nursery Cave: Shelley and the Maternal' (printed in *The New Shelley*, ed. G. Kim Blank, 1991). The essay mixes contextual study of the ideology of motherhood in Shelley's time with Julia Kristeva's notion of the 'semiotic'. Kristeva opposes the 'semiotic' (located in a pre-Oedipal play of impulses directed towards the mother) to the 'symbolic', the rational but repressive systems that the semiotic gives way to. Shelley, in seeking in *Prometheus Unbound* to overthrow tyranny, identifies it with the symbolic order. Gelpi analyses the syntax and language of passages from Act II to suggest Shelley's inclination towards the semiotic; his words and rhythms disrupt the rational, evoking a state where distinctions blur and the possibility of a new humanity emerges.

## *ii. The reader*

*Prometheus Unbound* has also been an important text for critics attentive, in the light of reader-response criticism (which holds that meaning is actualised by a reader), to the staging by Shelley's poems of scenes of reading. In *The Supplement of Reading*, for instance, Tilottama Rajan evolves a complex argument about *Prometheus Unbound*. She sees the lyrical drama as 'a consciously metafictional text' that dramatises its own desire to communicate an idealistic vision. Rajan elucidates the dialogue between Asia and Panthea (in II, i) as showing Shelley's sense of the importance of the reader who 'is given the responsibility of recovering and in some sense co-creating [the play's] vision'. The reader's involvement in interpretation ('hermeneutics') may, according to Rajan, either be deconstructed by the text's own deconstructive tendencies (tendencies illustrated in the dialogue between Asia and Demogorgon in II, iv.) or give rise to 'a range of reconstructive options from sympathetic understanding to demythologization'.[36]

In a much-quoted passage, Derrida refers to 'Nietzschean *affirmation*

. . . the affirmation of a world of signs without fault, without truth, and without origin which is offered to an active interpretation'.[37] Such 'affirmation' connects with Roland Barthes's notion that the death of the author is the birth of the reader. In the present volume it can be seen at work in Ronald Tetreault's discussion of 'Ode to the West Wind'. Tetreault views poetry, in the wake of deconstruction, as a game, a form of play, which, like other forms of play, needs conventions and rules if it is to be worth playing. Tetreault draws on Wittgenstein as much as Derrida for his sense of language as a game, an intellectual debt which makes possible some grounding of the degree of textual play. For Wittgenstein the language game makes meaning possible; for Derrida the game is itself open to deconstruction.[38] Tetreault emphasises Shelley's play with generic conventions, and sees him as providing in the 'Ode to the West Wind' 'a knowledge that results from the special language game that poets and readers agree to play'. The poem does not unambiguously engage in 'self-expression'; rather, it represents a subjectivity whose status is uncertain, 'simply "there", located in the play of signifiers' (p. 141). In the 'Ode', Shelley the sceptic suspends his disbelief in the parallel between political and natural cycles, 'and invites his audience to share in this act of poetic faith' (p. 142). Much critical theory is concerned to delimit aesthetic freedom; Tetreault, by contrast, uses deconstruction to deconstruct the Marxist assurance that art is the product of ideology. Instead, he gives a positive inflection to Louis Althusser's notion that ideology is not false consciousness but is part of the air we breathe, necessary to social existence; poetry can help to create 'better' rather than 'worse' climates of ideology because a poem gives rise to 'the community of the reading process' (p. 142), a process which allows readers to explore values imaginatively.

Tetreault cites Mikhail Bakhtin's notion of the 'dialogic' in support of his argument that the meanings of Shelley's finest, most liberating poems are negotiated between text and reader. Bakhtin contended that discourses always contain within themselves the potential for dialogue with other discourses, though this potential can be monologically repressed, and as a model for the reading experience dialogism has been appropriated freely. Shelleyan idealism is based on 'love', or that 'going out of our own nature' (*PP*, p. 487) described in *A Defence of Poetry*, and ought, therefore, to respect the reader's otherness. That is the idea, but the poetry's effect, according to William A. Ulmer in *Shelleyan Eros* (1990), is not so much dialogic as authoritarian. Ulmer mixes a variety of critical methods in his book, but they compose a relentless demystifying of Shelley's idealistic poetry. Shelley's idealism is expressed through rhetorical means that involuntarily concede the inevitable gap between self and other which the poetry seeks to elide; Ulmer argues that Shelley's favoured means for closing this gap is metaphor, used dubiously to establish identity at the cost of difference. The rhetoric of Shelleyan eros is, in part, deconstructed by Lacanian concepts: desire is unfulfillable lack and unity with the not-self is specular fantasy. Ulmer is severe on Shelley's 'metaphorical imperialism',[39] and opposes to it the emancipatory, non-hierarchical emphasis on difference which Jerrold Hogle, in fact, claims for the poetry (see below). Yet in his chapter on *The Cenci* (excerpted in the present volume) Ulmer brings together reception theory, deconstruction and feminism, ascribing to the text a pessimistic awareness of the effects of 'mimetic desire', a term derived from René Girard (via Hogle), who uses it to refer to the process by which a subject desires the desire of another (the Other); the potential results are rivalry, objectification, social conflict and hierarchy. In *The Cenci* the Count replicates in his daughter 'his willingness to murder' (p. 111), and history becomes the 'self-aggrandizing appropriation of otherness by power' (p. 112). Meanings are 'socially determined' (p. 113); therefore, Beatrice is suspicious of public discourse since ' "truth" ' is 'dependent on social reception' (p. 114). This dependency affects Shelley, too, whose representation (or non-representation) of Beatrice's rape undermines, according to Ulmer, the play's radical critique of patriarchy. Ulmer sees the play as deconstructing the author's avowed intention (in his Preface) to bring about self-knowledge in his audience, since 'if reception determines meaning as a public construct, and if readers' responses can be neither anticipated nor controlled absolutely, then texts are merely the histories of their own (mis)interpretation' (p. 118).

More cautious – arguably more balanced – in its treatment of the role of the reader and the thematisation of reception is Stephen C. Behrendt's *Shelley and His Audiences* (1989). Behrendt notes how the variety of genres in which Shelley writes corresponds to a variety of different strategies for shaping audience response. He draws on narratological theory – an offshoot of structuralist thought that seeks, among other things, to codify the kinds of reader presupposed by a work of fiction – for the idea of 'the virtual reader', that is, the reader on whom the author 'bestows', in Gerald Prince's words, 'certain qualities, faculties, and inclinations'.[40] Because Shelley knew little about any 'actual readers' and knew there was little likelihood of finding 'ideal readers', he concentrates on this class of 'virtual readers', attempting 'to regulate both the terms and the manner of discourse'. For Behrendt, Shelley's meanings are not so much unstable as multistable, and his poetry often seeks 'to convey different messages within the same work'.[41] There is little scope in Behrendt's view for readerly freedom to make meaning; but he writes well about Shelley's dealings with his imagined audiences. The extract I have chosen discusses the 'exoteric' or popular political poems of 1819 which, written after Peterloo, attempted to address primarily a working-class audience (in a volume which was not printed); Behrendt focuses on

Shelley's manipulation of 'stock iconography' (p. 128), his modulations of tone and voice, and his adaptation of genres.

## iii. *Related approaches*

Ulmer is more of a card-carrying post-structuralist than Behrendt; but they share a readiness to employ a mixture of critical discourses. Some of the most stimulating studies of Shelley's poetry to have appeared in recent years are suspicious of what Jerrold E. Hogle calls 'singular "critical positions"'.[42] Pre-eminent among these are three of the finest books to have been written on Shelley: William Keach's *Shelley's Style* (1984), Hogle's *Shelley's Process* and Stuart Sperry's *Shelley's Major Verse*. To these should probably be added a fourth, Richard Cronin's *Shelley's Poetic Thoughts* (1981). In its scrupulous attention to Shelley's handling of form and language, Cronin's book marks the moment at which a judiciously appreciative New Criticism caught up with Shelley; yet Cronin moves beyond a New Critical emphasis on organic unity, praising Shelley for his ability to 'lay bare [the] mechanisms'[43] which govern *Adonais*. Cronin put Shelley's style, rather than his ideas, back on the critical agenda, and William Keach's *Shelley's Style* is written out of a sense that the individual ways Shelley thought about and used words require highly particularised exploration. This he provides in a study that intelligently holds post-structuralist thinking about Shelley at arm's length, even as it looks carefully at the 'linguistic skepticism' apparent in *A Defence of Poetry*. What worries Keach is the post-structuralist carelessness about 'distinguishing the elusive activity peculiar to Shelley's writing from the problematic condition of language generally'. Keach's approach is, in his own description, 'formalist',[44] but it is a formalism whose theoretical self-consciousness is unusually sharp. As the printed extract (discussing the late poems to Jane Williams) shows, he is aware that Shelley was aware that the pressures of living and the disciplines of writing could not be neatly separated. Texts have their own life in Keach's book, but their contexts are not overlooked.

*Shelley's Major Verse* by Stuart Sperry shares Keach's view that 'although poems may acquire their own separate existence as verbal forms and fictions, they are never entirely free of the vicissitudes of those who write and read them' (Keach, p. 206). Sperry stresses that his is 'not a "thesis" book';[45] it employs whatever methods seem appropriate to the poem under discussion. But, along with a formalist emphasis on close reading, exemplified to fine effect by his analysis of the closing passage of *Prometheus Unbound*, Act III, Sperry gives generous space to biographical matters, more particularly to the psychodrama staged in Shelley's poems, which often seek to rekindle a lost, original sense of oneness or unity or to project such a sense into some imagined future. Prometheus's recalling of the curse is read, after Leon Waldoff (see Headnote, p. 152), as a form of therapy that allows the hero to re-enter and thus master the emotional state created by his Oedipal conflict with Jupiter. In the excerpt from his chapter on *Epipsychidion* reprinted here, Sperry offers a sympathetic, but keen-eyed, reading of the poem as 'a study in psychogenesis, an essay in the trials and difficulties of achieving poetic selfhood' (p. 153). Sperry does not idealise the Shelleyan theme of 'the limitlessness of human desire' (p. 161); rather, he sees it as necessary to Shelley's ability to write poems. Certainly Sperry makes concessions which another critic, antagonised by Shelley's idealising (of self, women, utopias) might wish to put to polemical use; the poem reveals the 'psychological cost of creating these idealized relationships' (p. 166). Christine Gallant's often ambivalent study of *Shelley's Ambivalence* (1989) comes to mind; Gallant, like Sperry, sees Shelley as yearning for some primal wholeness (hence the image of the Child in his poetry), and interprets much of Shelley's poetry as expressions of or fantasised solutions to his repressed feelings of ambivalence. But Sperry stops short of censure. *Epipsychidion* 'brings almost to conscious recognition the pattern of repeated effort and failure that underlies both the poetry and the life' (p. 166), while Shelley's poetry, generally, whatever its sources in the poet's unconscious life, is important politically because it 'describes not what humans are but what they might be'.[46]

Jerrold Hogle's *Shelley's Process* shares this sense that Shelley's poetry matters because it shows us what we 'might be'. Boldly grasping the nettle of value, he writes, 'Shelley's poetry is successful poetry . . . because it explodes the most established, conventional thought-relations into interconnections with others that were rarely thought to be analogous before.' Hogle's is easily the most sophisticated and independent reading of Shelley to have emerged since Wasserman's book. He takes from deconstruction its obsession with figurative displacement and substitution, but has no time for the nihilistic scepticism of de Man and his followers. Unlike William Ulmer (much of whose book seems written in a spirit of disagreement with Hogle), or, indeed, Stuart Sperry, Hogle does not see Shelley as the victim of some idealised longing for union with another. Even when Shelley most sounds as though he were invoking some 'Absolute Center', Hogle demonstrates, with great skill, that he is, in fact, revising traditional absolutes to make them accord with his preference for 'transference'. Transference is Hogle's master-term, a critical centre that adroitly decentres itself; it refers to the basic drive in Shelley to revise any position he provisionally assumes, any figure of speech he provisionally selects; the ethically and politically beneficial pay-off of the 'transference' enacted in the poems is that it expresses Shelley's 'persistent sense that each person should seek his or her "selfhood" by shifting his or her tendencies away from the present self towards "another and many others" [quoted from *A Defence of Poetry*]',[47] Hogle does justice both to Shelley's understanding of how transference can reify into false or stunted belief systems and the poet's search for transfer-based, creative modes of imagining or perceiving. Especially valuable is Hogle's ability to use the instruments of demystification which contemporary theory gives him in order to celebrate and explore Shelley's affirmative vision. In the excerpt included here, Hogle discusses the first act of *Prometheus Unbound*, arguing that Shelley does not try to create a myth in the lyrical drama; instead, he reworks old myths in such a way that their previously repressed potential is freed to participate in further connections with new and other thoughts.

## Ideological critique, new historicism, contextualism

This section discusses the influence on Shelleyan criticism of approaches that stress one or both of the following ideas: (1) literary works should be studied within their historical, intellectual or political contexts; (2) literature is a discourse that is historically produced and serves ideological purposes. The latter idea, drawn from the writings of Michel Foucault, is often bound up with a 'new historicist', Marxist or materialist reading of texts. New historicism is post-structuralist to the degree that it regards discourses as controlling humans and not vice versa, and in so far as it questions the status of the interpreter – who, after all, decides what 'history' is or what 'context' is appropriate and how can one's own assumptions not shape one's decisions? However, it departs from what it sees as post-structuralism's often ahistorical inclinations. Quasi-Marxist or culturally materialist readings oppose humanist 'essentialism' (the idea that there are unalterable 'essences' such as 'man' or 'nature' or 'the One') with what appears to be intended as anti-essentialism, but often turns out to be an alternative set of essences (certain ideological positions, to which the work discussed will be related).

Again, there is overlap between this section and previous sections. Jerrold Hogle, for one, is highly attuned to the political implications of 'transference'; William Ulmer relates *Epipsychidion*, very much in new historicist terms, to 'a historically specific mood of liberal alienation'.[48] In doing so, he reflects the influence of Jerome J. McGann's *The Romantic Ideology* (1983). McGann refuses to privilege Romanticism's favourite ideals, seeing them as produced in reaction to historical pressures; Shelley's idealism is the reflex of the times in which he lived. McGann is harder on other people's ideology than on his own, and is surprisingly ready to assert certain evaluative axioms as though they had the status of truths: 'Poetry's first obligation is to reveal the contradictory forces which human beings at once generate and live through';[49] a passage from *Prometheus Unbound*, Act III, is said not to perform this obligation. This specific critique seems unhelpfully wrong since the lines quoted – III, iv, 131–60 – are remarkable for their aliveness to contradiction. Yet McGann's influence has been great and valuable to the degree that it has reminded readers of Romantic poetry that poetry is not written in a vacuum but in a social and historical context. Marilyn Butler, too, has persuaded many readers of Romantic poetry to be 'sceptical of . . . theories which exalt the autonomy of art and the magus-role of the artist'.[50] She argues that Shelley's work has to be understood in relation to a nexus of ideological values shared with other liberal, anti-reactionary writers such as Thomas Love Peacock (about whose relations with Shelley she has written helpfully in *Peacock Displayed: A Satirist in his Context*, 1979).

A diluted Marxism is at work here and in McGann, in Butler's case seeking to allow both for the author's control over meanings and his responsiveness to ideological forces at work in his society. For the most part, both critics avoid imposing on the poetry a narrow ideological grid, and are concerned with the way the text reworks or displaces beliefs and pressures. They are joined in this endeavour by Marjorie Levinson who reads Shelley's *Posthumous Fragments of Margaret Nicholson* and *Julian and Maddalo* as poems that use the fragment form to explore the relationship between private and public, and as attempts by Shelley to maintain, or investigate the difficulty of maintaining, a radical politics. *Posthumous Fragments* is seen as 'a reactionary work in effect if not intention' because in it Shelley represents private anguish as the cause, not the consequence, of social malaise. *Julian and Maddalo* is, by contrast, far more perceptive in its understanding of the dialectic of the individual and history; it offers 'a bitter, self-lacerating critique of the effects of corrupt community upon individual consciousness, yet it casts a cold eye on those who retreat from that community'.[51]

Two critics who have illuminated Shelley's texts by reading contextually are Kelvin Everest and Timothy Clark, both of whom are represented in this volume. Everest supports Kenneth Cameron's view of Shelley's thinking about the relationship between consciousness and society as falling somewhere between the thinking of Godwin and Marx; he reads *Julian and Maddalo* as dramatising Shelley's understanding of 'the manner in which prevailing forms of consciousness work to preserve the structure of social power'.[52] At stake is the relationship between the 'political' and the 'aesthetic' in Shelley's work. Everest seeks to reconcile the two by ascribing to Shelley a capacity for ironic distance from poet-figures such as Julian, doubles whose ineffectuality points up Shelley's awareness of the problems facing the would-be radical poet. Such a poet must confront the conservative potential of his culture's language and poetic forms, and Everest is not alone in seeing Shelley as working with, but undoing the assumptions of, a particular form – in this case, the conversational poem.

Timothy Clark's *Embodying Revolution* (1989) also focuses on the representation of poet-figures in Shelley's work in order to bring out the crucial if paradoxical 'relation between introspection and radical politics' in the poetry. Clark argues that Shelley must be understood in terms of 'an aesthetic that was controversial in the 1810s but which has since been quite forgotten'. The poet exploring depths of the mind is, thereby, sensitised to revolutionary forces at work in his culture. Clark supports his case with a wealth of material drawn from Shelley's culture; he also emphasises the contradiction in Shelley's own philosophy of mind between affirming 'sensibility as a faculty of receptivity' and asserting 'the mind's voluntary power'.[53] *Alastor*, far from being a moral tale warning against the pursuit of solitude, is read by Clark as tragically dramatising the destructive as well as creative potential of the revolutionary imagination. As with much of the best contemporary criticism of Shelley, *Embodying Revolution* is alive to contradiction and paradox even as it gives Shelley credit for a subtle and impassioned poetic intelligence.

In choosing the essays for this volume, I have tried to select essays that cover many of Shelley's major poems, while illustrating a variety of contemporary critical approaches. The essays are ordered according to the chronology of the works which they discuss. (For details of the chronology of Shelley's works, see *Shelley's Poetry and Prose*, ed. Donald H. Reiman and Sharon B. Powers, pp. xvii–xix.) The volume can be read in a variety of ways. It can be read in the chronological order of the poems, beginning with Timothy Clark on *Alastor* and ending with Tilottama Rajan on *The Triumph of Life* and *Alastor*, a piece which itself works in anti-chronological order, moving backwards from the end of Shelley's career. Or the volume can be read, in some instances, for its pairings of essays on the same poem: Clark and Rajan on *Alastor*, Jerrold Hogle and Isobel Armstrong on *Prometheus Unbound*, Rajan and J. Hillis Miller on *The Triumph of Life*. Or it can be read for the dialogue of approaches established between different essays. I attempt to point out the presence of such dialogues in the Headnotes, but readers will find stimulating relationships – sometimes verging on opposition – between Hogle's and William Ulmer's perspectives, Ulmer's and Ronald Tetreault's, Hillis Miller's and Hogle's, and Clark's and Everest's, among others. Unless indicated otherwise, page numbers cited in the Introduction and the Headnotes refer to the present volume.

# Notes

1. TILOTTAMA RAJAN, *The Supplement of Reading: Figures of Understanding in Romantic Theory and Practice* (Ithaca and London: Cornell University Press, 1990), p. 341.

2. Hazlitt's unsigned review of Shelley's *Posthumous Poems* (1824) in *The Edinburgh Review* July 1824; quoted from THEODORE REDPATH, *The Young Romantics and Critical Opinion 1807–1824* (London: Harrap, 1973), pp. 388, 391, 389, 388.

3. *The Supplement of Reading*, p. 293.

4. Quotations from Eliot are taken from *The Use of Poetry and the Use of Criticism* (1933), excerpted in *Shelley: Shorter Poems and Lyrics*, A Casebook, ed. Patrick Swinden (London and Basingstoke: Macmillan, 1976), pp. 72, 76, 73.

5. Quoted from *Shelley: Shorter Poems and Lyrics*, A Casebook, p. 76.

6. Ibid., p. 32.

7. F.R. LEAVIS, *Revaluation: Tradition and Development in English Poetry* (First published 1936; Harmondsworth: Penguin, 1972), pp. 201, 200, 202, 198, 193, 193–4.

8. HAROLD BLOOM, *Shelley's Mythmaking* (First published 1959; Ithaca: Cornell University Press, 1969), pp. 1, 3, 10.

9. Stuart Curran finds Bloom's approach 'somewhat mechanical and reductive', 'Shelley', in *The English Romantic Poets: A Review of Research and Criticism*, ed. Frank Jordan, 4th edn (New York: Modern Language Association of America, 1985), p. 613.

10. *Shelley's Mythmaking*, pp. 126, 165, 184, 185, 125, 75, 193.

11. EARL R. WASSERMAN, *The Subtler Language: Critical Readings of Neoclassic and Romantic Poems* (First published 1959; Baltimore: The Johns Hopkins Press, 1968 paper), pp. 305, 307.

12. C.E. PULOS, *The Deep Truth: A Study of Shelley's Scepticism* (First published 1954; Lincoln: University of Nebraska Press, 1962), p. 8.

13. Quotations from Shelley's *On Life* are taken from *Shelley's Poetry and Prose*, ed. Donald H. Reiman and Sharon B. Powers (New York and London: Norton, 1977), pp. 476, 477, 478. Unless indicated otherwise, all quotations from Shelley's prose and poetry are taken from this edition, hereafter *PP*.

14. Introduction to *The New Shelley: Later Twentieth-Century Views*, ed. G. Kim Blank (Basingstoke and London: Macmillan, 1991), p. 6.

15. EARL R. WASSERMAN, *Shelley: A Critical Reading* (Baltimore: The Johns Hopkins University Press, 1971), pp. viii, 151, 395, ix, vii, 144, 238, 64.

16. LLOYD ABBEY, *Destroyer and Preserver: Shelley's Poetic Skepticism* (Lincoln and London: University of Nebraska Press, 1979), p. 9.

17. STUART CURRAN, *Shelley's Annus Mirabilis: The Maturing of an Epic Vision* (San Marino, California: Huntington Library, 1975), pp. xiv, 187.

18. DONALD H. REIMAN, *Percy Bysshe Shelley* (First published 1969; London and Basingstoke: Macmillan, 1976), p. 160.

19. M.H. ABRAMS, *Natural Supernaturalism: Tradition and Revolution in Romantic Literature* (New York and London: Norton 1971), p. 299.

20. ISOBEL ARMSTRONG, *Language as Living Form in Nineteenth-Century Poetry* (Brighton, Sussex: Harvester Press; Totowa, New Jersey: Barnes and Noble, 1982), pp. 115, 118.

21. Quoted from *Shelley: Poetical Works*, ed. Thomas Hutchinson, corr. G.M. Matthews (London: Oxford University Press, 1970), p. 478.

22. JONATHAN ARAC, 'Shelley, Deconstruction, History', in *Critical Genealogies: Historical Situations for Postmodern Literary Studies* (New York: Columbia University Press, 1987), p. 101.

23. In HAROLD BLOOM and others, *Deconstruction and Criticism* (London and Henley: Routledge & Kegan Paul, 1979), p. vii.

24. 'Shelley Disfigured', in *Deconstruction and Criticism*, pp. 64, 62.

25. 'Intentional Structure of the Romantic Image', in Paul de Man, *The Rhetoric of Romanticism* (New York: Columbia University Press, 1984), p. 6.

26. 'Shelley Disfigured', pp. 61, 66, 69.

27. 'Shelley', in *The English Romantic Poets*, ed. Frank Jordan, p. 658.

28. COLIN FALCK, *Myth, Truth and Literature* (Cambridge: Cambridge University Press, 1989, 1991 repr.), p. 25.

29. 'Shelley Disfigured', pp. 59, 69.

30. For further discussion of de Man, see CHRISTOPHER NORRIS, *Paul de Man: Deconstruction and the Critique of Aesthetic Ideology* (New York and London: Routledge, 1988), especially pp. xvi–xxi, and 'De Man's Rhetoric', in JONATHAN CULLER, *Framing the Sign: Criticism and its Institutions* (Oxford: Basil Blackwell, 1988), pp. 107–35.

31. 'Shelley Disfigured', p. 69.

32. TILOTTAMA RAJAN, *Dark Interpreter: The Discourse of Romanticism* (Ithaca and London: Cornell University Press, 1980), pp. 20, 21.

33. 'Stevens' Rock and Criticism as Cure, II', *The Georgia Review*, vol. 30 (Summer 1976), quoted by M.H. Abrams in *Modern Criticism and Theory: A Reader*, ed. David Lodge (London and New York: Longman, 1988), p. 272.

34. J. HILLIS MILLER, 'The Critic as Host', in *Deconstruction and Criticism*, p. 250.

35. Ibid., pp. 246, 243.

36. *The Supplement of Reading*, pp. 305, 307, 315.

37. JACQUES DERRIDA, 'Structure, Sign and Play in the Discourse of the Human Sciences', in *Modern Criticism and Theory: A Reader*, p. 121.

38. For a discussion of Derrida versus Wittgenstein, see JONATHAN CULLER, *On Deconstruction: Theory and Criticism After Structuralism* (London, Melbourne and Henley: Routledge & Kegan Paul, 1983), pp. 130–1.

39. WILLIAM A. ULMER, *Shelleyan Eros: The Rhetoric of Romantic Love* (Princeton, New Jersey: Princeton University Press, 1990), p. 9.

40. Quoted in Stephen C. Behrendt, *Shelley and His Audiences* (Lincoln and London: University of Nebraska Press, 1989), p. 4.

41. Ibid., pp. 5, 2.

42. Jerrold E. Hogle, 'The Dialectic of Transference and Tyranny: A Reply to Michael O'Neill', *The Wordsworth Circle*, vol. XXI, no. 4, Autumn 1990, p. 157.

43. Richard Cronin, *Shelley's Poetic Thoughts* (London and Basingstoke: Macmillan, 1981), p. 200.

44. William Keach, *Shelley's Style* (New York and London: Methuen, 1984), pp. 2, xii, xvii.

45. Stuart M. Sperry, *Shelley's Major Verse: The Narrative and Dramatic Poetry* (Cambridge, Mass. and London: Harvard University Press, 1988), p. x.

46. Ibid., p. 112.

47. Jerrold E. Hogle, *Shelley's Process: Radical Transference and the Development of His Major Works* (New York and Oxford: Oxford University Press, 1988), pp. 27, viii.

48. *Shelleyan Eros*, p. 141.

49. Jerome J. McGann, *The Romantic Ideology: A Critical Investigation* (Chicago and London: The University of Chicago Press, 1983), p. 121.

50. Marilyn Butler, *Romantics, Rebels and Reactionaries: English Literature and its Background 1760–1830* (Oxford: Oxford University Press, 1981), p. 185.

51. Marjorie Levinson, *The Romantic Fragment Poem: A Critique of a Form* (Chapel Hill and London: The University of North Carolina Press, 1986), pp. 149, 166.

52. Kelvin Everest, 'Shelley's Doubles: An Approach to *Julian and Maddalo*', in *Shelley Revalued: Essays from the Gregynog Conference*, ed. Kelvin Everest (Leicester: Leicester University Press, 1983), p. 69.

53. Timothy Clark, *Embodying Revolution: The Figure of the Poet in Shelley* (Oxford: Clarendon Press, 1989), pp. 1, 10.

# 2  Destructive Creativity: *Alastor* (1815)*

TIMOTHY CLARK

Timothy Clark's *Embodying Revolution: The Figure of the Poet in Shelley* (1989), hereafter *ER*, connects the 'two Shelleys' – the political radical and the introspective poet – by arguing that, for Shelley, private feelings point towards wider historical movements. Clark repudiates the split between the political and the metaphysical made by critics such as Earl Wasserman; nor does he endorse the ironic reading of the poetry favoured by Kelvin Everest (see Chapter 4 and Headnote). Instead, he draws from Shelley's prose a 'conception of the mind' which emphasises that 'self-analysis is related directly to historical processes' (*ER*, p. 7). Poets are the creators as well as the creations of their age; in them, 'the creation of new aspirations and wants is particularly intense' (*ER*, pp. 8–9). Sensibility becomes a political concept in Shelley's work since the capacity for intense feeling is the hallmark of writers attuned, like Rousseau and Byron, to the revolutionary energies of the age. A poet can, however, be victimised by the intense feelings that mark him out as 'a pioneer spirit' (*ER*, p. 8), and Clark's account of Shelley's career is especially eloquent on the growing presence in his work of motifs of 'loss and destruction' (*ER*, p. 10). That the revolutionary poet can be destroyed by the forces whose potential he helps, by virtue of his sensibility, to realise is an almost tragic double-bind explored by Clark's book. For Clark, Shelley's political optimism grows increasingly difficult to square with a contradictory theory of the mind that swings between emphasising control and receptivity. The book's procedures are historical. Drawing on material in the *Quarterly Review* and other periodicals, Clark shows how the ambivalences he describes in Shelley echo opinions in the

* Reprinted from Timothy Clark, *Embodying Revolution: The Figure of the Poet in Shelley* (Oxford: Clarendon Press, 1989), pp. 128–42 (footnotes renumbered from the original).

poet's culture. Clark's approach is more that of the intellectual historian than the new historicist (there is, for instance, no questioning of the status of history or of the vantage-point of the critic); yet this intellectual history is given a political dimension.

The following extract is taken from the chapter on *Alastor* which relates the poem to the 'issues of philosophy of mind' (*ER*, p. 9) that concerned Shelley. Clark opposes the didactic reading favoured by many critics which sees the poem as blaming the Poet for choosing self-centred solitude; by contrast, Clark argues that the poem accepts the 'necessary solitariness of the poet' and in the first part of the chapter (not reprinted here) explains the Preface's remark about the Poet's 'self-centred seclusion' as a 'sign of the unease with which Shelley regarded the destructive imaginative processes that make their first appearance in *Alastor*' (*ER*, p. 97). (See Introduction, pp. 22–3.)

It would seem that, for Shelley, any form of self-conscious mental reflexivity is incapable of reviving an original sensation as anything but a frustrating shadow of itself.[1] This has an obvious implication for the poet's quest in *Alastor* to refind the prototype of his dream through the medium of his own mind. The goal of the introspective project, closely related to *Alastor*, which Shelley describes in 'Difficulty of Analyzing the Human Mind' (1815–16),[2] is of an exact recurrence of a past sensation in all its immediacy, as well as an analysis of its nature – 'to be where we have been, vitally and indeed' and 'at the moment of our presence there' to 'define the results of our experience'. It is presumably the failure of this double demand that makes introspection 'so dizzying and so tumultous' (*J*, VII, p. 64). In *Alastor* (ll. 224–37) it is the return of the dream to the *newly self-conscious poet* that transforms it into a fiendish distortion of itself:

> driven
> By the bright shadow of that lovely dream,
> Beneath the cold glare of the desolate night,
> Through tangled swamps and deep precipitous dells,
> Startling with careless step the moon-light snake
> He fled.
>
> (ll. 232–7)

Like the soul in the poem 'Oh! there are spirits',[3] the dream is turned into the likeness of a fiend by the mind's inability to realize it. This anguish underlies the poet's fleeing from the experience, driven only by the dream's 'bright shadow' (l. 233). The syndrome of the repetition of past pleasure as present pain is evident in the scrambled way words such as 'hope' and 'despair' become almost synonymous. For example, when the poet first conceives of pursuing the image into the realms of sleep and death, this thought is immediately a 'doubt'. The sentence shifts at once from hope to despair: 'This doubt with sudden tide flowed on his heart, / The insatiate hope which it awakened, stung / His brain even like despair' (ll. 220–2). The most memorable expression of this syndrome of joy doubling as a fiend is the adaptation of the *Alastor* persona in *Adonais*. Here it is described in terms of a myth taken, like that of Narcissus, from the third book of Ovid's *Metamorphoses*, the myth of Actaeon.[4] Shelley reads the hounds that devour Actaeon as his own thoughts:

> Midst others of less note, came one frail Form,
> A phantom among men; companionless
> As the last cloud of an expiring storm
> Whose thunder is its knell; he, as I guess,
> Had gazed on Nature's naked loveliness,
> Actaeon-like, and now he fled astray
> With feeble steps o'er the world's wilderness,
> And his own thoughts, along that rugged way,
> Pursued, like raging hounds, their father and their prey.
>
> (ll. 271–9)

Jean Perrin has demonstrated the underlying presence of the Actaeon myth in the *Alastor* poet's curious flight.[5] The dream becomes a detached portion of the poet's own mind, attacking him from within. The poet, 'startled' by his own thoughts, looks around (l. 296), but the 'fair fiend' is only an alienated portion of himself, presumably the pursuing demon of solitude of the poem's title – 'There was no fair fiend near him, not a sight / Or sound of awe but in his own deep mind' (ll. 297–8). The alteration of the dream into a 'fair fiend' epitomizes the manner in which the dizzying, painful frustration of reflection underlies the image of the poet being pursued in fear through the landscape of his own mind. Introspection, as has been seen, is 'like one in dread who speeds through the recesses of some haunted pile, and dares not look behind'.[6]

The frustration evident in the memory of a lost pleasure would seem to be a familiar enough experience. However, it seems to have deeply disturbed Shelley, in particular in so far as it represents a certain deficiency in the power of imagination, never capable of repeating to itself its own former experience. It is *not* possible 'to be where we have been, vitally and indeed'.[7] The image for the mind in both the poem and the prose is of a stream that flows inexorably outwards, never returning upon itself. Shelley must have had in mind Heraclitus' description of flux,[8] that one never enters the same river twice. Mind is 'like a river

29

whose rapid and perpetual stream flows outwards. . .'.[9] Shelley may also
have been remembering a passage in which Mary Wollstonecraft expands
on the well-worn issue of the dangers of imagination. People, she writes,
are too often the dupes of their imagination, engaged in the profitless
pursuit of phantoms. From the nature of man's constitution 'he would
not find it very easy to catch the flying stream'.[10] This is Shelley's image
for the processes of thought in both *Alastor* and *The Revolt of Islam*, the
gathering stream impelling itself towards death.[11] Cyntha laments:

> 'Alas, our thoughts flow on with stream, whose waters
>   Return not to their fountain – Earth and Heaven,
> The Ocean and the Sun, the Clouds their daughters,
>   Winter, and Spring, and Morn, and Noon, and Even,
>   All that we are or know, is darkly driven
> Towards one gulf.'
>
> (ll. 3775–80)

Examination of the manner in which mental processes are described in
*Alastor* reveals a view of the mind very like that in 'Mutability' (written in
1814) and quite contrary to the hope that the will might attain command
over the active powers in the mind. The mind is a passive sensorium, the
scene of thoughts and passions sweeping upon it from an unknown
source. All that remains constant is the passivity of consciousness. For
instance, the dream is said to be 'sent' to the poet (l. 203). The poet is
several times described as the receiver of intense 'impulses' that spur him
on at critical moments (ll. 304, 415). At one point he is said to be 'Startled
by his own thoughts' (l. 296). Similarly, he is totally passive during his
mental development: 'Every sight / And sound from the vast earth and
ambient air, / *Sent to his heart* its choicest impulses' (ll. 68–70; emphasis
added). Most noticeable of all is the fact that mental processes are
described as happening not *in* the poet's mind but *on* it. Examples of this
peculiar usage are in the following lines: 'meaning on his vacant brain /
Flashed like strong inspiration' (ll. 126–7); 'A vision on his sleep / There
came' (ll. 149–50); 'sleep / Like a dark flood suspended in its course, /
Rolled back its impulse on his vacant brain' (ll. 189–91); and 'This doubt
with sudden tide flowed on his heart' (l. 220). Despite the brief period of
intense mental activity represented by the dream in *Alastor*, the notion of
the mind suggested is that of 'Mutability', an opaque realm of forces
beyond the control of will, the only relation to them being the passivity
of consciousness. The use of the image of the lyre for the mind reappears
in *Alastor*. The elegist of the poet describes himself awaiting inspiration
as 'a long-forgotten lyre / Suspended in the solitary dome / Of some
mysterious and deserted fane' (ll. 42–4). He is able only to await the
breeze of inspiration responsible for the main poem. The resemblance to

the description of the mind in 'Mutability' is very close. The minds of
men are 'like forgotten lyres, whose dissonant strings / Give various
response to each varying blast . . .'. The lyre is then described as a 'frail
frame'. This anticipates the description of the poet in *Alastor* as a passive
instrument who, as befits his especial sensibility, is 'A fragile lute, on
whose harmonious strings / The breath of heaven did wander . . .' (ll.
667–8). The wind on the passive strings represents the stream of
impressions coming from a mysterious source and the strings themselves
the passivity of consciousness. The image, not developed as Shelley was
later to do in such a way as to suggest a very minimal element of will,[12] is
in accordance with Shelley's repeated dogma that mind is only an organ
of perception, not a power in its own right.[13] Likewise, the introspective
crisis of the poet is both unwilled and traumatic. It is a sudden
confrontation of 'hopes that never yet / Had flushed his cheek'
(ll. 150–1).

While the notion that the active creative power is not at the behest of
conscious volition is familiar from *A Defence*,[14] this is hardly the
immediate context for *Alastor*. The hope of Shelley's study of mind in
1815 was that the active power of mind that constitutes genius could be
understood and directed by means of a scrupulous self-analysis.[15]

The most prominent, and also the most conventional, of images for the
mind's loss of autonomy to the alien forces of passion, are those of the
tempest and the wind. Lines 316–51 of the poem, in which the poet is
pictured sailing in a demented fashion across a tempestuous sea, provide
Shelley's clearest image for the relation between exquisite sensibility and
violent passion. John C. Bean has argued that this passage is symbolical
of 'mystical experience',[16] a description that fails to take account of the
totally empiricist context of the poem and the Preface. The argument that
the voyage represents the poet's state of mind after the dream is
convincing, however. One should not overlook the extraordinary
viciousness and destructiveness being described. The strange calm of the
poet in the storm passage is less reminiscent of any description of
mystical experience than of the liking of Godwin's Falkland, in *Things as
they Are* (1794), for violent landscapes as soothing expressions of his
tormented inner state,[17] or of the mood of Victor Frankenstein near Mont
Blanc in Mary Shelley's novel[18]:

> The waves arose. Higher and higher still
> Their fierce necks writhed beneath the tempest's scourge
> Like serpents struggling in a vulture's grasp.
> Calm and rejoicing in the fearful war
> Of wave running on wave, and blast on blast
> Descending, and black flood on whirlpool driven
> With dark obliterating course, he sate:

As if their genii were the ministers
Appointed to conduct him to the light
Of those beloved eyes, the Poet sate
Holding the steady helm.

(ll. 323–33)

The violent struggle of the snake and the eagle had already been used in lines 227–37 to describe the self-destructive and frustrated state of the poet after the dream. The image of passion as a destructive storm is, of course, a cliché.[19] Shelley modifies clichés like the following from Godwin's *Mandeville* by his emphasis on the self-conflicting nature of the violence within the poet ('wave running on wave, and blast on blast / Descending . . .', (ll. 326–7). Mandeville, the hero of the novel, describes the love for his sister Henrietta: 'Love was like the God of the tempestuous ocean, that controlled, and directed, and turned, like yielding gossamer in his hands, every wind that blew.'[20] The image of the destructive tempest was also a recurrent one, in the reviews, for Byron and the passionate heroes of his poems. Clearly, the contrast could hardly be more graphic between the hope that self-analysis would provide the key to mastery of the mind's powers and the picture of the poet's psyche as a self-destructive chaos.

Although the poet's passivity to imaginative forces was later to be emphasized by Shelley, *Alastor* embodies traces of a considerable ambivalence towards them. Their cultivation seems to lead only to tragedy.

It was commonplace, both in medical theory of this period and also in popular thought as reflected in the reviews, that the more man refines his sensibility and the more delicate he becomes, the more liable he is to be swept away by the force of some overwhelming passion.[21] Such, for example, is the fate of Godwin's Fleetwood, who becomes the victim of an almost pathological jealousy concerning his wife. In *Frankenstein* the hero exclaims:

Alas! why does man boast of sensibilities superior to those apparent in the brute; it only renders them more necessary beings. If our impulses were confined to hunger, thirst, and desire, we might be nearly free; but now we are moved by every wind that blows, and a chance word or scene that that word may convey to us.[22]

The passage is striking as a contrast to Shelley's own anti-primitivist position according to which civilization constitutes a refinement of sensibility and a desirable multiplication of wants of the heart and mind.[23] The notion that this process was actually an intensification of the mind's bondage to its own weakness and desires was hardly unfamiliar to Shelley, however.[24]

By the time Shelley was writing *Alastor* the belief had become widespread that civilization, as a refinement of wants, had altered general sensibility in such a way as to make man increasingly the victim of nervous and mental disorders. Certainly the *Quarterly Review*, for instance, while endorsing this view, would not have endorsed the political overtones of much contemporary primitivism:

> Nervous and mental affections of every kind are, in the present day, proverbially prevalent . . . the cause is to be sought for in that artificial state of society which grows necessarily out of a constant advancement in civilization. We multiply our comforts, and, by consequence, our cares and crosses. We beat out and expand our minds, as it were, and thus create a more extended surface of impression.[25]

This extract is from the article on insanity and madhouses published in July 1816. The corollary of this view, and certainly that endorsed by the Shelley of the notes to *Queen Mab*, is that madness is a state almost wholly confined to man's advanced social condition. As the *Quarterly Review* argues, both in the 1816 article and again in an article of October 1820, madness is 'an evil almost confined to the social state, [and so] it would seem a very natural supposition, that with the progress of refinement and the multiplication of artificial excitants, mental derangement and disease would increase in an equal proportion; and to a certain extent this is indisputably the case . . .'[26]

Despite Shelley's mature anti-primitivist conception of man's savage and his artificial states, a sense of the dangers of a refinement in sensibility is nevertheless apparent in *Alastor*. It is through 'too exquisite a perception' of Power that the 'luminaries' of the world are said to perish (Reiman and Powers, p. 69), a statement clarified further by Shelley's belief that it was fine sensibility that 'distinguishes genius from dullness'.[27] This clearly renders *Alastor* a tragic poem in which mankind seems liable to destruction by virtue of its very greatness. Lines 690–720 of the poem and the epigraph from Wordsworth's *Excursion* (1814) enact the same bleak pattern: 'The good die first, / And those whose hearts are dry as summer dust, / Burn to the socket'.[28] Only the insensitive can survive.

Shelley's study of mind at this time affirmed simultaneously the delicacy of sensibility and the power of the human will to direct the active powers of the mind to its own purpose. It would appear that these two affirmations, however, are almost contradictory. The correlation of delicacy of sensibility with a proportionate intensity of passion leaves little room for the hope that, as want and passion are intensified, the will can at the same time sustain the strength to direct these energies within the mind. The common belief, as Edward Duffy has shown,[29] was precisely the opposite. By Shelley's time sensibility, as a fashion, was out of favour precisely on the grounds that it reduced personal responsibility and rendered man a slave to his passions. This is the view already briefly quoted from *Frankenstein*. A letter Shelley wrote in August 1815 explicitly correlates human unhappiness with the imagination's power to awaken wants beyond the power of the will to realize. Even those who possess the limits of human power are not exempt:

> It excites my wonder to consider the perverted energies of the human mind. . . . Yet who is there that will not pursue phantoms, spend his choicest hours in hunting after dreams, and wake only to perceive his error and regret that death is so near? . . . Even the men who hold dominion over nations fatigue themselves by the interminable pursuit of emptiest visions; the honour and power which they seek is enjoyed neither in acquirement, possession or retrospect; for what is the fame that attends the most skilful deceiver or destroyer? *What the power which awakens not in its progression more wants than it can supply.*[30]

Since Earl Wasserman's reading of *Alastor*[31] the importance of the figure of the narrator or elegist of the idealized young poet has been recognized. This figure both introduces the poet and is pictured inconsolably lamenting his death at the poem's close. He first appears invoking Nature for the inspiration that is to guide his elegy. Wasserman sees the two figures as embodying a split in Shelley's own aspirations. Hence we are given one poet for whom Nature is a beneficent and adequate context for man, and another who rejects Nature in favour of the spiritual ideal dubiously apprehended in himself. While it is true that Shelley seems deliberately to use Wordsworthian phrases in the language of this narrating voice, even at one point inserting a quotation from Wordsworth's ode on 'Intimations of Immortality' (l. 713),[32] this does not endorse a view of beneficent Nature as Shelley's own. The power this figure addresses as a maternal and beneficent spirit has undertones that suggest it cannot be opposed (as Wasserman does) to the ambivalent forces responsible for the idealized poet's fate. The narrator invokes Nature as the force that will provide the inspiration for the elegy. In this he completely contradicts Shelley's repeated view of the sources of the energy that underlies creativity. Shelley ascribes it to the active forces of what he calls 'Power', as a totality of progressive *cultural* agencies, identifiable with what he calls 'Liberty' in the 'Ode to Liberty'. This is a preponderantly cultural entity, inseparable from man's social nature and the active perfectibility and refinement of civilization and opposed to a natural state which Shelley believed was selfish and barbarous. This would suggest that the narrator-poet is mistaken in his notion of a beneficent Nature. It is not surprising, therefore, that his invocation for power should acquire overtones of rape and violence in accordance with the violent workings of the mysterious active Power in the rest of the poem:

> I have made my bed
> In charnels and on coffins, where black death
> Keeps record of the trophies won from thee.
> Hoping to still these *obstinate questionings*
> Of thee and thine, by *forcing* some lone ghost,
> Thy messenger, to render up the tale
> Of what we are. In lone and silent hours,
> When night makes a weird sound of its own stillness,
> Like *an inspired and desperate alchymist*
> Staking his very life on some dark hope,
> Have I mixed *awful talk* and *asking looks*
> With my most innocent love, until *strange tears*
> Uniting with those *breathless kisses*, made
> Such magic as *compels* the charmed night
> To render up thy charge. . . .
>
>                    (ll. 23–37; emphasis added)

The fact that *Alastor* is about the nature of the mental processes involved in creation, not about a conflict of supposed natural and visionary impulses within Shelley, is evident from the fact that the narrator repeats, in the course of the elegy, the pattern of desire described in the Narcissus-poet. The poem enacts a repetition. Just as the dream-maiden represents to the poet the emblem of all that is excellent in human nature, so the poet bears this same relationship to his elegist. He is 'the loveliest among human forms' (l. 593), 'A lovely youth' (l. 55), and 'The brave, the gentle, and the beautiful, / The child of grace and genius' (ll. 689–90). The death of this beautiful figure, the object of an intense love on the part of his elegist, affects the latter just as the vanishing of the figure of his dream affected the poet. It leaves the natural world, previously a source of delight to both figures, a meaningless and dead husk.

The gradually intensifying nature of the narrator's state of mind as the elegy progresses can be traced to the point at which the whole world-view implicit in his initial self-dedication to Nature seems in ruins. At one point he seems to break down altogether with the extremely melodramatic section beginning 'O, storm of death . . .' (ll. 609–24), invoking the great 'Skeleton' of death as sole master of the world. Then he proceeds to give a series of variously bizarre and desperate

35

speculations about the elixir of life, only to conclude, as in an early letter of Shelley's,[33] that eternal life would merely constitute the most horrible of torments (ll. 675–81). Nature, no longer the 'great Mother' (l. 2) of the invocation, has become 'this phantasmal scene' (l. 697), a phrase recalling the vacancy with which the poet looked on the light of morning after awakening from the dream (ll. 200–2). All that remains in the world after the departure of the figure who summed up in himself all that was valuable in it are 'pale despair and cold tranquillity' (l. 718). The suggested resolution of the moralistic conclusion to the Preface, of dedication to social causes and human sympathy, is nowhere to be found. The poem concludes:

> Art and eloquence,
> And all the shows o' the world are frail and vain
> To weep a loss that turns their lights to shade.
> It is a woe too 'deep for tears', when all
> Is reft at once, when some surpassing Spirit,
> Whose light adorned the world around it, leaves
> Those who remain behind, not sobs or groans,
> The passionate tumult of a clinging hope;
> But pale despair and cold tranquillity,
> Nature's vast frame, the web of human things,
> Birth and the grave, that are not as they were.

(ll. 710–20)

The poet has effected an irreversible change in the narrating figure for whom things 'are not as they were'. *Alastor* enacts a chain of interrelated beauty and frustration that extends first from the dream-maiden to the poet and secondly from the poet to his elegist. Lisa M. Steinman has made the powerful suggestion that for the narrating poet, first seen in a state of heightened receptivity awaiting the active inspiration that will bring his elegy, the poem about the idealized youth is itself a manifestation of the Power impelling all things towards their more perfect likeness.[34] Steinman demonstrates from Shelley's prose that Shelley understood all human emotional reactions to the natural world as projections of an imaginative process whose true element was human relationship.[35] The nature of inspiration and Power for Shelley, as discussed above, supports Steinman's reading, despite her maintenance of the natural/visionary dichotomy inherited from Wasserman. Her argument is also corroborated by the initial similarity of narrator and poet. Both are first seen engaged on a quest to plumb the inmost secrets of life and the universe. Lines 81–2 describing the youth recall lines 19–22 describing his elegist:

> Nature's most secret steps
> He like her shadow has pursued. . . .
> > I have watched
> Thy shadow, and the darkness of thy steps,
> And my heart ever gazes on the depths
> Of thy deep mysteries.

When Shelley describes the poem as 'allegorical of one of the most interesting situations of the human mind' (Reimin and Powers, p. 69) he would seem to be describing a process enacted twice, in both figures. The violent erotic undertones in the narrator's invocation of Nature manifest the same want of an erotic counterpart as determines the hero's dream. The implications of the letter of August 1815 are clearly that the psychological forces leading to a state of love without an object are universal: 'What the power that awakens not in its progression more wants than it can supply'.[36]

Shelley's attempt to understand such a discrepancy in terms of human perfectibility and its relation to civilization as the development of want seems very muted here. *Alastor*, rather, seems to depict a process whereby the most highly developed representatives of civilization become a tragic blight both to themselves and others. In a sonnet of 1818 ('Lift not the painted veil', Reiman and Powers, p. 312), which Wasserman argues represents an *Alastor* in miniature,[37] the surpassing spirit who seeks some ideal in death is paradoxically described as 'A splendour among shadows, *a bright blot* / Upon this gloomy scene' (emphasis added). A manuscript version of the poem places its speaker in the same position as the narrator in *Alastor*. He laments, 'I should be happier had I ne'er known / This mournful man – he was himself alone.'[38]

In conclusion, the tragic syndrome enacted in *Alastor* is reminiscent of a note Shelley entered in Mary's journal in October 1814: 'Nothing should shake the truly great spirit which is not sufficiently mighty to destroy it'.[39] Much of Shelley's work during 1815 has strong affinities with Greek tragedy.[40] This is perhaps partly what Peacock had in mind when suggesting the title 'Alastor' or 'evil daemon'.[41]

Despite its consequences, there is no evidence to suggest that the education of the *Alastor* poet was less than ideal. The processes described in *Alastor* are thoroughly tragic in their inexorable relation between cultural excellence and destruction – 'that Power which strikes the luminaries of the world with sudden darkness and extinction, by awakening them to too exquisite a perception of its influences . . .' (Reiman and Powers, p. 69).

In the *Refutation of Deism* of 1814 Shelley had had the Christian character in the dialogue, Eusebes, describe as inconceivable a divinity that created only to destroy. However, this is just what the Power of *Alastor* seems to be:

> The same energy cannot be at once the cause of the serpent and the sheep; of the blight by which the harvest is destroyed, and the sunshine by which it is matured; of *the ferocious propensities by which man becomes a victim to himself*, and of the accurate judgement by which his institutions are improved.
>
> (*J*, VI, p. 48; emphasis added)

The most powerful denunciation of the agency of the *Alastor*-poet's fate occurs in lines 609–19, in which it is addressed as death itself:

> O, storm of death!
> Whose sightless speed divides this sullen night:
> And thou, colossal Skeleton, that, still
> Guiding its irresistible career
> In thy devastating omnipotence,
> Art King of this frail world, from the red field
> Of slaughter, from the reeking hospital,
> The patriot's sacred couch, the snowy bed
> Of innocence, the scaffold and the throne,
> A mighty voice invokes thee. Ruin calls
> His brother Death.

God is described as being 'Profuse of poisons' (ll. 675–6). In his journey the poet glimpses some beautiful flowers in his path. The Power, manifesting itself in the very impulses that move the poet on, is inseparable from his own desire. Shelley is depicting a total subversion of any possible autonomy of the will:

> the Poet longed
> To deck with their bright hues his withered hair,
> But on his heart its solitude returned,
> And he forbore. Not the strong impulse hid
> In those flushed cheeks, bent eyes, and shadowy frame,
> Had yet performed its ministry: it hung
> Upon his life, as lightning in a cloud
> Gleams, hovering ere it vanish, ere the floods
> Of night close over it.
>
> (ll. 412–20)

This obscure 'ministry' seems to be nothing other than the poet's destruction. The poet's solitude (l. 414) is, as these lines demonstrate, entirely an effect of the mysterious Power operating from a realm beyond the control of his will or consciousness and suddenly descending 'on his heart' (l. 414). There is no question here of the poet's solitude being a selfish moral choice receiving just requital. Moreover, this very image of violent Power will be affirmed in Shelley's later work as the very nature of poetic inspiration itself. Likewise, the destruction suffered by the hero of *Alastor* will become a necessary element of the poet's function.

## Notes

All references to Shelley's poetry are, when possible, to Donald H. Reiman and Sharon B. Powers (eds), *Shelley's Poetry and Prose* (New York: Norton, 1977), hereafter Reiman and Powers; otherwise to Thomas Hutchinson (ed.), *Shelley: Poetical Works*, corr. G.M. Matthews (London: Oxford University Press, 1970), hereafter *H*. All references to Shelley's prose are to Roger Ingpen and Walter E. Peck (eds), *The Complete Works of Percy Bysshe Shelley*, 10 vols (London: Ernest Benn, 1926–30), hereafter *J*. Shelley's letters are quoted from *The Letters of Percy Bysshe Shelley*, ed. Frederick L. Jones, 2 vols (Oxford: Clarendon Press, 1964), hereafter *L*.

1. This is manifest especially with Shelley's experience of memory. It is without exception the case that memory, in Shelley's work, whether of a pleasant or unpleasant experience, is in itself an experience of loss or pain. Its characteristic expression is an imagery of ghosts, phantoms, or other spirits with an ambiguous status between life and death, presence and absence (see 'The Past', *H*, p. 553, and 'Time Long Past', *H*, p. 632). The image of haunting is particularly apt because memory is not only a painful experience but also a compulsive one, as in the second half of *Alastor*. Shelley wrote to Peacock on 20 April 1818: 'The curse of this life is that whatever is once known can never be unknown. You inhabit a spot which before you inhabit it is as indifferent to any other spot upon the earth, & when, persuaded by some necessity you think to leave it, you leave it not – it clings to you & with memories of things which in your experience of them gave no such promise, revenges your desertion. Time flows on, places are changed, friends who were with us are no longer with us, but what has been, seems yet to be, but barren & stript of life. See, I have sent you a study for Night Mare Abbey' (*L*, II, p. 6). Memory, for Shelley, always confirms the implication of 'Mutability' that the self is essentially discontinuous.

2. For the date of the fragment and its relation to others entitled by Mary Shelley and placed under the general heading 'Speculations on Metaphysics', see my argument in *Embodying Revolution: The Figure of the Poet in Shelley* (Oxford: Clarendon Press, 1989), pp. 14–22.

3. 'Thine own soul still is true to thee, / But changed to a foul fiend through misery', ll. 29–30, *H*, p. 526.

4. *Metamorphoses*, ed. and trans. Frank Justus Miller, rev. G.P. Goold, 2 vols (Loeb Classical Library: 3rd edn, London, 1977), pp. 134–43 (III, ll. 138–252).

5. 'The Actaeon Myth in Shelley's Poetry', *Essays and Studies*, NS **28** (1975): 29–46.

6. 'Difficulty of Analyzing the Human Mind', *J*, VII, p. 64.

7. Ibid.

8. Heraclitus, *The Cosmic Fragments*, ed. G.S. Kirk (Cambridge: Cambridge University Press, 1954), p. 381.

9. 'Difficulty of Analyzing the Human Mind', *J*, VII, p. 64.

10. *Vindication of the Rights of Woman; With Strictures on Political and Moral Subjects* (London, 1792), p. 248. Shelley first ordered this book in 1812; see letter to Thomas Hookham, 29 July 1812, *L*, I, p. 319.

11. See also 'Rousseau's' description of the mind as a stream in *The Triumph of Life* (ll. 343–411) and the violence of the stream of mind in 'Mont Blanc' (ll. 1–11).

12. *A Defence*, *J*, VII, pp. 109–10.

13. See e.g. 'On Life', in which Shelley asserts that 'Mind . . . cannot create, it can only perceive' (*J*, VI, p. 197); Shelley affirmed this doctrine, in a letter to Hunt of 27 September 1814, as one of which he had long been persuaded, quoting a jotting of Charles Lloyd *contra* Berkeley which he had read during 1812, 'Mind cannot create; it can only perceive' (*L*, II, p. 123).

14. 'Poetry is not like reasoning, a power to be exerted according to the determination of the will' (*J*, VII, p. 135).

15. See 'What Metaphysics Are' (*J*, VII, p. 62).

16. 'The Poet Borne Darkly: The Dream–Voyage Allegory in Shelley's *Alastor*', *Keats–Shelley Journal*, **23** (1974): 65–6. Bean is correct, however, in reading the tempest passage as representing the influx of imaginative power on the weak, sensitive spirit of the poet, imaged as the frail boat.

17. *Caleb Williams*, ed. David McCracken (Oxford: Oxford University Press 1970), pp. 124–5.

18. Mary W. Shelley, *Frankenstein, or, The Modern Prometheus*, ed. M.K. Joseph (London: Oxford University Press, 1969), pp. 94–8.

19. Timothy Webb has drawn attention to Shelley's attraction for a line from the *Prometheus Vinctus* of Aeschylus in which the bound Prometheus is described as 'a plaything of the winds', a phrase Shelley noted twice in notebooks, 'Coleridge and Shelley's *Alastor*: A Reply', *RES*, NS **18** (1967): 408.

20. Godwin, *Mandeville: A Tale of the Seventeenth Century in England*, 3 vols (London, 1817), III, p. 310.

21. See e.g. David Unwins (attrib.), rev. of *An Essay on the Prevention and Cure of Insanity; with Observations on the Rules for the Detection of Pretenders to Madness*, by George Nesse Hill (and various other works on insanity), *Quarterly Review*, **30** (July 1816):

    Savages, unless in cases of palpable disorganization, are neither nervous nor mad; – they are not the subject of that variety of exciting agents which, while by a law of nature they prove destruction of their own good, are likewise liable, from their multiplicity and complication, to act in undue measure, and thus to set all wrong. 'In proportion as man emerges from his primaeval state, do the Furies of disease advance upon him, and would seem to scourge him back into the paths of nature and simplicity' (p. 398).

22. *Frankenstein*, p. 97.

23. See 'On the Nature of Virtue' (*J*, VII, p. 73).

24. A carefully argued case for the dangers of excessive sensibility is to be found in a medical book to which Shelley refers in the notes to *Queen Mab* (*H*, p. 833), *A View of the Nervous Temperament*, 2nd edn (London, 1807) by Thomas Trotter. However much Shelley may have understood *Alastor* in terms of the dialectic of active and passive powers already described, the case of an extreme sensibility destroyed by the sudden awakening of passion also conforms to Trotter's account: 'Sensibility to excess marks the constitution; and affliction cannot address it without meeting its sympathy. It is this degree of feeling, that too often makes it the sport and victim of passion. It loves and hates beyond bound. Hence those corroding sorrows, which sometimes overtake the most tender of all attachments, and which ultimately bring the possessor to the grave' (p. 164). Shelley had endorsed Trotter in his youth, affirming belief in a normative conception of a 'natural' state of moral and physical health from which civilization had degenerated (see the notes to *Queen Mab*, *H*, pp. 826–35). Trotter attributes the supposed vast increase in nervous diseases in the eighteenth century to, among other things, the tendency to live in cities, abuses of wealth and leisure, and the proliferation of novels. Shelley also ordered Trotter's *An Essay, Medical, Philosophical, and Chemical, on Drunkenness and its Effects on the Human Body*, 2nd edn (London, 1804) (letter to Clio Rickman, 24 Dec. 1812, *L*, I, p. 345).

25. Rev. of *Essay on the Prevention and Cure of Insanity*, by Hill, *Quarterly Review*, **30** (July 1816): 398.

26. David Uwins (attrib.), rev. of *An Inquiry into Certain Errors Relative to Insanity*, by George Man Burrows, *Quarterly Review*, **47** (Oct. 1820), p. 176.

27. Rev. of Hogg's *Alexy Haimatoff*, *J*, VI, p. 176.

28. *The Poetical Works of William Wordsworth*, ed. E. de Selincourt and Helen Darbishire, 5 vols (Oxford: Oxford University Press, 1952–59), rev. Helen Darbishire, V, p. 25. Charles E. Robinson has shown that Shelley did not derive these lines directly from Wordsworth's *Excursion*, but through a quotation from Coleridge's *The Friend*: 'The Shelley Circle and Coleridge's *The Friend*', *English Language Notes*, **8** (1971): 272.

29. *Rousseau in England: The Context for Shelley's Critique of the Enlightenment* (Berkeley, Calif.: University of California Press, 1974), pp. 46–71.

30. Letter to Hogg (end of Aug. 1815), *L*, I, pp. 429–30 (emphasis added).

31. *Shelley: A Critical Reading* (Baltimore: Johns Hopkins University Press, 1971), pp. 3–56.

32. *Wordsworth, Poetical Works*, IV, pp. 279–85, l. 204.

33. Letter to Hogg, 3 Jan. 1811, *L*, I, p. 35.

34. LISA M. STEINMAN, 'Shelley's Skepticism: Allegory in "Alastor"', *ELH*, **45** (1978): 255–69.

35. See 'On Love', *J*, VI, p. 202.

36. Letter to Hogg (end of Aug. 1815), *L*, I, p. 430.

37. *Shelley*, pp. 45–6.

38. Bod. MS Shelley adds. e. 12, pp. 22–3.

39. *Mary Shelley's Journal* ed. Frederick L. Jones (Norman: University of Oklahoma Press, 1947), p. 20.

40. See E.R. Dodds, *The Greeks and the Irrational* (Berkeley, Calif.: University of California Press, 1951). Dodds discusses the Greek–tragic notion of 'man's helpless dependence upon capricious Power' finding expression in 'a belief in daemons' (p. 45).

41. Thomas Love Peacock, *Peacock's Memoirs of Shelley; with Shelley's Letters to Peacock*, ed. H.F.B. Brett-Smith (London, 1909), pp. 55–6.

# 3 Shelley's *Mont Blanc*: What the Mountain Said*

### FRANCES FERGUSON

*Mont Blanc* (1816) is a rich and difficult poem in which Shelley conjures out of the Alpine landscape 'a voice . . . to repeal / Large codes of fraud and woe' (ll, 80–1) and investigates the interplay between the natural and the 'human mind's imaginings' (l. 143). Frances Ferguson's essay playfully reads the poem in post-structuralist terms as concerned with the process of signification. The poem on her account behaves as if it wished to posit the solemn confrontation between perceiving, sense-endowing mind and blank material object which many critics have discovered. But the poem's language works to undo such a confrontation; because it has to be named in words, the natural is already part of the web of relationship spun by language, a web which shows itself in what Ferguson calls the 'relational punning' (p. 47) of the poem. The river 'Arve raves in the ravine' (p. 47), she writes, the closeness of the words to one another implying that they are inextricably related. Shelley's language correlates epistemology (questions about knowing) not with ontology (the nature of being) but with love (the drive to create relationship); the act of address posits the reality of the addressee, gifting it with the status of an interlocuter. At the same time – and here as elsewhere the essay's fluid shifts obliquely correspond to those of the poem – the mountain is merely matter, and will say nothing, even if the poet-lover 'is still looking for a mountain who will understand him' (p. 52). And yet, as the final question reveals, the poem will not allow the mountain to remain simply material, since Shelley appropriates it for his own aesthetic purposes. Ferguson's post-structuralist wit redefines and draws to itself the paradoxical nature of Shelleyan sublimity: a state in which the mind discovers its worth in the act of showing its capacity for confusion. So the natural as

---

* Reprinted from *Romanticism and Language*, ed. Arden Reed (London: Methuen, 1984), pp. 202–14.

merely material or destructive is an idea projected by consciousness, which can never escape its responsibility for meaning and never elude its desire for relationship. (See Introduction, pp. 14–15.)

Critics seem to have agreed on one thing about *Mont Blanc* – that it is a poem about the relationship between the human mind and the external world. After that, the debates begin – over whether the mind or the world has primacy, over whether 'The veil of life and death' of line 54 has been 'upfurled' or 'unfurled' in line 53, over whether 'but for such faith' in line 79 means 'only through such faith' or 'except through such faith', and so on.[1] It is not surprising that debates should have arisen, because the poem moves through a variety of different ways of imagining the mountain and the power of which it is symbolic (or synecdochic); and although the poet may do the mountain in different voices, the variety of conceptions and the rapidity with which they succeed one another are possible largely because the mountain is like the tarbaby in Uncle Remus and says nothing.

The question that arises, of course, is, How is the mountain's silence any different from the silence of the subjects of any other poem? Grecian urns are likewise silent; and nightingales may sing, but they do not talk. In the case of *Mont Blanc*, the interest lies, curiously enough, in the palpable improbability of looking for anything but silence from the mountain, which is repeatedly seen as the ultimate example of materiality, of the 'thingness' of things, so that its symbolic significance is quite explicitly treated as something added to that materiality.

At moments Shelley seems to be almost defiantly trying to think of the mountain (and the entire landscape connected with it) as a brute physical existence. Such an effort would have to be at least somewhat defiant, both because of the inevitable difficulty of trying to imagine anything completely without history and context (and thus associations) and because of the multiplicity of associations that had accrued to the idea of this mountain. Whereas it is crucial to the mountain's force as an example of pure materiality that it can never know that it is the highest mountain in Europe, it – and the vale of Chamonix generally – had, as Richard Holmes nicely observes, developed a reputation among the 'travelling English' of the time 'as a natural temple of the Lord and a proof of the Deity by design'.[2] The famous story of Shelley's traveling through the region, entering his name in the hotel registers in Chamonix and Montavert, and listing his occupations as 'Democrat, Philanthropist and Atheist' serves to indicate the level of his indignation at the way in which religion attributes spiritual qualities to a brute material object when it assimilates such an object to a proof of the deity by design.[3] It serves as well to suggest how difficult it is to think of the mountain as a merely physical object. For in his efforts to counter the myth of natural religion that is attached to Mont Blanc, Shelley does not destroy the mountain's symbolic value but merely inverts it.

To say that Shelley attempts to conceive Mont Blanc in terms of sheer physical force may sound like a movement toward recognizing a gap between signifier* and signified* and toward trying to accept the mountain not just as pure physicality but also of necessity as pure nonreferentiality.† The mountain would function, in such an account, as a linguistic signifier that would reveal the ironic distance between its material presence and any possible signified. Yet I would argue that the poem insists, most importantly, on the inability of one's resting in such irony as it exhibits its own repeated failures to let Mont Blanc be merely a blank, merely a mass of stone: *Mont Blanc* leads to attempts to think of the mountain as physical and without metaphysical attributes, and fails; it attempts to imagine a gap between the mountain and the significances that people attach to it, and fails. But if one way of talking about the poem is to suggest that Shelley is here restricted because of the inadequacy of language, or the way in which language blocks one from saying certain things or certain kinds of things, the other side of that image of blockage – of the inability to break through – is a contrary movement made manifest by the way in which the relationships that are sketched out in the poem are not merely adequate but so abundant and well-fitting as almost to inspire claustrophobia. In this respect, the poem is more nearly akin to Wordsworth's lines about how exquisitely the human mind and the world are fitted to one another than even those lines that Harold Bloom and others have seen echoed in the opening section of *Mont Blanc* – the lines from 'Tintern Abbey' in which Wordsworth speaks of having 'felt / A presence that disturbs [him] with the joy / Of elevated thoughts . . . / A Motion and a spirit, that . . . / . . . rolls through all things' (ll. 93–102).[4]

Thus although the motive behind the poem appears to be conceiving of Mont Blanc not just as the white mountain but also as a massive version of blankness – or 'solitude / Or blank desertion' (*The Prelude*, I, 394–5), the poem has already in its first few lines become a poem about the impossibility of seeing the mountain as alien. As Earl Wasserman observes, the 'everlasting universe of things' is like the Arve flowing through the Ravine that is like the 'universal mind', and the Ravine of 'universal mind' and the Channel in which the brook of the individual

---

* [Ed. *Signified*: the conceptual aspect of a sign; *signifier*: the material form of a sign.]

† [Ed. *Referentiality*: the notion that language refers to extra-linguistic reality.]

mind flows merge with one another.[5] In the midst of all the convergence and congruence of the schema, however, Wasserman very convincingly notes a sensory overload in the image of the brook: 'The simile, which has no significant function except to transform the mode of vision, by its very tautology opens the door to an abundance of supposedly external objects that exceed the requirements of the comparison, as though the tendency to conceive of images as external were too great for the poet to resist.'[6]

Wasserman's central point here is that the poet conceives of metaphors in which he then finds 'a remarkably consistent objective correlative for his metaphor for a total universe that is indifferently things or thoughts and that is located in the One Mind'.[7] It is not, of course, particularly suprising that Shelley should see the scene, when he finally looks at it, in the terms in which he thought about it before he looked at it; what is, however, remarkable is not just that the interpretation and the perception are aligned with one another but that the various portions of the imagery are as well. The river, of necessity, fits the ravine perfectly – and in a way that makes it impossible to say which has priority and determines the other. Whereas a glass of water may be said to be prior to the water in it, in that its shape is one that any water in it must conform to, the course and shape of a riverbed may be said to be determined by the waters that flow through it just as much as the riverbed may be said to determine the course of the river. Yet it is not merely the river and the riverbed that are interdependent and mutually creative, for the height of the mountain and the depth of the ravine have an analogous relation to one another: there is a ravine – and a ravine this deep – because there is a mountain – and a mountain this high – and vice versa.

An additional complication appears, however, in the image of the brook that Wasserman describes as exceeding 'the requirements of the comparison'.[8]

> The source of human thought its tribute brings
> Of waters, – with a sound but half its own,
> Such as a feeble brook will oft assume
> In the wild woods, among the mountains lone,
> Where waterfalls around it leap for ever,
> Where woods and winds contend, and a vast river
> Over its rocks ceaselessly bursts and raves.
>
> (ll. 5–11)

The 'feeble brook' is not described simply as a tributary to the 'vast river'; instead, the river is said to 'burst and rave' over its – the brook's – rocks, thus introducing the question of whether a brook is still a brook when a river runs in its channel. Although the question itself seems like a bad riddle, it forcibly demonstrates Shelley's procedure throughout the poem of insisting on the changeableness of the identity of any individual entity. For the brook, in becoming a part of the river, both loses its identity as a brook and transcends itself, gaining access to a forcefulness it never had as a 'feeble brook'.

We have here, in the cluster of images that are continually put into relation with one another, an elaborate schema of reciprocity. The universe of things exists to be perceived by the universal mind, so that the mind does not create things in its acts of perception but rather keeps the things of the world from going to waste. The river that courses along the channel of the brook enables the individual mind to participate in thought and sensation without ever having to originate them for itself. As we do not make up the world of things as we go along, so we do not discover all of human thought on our own. The relationship between the river and the brook may be seen not only as analogous to that between all of human knowledge and an individual knowing subject but also as similar to all human language in relation to an individual speaker.

It is, however, when the terms that are put into relationship with one another get proper names that the poem begins to flirt with relational punning. Bloom has stressed the importance of Shelley's addressing the ravine and the mountain as 'Thou' and has seen it as emblematic of the poem's conjecturing 'the possibility of a Thou as a kind of universal mind in nature'.[9] Although there are no proper names in the first section of the poem, the second section offers not just the pronoun 'Thou' but also the names 'Ravine of Arve' and 'Arve'. The appearance of the names registers the shift from Shelley's imagining a schematic relationship for the ravine and the river to his seeing this particular ravine and this particular river. But the address to the ravine is repeated enough for it to become, as Wasserman might have said, 'excessive'. For when Shelley turns to look at and speak to the ravine, he calls it 'thou, Ravine of Arve – dark, deep Ravine', and in the nomenclature 'Ravine of Arve' is another way of suggesting the interdependence of the ravine and the river. There is also, however, a linguistic *tour de force* – or cheap trick – at work here: the river that has been imagined in the first section to 'burst and rave' ceaselessly is identified as the Arve, so that the 'Arve raves'. And it of course turns out that the 'Arve raves in the Ravine'. (If you drop the article 'the' from the previous clause, you have four words that are all contained in the letters of the word 'ravine', and it might, with a bit of work, be made into another song for *My Fair Lady*.)

This species of relational punning underscores the symbiosis of things and mind, of river and ravine, that Shelley has earlier been sketching. Further, it raises some interesting questions about the status of language in the poem. Although the punning is a kind of technological trick with language, it is hard to see how this language can really be described as duplicitous, for all it does is reiterate the earlier message: thought takes the world of things to be inextricable from the mind: the actual perception of the scene confirms this message, in taking the river to be inextricable from the ravine, and at this point in the poem the language itself rather glaringly insists that the Arve exists because it is in the Ravine of Arve. The importance of the language trick lies not, however, in the fact that this language is human and might thus reveal the primacy of the human and the priority of the human mind. Rather, the anagram suggests the inevitability of any human's seeing things in terms of relationship.

The significance of this love language, moreover, goes beyond the familiarity built into a poet's addresses to the personifications that he creates. For the questions about epistemology that Wasserman has very convincingly seen to dominate the poem appear very different if epistemology is correlated with ontology on the one hand or, alternatively, with love. In the one account – that which continually seeks to align epistemology with ontology so that one's knowing always struggles to coincide with the real existence of what one knows – the adequacy of one's ability to know is always suspect. In the other account – that which aligns epistemology with love – emotional profligacy that continually postulates and assumes the existence of an interlocutor supplants any notion of matching one's knowledge with things as they really are.

In the remarkable fragment 'On Love', Shelley approvingly remarks that 'Sterne says that if he were in a desert, he would love some cypress.'[10] In *Mont Blanc* Shelley falls in love with a ravine, a river, and a mountain not because of the nature of those objects but because of his own, his human, mind, which cannot imagine itself as a genuinely independent, isolated existence. Love is, he says,

> that powerful attraction towards all that we conceive, or fear, or hope beyond ourselves, when we find within our own thoughts the chasm of an insufficient void and seek to awaken in all things that are a community with what we experience within ourselves. If we reason, we would be understood: if we imagine, we would that the airy children of our brain were born anew within another's: if we feel, we would that another's nerves should vibrate to our own, that lips of motionless ice should not reply to lips quivering and burning with the heart's best blood. This is Love. This is the bond and the sanction which connects not only man with man but with everything which exists.[11]

When Shelley views the natural landscape, he immediately begins to speak familiarly to it, not just because poets traditionally personify natural objects and address them with terms of endearment, but because he cannot imagine himself without imagining an anti-type that will enable him to be assured of his own existence. For 'the invisible and unattainable point to which Love tends', he says, is 'the discovery of its anti-type; the meeting with an understanding capable of clearly estimating our own'.[12]

Edmund Burke had identified as sublime not only the experience of contemplating enormous heights and depths but also, and most particularly, the experience of being isolated from other humans.[13] From one perspective, Shelley seems to provide a textbook example of how to experience the sublimity of Mont Blanc as he registers his consciousness of the mountain's force while appearing to speak from a condition of isolation (where no human aid can intervene between him and the mountain's power). It is from this perspective unremarkable that Shelley's account of the mountain continually recurs to the subject of its wildness, of its being a wilderness remote from all that civilization involves. By a peculiar twist, however, Shelley converts the isolation of the mountain from a threat into an opportunity – as if he were not so much alone with the mountain as 'alone at last' with it. For the act of imagination or intellection by which he moves from the description of the portion of the mountain that remains hidden to him is an act of sympathy; although he speaks merely of the portion of the mountain that really exists, he in effect woos the mountain with an 'imagination which . . . enters into and seizes upon the subtle and delicate peculiarities' that the mountain (if it were human) would have 'delighted to cherish and unfold in secret'.[14]

Thus Shelley's addressing the ravine and the mountain as 'Thou' is only one aspect of the poet's effort to convert epistemological language into love language. For although *Mont Blanc* is a sublime poem upon a sublime subject, it projects an air of sociability. As soon as the poet depicts the 'Dark, deep ravine', he provides it with companionship in the persons of 'Thy giant brood of pines', those 'Children of elder time' (ll. 920–1). Even when he imagines Mont Blanc as a fierce and ravening force, he cannot imagine it as a real desert; it is 'A desart peopled by the storms' and a place where the poet immediately starts constituting a domestic circle as he asks, 'Is this the scene / Where the old Earthquake-daemon taught her young / Ruin? Were these their toys?' (ll. 71–3).

Yet Shelley's famous letter to Thomas Love Peacock describing his first viewing of Mont Blanc makes the poem's love-longing for the mountain seem particularly one-sided, not just unrequited but positively scorned:

I will not pursue Buffon's sublime but gloomy theory, that this earth which we inhabit will at some future period be changed into a mass of frost. Do you who assert the supremacy of Ahriman imagine him throned among these desolating snows, among these palaces of death and frost, sculptured in this their terrible magnificence by the unsparing hand of necessity, and that he casts around him as the first essays of his final usurpation avalanches, torrents, rocks and thunders – and above all, these deadly glaciers at once the proofs and symbols of his reign. – Add to this the degradation of the human species, who in these regions are half deformed or idiotic and all of whom are deprived of anything that can excite interest or admiration. This is a part of the subject more mournful and less sublime; – but such as neither the poet nor the philosopher should disdain.[15]

The logic by which Shelley regards the degradation of the humans in the vicinity as 'more mournful and less sublime' than Buffon's theory that the entire earth will become 'a mass of frost' may not be self-evident. But his central point here is that the deformity and idiocy of the inhabitants of the area are, quite literally, not sublime because such deformity and idiocy merely provide, in human form, a repetition of the mountain's role as pure materiality. Thus, although the mountain has the power to make these people less than human, that very power of oppression sets a limit to itself because it annihilates everything in the human that can understand the mountain's material aspect – with an understanding that Shelley speaks of in the fragment 'On Love'. Throughout *Mont Blanc*, Shelley's attention always moves from images of destructiveness to images of complementarity. In this sense, the poem appears to be almost an endorsement of Kant's remark that nothing in nature is sublime: 'All we can say is that the object is fit for the presentation of a sublimity which can be found in the mind, for no sensible form can contain the sublime properly so-called.'[16]

Shelley here focuses on a central paradox of the sublime – that we should take pleasure in the contemplation of anything that presents a threat to our tendency toward self-preservation. By falling in love with strenuous death, however, Shelley demonstrates the way in which nature's destructiveness is never centrally at issue in the experience of the sublime. Rather, because the human mind can attribute destructiveness to nature, nature needs us for it to be perceived as destructive and to continue to be destructive in any significant way. Thus *Mont Blanc* creates an image of sublimity that continually hypostatizes an eternity of human consciousness. Because even the ideas of the destructiveness of nature and the annihilation of mankind require human consciousness to give them their force, they thus are testimony to the necessity of the continuation of the human.

In the poem's first section, 'woods and winds contend' (l. 10); in the second, 'The chainless winds' (l. 22) come to hear the 'old and solemn harmony' (l. 24) that they make with the 'giant brood of pines' (l. 20).

The perspective of the mountain, presented in the third section, is the perspective of eternity where 'None can reply – all seems eternal now' (l. 75); and the fourth section offers the inverse of that eternal view – the perspective of mutability and mortality that sees that 'The race / Of man, flies far in dread; his work and dwelling / Vanish . . .' (ll. 117–19).

These different sections, although obviously similar, do not offer merely different versions of the same message. If the struggle between 'woods and winds' of the first section does not negate the possibility of seeing these same woods and winds creating a harmony between them, the relationship between the terms of eternity and mutability is even stronger. For it is not just that mutability and eternity are two different ways of conceiving time, but also that it becomes impossible for the poet to imagine eternity except in terms of mutability – the terms of generation in which earthquakes create epochs and broods of little earthquakes – or to image mutability except in the terms of eternity, in the form of a Power that 'dwells apart in its tranquillity' (l. 96).

The poet begins the fifth and final section with a magnificent feat of calculated vagueness and understatement:

Mont Blanc yet gleams on high: – the power is there,
The still and solemn power of many sights,
And many sounds, and much of life and death.

(ll. 127–9)

The understatement registers, among other things, the poet's awareness that his thoughts about the mountain have not changed the universe – or even the mountain. He seems almost to struggle to see the mountain's continued existence as a reason for him to return to his struggle to see it in its materiality. Yet this final section of the poem recapitulates the earlier movement into a language that inexorably begins to treat the mountain landscape as *someone* to be understood not merely through the understanding but through an understanding that operates to complete and magnify its object through an aggrandizement Shelley calls love.

The mountain has 'a voice' to 'repeal / Large codes of fraud and woe' (ll. 80–1) not because 'The secret strength of things / Which governs thought' inhabits it but because the poet is its voice as he finds himself in the process of recognizing the impossibility of taking the material as merely material. Just as one can see the letters that go together to make up 'Arve' and 'Ravine of Arve' as an example of the material aspects of language but cannot see them as language without seeing them as implying something more than matter, so one can see the mountain as an example of materiality but cannot see it even as a mountain without seeing it as involving more than matter. The mountain can repeal 'Large codes of fraud and woe' by making it clear that a love of humanity is easy if one can love a mountain that is physically inimical to man. And yet the final irony of the poem is that Shelley can conclude by asking the mountain his most famous question:

> And what were thou, and earth, and stars, and sea,
> If to the human mind's imaginings
> Silence and solitude were vacancy?

(ll. 142–4)

With this question, he reminds the mountain that it needs him. The relationship between man and world has been painted in such a way as to make it clear that complementarity rather than direct communication is at issue in his version of language. But although he reminds the mountain of its need for him, his questions also have all the poignancy of a speech by a lover who still needs to argue his case. He may be a fit anti-type to the mountain, but he is still looking for a mountain who will understand him.

Even though the poem ends with a question directed to the mountain, Shelley's interest in Mont Blanc is, of course, predicated upon the impossibility of the mountain's ever taking any interest in him and answering. The mountain is matter, and its power resides to a very considerable extent in that fact; just as Milton's Eve was once 'stupidly good',* so matter is, in Shelley's account, 'stupidly powerful', and powerful more because of its stupidity than in spite of it. That is, its power depends upon its never being able to move out of the world of death. Because it can never be alive, it can never be subject to death; because it can never be conscious, it can never experience fear (or love or any other emotion, anticipatory or otherwise).

In light of the poem's final account of the mountain, the first four verse paragraphs might seem to represent a massive epistemological error and a mistake in love as well. For the first two verse paragraphs argue for resemblance between the human and the natural worlds in claiming that the same model can be used for both (the Arve is to the ravine as the 'everlasting universe of things' is to the individual human mind) and in presenting the similarity between the two with a lover's air of pleasure in the discovery of himself in another. In this manner, Shelley addresses the ravine as if it were a version of himself:

> Dizzy Ravine, and when I gaze on thee
> I seem as in a trance sublime and strange

---

* [Ed. In fact, Milton's Satan; *Paradise Lost*, Book 9, l. 465.]

To muse on my own separate phantasy,
My own, my human mind. . . .

(ll. 34–7)

The reversion from thoughts of the ravine to thoughts of his own mind does not betoken any inappropriate narcissism but indicates, rather, the translation of the material to the human that is involved in any effort at making the scene intelligible. As both the formal analogy and the poet's familiar address to the scene argue for the equivalence between the material and the human, Shelley pursues this thinking by analogy down its fallacious course as he attributes sublimity to the mountain in making it appear to transcend itself. Thus he speaks of the 'Power in likeness of the Arve' as not like water but more than water as it comes 'Bursting through these dark mountains like the flame / Of lightning through the tempest' (ll. 16–19) and of those 'earthly rainbows stretched across the sweep / Of the etherial waterfall' (ll. 25–6) that refuse to occupy any single element or place; the transfer of attributes from one element to another lends each an all-inclusiveness that none would have individually.

Of course, the phenomena that are presented as more than themselves because of the transfer of attributes *are* palpably more than themselves, in that the rainbow, while being an interaction of water and air, is made 'earthly' whereas the waterfall produced by the passage of the water over the rocky earth is made 'etherial'. The distinct limit to the self-transcendence of these physical elements is, however, implicit in the conspicuous omission (for the moment) of the fire that emblemizes the animation of the elements. Although the water and the air, like the water and the earth, act together to produce a mutual self-transcendence of each, the crucial difference between these mutual magnifications and any real instance of sublime self-transcendence lies in the fact that these elements provide instances of action without representing agency.

If the apparent threat involved in any landscape that might be provocative of a sublime experience is that man (and mind) might be reduced to mere matter, the correspondent activity that occurs is that the poet's sublime account of Mont Blanc and the entire scene around it never allows matter to remain material but rather co-opts it or transmogrifies it by continually mistaking the activity of the material world for agency, by taking it to be as intentional as any human activity might be. Shelley insists virtually throughout the poem upon this confusion between activity and agency as he continually treats the mountain as a person (albeit a particularly large and powerful one). This programmatic confusion discloses a fundamental insight into the nature of sublime experience: in treating natural objects as occasions for sublime experience, one imputes agency (and therefore a moving spirit) to them.

Although such imputation would, in other hands, perhaps be the basis for seeing the designedness of nature as an argument for the existence of God, for Shelley it instead identifies the sublime as the aesthetic operation through which one makes an implicit argument for the transcendent existence of man – not because man is able to survive the threat posed by the power of the material world but because he is able to domesticate the material world for the purposes of aesthetics by converting such a massive example of the power of the material world as Mont Blanc from an object into a found object. For what the sublime does for nature is to annex all that is material to the human by appropriating it for aesthetics. In this sense, Shelley in *Mont Blanc* discovers the same assertion of human power that Kant did when he distinguished between the sublime and the beautiful on the grounds that 'we must seek a ground external to ourselves for the beautiful of nature, but seek it for the sublime merely in ourselves and in our attitude of thought, which introduces sublimity into the representation of nature'.[17] At Mont Blanc, in the assertion of human power that any sublime experience represents, Shelley thus revamps the argument from design to redound to the credit of the human observer who converts the object into a found object, not merely matter but matter designed by its perceiver.

Moreover, in treating the sublime experience of Mont Blanc as not merely adapting the material to the purposes of the human and the supersensible (or spiritual) but as a discovery of the human in nature, Shelley collapses Kant's account of the 'purposiveness without purpose' that we discover in aesthetic objects as he speaks of Mont Blanc as if it had purposes in relation to humans. Thus it is that the language of the poem continually moves from epistemological questions, questions of the poet's understanding, to love language in which all the questions are of his being understood.

## Notes

1.  The best brief survey of the various debates about the poem appears in the notes to the poem in *Shelley's Poetry and Prose*, ed. Donald H. Reiman and Sharon B. Powers (New York: Norton, 1977), pp. 89–93.

2.  Richard Holmes, *Shelley: The Pursuit* (London: Quartet Books, 1976), p. 342.

3.  See Holmes's account, pp. 339–43.

4.  Harold Bloom, *Shelley's Mythmaking* (Ithaca: Cornell University Press, 1969), p. 20. See also Bloom, *The Visionary Company* (Ithaca: Cornell University Press, 1971), p. 293.

5.  Earl R. Wasserman, *Shelley: A Critical Reading* (Baltimore: Johns Hopkins

University Press, 1971), pp. 221–38. Wasserman's reading remains, to my mind, the most impressive account of the poem.

6. Ibid., p. 224.

7. Ibid.

8. Ibid.

9. BLOOM, *Shelley's Mythmaking*, p. 23.

10. *Shelley's Prose, or The Trumpet of a Prophecy*, ed. David Lee Clark (Albuquerque: University of New Mexico Press, 1954), p. 171.

11. Ibid., p. 170.

12. Ibid.

13. EDMUND BURKE, *A Philosophical Enquiry into the Origin of Our Ideas of the Sublime and Beautiful*, ed. J.T. Boulton (Notre Dame: University of Notre Dame Press, 1958), pp. 43 and 71.

14. *Shelley's Poetry and Prose*, p. 170.

15. *Letters of Shelley*, ed. F.L. Jones, 2 vols (Oxford: Oxford University Press, 1964), I, p. 499. Quoted in BLOOM, *Shelley's Mythmaking*, p. 19, and in HOLMES, *Shelley*, p. 340.

16. IMMANUEL KANT, *Critique of Judgment*, trans. J.H. Bernard (New York: Hafner, 1966), pp. 83–4.

17. Ibid., p. 84.

# 4 Shelley's Doubles: An Approach to *Julian and Maddalo**

KELVIN EVEREST

Kelvin Everest's essay on *Julian and Maddalo* (from the second half of which the following extract is taken) addresses the 'paradoxical duality in Shelley's position as a profoundly radical poet of refined literary, and social, manner' ('Shelley's Doubles' (hereafter 'SD'), p. 75). Everest takes a materialist view of the relationship between consciousness and society. But he departs from the kind of crude Marxist analysis of Shelley typified by the quotation from Christopher Caudwell at the head of the extract. Everest cites Shelley's prose to prove convincingly that the poet saw a dialectical relationship between consciousness and social relations, and argues that poems such as *Epipsychidion, Adonais, Laon and Cythna,* and *Julian and Maddalo* present 'ironically distanced' doubles of the poet-figure; these doubles are placed in 'the controlling and qualifying context of larger poetic strategies' ('SD', p. 66). Everest adapts the idea of the 'double' from Freud, but gives it a more social inflection; the Shelleyan 'double', against his conscious intention, is 'rendered socially impotent by his tacit assent to the language, the mental forms, of the dominant social group' ('SD', p. 69).

Everest opposes the '"visionary" paradigm' ('SD', p. 68) of Shelley's career, according to which his poetry is marked by decreasing political radicalism and increasing idealism and subjectivity. Along with other critics he lays stress on Shelley's ability to question the values associated with a particular form or genre; the conversational idiom in which most of *Julian and Maddalo* is composed serves to ironise Julian's ineffectual acquiescence in the status quo. If Julian represents one type of double of the poet, a figure unable to make an authentic connection

---

* Reprinted from *Shelley Revalued: Essays from the Gregynog Conference*, ed. Kelvin Everest (Leicester: Leicester University Press, 1983), pp. 76–88 (footnotes renumbered from the original).

between ideas and social realities, the maniac, with his more disruptive style of speaking, represents another type, the radical poet misunderstood by society. Everest's essay deftly suggests Shelley's ability to make successful poetry out of his depiction of human failure, and should be read in conjunction with Timothy Clark's essay (Chapter 2 in this volume). Clark, too, treats the figure of the poet in Shelley, but opposes Everest's view of the poetry as 'the delicate instrument of an ironic intelligence' (*Embodying Revolution: The Figure of the Poet in Shelley*, p. 5); such a view, Clark argues, is alien to Shelley's avowed theoretical position (in *A Defence of Poetry*). Though Everest's discovery of irony in *Julian and Maddalo* seems an adroit critical strategy rather than the last word on the poem, it illuminates 'the subversive element in Shelley's handling of traditional literary forms' ('SD', p. 74). The resulting essay does justice to the ideological concerns and artistic skill of a poem increasingly regarded as central to Shelley's achievement. (See Introduction, pp. 22–3.)

[Shelley's] idealism is a reflection of the revolutionary bourgeois belief that, once the existing social relations that hamper a human being are shattered, the 'natural man will be realised' – his feelings, his emotions, his aspirations, will all be immediately bodied forth as material realities. Shelley does not see that these shattered social relations can only give place to the social relations of the class strong enough to shatter them and that in any case these feelings, aspirations and emotions are the product of the social relations in which he exists and that to realise them a social act is necessary, which in turn has its effect upon a man's feelings, aspirations and emotions.

(C. Caudwell, *Illusion and Reality*, 1937, p. 92)

Shelley's intellectual and emotional life is, in significant respects, the product of its social relations. While there can be no doubt that Shelley's desire to transform those relations was absolutely authentic, they are bound to enter somehow or other into his personality. He could not, for example, deny or revoke his own experience of family and sexual relations, whatever critique he might produce of their substance and shaping conditions. A growth into revolutionary consciousness is likely to involve elements of self-denial; 'false consciousness', the unconsidered tacit assent to a repressive reality, does not feel any less authentic for being false, to those who live within it. Shelley's personality bore for his contemporaries disconcerting traces of his class background; we cannot expect him, after all, to have erased all the contours of his lifetime's accumulated experience. There is a passage in Hogg's *Life of Shelley* that is pertinent here; there is, as usual, too much of Hogg himself in it, but it brings out an aspect of Shelley for which there is independent confirmation:

> 'Never did a more finished gentleman than Shelley step across a drawing-room!' Lord Byron exclaimed; and on reading the remark in Mr. Moore's *Memoirs*, I was struck forcibly by its justice, and wondered for a moment that, since it was so obvious, it had never been made before. Perhaps this excellence was blended so intimately with his entire nature, that it seemed to constitute a part of his identity, and being essential and necessary was therefore never noticed. I observed his eminence in this respect before I had sat beside him many minutes at our first meeting in the hall of University College. Since that day I have had the happiness to associate with some of the best specimens of gentlemen; but with all due deference for those admirable persons (may my candour and my preference be pardoned), I can affirm that Shelley was almost the only example I have yet found that was never wanting, even in the most minute particular, of the infinite and various observances of pure, entire, and perfect gentility.[1]

There is something back-handed in this enthusiasm of Hogg's, a certain suppressed smugness in his memory of the patent contradiction in his radical friend's manner. Shelley's gentility does not strike us now as a social so much as an intellectual manner; a fine intuition for discriminating refinement of mind. It is a manner that we meet often in Shelley's unillusioned and honest recognition of his intellectual and emotional superiority – something conferred, obviously enough, by his education and way of life – over the 'polluting multitude'. But the intellectual and social dimensions of this manner can be difficult to distinguish, as in Shelley's letter to Hunt of August 1819, where he discusses *Julian and Maddalo* in what appear to be the words of a rejected draft preface to that poem:

> I have employed a certain familiar style of language to express the actual way in which people talk to each other whom education and a certain refinement have placed above the use of vulgar idioms. I use the word *vulgar* in its most extensive sense; the vulgarity of rank and fashion is as gross in its way as that of Poverty, and its cant terms equally expressive of bare conceptions, and therefore equally unfit for poetry.[2]

This tone of voice, self-possessed and confidently judicious, has an unsettling ring; the 'vulgarity' that Shelley loftily dismisses, 'as gross in its way as that of Poverty', is a concept that takes its meaning from distinctions of manner that signify class difference. This is not, clearly, Shelley's intentional usage here, but his attitudes become entangled, in the passage, in the distracting associations of the language that he must use. In Shelley's work as a poet, these contradictions could be recognized, and employed to serve his representation of their larger context; in his life they must have operated to confirm the sad reality of his present world.

Shelley's gentility may have some relevance as well to the odd capacity he possessed for inspiring personal dislike in his contemporaries. Keats' undefined reserve about him is too cryptic to make much of; but others in the circle of the English Romantics, and particularly those who are most of the time quite incorrigibly gregarious, Benjamin Haydon, Henry Crabb Robinson, and Charles Lamb, all seemed to find something unpleasantly disconcerting in the manner of Shelley's radicalism. Those who knew him better did their best to defend him; Leigh Hunt, and Byron, who wrote to Murray after Shelley's death 'You are all mistaken about Shelley. You do not know how mild, how tolerant, how good he was in society; and as perfect a Gentleman as ever crossed a drawing-room, when he liked, and where he liked.'[3] There is no irony in Byron's remark, and certainly it is impossible to argue for anything in Shelley comparable to the self-conscious irony of Byron's own aristocratic radicalism, with its occasional flavour of a rhetorical pose. But when Shelley's potential audience was, from the beginning, so very small, it must have worried him that his manner created the reserved distance from which Lamb, for example, could come to react with such uncharacteristic callousness to the news of Shelley's death.

Most surprising of all is Hazlitt's impatience with Shelley. He generally formulates it as the irritation of the seasoned, hard-bitten radical campaigner, accustomed to the intractable realities of life, and confronted in Shelley by the pure idealist who has everything to learn, and who will not be convinced of that. Hazlitt objects to something quixotic in Shelley, a refusal to mediate his ideals for his own world, that puts us in mind of the visionary in *Alastor*. This particularly ironic distortion of Shelley stems in part, plainly, from Hazlitt's failure to grasp the complexity of Shelley's politics. But there is the hint of something else in Hazlitt's irritation, which is visible by indirect implication in, for example, the essay 'On Paradox and Common-Place', in *Table Talk*, and which is easier to see in the essay 'On the Qualifications Necessary to Success in Life', in *The Plain Speaker*:

> It is name, it is wealth, it is title and influence that mollifies the tender-hearted Cerberus of criticism – first, by placing the honorary candidate for fame out of the reach of Grub-street malice; secondly, by holding

out the prospect of a dinner or a vacant office to successful
sycophancy. This is the reason why a certain magazine praises Percy
Bysshe Shelley, and villifies 'Johnny Keats': they know very well that
they cannot ruin the one in fortune as well as fame, but they may ruin
the other in both, deprive him of a livelihood together with his good
name, send him to Coventry, and into the Rules of a prison; and this is
a double incitement to the exercise of their laudable and legitimate
vocation.[4]

It is hard to believe that Shelley's fellow-radical could so reduce him to
a mere strategy of invective in this way. But Hazlitt's bitterness is
justifiable in relation to Keats, and the Shelley he saw was the one visible
in Hazlitt's own perspective. Perhaps the problem would have
disappeared with time; it is important to stress that the right perspective
was even then available, as in a journal entry of Maria Gisborne's: 'We
talked much in praise of the Shelleys, and amused the Hunts by reading
parts of their letters to them; we laughed at Shelley's little occasional
aristocratical sallies, but we agreed that in general it is the aristocracy of
superior with regard to inferior intellect.'[5] But however difficult and
confused Shelley may have found the contradictions of social manner
and intellectual commitment, he found too that the contradiction had its
poetic uses.

Shelley explained to Hunt how he had attempted, in *Julian and Maddalo*,
to imitate the manner of conversation between people whom 'education
and a certain refinement of sentiment have placed above the use of
vulgar idioms'. Shelley's *'sermo pedestris'* style, as he himself called it, was
a manner adapted to the familiar idiom of the poetic audience, and as
such it was preferred and encouraged by Mary Shelley. In *Julian and
Maddalo*, and in *The Cenci*, it is a style appropriate to a specific poetic
intention; to present 'sad reality', as opposed to 'visions which
impersonate apprehensions of the beautiful and just', 'dreams of what
ought to be, or may be'.[6] The style is interestingly problematic for a
radical poet, for it involves the danger of acceding to the ideological
implications of that familiar idiom. And there is a strong possibility that
Shelley was fully alert to this problem in *Julian and Maddalo*, where the
single most striking rhetorical effect of the poem is the violently
contrasting idiom of the maniac's soliloquy, which is set against the
gentlemanly discourse of Maddalo and Julian.

There is a passage in Donald Davie's discussion of Shelley, in his
*Purity of Diction in English Verse*, that points up the problem:

The conversation that we have attended to in the poem is just as
civilized as the intercourse of Maddalo and Julian here described. It is

in keeping that Julian should know little of Maddalo and not approve of all that he knows, but should be prepared to take him, with personal reservations, on his own terms. It is the habit of gentlemen; and the poet inculcates it in the reader, simply by taking it for granted in his manner of address. The poem civilizes the reader; that is its virtue and its value.[7]

This does indeed catch a certain quality of tone in the poem; but Professor Davie's own tone here is more arresting, not simply in its oblivion to Shelley's whole manner of proceeding in the poem, where we are constantly offered qualifying and contrasting contexts for each passage, but in its bewildering identification of civilizing virtues and values with 'the habit of gentlemen'. It may be suggested that this identification is something that the whole movement of *Julian and Maddalo* is directed against, in its presentation of Julian's creative, 'poetic' potential as frozen within his quiescent commitment to the manner of a repressive and repressed dominant social group. The figure of the maniac may then emerge in the poem as the externalized representation of this buried poetic potential in Julian, a potential tragically unmediated for any audience and thus possessing the aspect of a tragic incoherence.

*Julian and Maddalo* opens in a tone of cultivated and relatively cool self-possession, which introduces into the voice of Julian, who speaks the poem, a note of wry self-distance, worldly, and not in fact very far from Maddalo's frank disillusionment. This tone is picked up from the preface, which we assume to be in some other voice, but a voice close in its estimate of Julian to Julian's own self-awareness. The preface tells us of Julian's 'passionate attachment' to certain 'philosophical notions', of how he is 'for ever speculating' how good may be made superior to evil. This is all goodhumoured of course, well-mannered; more *amusedly* tolerant than the sympathetic tolerance extended in the preface to Maddalo's lofty gloom, but still quite definitely not disaffected. The tone is echoed at various points by Julian's own perspective on his radical views:

> I love all waste
> And solitary places; where we taste
> The pleasure of believing what we see
> Is boundless, as we wish ourselves to be.
>
> (ll. 14–17)[8]

The phrasing and diction here – 'taste . . . pleasure . . . believing' – suggest something agreeably luxurious in the indulgence of such a whim. And again, in

> as we rode, we talked; and the swift thought,
> Winging itself with laughter, lingered not,
> But flew from brain to brain, – such glee was ours,
> Charged with light memories of remembered hours,
> None slow enough for sadness: till we came
> Homeward, which always makes the spirit tame.
>
> (ll. 28–33)

Talk is fine, but the possibilities it seems to open out must always be chastened as we recall the familiar substance of our actual lives. The tone of the poem's opening section is really the best medium for Maddalo, who, convinced in spite of his powers of the nothingness of human life, supports social life, as the preface tells us, by being in his manners surpassingly 'gentle, patient, and unassuming'. For all the balanced objectivity of Shelley's presentation of the argument between the two men, that argument is conducted in a manner in which Maddalo's position is more at home than Julian's. It is no more than we would expect from a style adapted to 'sad realities', rather than 'dreams of what ought to be, or may be'. Julian's radicalism is bound to appear diminished in strength, to have too much the aspect of a theory, 'refutation-tight / As far as words go' (ll. 194–5), when the words are organized on Maddalo's gentlemanly terms. And it does seem that this effect in the poem is intended by Shelley; for in the context of the whole poem, the argument between Maddalo and Julian will itself be diminished in strength, because we are exposed, in the maniac's soliloquy, to just precisely what it lacks. What unsettles us in Julian's manner is the absence of any critically disruptive emotional engagement with the conflict between social aspiration and social reality. His cultivated composure is tantamount to consent; so that the potential for change embodied in his ideas – a poetic potential, in Shelley's large sense of the 'poet' – is rendered inoperable. The maniac combines a passionate restatement of Julian's radical creed, with a grim enactment of its fate in the response of a society – an audience – that does not understand the language of that radicalism. This is in the order of a *poetic* failure, a failure of communication; Julian's ideals are not mediated for his society, and this consigns those ideals to an inarticulate limbo, like the madhouse.

*Julian and Maddalo* has grown steadily in critical esteem over the last fifteen years, and recent studies have rated it very highly indeed.[9] It is now assumed that the poem is a coherent whole, an executed design, and not the hotch-potch of autobiographical and other fragments that it once seemed. The difficulty of the poem's structure has always lain in what we are to make of the maniac, but it is now generally agreed that whatever his function in the poem he clearly provides us with a further perspective on the contrasting views of Julian and Maddalo. Julian believes, we can agree, that man has the capacity to imagine and create for himself a better world; Maddalo thinks that experience proves life to be unconquerably inimical to human aspirations and desires. The maniac, it is argued, shows us that the questions involved are too large for resolution, and that his presence in the poem throws the debate open for the reader's participation, to be decided in his own response to the maniac. As the preface says, 'the unconnected exclamations of his agony will perhaps be found a sufficient comment for the text of every heart'.

The progress of this argument is underpinned by the changing implications of the natural setting, however; and this makes a difference. The poem opens on:

> a bare strand
> Of hillocks, heaped from ever-shifting sand,
> Matted with thistles and amphibious weeds,
> Such as from earth's embrace the salt ooze breeds . . .

(ll. 3–6)

An ambiguously neutral territory, potentially fertile but barren in the immediate prospect, like the opposed grounds of the argument. Julian's optimism is confirmed in the beautiful Italian light, and in the lingering sunset over the distant mountains, and over Venice: 'in evening's gleam, / Its temples and its palaces did seem / Like fabrics of enchantment piled to Heaven' (ll. 90–2). But Maddalo manoeuvres Julian into what he calls 'a better station', from which the madhouse is seen outlined against the fading sunset, the emblem of mortality in Maddalo's view. As the discussion takes its sombre turn, nature assumes an increasing hostility: 'The following morn was rainy, cold and dim' (l. 141), and, as they approach the madhouse on their visit, they sail 'Through the fast-falling rain and high-wrought sea' (l. 213). This development implies the poem's tacit assent to Maddalo's pessimism, and for the maniac himself, at the nadir of hope, nature takes on an almost Hardyesque malicious indifference; human achievement perishes in its imperious and irrelevant necessities. Through the bars of the madhouse Julian sees 'like weeds on a wrecked palace growing, / Long tangled locks flung wildly forth' (ll. 224–5). The maniac himself is discovered 'sitting mournfully / Near a piano, his pale fingers twined / One with the other, and the ooze and wind / Rushed through an open casement, and did sway / His hair, and starred it with the brackish spray' (ll. 273–7). This specification of the natural context appears to imply man's subjection to the natural forces that govern him, independently and oblivious of the uniquely human consciousness that is the only part of nature not made immortal in its cycles. It is a position that Shelley arrives at, and transcends, in the first, darker half of *Adonais*. The ooze and brackish spray are tugging at the maniac's independent consciousness, threatening to resolve it back into meaningless elemental constituents; and this contrasts with Julian's earlier cheerful contemplation of the embrace of earth with the salt ooze, and his exultation at the way that 'the winds drove / The living spray along the sunny air / Into our faces' (ll 21–3). The negative implication of nature in the poem, up to the maniac's soliloquy, is countered to a certain extent by the more hopeful implication of the stress on perspective in the early part of the poem. From where Julian stands, and in his concentration on the sunset, nature can be made a beautiful and sympathetic setting for mind. Maddalo's differently chosen perspectives and emphases can confirm his different views; so that the status of nature is a matter determined by consciousness, which fits with Julian's argument. But this possibility is very definitely subdued in the first section of the poem, and the maniac's soliloquy opens to the accompaniment of a hostile natural world:

> all the while the loud and gusty storm
> Hissed through the window, and we stood behind
> Stealing his accents from the envious wind
> Unseen.
>
> (ll. 295–8)

The maniac's soliloquy begins at a point in the poem where Maddalo's perspective has as it were infected the rhetorical strategies of the poem.

The figure of the maniac is apparently based on parts of the real experience of Shelley and Byron, as of course are the figures of Julian and Maddalo, and this in itself suggests Shelley's concern to explore a disjunction of social and poetic identity that has some context in his own life. The maniac incorporates too details derived from Shelley's contemporary interest in Torquato Tasso, a striking example of the poet isolated and driven to madness, or the appearance of madness in the eyes of his audience, and thus frustrated by his social context. But we do not need to know these things to think of the maniac as a poet frustrated by the failure to achieve an audience. He is 'as a nerve o'er which do creep / The else unfelt oppressions of this earth' (ll 449–50); he strikes Julian as 'one who wrought from his own fervid heart / The eloquence of passion' (ll. 283–4), and he speaks 'as one who wrote, and thought / His words might move some heart that heeded not, / If sent to distant lands' (ll. 286–8). He speaks of his 'sad writing', and says at one point

> How vain
> Are words! I thought never to speak again,

Not even in secret, – not to my own heart –
But from my lips the unwilling accents start,
And from my pen the words flow as I write,
Dazzling my eyes with scalding tears . . . my sight
Is dim to see that charactered in vain
On this unfeeling leaf which burns the brain
And eats into it . . .

(ll. 472–80)

The maniac has two audiences in the poem; the absent ex-lover that his speech is addressed to, and the unseen Julian and Maddalo who overhear him, and whose urbane discussion pales into a passionless inadequacy in comparison with his words: 'our argument was quite forgot'. It is understandable that the maniac's suffering is the result of a broken love affair; the poet's need for an audience merges, in Shelley's thought, into his need for love (as in the lyric 'An Exhortation', published in the *Prometheus Unbound* volume), and the withholding of love by his audience, the failure of sympathetic and responsive consciousness, makes the poet seem inarticulate because he will not be understood. The maniac's state of mind is comparable with that expressed by the sixth Spirit in Act I of *Prometheus Unbound*, in the lines beginning 'Ah, sister, Desolation is a delicate thing.' The passage seems to have developed out of Shelley's recent work on a translation of Plato's *Symposium*, at Bagni di Lucca; he had been particularly impressed by the broad terms of Diotima's discussion of love, which expand the reference of the word to embrace the spirit of all creative human endeavour, in whatever sphere. The sixth Spirit's speech, closely following a passage in Diotima's discussion, articulates the especially devastating emotional effects of disappointment in our highest ideals; those who are most sensitive, and most delicately responsive to the human condition, are most severely vulnerable to its buffetings. But it is interesting to note that in the maniac's case, his desperate inarticulacy is itself partly the product of a hostility in the audience whose loss his manner of speech confirms.

This reading of the maniac's soliloquy, as a dramatization of the poet's position in a society whose attitudes severely hamper his creative potential, has been suggested by Donald Davie, although in a curiously inverted form:

It is in [his dealings with the abstractions of moral philosophy] that Shelley's diction is woefully impure. He expressed, in *The Defence of Poetry*, his concern for these large abstractions, and his Platonic intention to make them apprehensible and 'living' in themselves. In *The Witch of Atlas* he came near to effecting this; but more often, this programme only means that an abstraction such as Reason, or Justice

65

must always be tugged about in figurative language. The moment they appear in Shelley's verse (and they always come in droves) the tone becomes hectic, the syntax and punctuation disintegrate. In *Julian and Maddalo*, by inventing the figure and the predicament of the maniac, Shelley excuses this incoherency and presents it (plausibly enough) as a verbatim report of the lunatic's ravings.[10]

Even given the extreme and grossly misrepresenting hostility of this passage, Professor Davie has settled on a telling quality in Shelley's creation of the maniac; introduced into the discourse of Julian and Maddalo, the maniac's speech has an effect that reproduces the effect of Shelley's poetry on its contemporary audience (and indeed the effect that it frequently still has on readers unsympathetic or new to Shelley). It is worth emphasizing once more that the single most dramatic effect of reading the poem is its violent contrast of styles, between the urbane and wholly familiar manner of the two gentlemen, and the uncomprehended and thus despairingly isolated words of the maniac. His inarticulacy is simply the reflex, in Julian and Maddalo and in the ex-lover, of a consciousness that will not change until it can understand, and cannot understand except by being changed. The dramatic situation of the poem here externalizes a conflict that is implicit in the contradiction of Julian's radical creed and his passive acquiescence in the manners of a gentleman. Maddalo's attitude to the maniac is that he can but treat him with the decency owing to any man, 'evidently a very cultivated and amiable person when in his right senses', who has been defeated by life into a touching but wholly inarticulate intensity of despair. Maddalo attempts to alleviate the maniac's suffering by creating the illusion of a gentlemanly normality like the personal style with which Maddalo in fact supports his own sense of 'the nothingness of human life':

> I fitted up for him
> Those rooms beside the sea, to please his whim,
> And sent him busts and books and urns for flowers,
> Which had adorned his life in happier hours,
> And instruments of music – you may guess
> A stranger could do little more or less
> For one so gentle and unfortunate . . .

> (ll. 252–8)

Julian's response similarly reveals an inadequacy that is the measure of the limitations imposed by his social identity. He rightly detects something retrievable in the maniac's raving – it is very difficult for the reader too to decide whether the maniac is in fact mad, or really inarticulate – but his intention to work at the task of healing the maniac, of making him articulate again, is smothered by the commitment to a social existence that has no room for the maniac's experience. It is a perfectly appropriate irony that we can recognize in the maniac the outlines of Julian's own radicalism, and that this intellectual commitment is no less potently realized in the maniac's speech than in Julian's. The maniac is 'ever still the same / In creed as in resolve' (ll. 358–9), and, like Julian, he is especially sensitive to 'the else unfelt oppressions of the earth'. The maniac is recognizably Shelleyan too in his rejection of revenge, his sense of the fruitlessness of the desire to reciprocate wrongs. Shelley's ironic juxtapositioning of Julian and the maniac seems most overt in his representation of Julian's awareness of the poetic potential of the maniac, a potential that Maddalo is the more alert to:

> The colours of his mind seemed yet unworn;
> For the wild language of his grief was high,
> Such as in measure were called poetry;
> And I remember one remark which then
> Maddalo made. He said: 'Most wretched men
> Are cradled into poetry by wrong,
> They learn in suffering what they teach in song.'
>
> (ll. 540–6)

The maniac's 'high' language *is* 'in measure'; his speech is controlled and heightened by the same metrical convention that animates the speech of Maddalo and Julian. Here Shelley quite manifestly stands beyond his gentlemanly creations, and places them for us within the limitations that prevent them from recognizing themselves in the maniac.

The poem ends with Julian's failure or refusal to explain to 'the cold world' the story of the maniac, given to him by Maddalo's daughter. The daughter is a positive and hopeful but silent figure in the poem; she appears for the reader only through the idealizing medium of Julian's somewhat watery perception of her. We receive the impression, perhaps, from Julian's account of her – 'a wonder of this earth, / Where there is little of transcendent worth, – / Like one of Shakespeare's women' – that he is not prepared in practice to countenance the existence in his real world of simple human goodness, without the distancing perspective that experiences a realized ideal as somehow transcendent and remote in character. This note sounds more strongly in the passage towards the end of the poem in which Julian rationalizes his failure to attempt the rehabilitation of the maniac:

> If I had been an unconnected man
> I, from this moment, should have formed some plan
> Never to leave sweet Venice, – for to me

It was delight to ride by the lone sea;
And then, the town is silent – one may write
Or read in gondolas by day or night,
Having the little brazen lamp alight,
Unseen, uninterrupted; books are there,
Pictures, and casts from all those statues fair
Which were twin-born with poetry, and all
We seek in towns, with little to recall
Regrets for the green country. I might sit
In Maddalo's great palace, and his wit
And subtle talk would cheer the winter night
And make me know myself, and the firelight
Would flash upon our faces, till the day
Might dawn and make me wonder at my stay:
But I had friends in London too: the chief
Attraction here, was that I sought relief
From the deep tenderness that maniac wrought
Within me – 'twas perhaps an idle thought –
But I imagined that if day by day
I watched him, and but seldom went away,
And studied all the beatings of his heart
With zeal, as men study some stubborn art
For their own good, and could by patience find
An entrance to the caverns of his mind,
I might reclaim him from his dark estate:
In friendships I had been most fortunate –
Yet never saw I one whom I would call
More willingly my friend; and this was all
Accomplished not; such dreams of baseless good
Oft come and go in crowds or solitude
And leave no trace – but what I now designed
Made for long years impression on my mind.
The following morning, urged by my affairs,
I left bright Venice.

(ll. 547–83)

We witness here the process by which Julian accommodates his ideas to a social life which consigns them, inevitably, to the realm of the unrealizably ideal. He leaves the maniac, and Venice – the 'bright Venice' of his optimistic perception – and returns to the familiar tenor of his accustomed existence. Julian chooses not to articulate the maniac in himself, and aspires rather, appropriately, more to the life of Maddalo than of the maniac. It is Maddalo, and not the maniac, in whom Julian seeks to know himself.

*Julian and Maddalo* dramatizes the dangers that operate to nullify the creative radical potential of a man whose way of life identifies him with the class against which his radical critique is directed. These dangers were real enough, certainly in the view of contemporaries, in Shelley's own life, and they beset him still in the different form of the misleading expectations that his sophisticated literary medium produces in his readers. *Julian and Maddalo* overcomes the problem by building its rhetorical strategies upon it; so that the damaging limitations of Julian's situation emerge as the condition of his failure, in forming the materials of Shelley's poetic success.

## Notes

1. *The Life of Percy Bysshe Shelley as comprised in The Life of Shelley by Thomas Jefferson Hogg; The Recollections of Shelley and Byron by Edward John Trelawny; Memoirs of Shelley by Thomas Love Peacock*, ed. H. Wolfe, 2 vols (London: Dent, 1933), I, p. 130.

2. *The Letters of Percy Bysshe Shelley*, ed. F.L. Jones, 2 vols (Oxford: Clarendon Press, 1964), II, p. 108. 'Polluting multitude' in the previous sentence is quoted from *Lines Written Among the Euganean Hills*, l. 356.

3. *Byron's Letters and Journals*, ed. L.A. Marchand, 12 vols (London: John Murray, 1973–82), X, p. 69.

4. W. HAZLITT, *Complete Works*, ed. P.P. Howe, 21 vols (London: Dent, 1931), XII, p. 208.

5. MARIA GISBORNE and E.E. WILLIAMS, *Letters and Journals*, ed. F.L. Jones (Norman: University of Oklahoma Press, 1951), p. 47; and see in this context the very interesting comments by Leigh Hunt in his 1832 preface to *The Mask of Anarchy*, reprinted in *Complete Works of Percy Bysshe Shelley*, ed. R. Ingpen and W.E. Peck (10 vols) (1926–30; London: Benn, 1965), III, pp. 228–30.

6. Preface to *The Cenci, Shelley: Political Works*, ed. Thomas Hutchinson, rev. edn G.M. Matthews (Oxford: Oxford University Press, 1970), pp. 274–5. Shelley's own position here is probably influenced by Hunt's views on poetic diction in his Preface to *The Story of Rimini* (1816), pp. xv–xix (this important document has never been reprinted).

7. D. Davie, *Purity of Diction in English Verse* (London: Chatto and Windus, 1952), p. 144.

8. Quotations from *Shelley: Poetical Works*.

9. See for example Earl Wasserman, *Shelley: A Critical Reading* (Baltimore and London: Johns Hopkins University Press, 1971), Chapter 2, and G.M. Matthews, '"Julian and Maddalo": the draft and the meaning', *Studia Neophilologica* **XXXV** (1963): 57–84.

10. Davie, op. cit., p. 143.

# 5 Unchaining Mythography: *Prometheus Unbound**

### JERROLD E. HOGLE

Jerrold Hogle's *Shelley's Process* (1988), hereafter *SP*, detects in Shelley's work a drive, which he calls 'transference'. Transference is an operation that is at once linguistic and mental, and makes possible thought, literature and culture. The idea of transference is that thoughts and images exist by virtue of emerging from previous thoughts and images which they have remodelled and looking ahead to further thoughts and images. Transference can promote a desirable crossing between thoughts, but it can rigidify (if the transfer-based nature of thought is forgotten) into undesirable forms of objectification (such as the belief in a ruling deity). Shelley's work grows increasingly conscious, according to Hogle, of transference as underlying cultural production. This consciousness manifests itself as a continual interplay between shifting, reworked figures, and underpins the poet's mistrust of absolutes or centres. The poetry's refusal of closure tries to prevent intuition hardening into dogma, difference into hierarchy, art into convention. Hogle derives his alertness to the poetry's 'figural mobility' from deconstruction, but he is critical of deconstruction's 'bourgeois nihilism', castigating J. Hillis Miller and Paul de Man for slighting the will to meaning in Shelley. This will to meaning, for Hogle, has to do with the poet's politics, his 'radical sense of what people are and what the human race ought to become' (*SP*, p. 24). Hogle sees transference as 'the very essense – precisely by not being an essence – of [Shelley's] compelling moral vision' (*SP*, p. 27); part of what makes his own book compelling is the way he puts the concept of transference, and its concomitant demand that centres be questioned and revised, to 'moral'

---

* Reprinted from a chapter entitled 'Unchaining Mythography: *Prometheus Unbound* and its Aftermath' in Jerrold E. Hogle, *Shelley's Process: Radical Transference and the Development of His Major Works* (New York: Oxford University Press, 1988), pp. 167–9, 172–82 (footnotes renumbered from the original).

use. Hogle's critical approach is itself a model of what transference can be; he shows an unusually generous degree of responsiveness to the thoughts and opinions of a variety of critical schools even as he rarely gives total assent to any.

The extract below is taken (with cuts) from the discussion of *Prometheus Unbound*, Act I. *Pace* Bloom and Wasserman, Hogle denies that Shelley is engaged in making a myth in the lyrical drama, or that he is constructing a syncretic vision out of the work of predecessors; instead, the lyrical drama is engaged in demythologising past myths. Wary of mythopoesis (the construction of myth), *Prometheus Unbound* regards surviving myths as mythographs, by which Hogle means 'the written remains of what occurs when poetic interrelations become symbolic systems of control' (*SP*, p. 171). The poem experiences the regressive pull of these mythographs, but seeks to counter them with inventions that free elements from past myths into new and ever-altering relations with one another. (See Introduction, pp. 20–1)

## The anti-mythologist

When present-day experts try to distinguish Shelley from his most illustrious contemporaries, they frequently do so by describing him as the supreme 'mythmaker' among them, especially in *Prometheus Unbound* and the poems written in its wake. For some this label means that the poet returns longstanding Western myths to the effort that originally brought them about, to 'mythopoesis', the projection of human aspirations, fears, and desires for patterns of recurrence into the seemingly alien 'nature' that we perceive. Thus the Prometheus story to the younger Harold Bloom is reworked by Shelley into the aspiring of the alienated consciousness toward a total fusion of the subject with its objects at a distant point where the human psyche might fulfill its desires by obliterating all subject–object differences.[1] In the words of Northrop Frye, this struggle for coalescence confronts the human imagination with 'its own unifying capacity'; it now sees its method of 'linking analogy to analogy' as a way of composing a system of cultural and natural repetitions within which the individual can be positioned as an 'identity' among identities once there is a 'still center' of cycles providing a place for everything.[2] For others, who note the many different old myths that are drawn toward one another in *Prometheus Unbound*, Shelley is trying to develop the syncretizing tendencies in several myth-historians of the eighteenth and early nineteenth centuries. The poet very likely knew the many parallels between Western and Eastern myths proposed by Jacob

Bryant, Sir William Jones, Thomas Maurice, George Stanley Faber, Charles Dupuis, and Sir William Drummond, not to mention Thomas Love Peacock, who most probably suggested this entire course of reading. Hence, so the argument goes, Shelley follows his progress report on *Prometheus Unbound* in an 1819 letter to Peacock with his hope for a 'great work' of 'moral & political science', still 'far from me' at the present time, 'embodying the discoveries of all ages, & harmonizing the contending creeds by which mankind have been ruled' (*L*, II, p. 71). Shelley's lyric drama in this view is a first step in that integrative and totalizing direction. Previous myths for him, according to Earl Wasserman, are incomplete efforts at unifying the aspirations of all human minds and have been kept from fulfilling these 'syntactic potentials' by political and social restrictions on what can be joined with what.[3] *Prometheus Unbound* draws such potentials at last toward the interrelational oneness to which they have already aspired on their own. Moreover, if we believe Stuart Curran, the objective in that achievement is a joining of myths to reveal the most common ground they have always shared: the preconscious 'wisdom of the heart' trying to reveal its own 'dynamics of desire' to itself, to face up to its basic methods of self-repression, self-extension, and self-salvation.[4] Shelley, it seems, regards 'intellectual symbols', the more they are gathered into relations with one another, as producing 'the anatomy of a single mind' striving 'to establish coherence' in the 'fluid' world it keeps perceiving.

But such descriptions are resisted, I think, by Shelley himself and his rewritings of myth. As he shows most clearly in 'Mont Blanc', he does not propose drawing subject–object relations toward a point where they become one permanent union, be it a state of being or a cultural system. Although an 'I' does see an 'it' in terms of subjectivity for a time, making the 'it' a 'thou' (a 'Ravine of Arve') fulfilling the human desire for a counterpart, that transference must turn itself toward another relation (between, say, 'my separate phantasy' and the mountain-top) lest the exchange be frozen into a hierarchical fixity wherein the self must submit to the gaze of one Other or vice versa. Any point of apparent blending, too, such as the sending of the 'mind's imaginings' into the mist hiding the peak, must finally uncover the continual interplay of differences (light shining through already inter-lacing snowflakes) that is the process underlying the attempted connection and urging it toward this interaction and many others. The linking of one analogy to another has to reveal a primordial diversity that forms relations among its elements,[5] thereby exposing identity in a fixed system as an illusion to be overcome by 'doubt' or a 'mild' belief. Certainly, then, Shelley must oppose the governing aims and procedures of syncretic mythology. Whether they are orthodox Christians, speculative deists, or skeptical examiners of primal human projections, the syncretists of Shelley's time all draw the parallels they see back to some early truth, belief, place, construct, or patriarch (some one identity) from which all the variants descend and which they all reannounce as their similarities are rediscovered.[6] Even Wasserman and Curran must admit (if briefly) that such a reversion to a single past is anathema to Shelley,[7] and so, surely, is any would-be collapsing of stories into a single future monomyth or an all-conflating 'anatomy' of the always changing and changeable mind. Thus, when the poet speaks of a future 'harmonizing' of 'creeds' (and not in poetry), he is not really advocating syncretism at all. Given the words he uses, he is probably recalling the congress of all religious sects that ends the Comte de Volney's *Ruins of Empires*. There the callers of the assembly search for the 'means of establishing harmony' among announced cultural 'truths' that are really 'exercises' of political 'power'.[8] Following Volney's example would mean articulating each belief-system as his congress does to the point where each one's underlying power-plays are revealed,[9] where each would then emerge as equal to all the others in being a momentary, speculative solution to the mysterious depths behind our perceptions into which something prior seems to withdraw. For Shelley, to judge by the various old myths about Power's descent that he notes and quickly passes beyond in 'Mont Blanc', a mythic construct is far more peculiar to its time and culture, far more temporary and surpassable once its original purpose has been served, than any syncretist would be willing to admit in his search for the one order that all myths must have shared since the dawn of civilization. [. . .]

## Prometheus as transference: what confines and liberates him

Act I of *Prometheus Unbound*, in fact, is the most sustained battle in Shelley between the drawing power of established myths and the turning away from them in alternative figures. This is not just because, as the opening statement, it must emphasize the points of departure from which the entire drama would escape; there is also the fact that the focal point is Prometheus, a figure who has often enacted that very oscillation in several different schemes. Indeed, yet another reason for Shelley's attempt to liberate this particular myth is the transitional and disruptive actions of the Titan in his previous forms. These shifts make him very nearly the activity of transference incarnate and thus urge that he be released from any of the confines that seem to halt his movement. Whether Shelley beholds him in Hesiod and Aeschylus or finds him reappearing in the syncretists and other Romantic poets, Prometheus in all these cases, before his binding, is perpetually crossing, as a demigod, between old and new Olympians, Titans and Olympians, gods and men,

or father Heaven and mother Earth. He draws elements from the
heavens down toward the earth, or vice versa, as he brings Olympian
fire and forbidden knowledge to humankind or rises from his mother's
depths to supermundane power, even to the point of dethroning one
supreme ruling order (that of Kronos or Saturn) and replacing it with
another one formerly hidden in the earth (that of Kronos's son, Zeus or
Jupiter).[10] All this while, too, Prometheus is the foresight that draws
forth future reversals (such as the fall of Zeus) from the dreams or omens
of the past already tempting him into the heart of their enigmas.[11] In
these transpositions he also conceals or reconfigures what he has
appropriated and the fact of his possessing it. He hides the spark of life
belonging to the gods inside lifeless matter in several ancient versions of
his story.[12] He thereby molds the human figure from the fire–earth
combination into something metaphoric, something from one region
carried over into another, hence something always aspiring to be another
thing. The Titan then conceals from the human race its inevitable
mortality in yet another transfiguration. He veils in everyday awareness
the dissolution of the body – and thus the fear of death – that might keep
people from longing for greater, and even divine, levels of vision.[13]

Prometheus, in other words, before Shelley takes him up, has
transferred several human longings toward each other: the desires for
known origins, superhuman knowledge, punishment for overstepping
our limits (so that we know them), command over the elements,
protection from thoughts of death, courage to endure continual
adversity, and above all mediation connecting what is earthbound to
whatever is not. It is thus hardly surprising that he can be easily
transferred, as already a transitional figure between levels or states, from
these Greek creation-stories to far different configurations serving
different class and ideological ends. To later Neoplatonists, he can be
*Nous* or mind entering the body from an 'upper' level that only certain
initiates can apprehend;[14] to Renaissance humanists, he can be the good
will of the cultured, rational man trying to drive through and beyond the
confusions of fallen existence, as well as the laboring classes;[15] to
vegetarians, such as Shelley (for a time) and John Frank Newton (when
Shelley knew him), the Titan can embody the sad transition from natural
eating to cooking animal food with fire (Shelley's 'Notes on *Queen Mab*',
*PW*, p. 827); and to the syncretists who would make the gentile Bible the
Ur-myth, Prometheus can point either to Jehovah descending to create
man from the earth, to our Savior on the cross (God-in-man) suffering for
the sins of the mankind he made, or to a form of Noah, who recreated
the human race after the pattern wiped out by the Fall and the Deluge.[16]

In his effort, therefore, to release Prometheus from these old contexts,
Shelley intensifies the Titan's propensities, first for moving between
regions that are still kept different and then for changing one activity into

another that proceeds to mask its predecessor. The poet installs this drive
as the common principle in the earliest known deeds of Prometheus
when they are recalled by Asia in her second-act history of the world.
The Titan is remembered there as having transferred 'wisdom' and
'strength' from primitive humanity's desire for such seemingly distant
powers to a raised-up Jupiter (initially another reflector of several human
aspirations), with the proviso that people remain distinct and 'free' from
a wisdom that might impose its fancied strength on whatever it views (II,
iv, 43–5). Promethean foresight has also turned the early human
awareness of physical change and destruction into a perception, initially,
of the 'legioned hopes' for the future always bursting out of once 'folded'
blossoms and, later, into a sense of the relational 'Love' that can rapidly
'bind' again whatever is 'disunited' for the moment (II, iv, 59–65).
Finally, too, Prometheus has initiated the first thought-language
interplay in people. Now referents of language and interpretations of
each referent by thought form a 'Science' and an 'Art' in which our
perceptions (like the Titan's) both extract 'hidden power' and make
'divine' transformations out of all that we observe (II, iv, 72–82). These
are the motions that make Prometheus for Shelley 'the type of the
highest perfection of moral and intellectual nature, impelled by the
purest and truest motives to the best and noblest ends' (Preface, p. 133).

Hence, because this continuous, self-transforming, and frame-breaking
energy is the past of Shelley's title character into which he must again be
released, the poet must begin the sequence of disruptions in his new first
act with an opening speech by the bound Titan that attempts a number
of self-alterations. In the first several lines of the drama, to be sure, an
Aeschylean and Byronic Prometheus tightens his own 'mind-forg'd
manacles' by defying a 'Monarch' whom he still accepts as a 'mighty
God' even as he curses him for enslaving all nature (I, 1 and 17). But then
he suddenly foresees his overthrow of that emperor as a 'trampling' of a
newly debased 'slave' that might make the successful rebel as tyrannical
as his enemy (I, 51–2). At that point the Titan shifts abruptly, not just to
the sympathetic charity that many have noted,[17] but to the posture and
words of Jesus in Milton's *Paradise Regained* as they confront the
stratagems of Satan, whom Prometheus is here in danger of resembling
too much.[18] Just as Milton's portrait of his Savior lets Jesus empathize
with the 'poor miserable captive thrall' destined for a devil who has
'Lost' all 'bliss' (*Paradise Regained*, I, 411 and 419), Shelley's first act has
Prometheus (already a Christ-figure for some) 'pity' the 'Hell within' that
a tyrant must feel when confronting his will to power in another being
and the consequent enslavement of the former master by his supposed
slave (*Prometheus Unbound*, I, 53 and 56). The Titan, committed to a
warrior-aristocrat's epic heroism in the versions of Aeschylus and others,
is thereby joined to the explicit refusal of that posture by the Miltonic

Jesus.[19] Shelley's Prometheus consequently vows to replace the lust for empire with the patient 'sufferance', the hopeful endurance, and the sympathy for every other being's real needs that together can restrain destructive 'Passions, desires, and fears' (in the words of *Paradise Regained*, I, 160 and II, 466).

Meanwhile, though, Shelley's mythograph swerves again, this time to avoid the final ascent of Milton's Jesus to the position of Son assuming 'Rule in the clouds' and hurling Satan (or Jupiter) down to eternal misery 'under his feet' (*Paradise Regained*, IV, 626 and 618–21). Prometheus now aims at revoking 'The Curse' by which he has wrought the subordination of himself and all things (I, 59); he becomes the Son of *Paradise Lost* pitying all self-punishing sinners enough to help retract the 'decree' that once ordained their fall because they once tried to raise themselves to divine omnipotence (*Paradise Lost*, III, 126–241). Shelley, of course, unlike Milton, amalgamates the original decree with several other drives: the self-projection, enthroning omnipotence, the subsequent effort to assume that throne, and the anger directed at this always higher point that has denied the self's independent value. All of this becomes the early error of Prometheus that still imprisons his self-expansion. Milton's Son turned into Prometheus, as a result, turns into a freedom-loving and quietly determined rebel against all the heavenly supremacies of the Father that even Milton finally supports. We now behold the Jesus of Thomas Paine (and of Spinoza to a degree),[20] the revolutionary who in Shelley's 'Essay on Christianity' rejects God as a 'Jupiter [hurling] rain upon the earth' and preaches that man need never 'stand in awe before the golden throne . . . and gaze upon the venerable countenance of the paternal Monarch' (*CW*, VI, 230). The Promethean process of disruption and reconstitution clearly starts its return from suppression in Shelley's first few pages. It does so to such an extent that the modification of one version by a second (Aeschylus's by Milton's) insists on yet another redirection (Milton's to Paine's), which draws the second figure (Milton's Jesus) back toward the first (Aeschylean enthroning of Jupiter by the Titan) in order to leave both behind in the movement to a third.

This progression, however, does not simply drive on from liberation to liberation once it is begun; there is also that retrogressive movement, second figure to first, that must occur during any figural rebellion. Because of it, the Titan must wrestle repeatedly with the power of containment and reappropriation in the older figures (and ideologies) that have created the Prometheus of the best-known version. To free his inclinations from the injunctions of his commanding Other (Jupiter, his superego), he reconfronts a forgotten connection between three elements: his former rhetoric (the curse), his projection of the knowledge and power he wanted into a position above and beyond him, and the 'Phantasm' or mere figure of the self that Jupiter has been from the beginning. Moreover, when he asks to behold this combination, his mother Earth helps him see exactly what his relation is to the figural past, whether he is a mythograph, a transfer, a collation of desires, or an archetype of human aspiration and frustration. First she draws him toward yet another analogue for himself (an apparent unbinding) by seeing his encounter with his old self-reflection as resembling one of the moments when 'the magus Zoroaster . . . / Met his own image walking in the garden' (I, 192–3). She solidifies an already potential (and for Peacock and others a definite) link joining Prometheus, the bringer of fire, foreknowledge, and changes in government, to Zarathustra/ Zoroaster, the first known priest of fire-worship able to contemplate forms beyond present sight and to envision the passage from cosmic forces of oppression (Ahriman) toward the resurgence of world fecundity (the return of Oromaze).[21] Yet Earth also makes the faded, hollow phantasm of Jupiter analogous to the 'Fravashi' figure in the Zoroastrian *Zend-Avesta.* This celestial guardian or 'pre-existent soul' of a magus or of anyone, after all, has been depicted on 'widely reproduced religious icons' that show 'a heavenly duplication of the magi's earthly offices',[22] an exact spiritual precursor 'up there' of what is presently being performed 'down here'. The phantasm that is only a decaying construct is consequently reprieved by this connection, elevated to the status of a true predeterminer and double from beyond. The Fravashi image is meanwhile debased into a mere leftover shadow from a dead ideology that (like the Jupiter-phantasm) may have confirmed other controlling absolutes even as it probably tried to overthrow some of them. The observer of both figures in this transfer must see in each one a rejection *and* an affirmation of some dated method for arranging the world. The instant a present figure or thinker tries to break from his tradition into another, changing his identity, he finds he is haunted by the sort of formation – despite its uprooted, merely ghostly nature – that has made him much of what he has been and will never allow him a complete divorce from his past, only a passage between it and images in other archives. Even a literary revolution, as Pierre Machery has put it, is first the 'prisoner of [current society's] old dreams';[23] there is no other source of shapes for turning our present state into form, even for trying to transcend past figures by way of new formations.

The Earth of Act I, as it happens, is finally proof of that maxim herself and thus a revelation of what allows those dreams to retain the power they have. She does not directly announce what we have discovered in her Zoroaster analogy, since she fears the wrath of 'Heaven's fell King' descending upon her and hers if she 'dares [to] speak' the former words of Prometheus that prove Jupiter to be the image of an outdated concept (I, 140 and 186). Unlike her son, who sees beyond each temporal moment, she speaks out only in the patterns of the current rhetoric, the discourse of grudging submission to old monarchies in which the human race presently interprets her. She is therefore urged to repress the primacy of self-projection and temporal change, and what urges her is 'the language of the dead' (I, 138), the continuing influence of the old hierarchies once produced by those very movements. Soon, though, Prometheus reminds her that his original bursting out from and beyond her, the initial transfer of a shape from within her surface towards a different realm, is part of what she and her language retain in their memories (I, 157–8). The death of that movement within older shapes *creating* the 'language of the dead' turns out to be one aspect of a basic Promethean drive surging out of Earth's surface to produce new mythic figures (thoughts about thoughts of the earth). By helping to remind her of that primal movement, Prometheus reopens her discourse to the succession of emblems that have been formed by different 'readings' over the years, from the way in which visible figures or 'world'-orders seem to emerge from and rise beyond mother Earth. Now she is able to refer to the layers of interpretation piled up on her or driven into her depths, to such old productions of transference from Earth towards Heaven as the Fravashi of Zoroaster. She thus locates the figures that Prometheus wants to face again from his past in a realm of 'shadows' buried beneath the current method of representing her in language.

This vast crypt of once-perceived and once-articulated 'forms', including in it 'all that faith creates, or love desires' (I, 196 and 199) is the cultural archive of former images – a knowing revision of the Temple in *Laon and Cythna* – which underlies the discourse describing the earth in the supposedly 'latest' manner. Here lies the source of the Titan's inability *and* desire to break from the past. In this 'dwelling-house of symbols', which Yeats has called the 'Great Memory',[24] rest the 'writhing shade' of the Aeschylean Prometheus and the phantasm of Jupiter, 'the supreme tyrant, on his throne / Of burning Gold' (I, 203 and 208–9). To these remnants of ideology, now blatantly mythographs, the Prometheus of the present still remains (and *must* at least remain somewhat) attached like a monument deeply anchored in subterranean foundations and buried philosophies. Yet the vast cultural mausoleum also announces how much its 'ghosts' from many different times and systems are 'united' only by the death of their sources (I, 199), left 'vacant' of real conceptual force or truth and so able to be surpassed even while they are being repeated (I, 216).[25] The situation in which the Great Memory places one who would overcome it is inevitably double at all times. Any construct (such as Shelley's Prometheus) that takes a more recent or uncanonical figure (such as the Earth we now see or Thomas Paine's Jesus) as a point of departure, indeed a path of escape, finds itself at least half-repeating shapes in the repository of older forms that is the 'ground' of the new figure (however removed from old power-plays) and, whatever happens, cannot be left entirely for dead.

Hence the Titan in this drama, once he faces his own curses as shoring up the Jupiter-phantasm and 'repents' both his old works and his enthroning of a former self-image (I, 303), is not released from the Great Memory's bonds but actively assaulted by several of its other shadows, forced to deal (as Jesus confronting Satan) with many of the stratagems used to maintain the archive's influence over modern thought. First he must behold a version of 'Jove's world-wandering Herald, Mercury' (I, 325), who frequently resembles the Hermes urging submission to Zeus in Aeschylus's *Prometheus Bound*. Though far more obsequious (and thus duplicitous) to this Titan than Hermes was to his, calling Prometheus 'wise [and] firm and good' to his face as Milton's Satan does with Jesus (*Paradise Regained*, III, 10–11), Mercury argues that no power or origin is prior to the one possessed eternally and inherently by 'the Omnipotent' (I, 362), even though Prometheus has already revealed the historical and derived beginnings of such a projected figure. The herald of the master text then asks the Titan for the sort of submissive 'prayer' (I, 376) that would maintain the lie of a permanent originator not really engendered by a shifting process: 'clothe . . . in words', Mercury advises, the 'secret known' only to foresight (I, 375 and 371). This secret is not just, as in Aeschylus, the tyrant's future overthrow by his progeny (the resistance engendered by an imposition of power) but also the fact that Heaven's 'sceptre' must inevitably undergo 'transfer' to another place (I, 373), since that was the Promethean deed that first moved the sceptre to its current position. From Mercury's point of view, this motion must be immobilized if its transfer of power to Jupiter is to remain eternal. The incarnation of transposition (Prometheus) should be made to speak the 'Nature' of that drive once and for all in a single statement, thereby turning a sheer movement between words into a referent, a static 'essence', which one set of words can signify as occupying one unchangeable place 'over there'.

Fortunately, Prometheus has just the right response. He immediately identifies Mercury as Jupiter's 'thought-executing minister', a sort of press secretary determined to kill any self-transfiguring thought that might transgress the limits of the reigning ideology (I, 287). In doing so, the Titan recalls Lear's famous cry asking the stormy elements to hurl 'thought-executing fires' down from the heavens (*King Lear*, III, ii, 4). That speech shows Lear's desire for absolute power over his 'ingrateful' children projecting itself outward and upward into the sky, a clear analogue to the self-serving act by which Prometheus once enthroned Jupiter.[26] Prometheus has answered Mercury by revealing the herald to be another product of the transference that produced both Jove and Jove's attempt to suppress his foundations. No one interplay, then, is 'clothed in words' by the Titan. Instead, he assumes and rejects the posture of Lear, thus remembering and again repenting his making of Jupiter, and proceeds to transfer both allusive connections into the basis of Mercury's function. A single nature of transference is denied by a multileveled enactment of its process. Prometheus can therefore lecture Mercury on the many modes of transference there are (the *real* secret, whatever the herald of the Omnipotent may think). The Titan goes on to show how being 'trampled down' by a superior comes from the victim's giving 'all' his own power to another (I, 381–2). He then suggests that such created evil minds cannot escape the process creating them, despite achieving a sanction to dictate everything. They must 'change good to their own [evil] nature' in order to control it, obeying the very interplay they would master and contain (I, 380).

As a result, to stop Prometheus from dissecting the oneness of the Omnipotent and so revealing the many exchanges underlying and undermining Him, some other old mythographs, the Furies, join Mercury in his assault and try to make the Titan 'grow like' them by revealing another limitation in his movement (I, 450). Reincarnating old Greek nemesis figures who haunt younger generations with allegiances to or crimes against ancestors and former thoughts,[27] these caustic enforcers of history remind Prometheus (an impetus for change in human acts) of the past endeavors to which he remains attached and of the way these have always dwindled into the very restrictions and destructions he keeps trying to overcome. He is made to feel responsible for these fallings-off and still connected with them even when he would sever his links to them, whether they are the human-made 'cities [that finally] sink howling into ruin' (I, 499), the 'self-contempt' and 'fear' left behind by unfulfilled aspirations (I, 510 and 516), or the 'Kingly conclaves' produced in the end by what might have been republics (I, 530), all of which occurred in the hopeful and Promethean but then violent and tyrannical French Revolution (I, 650–5). Even the figure of Jesus *à la* Milton and Paine, to which Prometheus has allowed himself to be joined temporarily, contracts as the Furies present it into the always doomed fate (crucifixion) of those who try to cure the 'Deep wrongs [of] man' (I, 595) and then into the misconstrued center of a dictatorial religion that 'hunt[s people with] foul lies from their heart's [real] home' (I. 607). The Furies thus draw Prometheus toward believing that these entropic declines, these turnings of metaphoric relations into signs with fixed meanings, will be repeated henceforth without significant differences. Because the Titan transfigures the past *using* the past, all transfers (his and ours) will become hierarchies, all productions of life death, and all hopes fruitless, fulfilling the darkest forebodings of the Gothic sensibility; this is the 'destined agony' of Prometheus and ourselves that, if we believe in it, gives 'form' to the Furies (I, 471), to the human sense of being haunted by a primal state or sin that no revolutionary effort can alter or erase. The Furies thus suggest that nothing really changes as they enforce antiquated but dominant images of authority – so we might as well, they say, submit to what the most accepted ideology has enthroned, despairing of anything better, just as Mercury has advised. For the last time in Act I, facing this claim, Prometheus hovers between the attraction of that world beneath the 'grave', where at least there is the 'peace' of simply accepting outworn mythographs, and the determination to wait for entropy's other movement, its transformational answer to dissolution, at which point a thoroughly new system might be formed from old fragments containing 'no [unaltered] types of the things which are' at the moment (I, 638–45).

But the submissive option is never really the likely choice of Prometheus. Though his self-transformation does decelerate after he becomes a Jesus figure, his shift between different myths continues surreptitiously even as the Furies try to trap him in a consistent pattern. Just after he briefly adopts and surpasses the role of King Lear, the very arrival of the Furies makes the Titan a pursued Orestes recalling the end of Aeschylus's *Choephori* and much of the *Eumenides*. Prometheus is then saved from Orestes's submission to the patriarchal hierarchies affirmed in the latter play[28] by the resemblance of Orestes (and thus the Titan himself) to the Acteon of Ovid's less authoritarian *Metamorphoses*. The similarity makes the bound Prometheus, in the eyes of the Furies especially, a 'struck and sobbing fawn' pursued by 'the lean dogs' of his personal guilt (I, 454–5). His own would-be confiners help him reestablish the principle of metamorphosis (Titan becomes Orestes becomes Acteon becoming a wounded deer) that Shelley wants to revive in recent and rigidified mythic systems and in the mistaken beliefs they encourage about the fixity of human character. At the same time the crucified Christ-image breaks off from the Titan and recedes behind the 'Christianity' that Prometheus must disavow as a distortion helping the Furies to bind thought within notions of guilt and sin (I, 603–15).

Prometheus has kept his alteration going, we find, by playing out the role of the guilt-ridden ideologue only to turn round on it shortly thereafter and observe it from more of a distance. He is able – like Jesus in *Paradise Regained* (II, 466–71) yet precisely by *not* being the Son completely – to be 'king over himself', a current thought subjecting previous thought to different interpretations, 'rul[ing] / The torturing and conflicting throngs within', be they the Furies, other former mythographs, or feelings of resistance to old forms (I, 492–3). Concurrently, though, the Titan still gazes compassionately backward at all those enchained by the Great Memory as he has been himself; he especially 'pities' those so enwrapped by old self-images, so unreflective about what past ideologies can produce, that they are not 'tortured' by what the Furies point out (I, 633), by the fact that 'all best things are [so often] confused to ill' (I, 628). Prometheus thus becomes transitional again, almost in the fullest sense. His removal from the past's dominance is still an effort to look at that past, and he tries to pull it (and not something else) toward a different future (a new combination of self-rule and sympathy for others). When confronted by a relation so complex as to beget such a nonjudgmental judgment, the rigidly judgmental Furies, who gaze only backward, must fall silent (I, 634), leaving the past still in the memory but far less in control of the will.

Now the once-dominant cultural symbols in the collective unconscious can be denied exclusive power, and there can be a releasing from repression of the more 'subtle' and mobile 'spirits' inhabiting 'the dim [innermost] caves of human thought' too long forgotten by the modern consciousness (I, 658–60). These 'operations of the human mind' (to quote Shelley's Preface again, p. 133) are all passages between thoughts, or between locations of thought, where each pole is initially distant from the other in time or place or both. One form of this activity (a figuration of history) flees 'From the dust of creeds outworn' toward the revolutionary moment crying 'Freedom! Hope!' even to the point where the addition of a vengeful 'Death!' to that cry is kept from gaining dominance by 'the soul of love' bursting from the first crossing as its hidden impetus and later result (I, 697–705); another version (a mental traversing of life's known transitions) turns from a past 'storm' seen as a 'conquerer' to the redemptive calm that follows, while a rainbow 'arch[es]' to lift the scene from violence into resurgent beauty or a sailor dying from the tempest gives 'an enemy his plank' as he would never have done before (I, 707–22); and one more variation (a poet's sense of his basic process) sees imagination feeding 'on the aerial kisses [the fading coals] / Of shapes that haunt thought's wilderness' so that it may transmute an image of an image, a 'lake-reflected sun' for example, into 'Forms' that are 'Nurslings of [an] immortality' being kept immortal by reinterpretations of them (I, 741–9). Such transpositions have been at least quietly at work, if sometimes only in 'unremembered ages' (I, 672), throughout the whole span of the Great Memory's existence. The production of the domineering idols retained by that Memory would never have occurred had not these transfers of power between positions operated first, just as Prometheus has already told Earth. These transgressing movements compose the very 'breath' in 'the atmosphere of human thought' now and all through history protecting 'Heaven-oppressed mortality' from total self-imprisonment and guiding it toward outgoing self-extensions, if often quite unconsciously (I, 672–6).

As a matter of fact, this atmosphere is so breathed *out* of the psyche to exercise its relational action in some other realm – fulfilling itself in 'that which it resembles' – that the 'spirits . . . inhabit, as birds wing the winds, / [The] world-surrounding ether' while remaining 'human thought' (I, 659–62). The author has read in Berkeley, Volney, Erasmus Darwin, Sir Humphry Davy, George Dyer, and others that perceptions of what seems to travel invisibly from one object to another lead us to believe in an electrical fluid 'always restless and in motion' that interanimates and 'enlivens the whole [visible] mass', able 'to produce and to destroy' by way of 'forms it constantly sends forth and reabsorbs'.[29] At least as early as the *Refutation of Deism*, moreover, Shelley has accepted such an ether as the conductor of 'Light, electricity, and magnetism' and then seen all these as analogous to the 'tenuity and activity' of thinking (*CW*, VI, 50). Now, in *Prometheus Unbound*, since the world exists even more for him only as it is perceived and continually reinterpreted, thought's primordial transference refigures itself as a 'voyaging cloudlike and unpent / Through the boundless element', a transitional force in whatever seems to be outside it (I, 688–9). There is consequently an impulse for change (a redefined Necessity)[30] in things as they are, since they are but things as we interpret them. There is a Lucretian 'floating', the movement of a Venus (or a love) producing relationships, projected into 'all above the grave' of our past conceptions (I, 686). This force strives both to make 'buds grow red when snowstorms flee' (I, 791) and to recover the age-old desires for 'Wisdom, Justice, Love, and Peace' from within the prevailing rhetoric of power (the Mars) currently suppressing them (I, 796).

For the change to occur as it should, though, the 'spirits' (or various transferences) of thought that envision this resurgence must first gravitate – because the past image must be the point of departure for present alterations – toward the foreseer who has always achieved dethroning transformations in Western myths of history. They must announce their 'prophecy' but also the fact that it 'begins and ends' in an unbound Prometheus (I, 690–1), the agent of actual transfer who first sprang from the depths of the perceived earth as they are doing and who can therefore impel what they desire by visibly shifting between forms and levels of being. He is what they see themselves as being: the 'guide' and 'guardian' of 'Heaven-oppressed mortality' first projected by human longing in 'unremembered ages' *and* 'the thoughts of man's own mind' as they 'Float through all above the grave . . . Voyaging cloudlike and unpent / Through the boundless element' (I, 672–4 and 688–9). Indeed, once the spirits approach him as images of thought's process trying to be reimaged in his release from self-denial, he briefly becomes the mirror-images of what they envision. The reader recognizes in him, particularly since he is the 'reader' of the spirits' statements to him, the challenger of 'creeds outworn', the giver of the 'plank' to the 'enemy', and the poet refiguring 'haunting' thoughts in language,[31] each of which he is soon described as having been or begun in Asia's history of the world (II, iv,

43–79). The invisible crossings in our perceptions of existence thus further the slow unbinding of Prometheus from one configuration by revealing themselves, and seeing his movement, as the forgotten past behind the past's best-known constructs. They expose the projections by which such myths as 'the ether' have always been created, and they show the connection between those constructs and the outreach of thought to all its 'others' that, for Shelley as for many writers before him, is Love in the widest sense.

Shelley's Titan consequently moves closer to complete freedom by the end of Act 1 but cannot finally be the self-liberating agent on his own. Just as the spirits heralding Love's (or Oromaze's) renewal must be read and reincarnated by Prometheus to become 'what it is [their] destiny to be' (I, 816), so he must, as they fade into 'echoes' needing his extension of them to remain in human consciousness (I, 805), reach for his destiny by calling out his love to Asia, the wife of Prometheus in some ancient versions (according to Herodotus),[32] who has been 'far' from him (I, 808) – sequestered in the continent bearing her name – since the fixing of his identity under one male self-image stopped the Titan from 'drinking life from her loved eyes' (I, 123). His self-transcendence must be reflected back in her thoughts and actions, as we saw in the previous chapter, especially since that was the case in the distant past after the Titan sprang from the Earth toward Asia. Otherwise he cannot fully be again the becoming-self-by-becoming-different that he used to be when his 'being overflowed' into her 'chalice' and was there reshaped (born again) each time they made love (I, 809–10). The Titan here turns toward an image-pattern quite outside most of his previous ones. Again starting with but departing from the Aeschylean Prometheus, who begins the second half of *Prometheus Bound* by seeing his doom partly repeated and mitigated in the *telos* of the exiled Io,[33] Shelley's demigod recalls how much Wordsworth's speaker in 'Tintern Abbey' is unable to keep recreating the past in more recent perceptions unless that entire process is extended by the Dorothy Wordsworth (the 'Sister') of the final verse-paragraph[34] – though the process for Shelley is a more Lucretian and sexual pouring of backward-looking emissions into a soul that can redefine them. The new Prometheus, then, reconnects that kind of foresight to the stance Dante adopts toward Beatrice in the *Vita Nuova, Convivio* and *Commedia*. What the versified Dante can become, after all, is simply not made known to him without her love calling him toward her from a great distance through the mediation of other women, visible icons, fading dream-visions, and other poets.[35] By assuming Dante's posture, Shelley's 'foresight' announces plainly that his redemption must be completed by another being or figure, a 'reader' of his present movement across figurations, residing in a different place and performing somewhat different acts (the second act of the play), yet turning back toward him to lift him out of his current state.

At the same time the poet intimates that no such outreach can finally be extended unless the figure giving way to his other foregoes his claim to one identity, or at least to one established range of self-definition. Prometheus soon realizes that the major figures in a relation (for example, the subject and object in a sentence) must pursue each other through intermediate figures crossing the spaces between them, as in the Dante–Beatrice or poet–reader relationships. Prometheus and many of the mythographs confronting him have been partly interpreted for him, it turns out, by the intermediaries Panthea (literally a 'crossing over [between] all [the different] goddesses') and Ione (an 'Io' fearfully contemplating the figures of her destiny, here combined with the Roman version of Isis transmitting love between different beings, as she once did in Bacchic rituals).[36] Hence, after noting to Prometheus the fading of the spirits (I, 801–6), these shifts between more complex transfers volunteer to carry the desires and tendencies of the Titan to their reenactment, extension, and transmutation by Asia. The Titan accepts their intercession by giving his longings over to Panthea especially, and she then foresees dimly (adopting his most famous quality) the remingling of Asia and Prometheus in the speech that closes Act I (I, 825–33). Unlike Prometheus, though, who has too often sought a domineering selfhood, Panthea is so much an elsewhere-looking, selfless means of transmission that she can describe what is now occurring in the 'scene of [Asia's] exile' before she even leaves the Titan to fly there (I, 826–32) and can give in to her deepest dream-memories of the Titan's hidden potential (II, i, 62–90), allowing the 'presence' of his transmutation to 'flow and mingle through [her] blood' (I, i, 80).

The turn between Shelley's first and second acts, therefore, belongs as it should to Promethean transference purified of its need to retain any one past 'self' or the 'central' position in a mythographic construct. Prometheus has begun his liberation from any 'theisms' or plot-patterns that might still confine his drive by sending his primordial tendency away from the limitation of his name *and* his story in a feminine (not male-supremacist), pantheistic transfiguration that leaves some Western myths behind to form new links between those traditions and some from the Asiatic East. It is wrong, I think, to claim as some have that the whole of Shelley's lyric drama takes place in the mind of Prometheus or in some one mind by itself.[37] The ending of the first act leaps past such a restrictive frame to make Shelley's 'setting' the wide cultural and intersubjective range of mythic shapes (or self-projections of human desire) that can be urged into momentary contacts, with 'Prometheus' containing but some of the possible interplays and ultimately giving way to others by his own consent. In fact, that range is not really unfolded to the reader's awareness until Act I ends this way and so, by denying that any fixed state of being can draw the present back completely into the past begins to resolve the struggle between the mythographic archive and the possibilities of a future dance from mythic form to mythic form. Now the reader can focus purely, if only for a moment, on the surpassing of 'identity' by the sheer movement between orders defining the self as male qualities turn female, despair turns to love, speaker turns to reader, self turns selfless, West turns East, and Caucasian summit shifts to Indian vale, all in the direction of mythographic relations far beyond the Aeschylean limits of Act I.

# Notes

Unless noted otherwise, citations from Shelley's work are taken from *Shelley's Poetry and Prose*, Norton Critical Edition, ed. Donald H. Reiman and Sharon B. Powers (New York: Norton, 1977), abbreviated as 'NCE'. Other abbreviations used are 'CW' for *The Complete Works of Percy Bysshe Shelley*, ed. Roger Ingpen and Walter E. Peck, 10 vols (New York: Scribner, 1926–30), 'PW' for *Shelley: Poetical Works*, ed. Thomas Hutchinson, rev, G.M. Matthews (London: Oxford University Press, 1970) and 'L' for *The Letters of Percy Bysshe Shelley*, ed. Frederick L. Jones, 2 vols (Oxford: Clarendon Press, 1964).

1.  See *Shelley's Mythmaking* (1959; repr. Ithaca, NY: Cornell University Press, 1969), pp. 6–8 and 91–7. Note also the similar views of *Prometheus Unbound* in M.H. ABRAMS, *Natural Supernaturalism* (New York: Norton, 1971), pp. 299–307; JEAN HALL, *The Transforming Image: A Study of Shelley's Major Poems* (Urbana: University of Illinois Press, 1980), pp. 79–98; and RICHARD HARTER FOGLE, 'Image and Imagelessness: A Limited Reading of *Prometheus Unbound*', *Keats–Shelley Journal*, 1 (1952), repr. in Fogle's *The Permanent Pleasure: Essays on Classics of Romanticism* (Athens: University of Georgia Press, 1974), pp. 69–86.

2.  I quote Frye here from *A Study of English Romanticism* (New York: Random House, 1968), pp. 104 and 121, and *Anatomy of Criticism: Four Essays* (Princeton, NJ: Princeton University Press, 1957), p. 117.

3.  Earl Wasserman, *Shelley: A Critical Reading* (Baltimore: Johns Hopkins University Press, 1971), p. 275.

4.  *Shelley's Annus Mirabilis* (San Marino, Calif.: Huntington Library, 1975), pp. 102–3, 106, and 96–7.

5.  This sense of separation and distance redeclaring themselves in attempts at the interrelation of differences is what leads the early Bloom, though he does not say so, to point out Shelley's realization that the unifying effort of 'mythopoesis' must always remain incomplete and deferred. See *Shelley's Mythmaking*, p. 145.

6.  As thoroughly demonstrated by ALBERT J. KUHN in 'English Deism and the Development of Romantic Mythological Syncretism', *PMLA*, 71 (1956): 1094–116.

7.  In *A Critical Reading*, p. 271, and *Shelley's Annus Mirabilis*, p. 44. Indeed, more recently, Curran distances Shelley even farther from the assumptions of most eighteenth- and nineteenth-century syncretists while still maintaining the

poet's syncretic methods in 'The Political Prometheus', *Studies in Romanticism,* **25** (1986): 430–2.

8. Quoted from an anonymous translation of Count Volney, *The Ruins* (New York: Eckler, 1926), pp. 174–5.

9. See VOLNEY, *The Ruins*, pp. 130 and 175, and Shelley's exposure, during the very letter wherein he speaks of the 'harmonizing' treatise, of a power play disguised as an assertion of God's truth in Book V, Canto ii, of Spenser's *Fairie Queene*. Shelley refers, right after refusing to attempt a syncretic work, to 'cast[ing] what weight I can [instead] into the right scale of that balance which the Giant (of Arthegall) holds' (*L*, II, p. 71). The poet's refusal of syncretism, as Peacock says in annotating this letter, stems from a desire to avoid the imposition of a unifying order on an equalizing of differences. That very imposition is what occurs, Peacock remembers Shelley saying, when 'Arthegall's iron man knocks [the giant] over into the sea' after said giant has weighed different attempts to 'rectify the physical and moral evils which result from inequality of condition' (*L*, II, p. 71, n. 5). Shelley sees himself as 'of the Giant's faction', so he wants no part of a single-minded philosophy that tries tyrannically to subsume (and thereby drown) every particular method for overcoming hegemonies.

10. See HESOID's *Theogony*, ll. 561–9 and 453–91; AESCHYLUS's *Prometheus Bound*, ll, 108–14 and 209–20; and CARL KERÉNYI, *Prometheus: Archetypal Image of Human Existence*, trans. Ralph Manheim (New York: Pantheon, 1963), which, on p. 52, places the Titan explicitly in 'the position of the mediator, with the hovering in the middle typical of the messenger' Hermes, another longstanding figure of transference and one to whom the Titan is therefore connected in both Aeschylus and Shelley.

11. Cf. AESCHYLUS, *Prometheus Bound*, ll. 484–97 and 910–17, and KERÉNYI, *Prometheus*, pp. 96–9 and 105–6.

12. These are brought together in their most influential form in the Prometheus *plasticator* sequence of Ovid's *Metamorphoses*, I, 76–90. This segment in Ovid, as Shelley would surely have noticed, ends with a portrait of man as 'godlike' but not a god and therefore as gazing, more than animals do, toward the sky (toward the place from which parts of human nature have been transferred by Prometheus). That portrait then becomes the cue for Ovid to assert a self-transformative principle retained in the human form, a principle that can potentially lead to 'unknown species of mankind' if it is fully unleashed.

13. See PLATO, *Gorgias*, 523e.

14. See JACOB BRYANT, *A New System, or, An Analysis of Ancient Mythology* (London: Payne, Elmsly, White, and Walter, 1774), II, pp. 202–3; GEORGE STANLEY FABER, *The Origin of Pagan Idolatry* (London: Rivington, 1816), I, p. 172; and THOMAS TAYLOR, *The Six Books of Proclus the Platonic Successor* (London: privately printed for the translator, 1816), II, pp. 230–1. I should add that I have been directed to these sources and those mentioned in n. 26 and 27 of this chapter by CURRAN, *Shelley's Annus Mirabilis*, pp. 43–94 and 213–30.

15. As in Natalis Comes, *Mythologie, ou Explications des fables* (Paris: Chevalier, 1627), pp. 296–307.

16. For the sense of the Titan as Providence incarnate, see FRANCIS BACON, *The Wisedome of the Ancients* (1619; repr. New York: Da Capo, 1968), p. 124. For

Prometheus as a form of Noah, see BRYANT, *A New System*, II, pp. 206–7 and 274–5, and FABER, *Pagan Idolatry*, II, pp. 193–4. For several such incarnations – and especially for the analogies between Prometheus and Christ – listed all at once in a sequence of fourteen mythic uses of the figure, see the entry under 'Prometheus' in Alexander Ross's encyclopedia/dictionary of mythological beings, the *Mystagogus Poeticus, or the Muses Interpreter*, 2nd edn (London: Whitaker, 1648), pp. 366–8. On the Titan as Christ, see also KERÉNYI, p. 3 and WASSERMAN, *A Critical Reading*, pp. 293–7.

17. See CARLOS BAKER, *Shelley's Major Poetry: The Fabric of a Vision* (Princeton: Princeton University Press, 1948), pp. 96–101; PETER BUTTER, *Shelley's Idols of the Cave* (1954: repr. NY: Haskell House, 1969), pp. 169–77; MILTON WILSON, *Shelley's Later Poetry* (NY: Columbia University Press, 1959), pp. 54–62; BLOOM, *Shelley's Mythmaking*, pp. 92–3 and 100–2; and WASSERMAN, *A Critical Reading*, pp. 257–61.

18. Shelley's own preface discusses the resemblance of Prometheus to Satan and the poet's effort to divorce the Titan from that connection after a definite limit of similarity has been reached (*NCE*, p. 133). For a look at the most significant allusions to Milton's Satan in Act I, see WASSERMAN, *A Critical Reading*, pp. 294–5. For the first extensive list of the many echoes of Milton in *Prometheus Unbound*, see FREDERICK L. JONES, 'Shelley and Milton', *Studies in Philology*, 49 (1952): esp. 499–504.

19. See the assessment of Milton's Jesus in STUART CURRAN, '*Paradise Regained*: Implications of Epic', *Milton Studies*, **17** (1983), 210–17. Note, too, how Milton anticipates some of Shelley's concerns by using the name of Jesus (the revolutionary) rather than the word 'Christ', the symbol of a dictatorial institution. For a history of all the older critical readings that link Shelley's Prometheus with Christ – but without specifying the Jesus of *Paradise Regained* – see LAWRENCE JOHN ZILLMAN's *Variorum Edition* of *Prometheus Unbound* (Seattle: University of Washington Press, 1959), pp. 45 and 311.

20. Paine's clearest sense of Jesus as anti-hierarchical appears during *The Age of Reason* in *The Complete Writings of Thomas Paine*, ed. Philip S. Foner (New York: Citadel, 1945), I, pp. 469 and 480, and this characterization is accompanied by an attack (pp. 469–70) on the ways in which orthodox Christian mythology has legitimized itself by deceptively reworking the myth of the war between Jupiter and the Titans. *The Age of Reason*, in other words, is an additional influence on the entire anti-mythological stance of *Prometheus Unbound*. Spinoza's view can be found in the *Tractatus Theologico-Politicus*, which Shelley began translating in 1817. There Christ is contrasted with the Old Testament prophets, who slavishly followed 'the command of God' when they spoke His patriarchal will. Jesus is depicted as more of a participant in and continuation of the thought-process of universal law that *is* God for Spinoza; the apostles of Christ are therefore more inclined than a Moses or Elijah to argue for an ethical living-out of God's love in mind and action and to do so in statements worked out 'by the light of natural reason' instead of the glow of inspiration from above (*A Theologico-Political Treatise and A Political Treatise*, trans. R.H.M. Elwes (1883; repr. New York: Dover 1951), pp. 157, 18–19, and 161). See also MICHAEL HENRY SCRIVENER, *Radical Shelley* (Princeton: Princeton University Press, 1982), pp. 93–5 and 101.

21. See the definitive account of this connection in CURRAN, *Shelley's Annus Mirabilis*, pp. 67–71.

22. Curran's words in *Shelley's Annus Mirabilis*, p. 73. See also n. 58 on p. 223 of that book. Shelley probably drew this Zoroastrian vision from Abraham Anquetil du Perron's French translation of the *Zend-Avesta* (Paris: Tillard, 1771), II, pp. 254–76, and from Bryant's *A New System*, II, pp. 108–25.

23. *A Theory of Literary Production*, trans. Geoffrey Wall (London: Routledge, 1978), p. 237.

24. In 'The Philosophy of Shelley's Poetry' (1903) in *Essays and Introductions* (New York: Macmillan, 1961), p. 79. For a survey of the few readings since Yeats that even partially apply this idea to the realm of shades, see the ZILLMAN *Variorum*, pp. 360–1. Norman Thurston makes one of the most erroneous, yet in the end one of the most helpful uses of this concept in 'The Second Language of *Prometheus Unbound*', *PQ*, **55** (1976): 126–33. He wrongly argues that Shelley's world of the dead contains the 'true' language of the self that all earthly figures should try to approach in metaphors. Yet he rightly notes that the 'language of the *uncommunicating* dead' in this play (my emphasis), which I find to be the language of the forgotten Spirits suppressed by the ruling figures in the Great Memory, draws conscious language toward an openness to new verbal relations that can 'endlessly' expand human self-knowledge.

25. There is a strong resemblance, after all, between this resplendent underworld and the vast labyrinth adjacent to Lake Moeris in ancient Egypt where, according to Herodotus's *History* (Loeb Edition, Book II, section 148), the most wealthy kings placed memorials of the dictatorial power they held when they were alive. As Michael Grant briefly suggests, moreover (in *Myths of the Greeks and Romans* (New York: New American Library, 1962), p. 187), Shelley's drama may be alluding, particularly at this point, to Robert Blair's poem *The Grave* (1808) and especially to some illustrations appended to it by William Blake, perhaps the only work by Blake that Shelley may ever have perused. See ROBERT N. ESSICK and MORTON D. PALEY, *Robert Blair's* The Grave, *Illustrated by William Blake: A Study and Facsimile* (London: Scholar Press, 1982), esp. the page facing p. 11 of the poem. Shelley, however, prompted somewhat by Blair's lines at their least orthodox moments (as on p. 30 of the poem), clearly view the death of such older figures, mythographic or otherwise, the way James Parkinson regards dead bodies in the *Organic Remains of a Former World*: as shapes undergoing a chemical change in their decay that encourages the generation of 'new combinations' from the decaying materials (*Remains*, 2nd edn, I, p. 80). [. . .]

26. Wasserman is thus wrong to suggest, in *A Critical Reading*, p. 274, that 'Lear's [attempted] relation to his daughters' becomes conceptually 'inoperative' in this skewed repetition of it. Shelley, as he so often does, is ironically retaining that context of the words in order to announce the projective basis of the tyranny in them.

27. See Grant's *Myths*, pp. 170–1; Homer's *Odyssey*, XI, ll. 271–82; and Aeschylus's *Eumenides*, ll. 299–388.

28. At ll. 734–41 of the *Eumenides*, where Athena, despite her own femininity, intones the law of male dominance by terming man 'the master of the house' and noting her own birth from the mind of a male god without a 'mother' as intermediary (in the translation of Aeschylus by Herbert Weir Smyth).

29. Here I quote Berkeley from *Siris: A Chain of Philosophical Reflexions and Inquiries* (1744) in *The Works of George Berkeley*, ed. A.A. Luce and T.E. Jessup (London:

Thomas Nelson, 1953), V, p. 82. But I could make the same point using some of the other authors, especially Dyer, quoted on 'ether' by Curran in *Shelley's Annus Mirabilis*, pp. 106–9.

30. See STUART SPERRY, 'Necessity and the Role of the Hero in Shelley's *Prometheus Unbound*', *PMLA*, **96** (1981): 242–54. Sperry's essay, however, does raise the problem of whether Shelley is concerned primarily in this work with the potentials of the personal imagination, the submission of individual thought to a more interpersonal/historical drive, or the search for a harmony between the former and the latter. This problem has been raised again recently by John Rieder in 'The "One" in *Prometheus Unbound*', *SEL*, **25** (1985): 775–800, which argues that the play can only struggle to resolve an antagonism in Shelley's assumptions between 'individualist' and 'necessitarian' ideologies. Still, though Shelley is torn by ideological conflict, as my Chapters 3 and 5 try to point out, I find this problem elided in *Prometheus Unbound* by the fact that transference is opened up there as an interplay moving (1) through, beyond, and back toward individual perceptions at subliminal levels and (2) among the mythographs into which people have long projected their desires for more extensive transfigurations of the self. To focus on an increasing interplay of myth-figures across remembered and possible history, as this play does, is to face the mind with its own basic process in what resembles the process from outside it *and* to urge the process upon minds from outside their awareness because they are now too divorced from a sense of that motion's history, nature, and potential.

31. As in KENNETH NEILL CAMERON, *Shelley: The Golden Years* (Cambridge, Mass.: Harvard University Press, 1974), pp. 495–502; ANGELA LEIGHTON, *Shelley and the Sublime* (Cambridge: Cambridge University Press, 1984), pp. 80–2; and DANIEL HUGHES, 'Prometheus Made Capable Poet in Act One of *Prometheus Unbound*', *Studies in Romanticism*, **17** (1978): 3–11.

32. See the Loeb *Herodotus* Book IV, section 45, and CURRAN, *Shelley's Annus Mirabilis*, p. 45.

33. *Prometheus Bound*, ll. 700–72.

34. See ll. 111–59 of the poem and Frances Ferguson, *Wordsworth: Language as Counter-Spirit* (New Haven, CT: Yale University Press, 1977), pp. 144–54.

35. Examples in Dante include sections III, V, VI, IX, XXIII, XXV, XXX and XXXV of the *Vita Nuova* plus the *Inferno*, I, 112–35 and II, 52–126.

36. For the multiple sources of these names and figures, see CURRAN, *Shelley's Annus Mirabilis*, pp. 47–9. For one of the only senses prior to mine, though, of how both figures carry 'the sleeping potentiality of relationship' into 'some kinetic manifestations' see NEIL FRAISTAT, *The Poem and the Book* (Chapel Hill: University of North Carolina Press, 1985), pp. 152–3.

37. The most influential statements of this position are Baker's in *Shelley's Major Poetry*, esp. pp. 109–14; Frederick A. Pottle's in 'The Role of Asia in the Dramatic Action of *Prometheus Unbound*', in *Shelley: A Collection of Critical Essays*, ed. George M. Ridenour (Englewood Cliffs, NJ: Prentice Hall, 1965), esp. pp. 141–3; Wasserman's in *A Critical Reading*, esp. pp. 225–56; and Curran's in *Shelley's Annus Mirabilis*, where the play is 'at its most abstract level wholly a psychodrama' on p. 114. This view has been somewhat common, however, at least since WILLIAM ROSSETTI, 'Prometheus Unbound': A Study of Its Meanings and Personages' (1886), in *The Shelley Society's Papers*,

series 1, no. 1, pt 1 (London: Reeves and Turner, 1888), 50–72, and is articulated especially well in MELVIN SOLVE, *Shelley: His Theory of Poetry* (1927; repr. New York: Russell and Russell, 1964), pp. 90–1. One of the best refutations of this conception is Tilottama Rajan's in 'Romanticism and the Death of Lyric Consciousness', *Lyric Poetry: Beyond New Criticism*, eds Chaviva Hašek and Patricia Parker, (Ithaca, NY: Cornell UP, 1985) esp. pp. 202–7. Here the centripetal drive of any attempts at lyrical subjectivity in *Prometheus Unbound* is shown to be countered by a centrifugal, dramatic pulling of consciousness into the 'dialogic nature of language' whereupon any supposed 'lyrical voice is now situated among other voices that are not at one with it'.

# 6 Shelley's Perplexity [*Prometheus Unbound*]*

ISOBEL ARMSTRONG

Isobel Armstrong's *Language as Living Form in Nineteenth-Century Poetry* (1982), hereafter *LLF*, offers a sympathetic account of the workings of 'idealist language' in a number of Romantic and Victorian poets. Idealist language, Armstrong writes, 'assumes that the object is known as a category of mind' (*LLF*, p. xii). She contends, however, that the poets she treats cannot be accused of mystifying the relationship between consciousness and world; rather, their language 'struggles with the problem of relationship itself' (*LLF*, p. xiii), a struggle which has 'political implications (*LLF*, p. xiv) since the very complexity of poetic structures 'tells us something about the way in which language and history intersect' (*LLF*, p. 206). Armstrong does not pay allegiance to any particular school; but her interest in dualisms gives her readings something in common with structuralist analysis of texts as systems of signs organised by and round binary groupings. She also sees how Shelley's language acts as a forerunner of post-structuralist linguistic theory, his words constantly 'becoming a vaporising trace of prints and traces, fading in the wake of superseding sounds' (*LLF*, p. 114). Her book acts as a vigorous critique of the kind of Marxism that sees texts as 'caught in a predetermined pattern' (*LLF*, p. 207). At the same time, her attention to language, whilst showing a formalist virtuosity, is also energised by a sense that uses of syntax, say, illuminate philosophical and cultural issues.

The extract below comes from her chapter on Shelley and is concerned with *Prometheus Unbound*. Many of the issues explicitly theorised by deconstructionist or post-structuralist critics are subtly implicit in her pages. She, too, is concerned with the poem's treatment

* Reprinted from Isobel Armstrong, *Language as Living Form in Nineteenth-Century Poetry* (Brighton, Sussex: Harvester Press; Totowa, New Jersey: Barnes and Noble, 1982), pp. 122–40 (footnotes renumbered from the original).

of relationship, difference, narcissism, idealism, doubling, mirroring, and structures of dependence and oppression. She, too, notes that Shelley's language is paradoxically prompted by a sense of its own inadequacy, 'is always expressing the escape of the receding universe from the reach of consciousness and language' (*LLF*, p. 118). As Demogorgon says, 'a voice / Is wanting' (II, iv, 115–16). But what is especially impressive about Armstrong's analysis is the detailed clarity with which she shows how 'Shelley's account of triumphant reciprocity constantly quivers into the possibility of onesidedness' (*LLF*, p. 122). She values the poetry for confronting its own perplexities, bringing out the way in which 'the poem makes the ground of pessimism provide the reason for celebration' (p. 118). (See Introduction, pp. 9–10.)

The form of *Prometheus Unbound* comes into being because it creates a series of paradigms of relationship and its 'work' is almost ceaselessly to offer models which will be protected against a collapse to ungenerative, static opposites or into unequal dualism. Interestingly, and characteristic of Shelley, the poem is built up through a complex interrelation of repetition and doubling of itself. The form of the poem sets up the problem of repetition and reproduction. Like the Magus Zoroaster the poem meets its own image in different forms and grows by contemplating these. Shelley allows the poem's form, reflection, echo, to question itself and ask whether static replication and dependence rather than a propagative self-creation and interaction is the dominant model of relationship. It begins with a ritual act of repetition, the restatement of Prometheus' curse against Jupiter. The action of the poem is over almost as soon as it is begun, and is in any case a psychological act – 'for I hate no more' (I, 57).

The whole of the first Act turns on the significance of the repeated curse, and the rest of the poem turns on a multiple repetition of that significance and of the significance of repetition itself. Although 'no memory be / Of what is hate, let them not lose it now! (I, 71–2). The memory of *hate* must not be lost. Prometheus is seeking to revitalise the hatred of his curse through repetition in a magnificent testimony to the power of language. The reiterated, ritual incantation of his curse must not lose its power in 'thrice three hundred thousand years', even though a memory of his curse exists no longer. Significantly, the curse is transmitted through the reduplicating power of echoes. The Earth, however, interprets the 'power' of repetition pessimistically, assuming that it will concede to Jupiter and simply reproduce the universal disruption of its original. The first part of the poem is a dialogue between an affirmative and negative, fear-haunted account of repetition. For Prometheus repetition is a relearning of himself and his relationship to Jupiter. He meets his own image in a creative self-externalisation which to him is generative, like the spring which 'struggles to increase' (l. 797) at the end of the act. It is fitting that the *Phantasm* of Jupiter should speak the curse, an 'empty voice' (I, 249) informed by 'no thought', for the curse is a shadowing forth of the mind of Prometheus which achieves new being and dominance through repetition. The Phantasm of Jupiter belongs to the images of that secondary world which is 'underneath the grave' (l. 197), a shadowy, inverted reduplication of this world, coextensive with life and consciousness (*not*, like eternity, beginning where life ends). It is a place where thoughts, events and images of events exist together (ll. 195–207).

Earth sees this world as a dim, nether reflection of the upper world of being, estranged from it, as if thought and living consciousness, image-making and being, ideas and the forms of conscious life and action are cut off from one another and necessarily alienated. But these upper and nether worlds are restored to one another through the repetition of the curse. In Act III, which was originally the last Act of the poem, flanking the visit to Demogorgon's cave in Act II, the structural principle is an antithetical repetition or counterpart of the first Act. Jupiter descends in contrapuntal relationship to the liberated Prometheus, a negative double of his one-time victim. Thetis is thawed into a dew with poison, repeating in negative terms the vaporising of love as it dissolves the being of Asia, Panthea and Ione. The blowing of the conch parallels the utterance of the curse. The unified, fused worlds of sea and earth, air and water, where halcyons gaze at their own images and in which Proteus, humid nymphs and mortals live interchangeably, suggest the transparency of one to another, of upper and lower, inner and outer. These forms restate the estranged, double world of action and thought, being and memory, conceived by Earth as dim and alienated, in terms of crystalline interchange and reciprocity. The divisive dualism of the Furies and Spirits, who are doubles of one another in negative and positive forms in the first Act, locked in antithesis, is replaced by accounts of unity and wholeness. The repetition of the curse has restored a totality because the recognition of the potency and energy of hatred gives one power over it. Hatred is recognised in all its force and received into the consciousness as it *is* (Shelley never talks about the abolition of hatred) in order for Prometheus to be released from its subjugation. In unity with itself the world of Act III offers images of liberation and harmonious interchange. Set against the Furies and Spirits is the unifying propagative power of intellectual beauty. A form of the fountain which 'struggles to increase' (l. 797) at the end of Act I is freely playing in the cave of Act III. Language and speech are fully realised activities of communion rather than the struggling potential verbalisation and silent interchange of the first Act, in which Earth and Prometheus speak without understanding, without *exchanging* one another's words, and Asia and Panthea intuit each other's language.

One might say that the poem has brought its language into being and created its thought through repetition and doubling by this stage in its life, fusing shape and sense, forms and thoughts. Repetition uses repetition as its materials, externalising and constituting itself through a reflexive process of doubling and pairing. The repetition of the curse releases the possibility of reduplicating and enlarging its significance by the very fact that it can be seen as an externalised form. The first and third Acts are in binary opposition to one another, developing out of pairing, echo, reflection, and using the act of reduplication to create negative and positive mirrorings of one another. These antithetical mirrorings redefine the model of reflection as relationship (a model they both create and are created by) from one of reflection as subjugation to one of reflection as reciprocity. They redefine their own materials both formed by and liberated from them. It is not surprising that the central event of Act III is birth, or rather rebirth, as it repeats the myth of the birth of Venus, using language of a limpid, hard clarity unlike anything else in the poem, antithetically pairing it with the cruel myth of the crucifixion in the first Act.

The shifting or unbinding of the model of relationship as reflection from subjugation to reciprocity is clearly to be seen in the relation between the Furies and the Spirits in Act I and the relation between these and the great account of creativity in Act III. But – and this is the power of *Prometheus Unbound* – it is too clear, too easy. The opposition between the first and third Acts depends on an inversion which is won too easily, and which avoids the difficulties of a structure of repetition and reflection as a creative principle. The poem recognises this by creating the hiatus of Act II, the ritual catechism of Demogorgon, and offering another model of relationship even though it is one which also has its difficulties. Act II is left as a cluster of unanswered questions. Shelley also recognised the problems of the poem when he added the extraordinary visionary frolic of Act IV which restates the questions of Act II. Ultimately, the poem considers the permanent possibility of Prometheus' statement, 'Pain, pain ever, for ever' (I, 23–30), which locks up in its structure the principle of endless repetition.

To return to the attempt to redefine the model of reflection from Act I to Act III. The Furies and Spirits are doubles or echoes of one another, and through both Shelley explores the possibilities of the paradigm of reflection. They are doubles of the curse of Prometheus, an amplification of the 'image' (I, 296) he meets in it, because they evolve out of his recognition that 'ill deeds' and 'good' (I, 293) are 'infinite' (I, 294). For good and evil are alike *creative* of themselves, and depend for their being on the human imagination, for which the paradigm of reflection is used. The 'image' met by Prometheus is made objective to itself in their appearance. The Furies, 'ministers' (I, 452) of pain and fear as Mercury is, coming as he does to persuade Prometheus to submit, in particular testify to the human power to imagine. A minister is both an agent and a giver, an instrument and an attender upon need. The doubleness of the word brings out the way in which pain and fear are both agents of the imagination and substantive facts, using and used by the human mind. Unbelief and moral fear survive in the consciousness as an intense imaginative experience, a reality propagative of further imaginings even when their actual cause has departed: 'terror survives / The ravin it has gorged' (ll. 518–19). Unsated terror lives on after its prey is consumed, searching for an object, and since its prey is terror itself, it recreates itself as its object. The homonymic possibilities of ravine and gorge here, the deep physical gap or fissure which has been cleft, and the exchange of possibilities in the idea of a gorge or gap gorged, lend support to the primary meaning of substantive self-acting ruin in the activity of terror.

> In each human heart terror survives
> The ravin it has gorged: the loftiest fear
> All that they would disdain to think were true . . .
> The good want power, but to weep barren tears,
> The powerful goodness want: worse need for them.
> The wise want love; and those who love want wisdom.
>
> (I, 618–20; 625–7)

The poem rises to a rhetoric of hard, severe abstraction here, in an intransient recognition that Prometheus' change does not change the world. Playing on the idea of 'want' as both lack and need in a series of reversals the passage asserts that to 'want' is a capacity of the imagination, a kind of inversion of creativity, and goes on *creating* 'want'. 'The good *want* power. . . . The powerful goodness *want*.' The structure of the language expresses an infinite regress of impotent lack and incompletion as subjects lack objects to enable them to act, objects lack subjects to bring them into being. What might seem at first an unassimilated passage of moral categories is a living account of moral failure made by an inverted creativity which creates emptinesses. (Yeats, echoing this passage in 'The Second Coming', does not fully absorb the structural necessities of the language here, and Shelley's words become abstract in the borrowing.)

The Furies and Spirits erupt into the poem in a series of metrically complex strophes of great virtuosity, emerging out of a world of carnage and bloodshed which are both the cause and the consequence of the idealised psychological structures they represent. Both depend on the propagative principle of reflection, both are assimilated to forms of erotic feeling and sexuality. The Spirits 'feed' on 'aerial kisses' of thought; the Furies describe themselves as 'lovers'. They share one another's vocabulary – 'aerial', 'shape', 'form'.

> The beauty of delight makes lovers glad,
> Gazing on one another: so are we.
> As from the rose which the pale priestess kneels
> To gather for her festal crown of flowers
> The aëreal crimson falls, flushing her cheek,
> So from our victim's destined agony
> The shade which is our form invests us round,
> Else we are shapeless as our mother Night.
>
> (Second Fury, I, 465–72)

> Nor seeks nor finds he mortal blisses,
> But feeds on the aëreal kisses
> Of shapes that haunt thought's wildernesses.
> He will watch from dawn to gloom
> The lake-reflected sun illume
> The yellow bees in the ivy-bloom,
> Nor heed nor see, what things they be;
> But from these create he can
> Forms more real than living man,
> Nurslings of immortality!
>
> (Fourth Spirit, I, 740–50)

The Furies appropriate the passions of sexuality and religion to offer the mutually self-reflecting gaze of lovers and the transference of colour from see-er to seen and back as a paradigm of their activity. These are experiences where imagination is at its most intense and the intensity actually corroborates and creates the self-enclosed world of reflection. The victim's 'aëreal' thought (his terrors and fears) gives meaning and potency to and actually brings into being, 'form', the nature of the persecutor. 'Else we are shapeless.' The mutual self-creation of subject and object is perpetual, enabling the tormentor to give further terror as the victim invests him with further terror yet. 'The aëreal crimson falls, flushing': the convergence of 'falls, flushing' in the line suggests the reciprocity of the process. The aëreal crimson falls from rose, from flushing cheek alike; the flushing cheek is both a reflection and an organic blush which falls reciprocally back to the rose as 'aëreal' things create physical presences. The shade of the blush, of rose, of cheek, which 'invests' the formless with form in this orgiastic creativity is as

much a 'nursling' of immortality as the Spirits' forms. And in the Spirits'
words, the paradigm of creation out of self, of reflection made out of
reflection is exactly the same. The sun is 'lake-reflected', literally
compounded by its image. Reflection of sun into lake refracts against and
illuminates 'the yellow bees in the ivy bloom' as if the creative
transformation of light returns to a world ready to be transformed by it.
In this sense it does not matter 'what *things* they be', whether lake, light,
bees, ivy, for all are forms of thought or sensation because all
experiences, physical and mental, are transmuted by mind. Hence
'shapes', reflections of forms or forms themselves, 'haunt' thought's
*wildernesses*, spaces of mind barren of immediate sensation or '*mortal*
blisses': and yet, paradoxically, mind 'feeds' on the things of mind,
restructuring and transforming perceptual experience. This is a strange
world, warm and frigid, rich (yellow bees, sun, ivy) and yet empty,
barren, and yet propagative of 'nurslings', feeding and fed on itself. This
passage emphasises the restructuring nature of reflection but at the same
time, and more than the Furies, it stresses the waning aspect of
reflection. The light of the sun is at several removes from its source. The
refined sterility of the 'wildernesses' of thought overmasters this limpid,
sure transparent diction.

The account of creativity in Act III (iii, 30–63), attempts to break out of
the negative implications of reflection and echo. It is best described by its
most incisive commentator, I.A. Richards: 'This mind arising from "the
embrace of beauty" is no separate individual mind spellbound in
adoration of its own products . . . It is an ultimately inclusive whole
achieving in this way its own self-realisation.'[1]

> And hither come, sped on the charmèd winds,
> Which meet from all the points of heaven, as bees
> From every flower aëreal Enna feeds,
> At their known island-homes in Himera,
> The echoes of the human world, which tell
> Of the low voice of love, almost unheard,
> And dove-eyed pity's murmured pain, and music,
> Itself the echo of the heart, and all
> That tempers or improves man's life, now free;
> And lovely apparitions, – dim at first,
> Then radiant, as the mind, arising bright
> From the embrace of beauty (whence the forms
> Of which these are the phantoms) casts on them
> The gathered rays which are reality –
> Shall visit us, the progeny immortal
> Of Painting, Sculpture, and rapt Poesy,
> And arts, though unimagined, yet to be.

The wandering voices and the shadows these
Of all that man becomes, the mediators
Of that best worship love, by him and us
Given and returned; swift shapes and sounds, which grow
More fair and soft as man grows wise and kind,
And, veil by veil, evil and error fall:
Such virtue has the cave and place around.

(III, iii, 40–63).

The intervolved syntax here organises the statement in such a way that the activity of mind 'arising bright / From the embrace of beauty' is described in a parenthesis which 'embraces' a parenthesis '(whence the forms / Of which these are the phantoms)', and these parentheses are themselves embraced by phrase clusters describing what man is and what he will become. The embrace of beauty is no static thing (as Richards says, this is Intellectual Beauty, the pure essence of creative knowledge). The lovely apparitions which come ambiguously from the human world which sends to the cave its echoes and its 'music' – 'itself the echo of the heart', another parenthesis – and from the cave of beauty itself are in any case the shadows or phantoms of the forms created by beauty. So they are simultaneously phantoms and incandescent realities deriving both attributes from the same source, beauty. Source and derivations from it are inseparable. The mind, in union with beauty, is itself indivisible from it, and, like the sun's rays concentrated through a burning glass, casts on both phantoms and forms 'the gathered rays which are reality'. Distinctions of category dissolve: feeling and forms of feeling, experience and its embodiment. Everything is involved with everything else; beginnings and endings, phantoms and forms (shape and sense, as Shelley has it earlier) creators and creations, subject and object, negate distinctions in the act of making them. An embrace is an inclusion of each in each, a separation and a fusion, and the syntax declares this. Echoes and apparitions, simultaneously the shadows and the realities of beauty, are also the *progeny* of the arts. So these, too, become inseparable from beauty. The fluent, unitary sentence expresses the echoes and shadows of the human world as things of the present but simultaneously projections cast on to futurity. Projections are the 'mediators' of love, which is a movement beyond the present to the other, and the other, correspondingly, becomes reciprocally aware of the need to go beyond itself in an effort to grasp the meaning of this projection. This is 'want' defined creatively. Subjects find and create objects. Objects find and create subjects as they become identified. Shelley is describing the process of imaginative making, the creation of unknown possibility out of human thought.

The poem liberates itself from the closed world of reflection and echo here by acting out the transforming energy of the embrace. But it is at a cost. The syntax is so fluent, of such pouring ambiguousness and dissolution, that whatever its virtuosity the old charge of the obliteration of relationship cannot be forgotten. The poem takes a risk here and perhaps it is able to take a risk because before it, in Act II, another and different model of relationship has evolved which solves some of the problems of the paradigm of reflection. It does not conflict so much as runs parallel to it. This model is both supremely simple and paradoxical. It is intrinsic to the very nature of dramatic form itself – dialogue, or rather, question and answer. At the centre of the original poem is Asia's ritual interrogation of Demogorgon, a stark model of dramatic interchange. In it the central questions of the poem are given form: 'Who made terror, madness, crime, remorse?' (II, iv, 19); 'Who is the master of the slave?' (l. 114) It is the first point in the poem at which dialogue becomes really possible. As I have said, the interchange between Prometheus and Earth in Act I takes place without language, and there are no answers to the violent questions of Prometheus – 'I ask the Earth, have not the mountains felt?' (I, 25). It is as if he exists in a world without an object. The converse of Asia, Panthea and Ione is wordless: 'thy words / Are as the air: I feel them not'( II, i, 108–9). The journey to Demogorgon's cave, following echo inwards to its source, reverses the movement of the curse which sends out echoes, reduplicating its image in a cycle of repetition. Language comes into being in the act of interrogation, a kind of daemonic catechism. But paradoxically the form of the dialogue is a turning back of every interrogation on the asker, and what is discovered is arrived at because the formulation of the question dictates the formulation of the reply which reflects back the question. Demogorgon, 'a mighty darkness', 'Ungazed upon and shapeless; neither limb, / Nor form, nor outline' (II, iv, 5–6) is like the Furies, given form only by Asia's questions, which are an interrogation of formlessness, perhaps nothing. But being given form by the questions, he gives *them* form, returning them upon themselves, externalising them and enabling a recognition which is the growing point of all thought. Demogorgon can only repeat, simply, tautologically, 'He reigns', in answer to Asia's questions. 'All spirits are enslaved which serve things evil', he replies to her question 'Is he [Jupiter] too a slave?' (110–11). 'I spoke but as ye speak.' 'So much I asked before', Asia says, 'and my heart gave / The response thou hast given' (121–2). But the self here is not living in the hollow reverberation of its own echoes however much this pattern of dialogue might seem to repeat the paradigm of echo and reflection. The very structure of question and answer precludes the closed circle of repetition because dialogue is dialectic. The mind knows and possesses what it knows only by repossessing that knowledge. The act of reformulation – 'He *reigns*', 'All spirits are enslaved', is the

discovery of knowledge through a reshaping which enables further
questions to emerge. It is not simply the earlier knowledge in a new form
but the reforming is a new structure, a new experience. 'All spirits are
enslaved' introduces the vital new description, 'which *serve*'. To serve, to
be a minister, to be active or passive agent? This is how, in Shelley's own
words in *A Defence*, knowledge grows. Mind acting on thoughts
composes 'other thoughts'. Each contains within itself 'the principle of its
own integrity',[2] because thought is not an arbitrary principle of addition,
but a new content grows out of preceding forms of thought and is
genetically determined by it. Furthermore, the naming which goes on
here could not take place without the mutuality of self and other
returning one another's statement in objective form. The paradigm of
dialogue and dialectic breaks the relationship of domination. This is how
we deal with our Furies, by *mutual* interrogation. Prometheus' first
speech is caught in a syntax of domination and opposition which
precludes the dramatic structure of mutuality. The pronouns oppose
'Thou and I', thou and me, thy and mine remorselessly as one fights the
subjugation of the other.

> Monarch of Gods and Daemons, and all Spirits
> But One, who throng those bright and rolling worlds
> Which Thou and I alone of living things
> Behold with sleepless eyes! regard this Earth
> Made multitudinous with thy slaves, whom thou
> Requitest for knee-worship, prayer, and praise,
> And toil, and hecatombs of broken hearts,
> With fear and self-contempt and barren hope.
> Whilst me, who am thy foe, eyeless in hate,
> Hast thou made reign and triumph, to thy scorn,
> O'er mine own misery and thy vain revenge.

$$(I, 1-11)$$

And so, in reasserting *drama* as the centre of the Demogorgon
catechism the poem justifies its own structure and liberates the
possibility of its growth, releasing new modes of relationship.
Characteristically, though, it does not *seem* to do this. Demogorgon
asserts that an ultimate truth is unknowable. 'But a voice / Is wanting,
the deep truth is imageless.' Shelley is very fond of the negative '-less'
suffix, where perception is made possible only by being defined as what
it is not, or cannot do. Demogorgon seems to be conceding to a notion of
numinous transcendent essence, an ever-hidden source, unseen,
unknown. He seems to concede to an unreachable beyond, and with it to
a Romantic nihilism about language, which vaporises, turns into the mist
and foam of its vanishing point, destroying itself in the effort to reach

beyond. And yet there is a counterpart to this account of things, Asia's 'and speech created thought' (II, iv, 72), which precedes Demogorgon's statement, and is not in fact incompatible with it. The mind can only know what language can image. But language and relationship emerge at the point of negation. The deep truth is imageless. It is at this point that a voice is lacking, but at which language is *needed*. The word 'want' moves from its designation as deprivation to a more positive designation of *need*. Imagelessness calls images into being, if only by being defined as such. The not, the -less, is an *is* not. 'Poetry enlarges the circumference of the imagination,' Shelley wrote in *A Defence*, 'by replenishing it with thoughts of ever new delight which have the power of attracting and assimilating to their own nature all other thoughts, and which form *new* [my italics] intervals and interstices, whose voice for ever craves fresh food.'[3] The ambiguity of 'wanting' as both negation and affirmation, lacking and *needing*, shifts the definition of want offered by the Furies – 'the good *want* power' – in a positive direction, and points to the possibilities inherent in Demogorgon's pessimistic statement. The act of negation is a creative structuring of the world. The definition of lack simultaneously creates and discovers need. By seeing want, indivisibly lack and need, as *not*, as other, what is not known, the void and interstice is brought into being and into relationship with the self. To acknowledge that experience is 'imageless', is a way not of closing but of liberating areas of experience for definition and discovery. The act of verbalising gives form to imagelessness and creates the possibility of further form which in turn depends on the opening up of new spaces. Demogorgon occupies a realm of negation, where perceptual experience is dissipated in dew blanching, breezes dying, light scattering. It is just such 'thought's wildernesses' that the poet opens up, on the edge of perception. In her final song Asia moves amid a 'paradise' of 'wildernesses' and 'wildernesses calm and green' (II, v, 81, 107).

The act of negation, of course, is a self-creation in Hegel's sense because it defines the subject against the not incorporating it as part of being. But the labour of the negative here is also a differentiation, an interval which is inalienably other. And so the wilderness both creates and negates being. Want creates need, need creates want and lack. If the shapeless, limbless Demogorgon is to be described as anything (Necessity? the life force? the deep truth? the unknowable source?) he is the moment of coming into being, the moment of definition which is other to the self and both primal and recurrent, the coming into being of negation, the moment of want which needs a voice to create thought and relationship by constituting that void *as* void. Interestingly, behind both the *Defence* and *Prometheus* is an atavistic account of primal lack in terms of food and sexuality – 'craves fresh food', 'aëreal kisses'. It is as if language arises from an analogous deprivation and gives structure to it.

To create the not is to create thought. With spectacular consistency the Demogorgon scene evolves the song of the Voice in Air, the voice which is wanting, the voice from the air, the voice comong out of nothing and made out of nothing. It answers the pure, wordless sound of the nightingale in Demogorgon's realm, which is perpetually dying and recreated, inexhaustible but repetitive, only expressive of itself, sung (like the Nightingale poet in the *Defence*) to 'cheer its own solitude', a sound without a language. The opposition of pure sound is not only silence but language or meaning, just as the antithesis of Demogorgon's shapelessness is a double opposition which is both form and emptiness. Converse, dialogue, emerges through the interaction of all three 'converse' elements. The language seeks to express the converse. This is why the proper mode of discourse in the song of the Voice in Air, celebrating the mystery of Asia's being, is paradox. The *cold* air is *fire*, *dim* shapes are clad with *brightness*. Paradox depends upon opposition and negation. It says that something is and is not simultaneously. It is the embodiment of that flicker, quiver or tremble which is the principle of Shelley's language. Its being is oscillation.

> Life of Life! thy lips enkindle
>> With their love the breath between them;
> And thy smiles before they dwindle
>> Make the cold air fire; then screen them
> In those looks, where whoso gazes
> Faints, entangled in their mazes.
>
> Child of Light! thy limbs are burning
>> Through the vest which seems to hide them;
> As the radiant lines of morning
>> Through the clouds ere they divide them;
> And this atmosphere divinest
> Shrouds thee wheresoe'er thou shinest.
>
> Fair are others; none beholds thee,
>> But thy voice sounds low and tender
> Like the fairest, for it folds thee
>> From the sight, that liquid splendour,
> And all feel, yet see thee never,
> As I feel now, lost for ever!
>
> Lamp of Earth! where'er thou movest
>> Its dim shapes are clad with brightness,
> And the souls of whom thou lovest
>> Walk upon the winds with lightness,

Till they fail, as I am failing,
Dizzy, lost, yet unbewailing!

(II, v, 48–71)

This is a transposition of the traditional language of spiritual extremity
into philosophical terms and achieves that peculiar fusion of rationality
and ecstasy which is characteristic of *Prometheus Unbound*. The structure
of paradox enables negation, and affirmation, creation and denial, to be
experienced simultaneously – 'make the cold air fire': cold air is, is not
cold air: cold air is, is not fire: fire is, is not fire: fire is, is not cold air. It is
not simply that the impossible transgression of sensation from cold to
heat ignites the 'is not' into an 'is', converting negative into positive, cold
into heat (and, it follows, cold air unseen into heat felt and *visible* fire);
one sensation succeeding another. Paradox will not allow such
supersession because it does not depend on the substitution of one
quality for another. The substitutions continually construct and
deconstruct themselves. The new meaning it insists upon is a new
category evolving out of a new relationship between *is* and *is not* which
are continually changing places, 'is not' defining 'is', 'is' defining 'is not',
'is not' becoming 'is', 'is' becoming 'is not' – visible air, invisible fire,
burning cold, cold heat. The language flickers, quivers endlessly between
negation and assertion and this quivering oscillation discovers new
definitions. It is not merely a paradigm of the activity which forms
intervals and interstices whose void forever craves fresh food, but it *is*
that activity, constituting meaning in and through its structure. Paradox
is language moving to the edge of itself, where new definition just hovers
into being through the assertion of negation. It is language discovering
the void in the double sense of finding and exploring it, reaching out to
possess the spaces it opens almost to the point of attenuation. With each
successive statement of paradox and with that characteristically physical
quality, a sensuous knowledge of non-being which is itself paradoxical,
the voice faints, loses itself, fails – 'Faints . . . lost forever . . . till they
fail, as I am failing / Dizzy, lost, yet unbewailing!' Sounds melt down into
one another through the stanza as rhymes soften and fail with the
dissolution of line endings. The grammar faints: 'then screen them / In
those looks', 'hide them', 'divide them'. The persistent ambiguity of
'their', 'them' is 'entangled in *their* mazes'. 'Their', 'them' either serves
two subjects at once, failing the differentiation between separate entities,
or returns upon the subject as its own object: 'thy lips enkindle / With
*their* love the breath between *them* [lips]': 'then screen *them* [lips, smiles] /
In *those* looks [smiles], where whoso gazes / Faints, entangled in *their*
mazes' (the mazes of the smile, the onlooker's own amazement). But with
each sinking or failure of relationship, with each entry into annihilation,
paradox re-emerges in a new form as a means of constructing experience,

coming into being out of nothing, as it were, but with a structure made possible by that condition.

Paradox is a living example of the transformation of categories and the creation of new ones. What it construes here, with characteristic daring and virtuosity, is that experience of 'is' and 'is not' which is the condition of the expansion of language and knowledge. Asia is unknowable, imageless, concealed and yet revealed. With a dazzling rearrangement and reversal of paradoxical statement in negative and positive terms, each of which grows out of antecedent forms (the dazzle is in the words – enkindle, fire, burning, radiant, shinest, brightness), the paradoxical structure asserts that to construe a not seen is to shape a seen, that to construe a seen is to define a not seen. 'Screen them', 'hide them', 'shrouds thee', 'folds thee', 'clad with brightness'. The poem risks mystical language and the metaphor of the veil and barrier to knowledge (with its cognate implication that language is the inadequate dress of thought), and yet enables these to contradict themselves. 'Then screen them / In those *looks*, where whoso *gazes*.' To screen is to constitute a presence as well as to hide it: there could be no screen without something behind it. Reciprocally, a presence brings into being a screen. And so a visible screen brings the possibility of 'looks' and 'gazes' into being. Screen generates its opposite, seen is not, is. Those looks, the syntax allows, are the screen, and also what is screened, 'them', the smiles which are consequently, simultaneously, consecutively, reflexively, screening themselves. Appropriately, as smiles are present and absent, given transient form in physical features without being physical features themselves, and giving form to physical features and indeed requiring them for its existence. A smile is neither the body nor the disembodied, but it might be called the 'Life of Life' in the strict sense that it both animates and is animated by the physical, a presence which cannot come into being without the physical, cannot be subtracted from it and yet mysteriously does not belong to it, is not *of* it. What the paradoxes have done is to give new content to the paradox of 'Life'. The first paradox moves towards creating a being for 'imageless' 'Life'. The poem gives itself the right to call Asia 'Child of Light' in the next stanza. She is made of light, generated by it, but also the progeny of knowing, born out of what is known, as the next stanza is born out of the paradoxes of the first.

It is the negative side of the known, not known, revealed, concealed paradox which is uppermost in the second stanza. Screen, seen, 'shrouds', 'shinest': the contradictory words become closely allied in sound. Shrouding is dependent upon shining for its activity. The not seen creates the seen and yet is intuited through it, known by what conceals it. 'Thy limbs are burning / *Through* the vest which seems to hide thee.' 'Seems' here, appropriately, asks the perceptual question arising from the ambiguity of 'through'; burning behind and shining through, burning by means of, burning up, penetrating through, but in all cases the nature of covering vesture and limbs is interdependent, the one coming into being as known through the other 'As the radiant lines of morning / *Through* the clouds ere they divide them': the ambiguous syntax here allows a similar reciprocal interdependence of being to radiant sunrise and concealing clouds. Either clouds divide, *expose* radiance, or radiance divides, penetrates, clouds. 'Them' is radiance and cloud indivisibly. We cannot see a voice or the source of a voice, so the third stanza proposes; and yet being is folded in sound like a shroud. It can be sensed. Again, and paradoxically, absence is intuited as present and therefore presence from the sourceless song. Again, presence is negatively intuited from positive absence in a fluid grammar: 'for *it* folds *thee* / From the sight, that liquid splendour'. The song, 'it', is liquid splendour and so is 'thee', the being of Asia, and so is 'sight' which designates both self and seen, liquid splendour created by and creating splendour. Being is *flowing* radiance, or beauty as splendour, is taken back to its primal sense as lustre. The source and its derivation are fused as the not seen creates, not the seen, but the known. And the lyric proceeds to its final paradox – 'Its dim shapes are clad with brightness.' The concealing element is light itself as screen and shroud reverse their sense of obliterating physical barrier. Dimness is created by brightness. The deep truth is imageless and known, but, the paradox of the paradox, each condition enables, creates the other and this in itself is being. It is also language, as speech creates thought and is indivisible from it.

The poem fulfils itself here, one would have thought, creating and denying negation as the principle of growth and allowing speech to create thought by fusing shape and sense, form and meaning. Perhaps the new confidence in the use of reflection as a paradigm of relationship which is returned to in Act III, and the emphasis on its restructuring and creative possibilities, is born of the discovery of the possibilities of dialogue and creative negation in Act II. Indeed, the 'interval' of Act II would enable one to see the insistent pairing doubling and antithesis of ideas of reflection in Acts I and III as an attempt to create not a simple opposition but a paradox out of the contradictions of reflection itself. It is, and is not an enclosed self-creation of object by the subject. The poem solves some of its problems in Act II, proposing the finding of an object in the very fact of its negation and the fact of lacunae by turning want into need, the need which creates a new object and new knowledge. However, the rigour of this lyric, and of the whole poem, is unremitting. They carry their own criticisms along with them. Since the finding of the object depends on the losing of it, on lacunae, a reading of Act II does not entirely resist an account of it as that condition in which mind constructs itself as other, not the thing but thought. 'Faints', 'lost

forever', 'failing', 'Dizzy': these words do not withstand the familiar
attack on idealism. The negation created as other, the hungry void and
interval craving for being, can be defined, as Marx defined it, as that void
from which reality is continually disappearing, reaching its vanishing-
point where the distinction between subject and object dissolves into
thought's wildernesses. The gazer entangled in the amazement of the
'mazes' of what it sees, 'those looks' is also entangled in 'their' or his *own*
mazes, and through the ambiguity of the syntax 'those looks' are his own
seeing and the seen without distinction. In the same way the 'sight' is
the 'see-ers' sight and the sight he sees, as the fluent syntax of 'that
liquid splendour' moves inderminately between 'it' as voice, 'thee' as
Asia and 'sight' as perceiver and perceived.

The last line of Act III, 'Pinnacled dim in the intense inane' (l. 204),
unintentionally corroborates these doubts, and, despite its certainties,
the triumphant assertion of freedom is less confident than it might seem.
Nor yet exempt, though 'ruling them like slaves, / From chance, and
death, and mutability' (III, iv, 200–2): men rule the slaves of chance and
death, but, the syntax allows, exposing the complexities of power and
freedom, they also rule them as slaves rule. If the poem had ended at Act
III it would have left too many things closed and too many things open.
The rapturous coda of the fourth Act is a necessity. Neither Act II nor Act
III entirely free themselves into a universe of reciprocity, despite the play
of energy, of motion and flight, of rush and speed, of beings drawn and
driven, impelling and impelled, active and passive, fleeing and pursuing,
first and last. The models of relationship evolved raise doubts as the
paradigm of reflection reasserts itself, either suggesting the subjugation
of secondary forms as the self encloses the object in a reduplication of
itself or creating a state where relationships are obliterated altogether in
undifferentiated exchange of qualities. The coda of Act IV does not leave
aside the perplexities of the poem. Instead it releases itself into the
energies of freedom and delight by another act of repetition – the
interpenetration and flow of light, wind, water, the leap of energy
through and into being and being, the synaesthesic fusion of like and
unlike. Act IV repeats the images of the earlier poem, recirculating them
to act out the energies of circulation and movement. It is constructed out
of dialogue and dance, echo and reflection but gives primacy to none of
these paradigms of relationship, simply including them all. Included,
too, but redefined by the released energies of delight and compassion,
are the implications of subjugation and dissolution which so threatened
the earlier acts. They are not forgotten. The poem includes and
acknowledges its perplexities within itself. It can do this because it is a
celebration of *Hope* rather than an achieved triumph. Hope, creating
'From its own wreck the thing it contemplates' (IV, 573) is another and
more affirmative definition of want. Meanwhile, reminding itself of the

107

recurrent pattern of dependence and subjugation, the moon, circling in dizzy maenad-like movement round the earth, dependent on it for light, repeats the structure of the Furies' relation to Prometheus in Act I, though not its form.

> Drinking from thy sense and sight
> Beauty, majesty, and might,
> As a lover or a chameleon,
> Grows like what it looks upon.

> (ll. 481–4)

As the moon dissolves in the light of the sun, Earth answers, 'And the weak day weeps / That it should be so' (ll. 493–4), mourning its own and the moon's dependence on the sun. The mourning here, amid the celebrations of Act IV, sounds the great perplexity of this poem, which cannot obliterate the pattern of dependence and subjugation. Nor, correspondingly perhaps, can it entirely acknowledge that language 'rules' (IV, 416) and creates thought.

## Notes

Quotations from *Prometheus Unbound* are taken from *Shelley's Poetical Works*, ed. Thomas Hutchinson, rev. edn G.M. Matthews (Oxford: Oxford University Press, 1970).

1.  *Beyond* (New York and London: Harcourt Brace Jovanovich, 1973), p. 199.

2.  *A Defence of Poetry*, *Shelley's Prose*, ed. David Lee Clark (Albuquerque: University of New Mexico Press, 1954), pp. 276, 276–7.

3.  *A Defence of Poetry*, *Shelley's Prose*, p. 283.

# 7 The Politics of Reception [*The Cenci*]*

WILLIAM A. ULMER

In *Shelleyan Eros* (1990), hereafter *SE*, William Ulmer combines various critical approaches – especially deconstruction, reception theory, feminism, and psychoanalysis – in order to probe Shelley's poetic treatment of desire. He questions the growing critical consensus that Shelley is best understood as a sceptic rather than idealist, and takes issue with the view put forward by Ronald Tetreault (see Chapter 9 of this volume) that Shelley avoids determinate meaning so as to celebrate the freedom of the reader. Ulmer has no time for this celebratory form of deconstruction and reminds us of 'the inability of deconstruction to escape logocentrism' (*SE*, p. 16), reading the poetry as driven by a strong but often unattainable wish to communicate an idealist vision. Ulmer's Shelley strives for closure as much as for indeterminacy, but is constantly baffled in his idealistic project by the nature of language, the instrument through which he seeks to communicate his vision of life. For one thing, the idealist venture, as Shelley saw it, depends on eliminating the difference between author and reader, yet his poetics of love demanded that he yield the reader some measure of autonomy. Another contradiction, in Ulmer's view, is that between Shelley's avowed feminism and his reinvestment in 'patriarchal norms' (*SE*, p. 23). Moreover, metaphor, on Ulmer's account the principal means by which Shelleyan unity is posited, works by appropriating otherness and repressing difference; its use by Shelley betrays a 'unitive poetics divided against itself' (*SE*, p. 7). As a result, Shelley's idealism is involved in displacement, his later poems 'diverting love from worldly mediations to transcendent absolutes' (*SE*, p. 23).

The following extract is drawn from Ulmer's discussion of *The Cenci*.

---

* Reprinted from William A. Ulmer, *Shelleyan Eros: The Rhetoric of Romantic Love* (Princeton, N.J.: Princeton University Press, 1990), pp. 118-29 (footnotes renumbered from the original).

He sees this work as investigating and caught up in a series of tortuous, fascinating tensions. Its images of mirroring enforce the Lacanian point that the subject is constituted in a specular fashion, responding to what it takes to be its reflection in the eyes of others, escaping aloneness at the cost of integrity; such images, like the play as a whole, thematise Shelley's own anxiety about how his words will be received. The play becomes, on Ulmer's reading, a pessimistic fable about 'the indeterminacies of public discourse' (*SE*, p. 118) that deconstructs its desire to involve the spectator in a process of cathartic recognition; ironically both play and dramatist are implicated in the very oppression they set out to expose. (See Introduction, pp. 17–18.)

## Metaphor and Violence

As the negation of Shelley's Promethean myth, *The Cenci* both reflects and disfigures the metaphorical idealism of *Prometheus Unbound*. If the tragedy's distorting mirror makes metaphor the trope of power, it makes power the motive of desire. Francesco Cenci's cruelty must be attributed partly to 'a perverted sexual drive', an investment of libido in the luxurious refinements of pain and fear.[1] 'I was happier than I am', the aging Count admits,

> While lust was sweeter than revenge; and now
> Invention palls: – Aye, we must all grow old –
> And but that there remains a deed to act
> Whose horror might make sharp an appetite
> Duller than mine – I'd do, – I know not what.
> When I was young I thought of nothing else
> But pleasure; and I fed on honey sweets:
> Men, by St. Thomas! cannot live like bees
> And I grew tired: – yet, till I killed a foe,
> And heard his groans, and heard his children's groans,
> Knew I not what delight was else on earth,
> Which now delights me little.

(I, i, 96–109)[2]

Agony replaces 'honey sweets' because of the connection of eroticism and subjugation. Cenci can easily make sexuality a means of aggression – the murderer turning rapist – because his aggressions were always merely displaced sexuality. *The Cenci* envisions eros as a derivation of the will to power. Desire 'authenticates' individuals, allowing them to forget their emptiness by making another person the reflection and instrument of their will. Such mimetic desire ends in addiction and futility, in the accelerating exchanges of mastery and abjection that Hogle anatomizes so brilliantly.[3] But until these specular appropriations exhaust themselves, they destroy voraciously.

The sexual violence they traffic in is a metaphorical violence. The dramatic image of metaphor dominating *The Cenci* is the Count's rape of Beatrice. Like the phantasm of Jupiter repeating the words of Prometheus, or the '*O, follow, follow*' dream shared by Asia and Panthea, the rape signifies metaphor-in-action, establishing a point of coincidence for disparate beings. As the rape's incestuous character shows, the basis of this convergence is similitude. Only because Beatrice is a 'particle of [his] divided being' (IV, i, 117) linked to him by family resemblance can Cenci break the taboos that goad his appetites. His sexual possession will formalize that resemblance. Beatrice will eventually share his infamy and even his venereal infection, he boasts. 'What she most abhors', moreover, 'Shall have a fascination to entrap / Her loathing will' (IV, i, 85–7). The rape can thereby psychologically transform her in the image of her father's depravity, her moral will 'by its own consent [stooping] as low / As that which drags it down' (IV, i, 11–12). If Beatrice 'ever have a child', Cenci implores,

> May it be
> A hideous likeness of herself, that as
> From a distorting mirror, she may see
> Her image mixed with what she most abhors,
> Smiling upon her from her nursing breast.
> And that the child may from its infancy
> Grow, day by day, more wicked and deformed,
> Turning her mother's love to misery:
> And that both she and it may live until
> It shall repay her care and pain with hate,
> Or what may else be more unnatural.
>
> (IV, i, 145–55)

In *The Cenci*, regrettably, this genealogical fantasy is an exemplary act of imagination. Beatrice's imagined infant will image 'what she most abhors', her father, by memorializing the violence that impregnated her. Through a metalepsis of cause and effect, rape and child, Cenci presents the imposed similitude of his rape as itself a 'distorting mirror' – metaphor as a 'distorting mirror'. Metaphor becomes by association a form of rape.

The metaphorical transmission of evil enjoys a success Cenci never foresaw when, replicating in Beatrice his willingness to murder, the victimizer becomes a victim of his own methods. All the specular encounters of *The Cenci* leave violence uncontrollable. The dynamic of self and other produces power as a consequence of uncentered exchanges in which the interdependence of self and other renders the locus of power indeterminate. Still, we would be unwise to stress the elusiveness of force in Shelley's play. Whatever their ultimate import, the indeterminacies of specularity work mainly to enfranchise power, allowing it to systematize itself by appropriating values not securely anchored elsewhere. Shelley can consequently use the self/other paradigm as his model of history unfolding. We have only to recall Romanticism's greatest theorist of history, Hegel, to recognize the potential for historical explanation inherent in self/other constructs.[4] *The Cenci* can in fact appear a negative image, in miniature, of Hegelian dialectic. Shelley exchanges state for Hegelian Spirit, but still conceives of political history as the self-aggrandizing appropriation of otherness by power.

Although not directed to large-scale historical representations, *The Cenci* shows the initiatives of public power at one crucial point: the papal legate's arrival with an official warrant for Cenci's death. The irony of Savella's arrival, moments after Cenci's murder, is so heavy-handed as to suggest that Shelley 'saw the effect as vital to the significance of his play'.[5] What need does this ironic event fulfill? Stuart M. Sperry describes Cenci's death as 'the very end that *society* itself has belatedly ordained.'[6] Savella's entry shows that there have been *two* plots to kill Francesco Cenci: the private plot of self-defensive vengeance and the public plot of legally sanctioned execution. The second, papal plot accords dramatic action a metaphorical structure in *The Cenci* by making Cenci's death occur at the (near) juncture of two analogous sequences of events. We cannot reconstruct Vatican machinations in any detail; the motives behind Cenci's condemnation may include his public blasphemy at the banquet or the near-depletion of his wealth, a source of papal revenue. Savella's arrival nonetheless throws open a door on the plot of history, the strategies through which public power seeks its ends.

The pope serves then as a figure of the historical process.[7] It is a process that externalizes itself only in glimpses – the pope himself never appears in *The Cenci* – because it acts solely through surrogate forms of itself. History, or political power, kills Francesco Cenci through the intercession of Beatrice and her conspirators, puppets driven to action by the state's strategic refusal to act. The pope is by no means the deliberate or self-conscious motive force of the private plot. He figures history as a vast field of impersonal relations motivated by various pressures. He also figures the injustice of social mandates. Like all parallel lines, the two concurrent death plots never converge. Savella arrives too late; there is no coincidence of public and private violence. That disjunction allows the pope to shape the essential form of Beatrice's actions, as tenor shapes vehicle, and then deny his complicity by disavowing mutual similarity. The metaphorical relation of Shelley's two plots succumbs to another appropriation of otherness by self. When the pope rescinds his toleration of Cenci and pronounces his death sentence, history secretly refashions Beatrice in the image of its newfound imperatives as Orsino manipulated Giacomo. Social events transpire as externalizations of power into duplicative agencies that power, as another exploitative father, engendered but will not recognize. Beatrice and her coconspirators are the bastard offspring of History.

Power's strategies for concealing its operation are what interest Shelley most in *The Cenci*. Lacking a means to reverse or redirect authority, the tragedy turns from revolutionary agendas to ideological representations. Shelley recognized the authoritarian values latent in language from at least 1817, when *The Revolt of Islam* declared words one of evil's habitations (ll. 388–9). In *The Cenci* he emphasizes the treachery of language when Savella's suspicions are substantiated by the discovery of Orsino's letter to Beatrice (IV, iv, 90–5). With their conviction virtually assured by this note, the surviving Cencis find themselves betrayed by *writing*. Shelley hints at the role of language in their deaths with the *double entendre* of the pope's death sentence: 'Here is their *sentence*; never see me more / Till, to the *letter*, it be all fulfilled' (V, iv, 26–7, emphases added). Metaphor in particular serves tyranny best. The drama's patriarchal hegemony presupposes metaphor: since the pope considers 'paternal power, / . . . the shadow of his own' (II, ii, 55–6), and since God reigns as 'the great father of all' (I, iii, 23), power establishes itself here by organizing the familial, social, and religious spheres as interconnected versions of the trope of paternity, which is therefore made to appear inevitable through its sheer ubiquity. Metaphor sets the terms for both conformity and rebellion. It provides docile citizens reifying representations 'that forever recast the life of the mind into their own image'.[8] Yet the non-conforming Beatrice merely conforms at an ulterior level: her 'psychological enslavement to the father principle' allows her to combat one father only by appealing to another in her prayers, validating the patriarchal ideology that destroys her.[9]

Shelley's treatment of ideological appropriation reflects his psychological argument. As the self is socially constructed, so are meanings socially determined. As specular exchanges of self and other are coopted by the more adroit manipulator, so is the determination of truth subject to power. The impotence of words to arrest truth in a determinate formulation helps explain Beatrice's refusal to declare what happened to her:

If I could find a word that might make known
The crime of my destroyer; and that done

My tongue should like a knife tear out the secret
Which cankers my heart's core; aye, lay all bare
So that my unpolluted fame should be
With vilest gossips a stale mouthed story;
A mock, a bye-word, an astonishment: –
If this were done, which never shall be done,
Think of the offender's gold, his dreaded hate,
And the strange horror of the accuser's tale,
Baffling belief, and overpowering speech;
Scarce whispered, unimaginable, wrapt
In hideous hints . . . Oh, most assured redress!

(III, i, 154–66)

To speak is to risk becoming 'subdued even to the hue / Of that which thou permittest' (III, i, 176–7) – to risk according rape a vicarious life of its own in the annals of public discourse. Beatrice will reiterate these fears even after Cenci's death. They reflect her sense of the malleability of a 'truth' dependent on social reception. Her trial (along with much else) justifies such fear. What establishes Beatrice's guilt is a substitutive logic directed to predetermined ends. Paolo Santa Croce, a sibling like Beatrice, killed his mother, a parent-figure like the pope; Paolo escaped, but social order requires the state to defend its prerogatives by killing Beatrice as a surrogate Paolo (V, iv, 18–27). The findings at Beatrice's trial precede the hearings that produce them. Marzio's confession is made and believed, then retracted but believed anyway; Beatrice's resolute silence alters nothing: 'She is convicted, but has not confessed' (V, iii, 90). Her conviction effects a closure of myriad possibilities into a narrative of truth institutionally recorded and fixed in judicial archives.

## Imagination on Trial

The courtroom scenes that dominate Act V of *The Cenci* force judgments from readers. But who or what do these scenes put on trial? Beatrice, certainly, and with her the world she inhabits. Yet Baker remarked wittily that 'in reading criticisms of the trial scene one sometimes gains the impression that it not so much Beatrice as the author himself who is up for judgment'.[10] In truth, Shelley *is* on trial in *The Cenci*, and with him the poetic imagination as a means of moral renovation. The play's ending gathers up imaginative problems developed earlier in order to probe their implications for the politics of writing. The reversible mirrorings that leave meaning socially constructed and ultimately indeterminate, the opportunity for misreading presented by such indeterminacy, the metaphorical structure of ideology – all recur in Beatrice's public addresses in Acts IV and V. Beatrice consequently emerges as the play's predominant poet-figure.[11] Like Shelley himself, Beatrice must communicate a vision of sexual violence so as to promulgate justice, but cannot articulate that violence explicitly. Her courtroom rhetoric is an exercise in reconciling these irreconcilable demands.

The contradictions embroiling Beatrice have precise correlatives in Shelley's own efforts to address a public sitting in judgment. As Beatrice must stress the brutalization she underwent, explaining her motives to exonerate herself, so must Shelley stress the brutality of rape. This necessity accounts for an otherwise unaccountable circumstance. Shelley's version of the Cenci legend emphasizes not only the terror, but the very *fact* of Beatrice's rape. His main manuscript source, the *Relation of the Death of the Family of the Cenci*, merely stated that Cenci 'often endeavoured, by force and threats, to debauch his daughter Beatrice'.[12] Shelley dramatically realizes this force, transforming 'an originally questionable incest into a central event'.[13] Since the centrality finally forestalled production of *The Cenci*, Shelley's decision to heighten the rape should seem curious. Why did he dilate on a sexual violence his sources minimized? In part because such violence struck him as basic to the story's tragic potential. And in part because *The Cenci* had to establish Beatrice's victimization in order to wrest the appropriate moral and political exempla from her plight. Only the representation of rape could leave spectators suitably horrified by the injustices of entrenched patriarchal privilege. We can explain the centrality of rape in *The Cenci* only by assuming Shelley's belief in it as fundamental to the moral catharsis he sought.

But what *The Cenci* offers with one hand it retracts with the other. The tragedy performs a dance of attraction and repulsion around the rape as an object of representation. We necessarily and easily infer rape in making emotional and dramatic sense of the drama, yet our need to infer is itself telling. The rape occurs offstage, as a lacuna between acts. It signifies a violence that spreads through Shelley's plot without directly entering it, never achieving representation except through the depiction of its consequences. Staging Beatrice's rape was unthinkable: that would have affronted theatrical censors, contemporary sensibilities, and even classical preferences for offstage cruelty. Shelley's play leans most heavily on Renaissance tragic conventions, however, and hardly exhausts the limited staging options available to it, granting Francesco a few leers and innuendos but forbidding him even a brief appearance in Beatrice's bedroom. There should be no doubt as to Shelley's deliberate elision of sexual violence, for it extends from action to dialogue. *The Cenci* refuses even to name the rape, as Shelley fully realized: 'In speaking of his mode of treating this main incident, Shelley said that it might be remarked that, in the course of the play, he had never mentioned expressly Cenci's worst crime. Every one knew what it must be, but it was never imaged in words.' ('Note on The Cenci. By Mrs Shelley', *CW*, 2, p. 158). Beatrice's inability to report her father's crime reflects Shelley's aversion to verbalizing the facts of sexual assault. Rape thereby serves as a nexus of the play's ambivalence toward representation itself as a social act. Underlying the ambivalence is fear of the vicarious power of reimaged experiences, as Michael Worton suggests,[14] and a deep insecurity about audience. What we must recognize above all are the communicative costs exacted by this ambivalence.

In court Beatrice cuts an impressive figure, and not merely to Marzio. Conviction rings in her voice, compelling a sympathy born of accurate intuitions. Camillo describes himself defending Beatrice as someone 'Pleading, as I could guess, the devilish wrong / Which prompted [her] unnatural parent's death' (V, iv, 16–17). To some auditors, at least, Beatrice's silence clearly speaks volumes. But it still leaves far too much unsaid in her encounters with authority. Beatrice fears playing into her enemies' hands through words. Like radical poets of Shelley's era, she clings to her 'awareness of the conservative force of language and [engages] in a self-conscious struggle against it.'[15] She tries to circumvent the inherited conservatism of language by placing words in novel contexts that estrange inherited meanings and dislocate preconceptions – Shelley's own strategy with the monarchical diction of *Prometheus Unbound*. ''Tis most false / That I am guilty of foul parricide', Beatrice tells Savella (IV, iv, 145–6). She believes herself guiltless presumably because the parricide was not truly 'foul'. She remains 'more innocent of parricide / Than is a child born fatherless' (IV, iv, 112–13), similarly, because in no sense that truly counts was Francesco Cenci a 'father'. Unfortunately this privileging of context over diction is subject to the same reversals that undermined certainty in the play's mirroring scenes. Beatrice's words do not remake audience expectations; audience expectations subvert the efficacy of Beatrice's words. Statements such as ''Tis most false / That I am guilty of foul parricide' hardly redefine 'guilt' effectively. Instead, they seem brazenly hypocritical – Orsino-like corroborations of others' assumptions when those assumptions are known to be misled. In Beatrice's rhetoric indirection becomes equivocation. By mixing her disingenuous evasions with outright lies (her denial of seeing Marzio before), Shelley portrays her language as 'legal quibbling and logic chopping'.[16]

Yet the Romantic ventriloquism of *The Cenci* makes Beatrice's failure Shelley's at one remove. With Shelley too, the problems of dramatic indirection refer back to the merely implied occurrence of the rape. If we infer rape as the offstage event that *The Cenci* cannot name, we also infer rape as the wellspring of Beatrice's character development from Acts III to V – a transition from saint to murderer that remains one of the most teasing and contested cruxes in Shelley studies.[17] The mysteries of her character arise as unresolved issues in the psychology of violence as *The Cenci* engages it, or fails to. Count Cenci pursues the destruction of his daughter's moral will through the fascination of the abhorrent. When Shelley internalizes the issue in this way, forcing us to ask what Beatrice undergoes spiritually, he foregrounds the inscrutability of her development. At some point we may begin 'to suspect that the rape did more to expose than to pollute'.[18] What are the subjective correlatives of the coarsening that gradually recasts Beatrice in her father's role? Did she put on his knowledge with his power? Did she discover an affinity for the forbidden in the midst of revulsion, a revelation, beyond any later power to forget, of the ego's wanton complicity in its own dissolution? Did she kill to prevent further rapes or to avenge the one that occurred? From what precisely is Beatrice recoiling in horror as she speaks so wildly at the beginning of Act III? Posing these unanswerable questions, *The Cenci* revolves around an absent center.

This absence is obviously overdetermined. It derives partly from strategies Shelley embraced in adapting his play to prevailing criteria of stageworthiness: incest would 'form no objection', would 'be admitted on the stage', Peacock was reassured, due to 'the peculiar delicacy' of Shelley's dramatization.[19] Precisely this notion of the language of tragedy makes *The Cenci* a tragedy of language. As the reflex of an evasive 'delicacy', Beatrice's inability to say 'my father raped me' shows the play internalizing the moralistic strictures of bourgeois propriety. Rape is eradicated from Shelley's writing, and from Beatrice's speech, by an imposition of power disturbingly rape-like itself. Violence becomes the violence of society, rape-as-blankness an aporia inscribed in Shelley's text by the unenlightened conservatism he detested. The unvisualized summit of Mont Blanc, the unsayable language of the dead in *Prometheus Unbound* – these vacancies promote revolutionary change by exposing the baseless fabric of power. The unimaged deep truth of *The Cenci* creates indeterminacies that allow authority to co-opt Beatrice through a misappropriation that validates privilege by confirming power. We witness a final metalepsis,* the play's corruption by the debased world over which it aspired to wield reformative influence. Instead of compelling spectators to see themselves reflected in Beatrice, the distorting mirror of *The Cenci* compelled Shelley to see himself reflected in the forces that deny rape access to stage, courtroom, and even consciousness.

---

* [Ed. *Metalepsis*: used, often in connection with poetic figures, to describe a wrenching from one context to another.]

This complicity provides Shelley's investigation of writing its final tragic irony. *The Cenci* makes the poet a cooperative participant in the reconsolidation of oppression – a possibility Shelley may deny elsewhere but finally cannot deny here. The errancies of public reception shadowed Shelley's entire career. But *The Cenci* self-consciously thematizes those errancies. The play argues that, if reception determines meaning as a public construct, and if readers' responses can be neither anticipated nor controlled absolutely, then texts are merely the histories of their own (mis)interpretation. If circumstances reduced 'Beatrice Cenci' to the 'deep and breathless interest' (Preface to *The Cenci*, p. 239) gossip takes in scandal, Beatrice herself prophesies that fate:

> Are centuries of high splendour laid in dust?
> And that eternal honour which should live
> Sunlike, above the reek of mortal fame,
> Changed to a mockery and a bye-word? What!
> Will you give up these bodies to be dragged
> At horse's heels, so that our hair should sweep
> The footsteps of the vain and senseless crowd,
> Who, that they may make our calamity
> Their worship and their spectacle, will leave
> The churches and the theatres as void
> As their own hearts? Shall the light multitude
> Fling, at their choice, curses or faded pity,
> Sad funeral flowers to deck a living corpse,
> Upon us as we pass to pass away,
> And leave . . . what memory of our having been?
> Infamy, blood, terror, despair?
>
> (IV, iii, 30–45)

Although they project empty theaters, these extraordinary lines were written to be declaimed in a crowded theater. They publicize Shelley's awareness of the people's ability to trivialize the most morally harrowing 'spectacle', including *The Cenci*. By associating 'the churches and the theatres', Shelley blames religion for the degeneration of 'Beatrice Cenci' into an idle amusement, a cautionary tale reminding the multitude of the cost of ignoring papal law. Yet his words indict the poet too. Delivering Beatrice into the hands of the public, Shelley potentially makes the Cenci name 'a mark stamped on [an] innocent brow / For men to point at as they pass' (V, iv, 151–2), and enlists himself with the man Beatrice imagines saying, 'I with my words killed her and all her kin' (V, ii, 143).

We should understand why even Beatrice's fear of death signifies fear of reading. Envisioning a death-world of repetitions that will restage her rape endlessly (V, iv, 60–7), she fears a figure for the vicarious afterlife granted fictions by empathizing readers. Shelley critics often represent the aporias* of his texts as strategic irresolution that 'rouzes the faculties to act' (as Blake might say) with inevitably beneficial consequences. The simultaneous nobility and depravity of Beatrice 'may, by engendering our internal debate, cause us to know ourselves' – as if self-knowledge always proved therapeutic, so that the play's moral conflicts miraculously heal themselves merely in entering the affective register.[20] If there are unfailing reasons to celebrate the activation of the human will, they appear in the newspapers of neither Shelley's day nor ours. Yet Shelley criticism abounds in idealizations of the reader as the poem's actualization and resolution. These viewpoints forget would-be Werthers driven to suicide; they forget other reader-responses neither enlightened nor ethical. They use the 'reader' to personalize and depoliticize the institutional forces that control the place Shelley has been granted in contemporary culture, a place of reading suspect in many ways. We cannot simply invoke the reader to save *The Cenci* for a provisional optimism. We read the play poorly in seeking to do so, for through its specular figures, *The Cenci* deconstructs its own theory of morally educative catharsis.

## Notes

1.  CARLOS BAKER, *Shelley's Major Poetry: The Fabric of a Vision* (Princeton: Princeton University Press, 1948), p. 144.

2.  Quoted from *Shelley's Poetry and Prose*, ed. Donald H. Reiman and Sharon B. Powers (New York and London: Norton, 1977).

3.  In particular, see the discussion of mimetic desire, objectification and abjection in JERROLD E. HOGLE, *Shelley's Process: Radical Transference and the Development of His Major Works* (New York: Oxford University Press, 1988), pp. 155–9.

4.  Alan Richardson discusses Shelleyan mirroring from a Hegelian perspective in *A Mental Theater: Poetic Drama and Consciousness in the Romantic Age* (University Park: Pennsylvania State University Press, 1988), pp. 100–23.

5.  STUART M. SPERRY, *Shelley's Major Verse: The Narrative and Dramatic Poetry* (Cambridge: Harvard University Press, 1988), p. 132.

6.  SPERRY, *Shelley's Major Verse*, p. 132 (emphasis added).

7.  The pope ironically personifies the 'larger socio-political movement' that might alone save Beatrice for Laurence S. Lockridge, in 'Justice in *The Cenci*', *The Wordsworth Circle*, **19** (1988): 98. For Shelley's representation of a historical process inimical to the individual will in *Prometheus Unbound*, see John Rieder's

* [Ed. *Aporia*: insoluble doubt or hesitation created in reading a text.]

discussion of 'the plot of necessity in 'The "One" in *Prometheus Unbound'*, *SEL*, **25** (1985): 787–800.

8.  David Quint's phrase, in 'Representation and Ideology in *The Triumph of Life'*, *SEL*, **18** (1978): 639.

9.  MICHAEL HENRY SCRIVENER, *Radical Shelley: The Philosophical Anarchism and Utopian Thought of Percy Bysshe Shelley* (Princeton: Princeton University Press, 1982), p. 195.

10. BAKER, *Shelley's Major Poetry*, p. 147.

11. JEFFREY N. COX, in *In the Shadows of Romance: Romantic Tragic Drama in Germany, England, and France* (Athens, Oh.: Ohio University Press, 1987), p. 163, comments, 'Shelley sees the dramatic poet as facing a situation much like that which Beatrice confronts. Like her, the dramatist must struggle against the "circumstance and opinion" of his place and time in history to discover a mode of language that will communicate with those around him without betraying his imaginative vision.' For Beatrice's experience as 'a parable of the poet' tragically wedded to a single meaning, see RONALD TETREAULT, *The Poetry of Life: Shelley and Literary Form* (Toronto: University of Toronto Press, 1987), p. 131. Ronald L. Lemoncelli uses the *Defence of Poetry* to depict Francesco as a poet-figure in 'Cenci as Corrupt Dramatic Poet', *ELN*, **16** (1978): 103–17. Stuart Curran treats Cenci as a Renaissance Genet, an artist conceiving of crime as an immortalizing art form (*Shelley's 'Cenci': Scorpions Ringed with Fire* (Princeton: Princeton University Press, 1970), pp. 73–5).

12. *Relation*, reprinted in *The Complete Works of Percy Bysshe Shelley*, eds Roger Ingpen and Walter E. Peck, 10 vols (London: Ernest Benn, 1926–30), hereafter *CW*, 2: 160. The versions of the Cenci legend examined by Truman Guy Steffan in 'Seven Accounts of the Cenci and Shelley's Drama', *SEL*, **9** (1969): 601–18, at most limit Francesco to attempted rape. There is no rape in Pieracci's tragedy on Beatrice, which may have influenced Shelley, according to GEORGE YOST, *Pieracci and Shelley: An Italian Ur-Cenci* (Potomac, Md.: Scripta Humanistica, 1986).

13. CURRAN, *Shelley's 'Cenci'*, p. 43.

14. MICHAEL WORTON, 'Speech and Silence in *The Cenci'*, in *Essays on Shelley*, ed. Miriam Allott (Totowa, N.J.: Barnes and Noble, 1982), pp. 108–9.

15. Richard Cronin's phrase, from *Shelley's Poetic Thoughts* (New York: St Martin's Press, 1981), p. 8. For Cronin, this is one of the two options confronting radical poets forced to employ a language saturated with conservative connotations, and the one Shelley ordinarily chose.

16. MELVIN R. WATSON, 'Shelley and Tragedy: The Case of Beatrice Cenci', *KSJ*, **7** (1958): 19.

17. A useful synopsis of debate on the moral enigma of Beatrice appears in SPERRY, *Shelley's Major Verse*, 130–1. The first influential argument for Beatrice's moral corruption was Robert F. Whitman, 'Beatrice's "Pernicious Mistake" in *The Cenci*,' *PMLA*, **74** (1959): 249–53, which supplanted earlier interpretations stressing Beatrice's moral heroism, and which has been challenged by Curran's existentialist interpretation.

18. TERRY OTTEN, *The Deserted Stage: The Search for Dramatic Form in Nineteenth-Century England* (Athens, Oh.: Ohio University Press, 1972), p. 30.

19. *The Letters of Percy Bysshe Shelley*, ed. F.L. Jones, 2 vols (Oxford: Clarendon Press, 1964), 2, p. 102.

20. EARL R. WASSERMAN, *Shelley: A Critical Reading* (Baltimore: Johns Hopkins University Press, 1971), p. 121. Despite both the careful *may* in this statement and the acknowledgment that Shelley did not believe self-consciousness to be always cathartic (pp. 111–12), Wasserman views skeptical irresolution in *The Cenci* (and in *Alastor* and *Julian and Maddalo* as well) as a deliberate strategy for forcing readers to resolve the text's dilemmas for themselves. Sperry has recently offered a version of the same reader-response argument. His analysis of the emotional dynamics of catharsis in *The Cenci* recuperates thematic disunity as a unifying lesson in love. Sperry's 'spectator is propelled violently back and forth between two poles of supposition' until those poles become the limits of a more inclusive understanding of love as 'an act incorporating but transcending mere forgiveness' (pp. 134, 140). To develop this viewpoint, Sperry must assume, or mandate, a particular response – here a sympathetic love for Beatrice that many readers and viewers no longer feel by Act V.

# 8 The Exoteric Political Poems*

STEPHEN C. BEHRENDT

In November 1819 Shelley wrote to Leigh Hunt concerning *The Mask of Anarchy* (written in response to the Peterloo massacre): 'You do not tell me whether you have received my lines on the Manchester affair. They are of the exoteric species . . .' (*Letters*, ii, p. 152). The extract below considers the context and strategies of Shelley's 'exoteric' poems of 1819, poems written in a relatively straightforward style and designed to stir a working-class readership into responsive and responsible political action. Throughout *Shelley and His Audiences* (1989), hereafter *SA*, Stephen Behrendt ascribes to Shelley an acute awareness of the 'delicate relationship between artist and audience' (*SA*, p. 4), contending that 'as a skilled rhetorician Shelley routinely and deliberately attempted to manipulate his audiences into positions favourable to him and his designs' (*SA*, p. 7). This stress on Shelley as rhetorician leads Behrendt to examine the diversity of styles and genres employed in the poetry (and prose). Behrendt's dealings with contemporary theory are coolly eclectic. He is conscious that Shelley can be seen as a proto-post-structuralist, fascinated by indeterminacy, but he prefers to regard the poet as exploiting literature's capacity for 'multistability', the conveying of 'multiple messages simultaneously' (*SA*, p. 2). And though his pages show the influence of reader-response criticism, with its interest in the reader as constructor of meanings, Behrendt remains committed to the idea of Shelley maintaining authorial control over any dialogue with an imagined audience set in motion by his work. (See Introduction, pp. 18–19.)

---

* Reprinted from a chapter entitled 'Public Politics Once Again: 1819 and after', in Stephen C. Behrendt, *Shelley and His Audiences* (Lincoln and London: University of Nebraska Press, 1989), pp. 187–201 (footnotes renumbered from the original).

the spring rebels not against winter but it succeeds it –
the dawn rebels not against night but it disperses it
(Shelley, manuscript fragment)

Of all Shelley's work, the exoteric political poems of 1819 best
demonstrate the validity of Marilyn Butler's observation that the arts 'do
not exist faithfully to reproduce political realities or real-life political
arguments'.[1] The artist routinely transforms both the external details and
the inner nature of temporal events for particular aesthetic, intellectual,
or sociopolitical purposes. This point is especially relevant to the overtly
political poems Shelley composed after the Peterloo incident of 16 August
1819, when in Manchester a peaceable mass meeting for reform had been
forcibly broken up by local yeomanry and government troops, resulting
in a number of deaths, many injuries and the arrest and imprisonment of
both the main speaker (Henry 'Orator' Hunt) and several leaders of the
reform movement.

English publishers had been made understandably fearful by the
government's subsequent passage in November and December 1819 of
the Six Acts, legislation specifically designed both to weaken the reform
movement and to head off armed rebellion first by curtailing the rights to
public assembly and the bearing of arms, and second by largely
eliminating all printed opposition.[2] Coming in the wake of the
prosecution of the radical publisher Richard Carlile . . . the Six Acts sent
a clear warning to the liberal and radical press. The consequences for
Shelley are obvious from the refusal of the moderate Hunt to print the
political poems – The Mask of Anarchy, for example – Shelley sent him late
in 1819. From his removed position in Italy Shelley could not fully
appreciate Hunt's very practical reasons for suppressing the poems.
Hunt seems typically to have chosen silence rather than frankness when
declining to publish any of Shelley's pieces, as is evident from Shelley's
comment that 'you do not tell me whether you have received my lines on
the Manchester affair'[3].

Given the hesitancy of both Hunt and Ollier, it is curious that Shelley
apparently never approached Carlile, Eaton, or any other notable radical
publisher as a potential publisher for his own works, and especially for
the exoteric poems. Perhaps Shelley felt morally bound to commit
himself to a single publisher in each area (periodical and book). Probably,
too, he retained hopes of convincing his regular publishers of the need
for greater political commitment, as is clear from his effort to nudge Hunt
in that direction:

You will never write politics. I dont wonder; but I wish then that you
would write a paper in the Examiner on the actual state of the country;
& what under all the circumstances of the conflicting passions &

interests of men, we are to expect; – Not what we ought to expect or
what if so & so were to happen we might expect; but what as things
are there is reason to believe will come; & send it me for my
information. Every word a man has to say is valuable to the public
now, & thus you will at once gratify your friend, nay instruct & either
exhilarate [sic] him or force him to be resigned & awaken the minds of
the people –

(*SC*, VI, pp. 1107; 23 December 1819)

Here are the familiar Shelleyan tactics: the appeal to Hunt both as
private, personal friend and as public, liberal publisher, the posture of
expecting to derive both satisfaction and instruction from Hunt's
exertions, and the overt suggestion that it is Hunt's duty to 'awaken the
minds of the people'.

The radical press had begun to play an increasingly important and
highly visible role in English affairs, especially after the government's
suspension of habeas corpus early in 1817. Shelley must have known, for
instance, about the popularity of papers like Wooler's *Black Dwarf*, the
circulation of which reached some twelve thousand in 1819.[4] The printed
word, particularly as it appeared in the periodical press, had become by
the time of the Manchester affair a vehicle for leading and inspiring the
emerging lower- and lower-middle-class readership. Cobbett's *Political
Register*, especially, had fostered a new journalism that overtly took to
task the prevailing political, social, economic, and even religious status
quo. That so much of the radical journalism of the period draws upon
stylistic models as diverse as the Bible, popular songs, and folktales is
little surprise; in deliberately adopting these familiar patterns the radical
journalists mounted an effective subliminal appeal to their readers,
preconditioning their assent by addressing them within familiar
rhetorical and stylistic frameworks. Indeed, this new class of readers was
coming to regard the printed word as 'a new revelation' that was
'infinitely more applicable to their immediate situation than the Scriptural
precepts expounded in religious tracts'.[5] Like all revolutionary art, radical
journalism subverted the Establishment from within as well as from
without, turning against it its own terminology and rhetorical models.

Shelley was not unaware of these developments, nor did he fail to
appreciate the value at this juncture of yet another attempt to reach 'the
people' in a language and a style appropriate to what he regarded as
both their limited sophistication and their potentially dangerous
character. He writes Peacock eight days after the Manchester incident
had occurred but before he had received word of it: 'England seems to be
in a very disturbed state, if we may judge by some Paris Papers. . . . But
the change should commence among the higher orders, or anarchy will
only be the last flash before despotism. I wonder & tremble.'[6] When he

learns of Peterloo his response to his correspondents is revealing: 'The torrent of my indignation has not yet done boiling in my veins. I wait anxiously [to] hear how the Country will express its sense of this bloody murderous oppression of its destroyers' (*Letters*, II, p. 117; 6 September 1819). Perhaps thinking of Cobbett, the political and economic shrewdness of whose work he had come to respect, Shelley again links the violence with its economic causes and consequences when he writes to Peacock:

> These are, as it were, the distant thunders of the terrible storm which is approaching. The tyrants here as in the French Revolution have first shed blood[;] may their execrable lessons not be learnt with equal docility! I still think there will be no coming to close quarters until financial affairs decidedly bring the oppressors & the oppressed together.
>
> (*SC*, VI, pp. 895–6; 9 September 1819)

Although Shelley had been coming gradually to appreciate the purely economic issues involved in class oppression and class consciousness, he had likely read and approved much of Robert Owen's recent essay, 'An Address to the Working Class', which had appeared in the *Examiner* on 25 April and which he would have received in Italy. Owen stresses that 'the rich and the poor, the governors and the governed, have really but one interest',[7] a point with which Shelley agreed entirely.

Widely acknowledged as Shelley's *annus mirabilis*, 1819 marked the confluence of his creative powers, his sociopolitical and artistic commitments, and his manipulation of genre and style in perhaps the greatest array of works and forms ever produced in a relatively short period by a single author in English literary history. Not only the two great dramatic works but also the exoteric political poems, the letter on Carlile's trial, and *A Philosophical View of Reform* explore closely related, often identical, issues from a variety of perspectives, in a variety of voices, and for a variety of audiences. Even as we attempt to consider these works individually, we must try to appreciate their relations to one another and to the coordinated literary program Shelley was pursuing at the time. Late 1819 marked a crucial moment for his hopes as author and activist. Both *Prometheus Unbound* and *The Cenci* had been sent off to England, attended by Shelley's high hopes particularly for the latter; if it succeeded, the former might gain by association. *Julian and Maddalo* was in Hunt's hands, and *The Mask of Anarchy* had been posted to him at the end of September. It does appear, however, that Shelley did not intend for his name to appear with *The Mask*, even had it been published, although at a later, 'safer' time he would doubtless have been willing to acknowledge it as his own poem. What I have already said in this light about *Queen Mab*, his authorship of which Shelley had likewise initially attempted to shield if not conceal, might be applied to *The Mask* as well. Shelley was, at this time, already at work also on both the 'popular songs' and *A Philosophical View of Reform*, and the long letter to Hunt (as editor of the *Examiner*) on Carlile's situation is dated 3 November 1819. Had *The Mask* appeared promptly and *The Cenci* been acted, they might have gained Shelley the visibility and credibility his public campaign required. That Hunt silently suppressed *The Mask* both puzzled and hurt Shelley, as is evident from the transparent nonchalance with which he subsequently writes to Hunt about his more political works. A telling example comes in an inquiry to Hunt in 1820: 'I wish to ask you if you know of any bookseller who would like to publish a little volume of *popular songs* wholly political, & destined to awaken & direct the imagination of the reformers. I see you smile but answer my question' (*Letters*, II, p. 191; 1 May 1820).

Hunt had reacted to Shelley's political poems in December of 1819, when he warned him about the new associations Ollier seemed to be making: 'I will write more speedily, & tell you about your political songs & pamphlets, which we must publish without Ollier, as he gets more timid & pale every day; – I hope I shall not have to add time serving; but they say he is getting intimate with strange people' (*SC*, VI, p. 1090). Hunt's suggestions about Ollier probably contributed to the suspicion with which Shelley subsequently regarded his publisher, who he felt lacked both courage and enthusiasm.[8] The 'strange people' likely alludes to Ollier's growing connections with *Blackwood's Edinburgh Magazine*, which praised him as publisher and author and to which in 1821 he contributed at least two articles, one of which discusses *Epipsychidion* (*SC*, VI, p. 1090). Shelley had not abandoned the idea of a book of topical, politically committed 'popular poems' like the one he had broached to Thomas Hookham in 1813 in connection with his Esdaile Notebook poems. This new effort would doubtless have been a mixed bag: somehow 'the reformers' suggests an audience different from that for 'A New National Anthem' or 'Song to the Men of England'. Probably some of the poems (such as 'Ode to the West Wind' and 'Ode to Liberty') that eventually appeared in the *Prometheus Unbound* volume would have found a place in this collection, perhaps wth poems as different stylistically and aesthetically as *The Mask of Anarchy*.

Poems of 'the exoteric species' on 'ordinary topics' Shelley intended for both his disciples and the general public.[9] *The Mask of Anarchy*, though distinguished by its greater length and complexity, shares with the other exoteric poems of late 1819 an immediate and overt topicality as well as a stylistic ruggedness that has often been mistaken for inartistry.[10] These poems are not comparable with Shelley's esoteric verses, of course, but they were never intended to be. To devalue them on the basis of their apparent roughness, though, is to misunderstand Shelley's vehicle and to judge the poems by the wrong standards. It is to deny the stylistic and rhetorical acuteness that is so evident in everything Shelley wrote. The criteria for comparison here are not Byron and Aeschylus but Wooler and Hone, not *Childe Harold's Pilgrimage*, 'Prometheus', or *Prometheus Bound* but 'The Political House That Jack Built' and 'A Political Christmas Carol'. Shelley's exoteric poems exhibit a surprising familiarity with both the texts and the iconography of the radical press and the pamphlet war of the latter stages of the Regency.[11]

Accurately characterized by Timothy Webb as 'poems of exhortation, of vituperation and of fundamental political analysis, designed for the popular reader',[12] these poems employ a common and straightforward diction and syntax for the most part, as well as plain allegories and generally familiar, simple poetic structures. Like the radical journalists, Shelley drew upon familiar models ranging from the Bible through the colloquial ballad forms of popular culture. 'A New National Anthem', for instance, draws power from its obvious parodic relationship to the conventional anthem. As he had done in his essay on the death of Princess Charlotte in 1817, Shelley invokes the figure of martyred Liberty:

> God prosper, speed, and save,
> God raise from England's grave
>     Her murdered Queen![13]

If the Bodleian manuscript (MS Shelley adds. e. 6) is the first draft, as it appears to be, Shelley apparently composed stanzas 1, 3, 4, and 5 first, revising the first heavily as he worked. Once under way, he must have composed more easily and more surely, for the next stanzas, written like the first in pencil, are only lightly revised (MS pp. 19–20). Apparently part of 'The Cloud' was already in this notebook, for the next page of the manuscript contains a draft with revisions of 'The Cloud', lines 60 through 66. It appears that Shelley stopped after what is now stanza 5 and then later returned to the anthem, making some revisions in ink, adding sideways on the page next to the first stanza what is now stanza 2, and then cross-writing in ink, over the lines from 'The Cloud', the final stanza. When Mary Shelley later published the poem, she several times substituted in the final line of a stanza the phrase '*the* Queen' where Shelley had written '*our* Queen'. A seemingly minor change, this substitution of the definite article for the inclusive personal pronoun makes a major difference in the distance it establishes between author and audience. Had she forgotten that throughout 1819 and on into 1820 Shelley had expressed to Hunt, Peacock, and others his hope to return to England? Perhaps she simply miscopied, or perhaps the printer erred.

127

But such lapses (or deliberate alterations) contributed to the myth that Shelley renounced England and his countrymen. Indeed, in the first occurrence of the phrase in the original draft of line 16, he initially wrote 'God save the Queen!' but canceled 'the' and substituted 'our', which revision clearly indicates his numbering himself among the English people in whose collective voice he is attempting to speak.[14]

The exoteric poems of 1819 are battle cries; they are calls not to mere contemplation but to action, filled with masterful manipulation of stock iconography. The bitter, devastating invective of 'To S——th and C——gh', whose title Medwin and Mary Shelley subsequently sanitized and depersonalized as 'Similies for Two Political Characters of 1819', exhibits a savagery not ordinarily associated with Shelley:

> . . . ye, two vultures sick for battle,
>    Two scorpions under one wet stone,
> Two bloodless wolves whose dry throats rattle,
> Two crows perched on the murrained cattle,
>    Two vipers tangled into one.

(*Works*, p. 573)

These poems, in which Shelley asserts an empathic solidarity with the brutalized and maimed victims of Peterloo and all it stands for, attain a level of personal, passionate intensity found also in poems like 'To the Lord Chancellor',[15] which address the personal injuries to which Shelley felt he had been subjected. The formal posture of public suffering is, however, integral to poems of this sort; the outbursts against outrage and injustice underscore the undeserved nature of the outrage, imaging the persecutions of the public martyr. Although these heavily revised poems are, to some extent, exercises in therapeutic writing, Shelley's desire to publish them indicates a serious purpose: they are both models and examples of the community of shared suffering that unites all humanity when the most basic human rights – whether of political freedom or of possession of one's children – are violated by a seemingly mindless patriarchal tyranny.

These poems illustrate Shelley's penetrating understanding of economic and social issues. 'Song to the Men of England', for instance, expresses the same rejection of economic vampirism we have already observed in his Irish writings of 1812. Most obviously of all the 'popular songs', this one explicitly adopts the rhetorical features of working-class radicalism. Its central image of 'Bees of England' is a trope that had been politicized and repopularized by Paine, Spence, and Wooler and that was used almost exclusively at this time by working-class socialists and radicals.[16]

Men of England, wherefore plough
For the lords who lay ye low?
Wherefore weave with toil and care
The rich robes your tyrants wear?

Wherefore feed, and clothe, and save,
From the cradle to the grave,
Those ungrateful drones who would
Drain your sweat – nay, drink your blood?

(*Works*, p. 572)

Shelley concludes in a disturbing tone of bitter irony:

Shrink to your cellars, holes, and cells;
In halls ye deck another dwells.
Why shake the chains ye wrought? Ye see
The steel ye tempered glance on ye.

With plough and spade, and hoe and loom,
Trace your grave, and build your tomb,
And weave your winding-sheet, till fair
England be your sepulchre.

(*Works*, p. 573)

Shelley's poem does not vacillate between exhortation and contemptuous satire nearly so much as it is often said to do. Shelley's strategy here must be seen in light of both his intended audience and his notion of how to arouse that audience from its self-induced torpor. Like the 'Ode Written in October, 1819, Before the Spaniards Had Recovered Their Liberty', the 'Song' adopts an 'ardent missionary style'[17] in commemorating the committed patriots who have fought, suffered, and (temporarily) been defeated and in looking forward to the day when nations 'arise' and 'awaken' to shake their chains to dust (*Works*, pp. 575–6). Like the 'Ode', the 'Song' is hortatory and declamatory: as a song it is both anthem and marching song in the manner of *La Marseillaise*. But its tone is ironic, its argument skeptical. To the questions that occupy the first four stanzas, the invented audience must necessarily respond, 'Why, indeed?' Stanza five states the present dilemma, driving home the reality of labor's exploitation. Stanza six counsels continuing the same activities but for a different purpose: for the dignity that *self*-support provides. Further, it recommends taking up arms – 'in your defence to bear'. This is a difficult point; Shelley seems to imply that violence in self-defense is acceptable, which contradicts his position elsewhere. I would suggest that his sustained consideration of an analogous situation in *The Cenci* had made him more willing to countenance a united show of force

129

against the oppressors, despite the terrible risks (and despite the idealistic response *Prometheus Unbound* proposes). This poem comes as close as Shelley ever comes to sanctioning violence as a last resort, and I believe that the reversal in both sense and tone in the final two stanzas suggests that he did not consider the 'men of England' actually capable of so decisive an assertion. Even though subsequent poems such as 'Ode to Liberty' support the cause of overt revolution in other countries, Shelley's position regarding change in England remains remarkably consistent: change must come gradually through the joint exertions of enlightened leaders and an awakened populace capable of appreciating basic human dignity and seeking it not through violence and retribution but through reconciliation and community.

Hence though the conclusion of the 'Song to the Men of England' ironically chastises its audience, it does so the more powerfully to alert them to the error they have already too long perpetuated. Like the ode on the Spanish situation, with which it is contemporaneous, the 'Song' transcends purely national issues in its determined focus on the human issues that link all nations, all peoples. It shares with that ode, as it does with *Hellas*, written eighteen months later and under different circumstances, the conviction that the oppressed of all nations share a common cause even as they share in the 'one human heart': they are participants in different scenes of the same drama.[18] The poem's conclusion is a variation on the reverse definition. Having presumably raised the audience's ire in the opening stanzas, and having stated the 'sad reality' of their condition in the middle stanzas, Shelley concludes with a vision of the inevitable consequences of continued failure to alter the status quo. Neither a concession to the impracticality of his suggestions nor a contemptuous verbal gesture of despair over his inability to stimulate change, Shelley's final lines are a calculated challenge to the audience to reject their subhuman images as rats, moles, and bees ('your cellars, holes, and cells', l. 25) and to assume their full status as human beings.

The fragmentary 'To the People of England' affords another example of Shelley's approach both to his subject matter and to his working-class audience:

> People of England, ye who toil and groan,
> Who reap the harvests which are not your own,
> Who weave the clothes which your oppressors wear,
> And for your own take the inclement air;
> Who build houses . . .
> And are like gods, who give them all they have,
> And nurse them from the cradle to the grave . . .

                                                   (*Works*, p. 573)

As in 'Song to the Men of England', of which this poem may have been an early version, Shelley makes the point that the oppressors are utterly dependent upon the victims' acquiescence in their own exploitation. If the people ever awaken, as the poems of this period repeatedly exhort them to do, they will not need to seize power for it is already theirs: it is in the people, not in the prevailing élitist minority, that true power resides.

Owen had made this same point:

> You [the working classes] now possess all the means which are necessary to relieve yourselves and your descendants to the latest period, from the sufferings which you have hitherto experienced, except the knowledge how to direct those means. . . . this knowledge is withheld from you only until the violence of your irritation against your fellow-men shall cease; that is, until you thoroughly understand and are influenced in all your conduct by the principle, 'That it is the circumstances of birth, with subsequent surrounding circumstances, all formed *for* the individual (and over which society has now a complete controul) that have hitherto made the past generations of mankind into the irrational creatures exhibited in history, and fashioned them, up to the present hour, into those localized beings of country, sect, class and party, who now compose the population of the earth.'[19]

Because individuals tend to be motivated by self-interest and to depend on others rather than on themselves, the oppressors exploit these propensities to subjugate their victims, cultivating among them the illusion that the welfare and security of all depends upon the unquestioned maintenance of the prevailing power structure, regardless of the cost to the suffering populace. Their insecurities thus nurtured and reinforced, the deluded masses fall into the habit of nursing their oppressors, literally 'giving them all they have' rather than risk the destabilizing trauma of resisting this unjust arrangement.

As in *The Mask of Anarchy*, Shelley attempts in the unabashedly inflammatory 'To the People of England' to awaken his readers to the extent of their own misery. And as in *The Mask*, the catalyst is a reverse definition designed to remind them of all that they are presently denied. Though the poem is only a fragment of what Shelley appears to have intended as a sonnet, it shares with the 'Song to the Men of England' the familiar, generalized images of domestic labor and the emphasis on the disproportionate relationship between labor and reward. Although during the war years a journalism had appeared that was dedicated to mobilization over national issues, after the war radical journalists in particular began more insistently to stress domestic issues and the actual condition of the people. The praxis of popular radicalism was rooted in tangible experience, in the realities of individual hardship, and in the alienation of the people from the political process.[20] Hence personal hardships like hunger, unemployment, and the frustration of petitions for industrial regulation contributed far more to the pressure for reform than did more abstract notions about liberty. Shelley's exoteric poems attempt to capitalize on the plain fact that ideological conversion is made easier when it is tied closely to the common people's direct experience of hardship.

Shelley's esoteric poems – *Prometheus Unbound*, for example – involve a rarefied intellectual atmosphere: their elevated diction and complex periodic syntax, their intricate symbolism, their wealth of sophisticated and erudite background materials, and their broad 'sociohistorical' sweep far outstrip anything we may classify as an exoteric poem, even including *The Mask of Anarchy*.[21] Whereas the esoteric poems focus on fresh, even apocalyptic myths of the *new* man, the exoteric poems dwell with the righteous indignation of Jesus among the money changers on the dilemma of the *old* man crushed by the old, exploitive intellectual and sociopolitical system. The exoteric poems aim to play a significant role in the repudiation of the old power structure by the oppressed Britons who are seemingly beginning at last to awaken and to assert themselves. Hence while Shelley instructs the enlightened few who might comprehend the political program advocated in *Prometheus Unbound*, he also prepares the masses (or so he believes) for the institution of that new and benevolent system, beginning gradually to give them the 'knowledge' of which Owen speaks in the passage quoted above.

The very real danger posed to all parties by the explosive situation, even well before Peterloo, is implicit in *The Cenci*, where everyone loses. John Farrell has written that violence is essential to revolution:

> Revolution assaults a set of legitimizing norms, the prevailing paradigm. One of the distinguishing features of this paradigm is that it explicitly excludes whatever it is that the revolution wants. There is nothing in the paradigm to sanction its revolutionary replacement. Violence alone can alter this situation by enforcing the authority that revolution confers upon itself.[22]

Shelley understood this, of course, which explains why he advocates for England not revolution but nonviolent *reform*, believing that both the hostile and the apathetic members of the working classes could be enlisted in reasonable courses of action, 'if reason could once be got inside their defences'.[23] Shelley counsels not violence but insubordination, not revenge but education, not retaliation but resistance. If history is 'a roll call of iniquities' and 'an unanswerable indictment of the present structure of society',[24] its transformation cannot come by any of the methods that history has already proven ineffective: something new and daring is called for. Mary Shelley stated the case well in 1840:

> His indignant detestation of political oppression did not prevent him from deprecating the smallest approach to similar crimes on the part of his own party, and he abjured revenge and retaliation, while he strenuously advocated reform. He felt assured that there would be a change for the better in our institutions; he feared bloodshed, he feared the ruin of many. . . . 'The thing to fear', he observes, 'will be, that the change should proceed too fast – it must be gradual to be secure'.[25]

Here the 'Scotch philosopher' Robert Forsyth, whose *Principles of Moral Science* (1805) discusses the 'passion for reforming the world', [quoted in the Preface to *Prometheus Unbound*] is helpful. Forsyth, whom Peacock – and probably also Shelley – had read, deprecates as Godwin had done the inclination toward violent and precipitious social and political change:

> In times of public contention or alarm, . . . it is the duty of a virtuous man to recollect often, that human affairs are . . . so contrived, that their amelioration is slow and progressive, and that great good is never suddenly or violently accomplished. It is also his duty to render the passion [for immediate change in the world] . . . unnecessary in his own mind, by acquiring that self-command which . . . may enable him to do his duty to society, without suffering himself either to be so much inflamed by opposition, or so much blinded by attachment to particular projects or notions, as to forget that force is not reason, that the edge of the sword introduces no light into the human mind, and that the certain and immediate commission of sanguinary actions can seldom be balanced by the doubtful prospect of future good.[26]

Shelley shares Forsyth's estimate of the danger of allowing one's own political, social, moral, or intellectual program to blind him or her to society's best interests. Such a view is apparent, for instance, in Shelley's Aristotelian insistence that works like *The Cenci* and *Prometheus Unbound* not be burdened (or disfigured) by the superimposition upon them of the author's program, but rather that any ideological implications ought to inhere in and arise naturally from the materials of the works themselves.

*The Mask of Anarchy*, the longest and most complex of the exoteric poems, is also the most ambivalent. It is a poem of appearances, from its ambivalent descriptions of the characters – Murder, for example, who 'had a mask like Castlereagh' – to the distracted 'maniac maid', whose actual identity is uncertain ('her name was Hope, she said: / But she looked more like Despair') to the 'Shape arrayed in mail' that appears between the maid and the hooves of the approaching horses. *The Mask* again addresses the problem of finding a viable way to resist an oppressive patriarchal establishment. Here the 'maniac maid' lies down in the path of Murder, Fraud, and Anarchy and thus impedes their progress.[27] Her deliberate gesture of self-sacrifice offers a very different and very public alternative to Beatrice Cenci's method of dealing with a bad father. That the maid's course of action is inherently more correct is indicated first in that she is not simply trampled and, second, in that a sort of 'miracle' occurs in the appearance and the subsequent speech of the inscrutable Shape.

That Shape constitutes another of the poem's ambiguities. When it apparently speaks, for instance, the speech – even though it is quoted as direct address – is presented within the framework of a simile: a transfiguration occurs, and, like the voice of God speaking to Moses from the burning bush,

> A sense awakening and yet tender
> Was heard and felt – and at its close
> These words of joy and fear arose
>
> *As if* their Own indignant Earth
> Which gave the sons of England birth
> Had felt their blood upon her brow,
> And shuddering with a mother's throe
>
> Had turned every drop of blood
> By which her face had been bedewed
> To an accent unwithstood, –
> *As if* her heart had cried aloud:
>
> > (*Shelley's Poetry and Prose*, ed. Donald H. Reiman and Sharon
> > B. Powers, p. 305; my italics)

We may infer that the words are the apparition's, but Shelley's equivocation permits us equally to infer that they are those of a universal spirit of England not unlike the elemental spirits who speak in *Prometheus Unbound*. This spirit's clear ties with the unseen and 'awful shadow of some unseen Power', the Spirit of Intellectual Beauty, are indicated by the fact that while human beings cannot see it, they still know it is present.[28]

Even the poem's voices are ambivalent. The naive narratorial voice, whose rhetoric and figures are those of the popular ballad style, is countered by the more sophisticated authorial voice that, even when it intentionally mouths the balladeer's style, is often deliberately ironic and always reflective of Shelley's own isolation in Italy, where he, too, hears a disembodied 'voice'.[29] This doubling of voice reflects the poem's grounding in the skeptical debate. In an angry poem on a subject of pressing national concern, addressed principally to an audience of the aggrieved oppressed, this ambivalence of voice is potentially dangerous, for the poem implicitly condones a variety of the violence it explicitly condemns. Cautioning the people against retaliating agains the soldiers who cut them down, the Voice nonetheless exonerates the multitude from guilt over 'the blood that must ensue' (l. 338).

Indeed, the vigorous actions the Voice recommends to the people in the 'Rise like Lions' refrain and elsewhere contradict the notion of passive resistance. Hunt saw this and explained why he suppressed the poem until 1832:

> I did not insert it [in the *Examiner*], because I thought that the public at large had not become sufficiently discerning to do justice to the sincerity and kind-heartedness of the spirit that walked in this flaming robe of verse. His charity was avowedly more than proportionate to his indignation; yet I thought that even the suffering part of the people, judging, not unnaturally from their own feelings, and from the exasperation which suffering produces before it produces knowledge, would believe a hundred-fold in his anger, to what they would in his good intention; and this made me fear that the common enemy would take advantage of the mistake to do them both a disservice.

Hunt even had stanzas 81–3 set in italics, with a footnote informing the reader he had done so to stress 'the sober, lawful, and charitable mode of proceeding advocated and anticipated by this supposed reckless innovator. "*Passive obedience*" he certainly had not; but here follows a picture and a recommendation of "*non-resistance*", in all its glory.'[30]

More lay behind Shelley's desire for *The Mask* to appear in the *Examiner* than his mere acquaintance with Hunt, though, for the poem invokes Hunt's own words on the Manchester incident in the *Examiner* for 22 August 1819. Stressing the speakers' and the crowd's peaceable intentions and demeanor. Hunt had stated the official perpetrators of the violence, asking what would have been the consequences had 'the military' succeeded in its apparent determination 'to cut [Henry Hunt] in pieces':

> Do we think that thousands and thousands of Englishmen would any longer have contented themselves with tamely looking on; or with execrations, or with brickbats and staves? No, most assuredly. *They would have risen in the irresistible might of their numbers.* . . . With what feelings can these *Men in the Brazen Masks* of power dare to speak lamentingly of the wounds or even the death received by a constable

or soldier or any other person concerned against an assemblage of Englishmen irritated by every species of wrong and insult, public and private?[31]

Shelley was attuned to both the tone and the substance of the popular press. Had *The Mask* appeared in the *Examiner*, a perceptive reader, noting the verbal echoes, might have been moved by the reminder.

Shelley appreciated that demonstrations of their unsuspected strength often tempt the impatient oppressed into employing that strength to avenge past wrongs, so the goad provided by *The Mask* was a calculated risk. Had Hunt published Shelley's poem in *The Examiner* or arranged for its publication elsewhere, it would certainly have attracted the notice of the aristocracy (liberal or otherwise) and of others outside the working classes. Shelley undoubtedly intended to address to these readers as well his warning of the clear and present danger of continued failure to enact real social, political, and economic reform. Technically not a part of the oppressed classes, the possessors of power and influence are nevertheless implicated by their own acts of omission in allowing injustice to continue. To this audience, as to the physical victims of Peterloo and to their sympathetic comrades throughout England, the brutality of the bullying yeomanry in Manchester was both an insult and a humiliation. As in *The Cenci*, Shelley wishes to instruct his audiences about present issues by exposing the terrible blunders of the past. Here, however, the example invoked is more immediate: the shed blood is English, not Italian, and the latter-day Beatrices – whose emblems Shelley found in press reports of the wounded Manchester women and who represent the entire populace – are nearer than ever to choosing a form of national patricide as a means of redressing their wrongs.

But if *The Mask* presents both a program (to one audience) and a warning (to another), it envisions an ultimately millennial transformation. Though Shelley never mentions the painting, he could scarcely have been unaware of Benjamin West's popular *Death on a Pale Horse* (1783), which had strongly impressed Hunt and for which West had sketched revisions in 1787 and 1802.[32] Indeed, the subject became very popular during the French Revolutionary period among both liberal and conservative artists, each of whom viewed its applicability to contemporary events according to his personal political orientation. Shelley's poem invests this verbal and visual topos with the status of myth to suggest 'how humanity may wrest the millennium out of God's hands' in an act of collective self-purification that reestablishes human community from the ruins of class warfare.[33] Like James Gillray, whose brilliant caricatures are characterized by a sophisticated intertextual allusiveness, Shelley understood that a central aspect of revolutionary art is its revisionist treatment of existing, traditional forms: outmoded, irrelevant, and ideologically unacceptable elements are cast off while what is retained forms the basis of a new work whose visible generic and thematic relationships to the old serve further to destabilize the old. In any such work of 'redeployment', the old work is 'harnessed', together with its characteristic effects, to an entirely new purpose.[34] This is precisely what Shelley is about in *The Mask*, inverting a conventional image of the Apocalypse so as more powerfully to suggest that both individual and collective destiny are the responsibility of each member of society and may not be surrendered to external agents without oppression as a certain result. Deliberately willed realignment of social values and behavior can generate the rise, Phoenix-like, of life from the present death-in-life state.

## Notes

1. MARILYN BUTLER, *Romantics, Rebels and Reactionaries: English Literature and its Background, 1760–1830* (Oxford: Oxford University Press, 1981), p. 15.

2. RICHARD D. ALTICK, *The English Common Reader: A Social History of the Mass Reading Public, 1800–1900* (Chicago: University of Chicago Press, 1957), pp. 327ff.

3. *Shelley and His Circle, 1773–1822*, ed. Kenneth Neill Cameron and Donald H. Reiman, 8 vols (Cambridge, Mass.: Harvard University Press, 1961–86), VI, p. 1080; [16] November 1819. This series is hereafter cited as *SC*.

4. ALTICK, *English Common Reader*, p. 326.

5. Ibid., pp. 326–7.

6. *The Letters of Percy Bysshe Shelley*, ed. Frederick L. Jones, 2 vols (Oxford: Clarendon Press, 1964), II, 115; 24 August 1819. This work is hereafter cited as *Letters*.

7. *Examiner* (25 April 1819), p. 259. The *Examiner* gave prominent notice to Owen, whose speeches it also printed on 29 March, 5 April and 4 July 1819.

8. Mary Shelley's letters likewise record the growing estrangement from Ollier, whom on 7 July 1820 she calls 'a ninny or worse'. By 7 March 1822 she is even more emphatic in her judgment that 'he is a very bad bookseller to publish with' (*The Letters of Mary Wollstonecraft Shelley*, ed. Betty T. Bennett, 3 vols (Baltimore: Johns Hopkins University Press, 1980–87), I, pp. 153, 222).

9. I have discussed this matter in greater detail in 'The Exoteric Species: The Popular Idiom in Shelley's Poetry', *Genre*, **14** (Winter 1981): 473–92.

10. Timothy Webb, for instance, regards these poems as vastly inferior, even crude (*Shelley: A Voice Not Understood* (Atlantic Highlands, N.J.: Humanities Press, 1977), p. 93).

11. See STUART CURRAN, *Shelley's Annus Mirabilis: The Maturing of an Epic Vision* (San Marino, Calif.: Huntington Library, 1975), Chapter 6; and Michael Henry

Scrivener, *Radical Shelley: The Philosophical Anarchism and Utopian Thought of Percy Bysshe Shelley* (Princeton: Princeton University Press, 1982), pp. 196–210.

12. Webb, *Shelley*, p. 89.

13. Quoted from *Shelley: Poetical Works*, ed. Thomas Hutchinson, corr. G.M. Matthews (Oxford: Oxford University Press, 1971); hereafter cited as *Works*.

14. Bodleian MS Shelley adds. e. 6, p. 19. Scrivener, *Radical Shelley*, pp. 227–8, rightly laments the distortions of the texts of these poems by their various editors.

15. In Bodleian MS Shelley adds. e. 9, pp. 180ff. the poem is titled 'To the C.——.' The subsequent revised transcription in the Harvard Shelley notebook bears the title 'To the Lord Chancellor', though 'Lord Chancellor' has been line-canceled. The table of contents at the back of this incomplete notebook refers to the poem as 'To Lord Cxxxr'.

16. P.M.S. Dawson, *The Unacknowledged Legislator: Shelley and Politics* (Oxford: Clarendon Press, 1980), p. 51.

17. James Brazell, *Shelley and the Concept of Humanity: A Study of His Moral Vision*, Salzburg Studies in English Literature, Romantic Reassessment, no. 7 (Salzburg: University of Salzburg, 1972), p. 76.

18. Ibid., p. 138.

19. *Examiner*, no. 591 (25 April 1819), p. 259.

20. John Bohstedt, *Riots and Community Politics in England and Wales, 1790–1810* (Cambridge, Mass.: Harvard University Press, 1983), p. 219.

21. See also Kenneth Neill Cameron, *Shelley: The Golden Years* (Cambridge, Mass.: Harvard University Press, 1974), Chapter 9, on this distinction.

22. John Farrell, *Revolution as Tragedy: The Dilemma of the Moderate from Scott to Arnold* (Ithaca: Cornell University Press, 1980), pp. 51–2.

23. R.K. Webb, *The British Working-Class Reader, 1790–1848: Literacy and Social Tension* (London: George Allen & Unwin, 1955), p. 35.

24. See Brazell, *Shelley and the Concept of Humanity*, p. 129. Butler notes (*Burke, Paine, Godwin, and the Revolution Controversy*, ed. Marilyn Butler (Cambridge: Cambridge University Press, 1984), p. 5) that insubordination was the leading message by the 1780s and early 1790s, in the rhetoric of liberty evolved by Priestley and other Dissenting intellectuals who were developing a rhetoric that addressed *individual* – rather than class – consciousness, a rhetoric that 'has no class accent' (p. 5).

25. Percy Bysshe Shelley, *Essays, Letters from Abroad, Translations and Fragments* ed. Mary Shelley, 2 vols (London: Edward Moxon, 1840), I, xxv–xxvi.

26. Robert Forsyth, *Principles of Moral Science* (Edinburgh, 1805), pp. 291–3.

27. Scrivener claims that her act instigated the revolution (*Radical Shelley*, p. 207), but especially in view of her 'maniac' nature this seems to me to overstate the case. On *The Mask*, see also the Garland Press facsimile in *The Manuscripts of the Younger Romantics* (Shelley, vol. II, 1985).

28. See Paul Foot, *Red Shelley* (London: Bookmarks, 1984), p. 176.

29. See also Richard Cronin, *Shelley's Poetic Thoughts* (New York: St Martin's

Press, 1981), pp. 42–3; and Donald H. Reiman, 'Shelley as Agrarian Revolutionary', *Keats–Shelley Memorial Bulletin*, **30** (1979): 12–13.

30. *The Masque of Anarchy*, preface by Leigh Hunt (1832; London: J. Watson, 1842), pp. 3, 21–2.

31. *Examiner*, no. 608 (22 August 1819), pp. 530–1. (My italics.)

32. See *SC*, VI, 894n; Robert C. Alberts, *Benjamin West: A Biography* (Boston: Houghton Mifflin, 1978), pp. 223–4; and Morton D. Paley, *The Apocalyptic Sublime* (New Haven: Yale University Press, 1986), pp. 18–31.

33. Curran, *Shelley's Annus Mirabilis*, p. 185.

34. Butler, *Romantics, Rebels and Reactionaries*, p. 54.

# 9 The Dramatic Lyric ['Ode to the West Wind']*

RONALD TETREAULT

In *The Poetry of Life* (1987), hereafter *PL*, Ronald Tetreault describes Shelley's creation of a poetry that engages 'the reader in the play of interpretation' (*PL*, p. 16). Tetreault seeks to reconcile Shelley the political reformist with Shelley the imaginative poet by way of what might be called positive or celebratory deconstruction; his readings rehabilitate subjectivity, albeit in decentred form, and describe poetry as play, a game that does not claim to be true but does offer to liberate its readers' imaginations. Shelley's philosophical scepticism is not, for Tetreault, disabling since what matters 'is not what poetry is but what it does for us' (*PL*, p. 10). Tetreault also calls upon Mikhail Bakhtin's notion of discourse as dialogical, of meaning as a joint venture involving text and reader, to illuminate Shelley's poems. The book is organised to bring out the different effects aimed at and achieved by Shelley's use of different literary forms: epic, tragedy, comedy and lyric.

In the extract printed below, Tetreault discusses the 'Ode to the West Wind' as a poem that moves from solitary subjectivity to a more social discourse. At work throughout the extract is a view of art as the shaper rather than the product of ideology: a shaper of ideology not because it imparts messages but because, in the case of the 'Ode', it enfranchises the reader who is free, if he or she wishes, to reverse the poem's final deconstructive gesture and share in the faith that the form of the concluding question momentarily destabilises. (See Introduction, p. 17.)

In the *Ode to the West Wind*, Shelley shapes a dramatic voice that first gives form to an ideology of social renewal and then mimes the process

---

* Reprinted from Ronald Tetreault, *The Poetry of Life: Shelley and Literary Form* (Toronto, Buffalo and London: University of Toronto Press, 1987), pp. 210–20 (footnotes renumbered from the original).

of its dissemination. Despite its apparent concentration on the self, the poem dramatizes the speaker in such a way that his discourse is projected outward, first toward the mighty forces of nature which he engages in verbal agon, but finally toward an implicit audience for whom his struggle provides a powerful focus of emotion. The *Ode*, then, unfolds a dramatic process of development from one stage to another in which the voice of the poet moves from the solitude of creative subjectivity to a social discourse that finds its *telos* in its audience.

Once we admit that lyric poems embody a speaking subject, we must leave the world of objectivity and truth for the realm of dream, ideology, and play. Dramatization of this lyric impulse, however, lends a degree of ambiguity to self-expression. The dramatic lyric does not express emotion; rather it is a public representation of emotion and of the self, a mimesis in which what would otherwise be absent is given presence, a presence, however, whose ontological status must remain uncertain. We cannot say of this represented subjectivity that it is true or false, real or illusory. It is simply 'there', located in the play of signifiers. The question is not whether this subjectivity is correct; instead, the question becomes how this subjectivity comes to be shared, that is, how it is transformed into intersubjectivity. The knowledge such a poem provides is not so much objective as it is that knowledge based on acknowledgment of which Wittgenstein speaks.[1] It is a knowledge that results from the special language game that poets and readers agree to play.

Ideology is very much a part of the language game that political poetry plays, and that game is one of the chief ways by which ideology enters our lives. Far from being 'false consciousness' or what our enemy believes in, ideology (as Louis Althusser writes) is as necessary to all humankind as the air they breathe, and, we may add, no more substantial.[2] Its value resides not in its claim to metaphysical or scientific truth but in its capacity to sustain life and to form the basis of social activity. Every society requires a system of mass representation by which its citizens are formed, transformed, and equipped to endure the conditions of life. That system is an atmosphere of myths, beliefs, conventions, and values which animates human activity and gives buoyancy to human aspiration. It is a product of the human historical and social imagination, and as such it is in a constant process of development. To say that art is merely a product of ideology is naive, for when art gives a determinate form to ideology it thrusts ideology into the dialectic of history by revealing the limitations of a particular set of values and projecting possible alternatives that transcend them. Art is an active partner in the process by which ideology evolves.

Shelley seems to have caught a glimpse of this dialectic when he wrote his peroration to the *Defence of Poetry*. Poets may be 'the unacknowledged legislators of the world'[3] if their poems embody beliefs and attitudes that can guide the ethical (and sometimes even the metaphysical) life of humanity. As we are becoming increasingly aware, literature at least since Arnold and Carlyle has been asked to shoulder the burden of belief, even though its ambiguous fictional status gives it a tenuous claim to satisfy our profounder psychological needs. Literary art has for some time been required to provide the metaphysical solace religion once did, on the assumption that the objects of literary imagination were signs of some higher level of being. If, on the other hand, literary works signify only themselves, something of Shelley's dilemma as a public poet becomes apparent. A man of sufficient skepticism to accept the inaccessibility of ultimate truth, he nevertheless knew that humanity was in profound need of faith. For life to be possible, as Tennyson found, we must believe where we cannot prove. Taking up the Aristotelian dictum that the end of life is not a thought but an action, Shelley devoted his poetry to the furtherance of life and human social activity by directing poetic faith toward ethical progress rather than metaphysical definition. Poetry might never know the truth, but it might engage us in acts that work 'the moral improvement of man' (J, VII, p. 117).

As a dramatic utterance, then, Shelley's *Ode to the West Wind* may be read as an act of faith in the form of a sustained prayer. The faith it seeks to generate, however, has less to do with religious ideology than an emerging political one. A belief in the necessity of social renewal was indispensable to an age of revolution, and if this renewal could be seen as somehow akin to a 'natural' process the ideology of political change might come to be regarded as less radical and impractical than many might think. The faith evoked in the *Ode*, therefore, is neither a faith in Providence nor even in some immanent teleology at work in nature, but rather a variety of poetic faith in which the reader will accept the parallel between natural regeneration and social renewal through the convention of tropic substitution. What happens in nature, we are asked to believe, will happen in politics – all change is a form of renewal. Or perhaps it is more accurate to say that Shelley the skeptic, as always in the creative act, for the moment of this poem willingly suspends his disbelief in this parallel and invites his audience to share in this act of poetic faith.

As we have seen, Shelley regarded faith as very much a political virtue because he considered 'belief . . . at once a prophecy and a cause'.[4] Belief has 'a power of producing' the effects that it envisions when the act of faith becomes a shared experience. Just as ritual makes private myth into public dream, so poetic language, when it assumes dramatic form, removes the process of sign-making from the solitude of the poet's subjectivity into the community of the reading process. Those who are poets 'in the most universal sense of the word', writes Shelley in the *Defence*, are those in whose work 'the pleasure resulting from the manner in which they express the influence of society or nature upon their own minds communicates itself to others and gathers a sort of reduplication from that community' (*J*, VII, p. 111). The *Ode to the West Wind* is no mere private meditation but the public invocation of a myth which provides a focus for that community of worshippers Shelley hopes will transform the world. The poem begins by presenting a self in communion with nature, but as it develops, this self is dramatized in a context of repeated action and in accordance with a conventional decorum and structure.[5] As a dramatic utterance, the poem inscribes an audience even while it avoids addressing them directly. Although the poem is addressed to the wind, its conative function does not exclude auditors any more than the liturgy excludes the congregation. Shelley's *Ode* has a powerful ritual dimension which sweeps up its hearers into the myth it dramatizes, inviting them to participate in this act of poetic faith in which the speaker plays the role of high priest.

The role of the ritual celebrant in this poem is played out in speech. Once again, Shelley adopts the strategy of deploying a dramatic voice in order to focus the experience of the poem. This voice derives its authority from no other source than the fact that it speaks, although the peculiar mode of its speech generates effects characteristic of rhetorical trope. Simple and complex instances of repetition, from the reiterated 'oh, hear!' to the evolving structure of metaphorical respondents to the wind, induce a trance-like effect attributable to what Shelley himself calls 'the incantation of this verse'. This incantatory power of Shelley's poetic language is vitally linked to the ritual and dramatic dimensions of the poem as public dream. Jacques Lacan, in the process of offering his own version of the theoretical topos that discourse is itself an origin, writes provocatively of the psychic energies stirred by the power of this kind of represented speech:

> Hypnotic recollection is, no doubt, a reproduction of the past, but it is above all a spoken representation – and as such implies all sorts of presences. It stands in the same relation to the waking recollection of what is curiously called in analysis 'the material', as the drama in which the original myths of the City State are produced before its assembled citizens stands in relation to a history that may well be made up of materials, but in which a nation today learns to read the symbols of a destiny on the march.[6]

In Shelley's dramatic lyrics, the drama of the myth-making speaker evokes a corresponding psychodrama in the audience in which the speaker's improvisations become the prototypes of a new mythus. Some such shadowy recognition of how the production of myth comes to be read as 'symbols of destiny on the march' may be asserting itself in Shelley's fascination with the Italian improvisatore, Sgricci (*L*, II, p.

266n). By similarly embodying a private urge to self-expression in a public performance, Shelley has learned to transform those 'delineations of human passion' so admired by his wife into tales of 'human nature and its destiny, a desire to diffuse which was the master passion of his soul' (J, II, p. 158).

In the *Ode to the West Wind* (J, II, pp. 294–7), the ritual action is provided by the repetition and modification of metaphorical presences that illustrate the influence of the wind. Because the wind itself is like Intellectual Beauty an 'unseen presence', it can be known only by its effects. In the first stanza, it is manifest when it drives the dead leaves of autumn into their 'wintry bed'. Among the leaves are seeds which do not die but merely lie dormant until 'Thine azure sister of the Spring' reanimates them. The mythopoeia of regeneration thus asserts itself early in the poem through a structure of repetition and difference. The old life goes and a new life returns with the seasonal cycle, a cycle marked by the trace of the autumnal west wind in its springtime counterpart. It is the same west wind, but different, just as the newly germinating seeds bear a trace of the same life force that departed in the fall. 'Destroyer and preserver', the wind plays a double but continuous role in a myth of cyclical renewal, the pattern of which is established in the play of repetition among the signifiers of the first stanza.

The second and third stanzas extend and modify this developing pattern of cyclical regularity. The wind's effects on the land are repeated, first in the sky, then in the sea. The clouds, likened to leaves, are also swept across the sky until finally their pent-up energy is released in the storm that is the climax of the second stanza. Intimations of the water cycle lead through poetic logic to the third stanza, where the Mediterranean waves also answer to the wind's force, creating an endless round of motion. The water itself now provides an instance of repetition, reflecting the 'old palaces and towers' of the shore 'within the wave's intenser day' and revealing a curious marine 'foliage' that again repeats the seasonal cycle of the land. Having by now shown how cyclical regularity pervades the whole natural world, the poem requires only one step in its own logic to discover a similar pattern repeated in the world of social and political life.

This step requires the inclusion of the poet's voice in the structures of repetition and difference that help generate the poem's meanings. The poet's response to the wind initially repeats the response of nature. Because the wind is a mysterious cause whose existence is evident only in its effects, it makes an apt symbol for the unknown 'power' that animates all life. The wind is more suitable than a mountain in this respect, though, because its trace may be found in both nature and the poet – it may denote both the 'breath of Autumn's being' and the breath which gives voice to the speaker of these lines. 'Wind', therefore, is invoked in the poem not just as a natural force but also as a symbol for inspiration. Where the human world is concerned, however, passive response to external forces is not enough to renew the conditions of existence. Nature may provide a stimulus, but it is the poetic consciousness itself that must give voice to nature and articulate its meanings. In that act of 'giving voice', the poet shapes the voiceless wind into articulate speech, absorbs brute nature into the human world of signs and meanings, and in this verbal transformation of the natural world asserts his creative subjectivity. In this poem, we are constantly aware of hearing the voice of the poet, not the displaced fictional voices of nature. The *Ode* completes the promise of *Mont Blanc* to reveal 'the precious portents of our own powers',[7] by showing how the aesthetic subject interprets and makes felt the promptings of nature.

The poet's role in this action (as James Rieger suggests) is that of the shaman, whose incantations shape a new language and weave a tribal myth.[8] His vocal display generates an occasion for shared homage in which a private agon is transformed into a collective myth. In his supplication of nature, the speaker has invoked the wind as the energy which drives the cycle of natural renewal. With the interests of the tribe in mind, the incantatory voice of the poem seeks the trace of that energy in human affairs. In human life there also must be a cycle of renewal, akin to the seasonal cycle in nature, on which an ideology of social renovation can be based. In his attempt to generate a new social mythus, however, Shelley finds himself once again speaking the language of desire:

> If I were a dead leaf thou mightest bear;
> If I were a swift cloud to fly with thee;
> A wave to pant beneath thy power, and share
>
> The impulse of thy strength, only less free
> Than thou, O uncontrollable!

The conditional verbs of these lines show how futile this wish is: the human speaker is fundamentally different from a wave, a leaf, or a cloud, by virtue of the very fact that he is conscious and can express that consciousness in speech. This irreconcilable difference between man and nature brings the poem to a crisis, works its peripeteia, and discovers a new meaning in the function of the wind. The myth of natural force is destroyed and preserved (Hegel's term is 'sublated') in the myth of dissemination.

This process of dialectical transformation is initiated by the poetic logic of irony. It is ironic that if the speaker's wishes were granted he would find himself 'only less free' than the force that drives him. The 'only' seems less a minimization than a reservation – it suggests 'but' and 'unfortunately'. If the speaker could be as a wave, a leaf, or a cloud, he must accept a diminution of his freedom. If he could sustain childhood's unconscious, unreflecting, unspeaking (*infans* after all means 'unable to speak') relation to nature he would not have to make this impassioned prayer in the first place:

> If even
> I were as in my boyhood, and could be
>
> The comrade of thy wanderings over heaven,
> As then, when to outstrip thy skiey speed
> Scarce seemed a vision, I would ne'er have striven
>
> As thus with thee in prayer in my sore need.

The mature poet is no longer one with nature but must contend with it. He must strive with nature to satisfy his 'sore need' for reassurance and faith in the future. The struggle to wrest meaning from life and the world is not easy, however, and the poet must fall back on the conventions of language and myth in his strife with the forces of an indifferent universe. He cannot do otherwise than to admit his frailty, for the task of human redemption customarily consumes the saviour:

> O life me as a wave, a leaf, a cloud!
> I fall upon the thorns of life! I bleed!

The priestly intermediary must be ready to surrender to the pains of ritual sacrifice. Being human and not divine, Shelley often thus sank under the burden of verbalizing desire. His poetry would be less authentic if it did not occasionally dread the inadequacy of language to his needs, the poet less admirable if he did not from time to time doubt his own adequacy to the task he has assumed. What is important is not so much the tone of this passage as the fact that this forthright admission of mythopoeic impotency does not allow the poem to collapse. Even from within the prison-house of language, the speaking voice reasserts its equivalency with the wind:

> A heavy weight of hours has chained and bowed
> One too like thee: tameless, swift, and proud.

Ironically, time can still the voice of the poet no more than it can tame the wind. Words defy time with their semantic persistence, vibrating in the memory and continuing their play of meaning long after the voice that uttered them is stilled. And that commitment to shaping a language, that dynamic verbal energy which delights in the play of signifiers, drives the poem forward to its conclusion.

The fifth and final stanza of the poem recapitulates the agon of man and nature developed in the first four. The stages of this dramatic process are recapitulated by the rival musical metaphors which balance the beginning and ending of this concluding passage. The first depicts the poet as a natural and dying being in passive response to the wind:

> Make me thy lyre, even as the forest is:
> What if my leaves are falling like its own!
> The tumult of thy mighty harmonies
>
> Will take from both a deep, autumnal tone,
> Sweet though in sadness.

This elegiac tone is one possibility for any poet who chooses to rely on natural structures alone. To be born is to begin dying, and the leaves measure the passing of time. But the 'mighty harmonies' of nature are challenged in the next few lines by 'the incantation of this verse'. Commitment to the poetic act, with its man-made structures and its own temporal measure, achieves the dramatic peripeteia* of Shelley's *Ode*. The verbal formula 'Be thou me' reverses the relation of instrument to agent in the next lines. The speaker does not simply identify himself with the wind; instead he swallows it, absorbing nature into his own being so that he might use it instead of being used by it:

> Be thou, spirit fierce,
> My spirit! Be thou me, impetuous one!
>
> Drive my dead thoughts over the universe
> Like withered leaves to quicken a new birth!
> And, by the incantation of this verse,
>
> Scatter, as from an unextinguished hearth,
> Ashes and sparks, my words among mankind!
> Be through my lips to unawakened earth
>
> The trumpet of prophecy!

The winds of inspiration, now internalized as 'spirit fierce, / My spirit', are shaped by the poet's lips into articulate speech likened not to a passive aeolian lyre but to an active trumpet that heralds 'destiny on the march'. The imperative verbs here demand of the wind that it serve the

---

* [Ed. *Peripeteia*: reversal (of fortune, situation).]

poet, that it become the medium to disseminate his thoughts. They may 'scatter' as he utters them, but if they can reach their destination in the audience they may 'quicken a new birth'. The thoughts themselves are withered leaves, but in the act of speech his words are not just ashes but also sparks to ignite other human consciousnesses with a repetition and reduplication of his vision.

As Donald Reiman has noted, the imagery of this climactic passage recurs in two other perorations among Shelley's works.[9] At the conclusion of the first chapter of *A Philosophical View of Reform*, Shelley writes:

> It is impossible to read the productions of our most celebrated writers, whatever may be their system relating to thought or expression, without being startled by the electric life which there is in their words. . . . They are the priests of an unapprehended inspiration. . . . the trumpet which sings to battle and feels not what it inspires; the influence which is moved not but moves. Poets and philosophers are the unacknowledged legislators of the world.
>
> (J, VII, p. 20)

As always, origins are less important to Shelley than ends. The poet may be passive and lyre-like in relation to inspiration, which comes from 'unapprehended' and mysterious sources. But in relation to his audience he is a trumpet, a sufficient origin in itself that inspires and moves its auditors. The inspiration that matters most to Shelley is not that which originates his poems but the influence they will exert when they are scattered throughout the world.

When almost two years later Shelley adapted this passage to close his *Defence of Poetry*, the only substantial change he made was to alter 'priests' to 'hierophants'. The change introduces an ambiguity that must not be overlooked: the priest reveals the divine, but the hierophant is literally a 'shower forth', one who engages in the act of expounding, one who sets forth some sacred mystery. This shift in terms to describe the poetic act may be read as an admission on Shelley's part of the element of mystification in poetic language. After all, repetition is a rhetorical device that lends significance to discrete events. It links the wind of autumn with the wind of spring and asserts their identity despite their difference. This identification depends on a trope of analogy which substitutes one for the other merely verbally, and which is reinforced by further analogies drawn from the sky and the sea. But a contradictory conclusion could just as easily be drawn: if each leaf, cloud, and wave is unique, so may the winds be distinct from another, and so may be the events they represent. The rhetoric of the poem, however, has chosen to emphasize their affinities to the exclusion of their differences, and so has made them into signs for recurrence. We read a myth of cyclical renewal into nature because the rhetoric of the poem instructs us to do so, but this notion of repetition is a strictly semiotic phenomenon that depends on the poem's deployment of signs. The authority of this particular arrangement of signs derives not from the objective structure of nature but from our experience of the order of the poem's language.

Nevertheless, poetry bears a relation to human historical and social activity because its language encourages the exercise of belief. The dialectic between belief and political change is explored in the *Philosophical View*, written in the months immediately following the composition of the *Ode*. Here Shelley articulates in prose his mature understanding of the relationship between poetry and practical life. Political change, he writes, depends as much on the sentiment that change is inevitable and desirable as on actual social conditions (*J*, VII, p. 21). He shows his awareness that expectation can influence circumstances as much as circumstances affect expectation; and he knows that when poetry gives determinate form to ideology it raises expectations. Ideology, after all, does not describe reality so much as express a will or a hope that operates, says Althusser, in the realm of imagination.[10] Shelley's *Ode to the West Wind*, by expounding the orderliness of natural change, seeks to generate just such expectations of order and necessity with regard to political change. The poem is less description of objective conditions in nature and society than an attempt to evoke in its auditors that belief 'which is at once a prophecy and a cause' of future events.

For Shelley, the measure of a poem's worth resided not in its value as truth but in its effects upon an audience. Shelley knew that the analogy between the seasonal cycle and political renovation was rhetorical and not logical; therefore he refrains from enforcing a moral at the end of the poem. Instead of a flatly declarative conclusion that compels the reader, he uses a rhetorical question in order to defer meaning to the reader:

> O, wind
> If Winter comes, can Spring be far behind?

As Paul de Man has written of such questions, 'rhetoric radically suspends logic' and opens the way to endless possibilities.[11] The question that the *Ode* finally poses is the question implicit in the analogical rhetoric of the first three stanzas: is winter a sign of spring, or not; that is, is there a necessary connection between signifier and signified, such that the appearance of the former involves the expectation of the latter? The poem has worked mightily to rouse such an expectation of meaningful relations in the natural and the political worlds, but its final lines defer those meanings from the text to the reading process itself.

Readers who can detach themselves from the poem's rhetoric might easily pose the counter-question: if Autumn comes, can Winter be far behind?

The rhetoric of Shelley's poetic language in this poem thus reflects the by now familiar distinction between insemination and dissemination. Because the poem's rhetoric can be so readily deconstructed, it cannot inflict its code on the reader. The poem cannot impregnate its reader either genetically or ideologically, but can only give itself up to be read just as Shelley surrenders his voice to the wind:

> Drive my dead thoughts over the universe
> Like withered leaves to quicken a new birth!
> And, by the incantation of this verse,
>
> Scatter, as from an unextinguished hearth
> Ashes and sparks, my words among mankind!

The poem cannot 'quicken' its readers without first allowing itself to be 'scattered'. Shelley finally surrenders his words to the wind because he trusts the reading process enough to prefer dissemination to insemination. He has become enough of an artist not to force his meaning on his auditors but to yield them their autonomy. His discourse does not transmit meaning but instead now truly 'generates occasions' (J, V, p. 253) for meanings. He no longer wields words as weapons, though he persists in playing the language game of poetry. He is confident that his readers will freely join in that game, and pursue the relations between signifiers and signifieds in the process of playing it. In a lyric which dramatizes desire, Shelley willingly surrenders his authority as poet to the reader, who can if he chooses cancel the deconstruction of the text and recover the authority of the sign in the pursuit of meaning. Such willing suspensions on both sides are essential to the erotics of Shelley's poetry.

## Notes

1. LUDWIG WITTGENSTEIN, *On Certainty* (Oxford: Basil Blackwell, 1969), p. 49. Wittgenstein adds (p. 74) that 'the concept of knowing is coupled with that of the language game'.

2. See LOUIS ALTHUSSER, *For Marx*, trans. Ben Brewster (London: Allen Lane, 1969), where he says (p. 232): 'Human societies secrete ideology as the very element and atmosphere indispensable to their historical respiration and life.'

3. *The Complete Works of Percy Bysshe Shelley*, eds. Roger Ingpen and Walter E. Peck, The Julian Edition, 10 vols (London: Ernest Benn, 1926–30), VII, p. 140.

All references to Shelley's poetry and prose, excluding his letters, are taken from this edition, hereafter cited as *J*.

4. *The Letters of Percy Bysshe Shelley*, ed. Frederick L. Jones, 2 vols (Oxford: Clarendon Press, 1964), II, p. 191; hereafter cited as *L*.

5. Shelley's *Ode* conforms to what Northrop Frye calls 'the primitive idea of drama, which is to present a powerful sensational focus for a community' (*Anatomy of Criticism*, Princeton: Princeton University Press, 1957, p. 282). Frye adds that in 'the more public type of religious lyric . . . the "I" of the poem is one of a visible community of worshipers'. Irene Chayes, in 'Rhetoric as Drama: An Approach to the Romantic Ode', *PMLA*, **79** (1964), p. 72, writes that the *Ode* 'takes the form of a dramatic recovery and reversal by way of a pattern of rhetoric'.

6. JACQUES LACAN, *Ecrits*, trans. Alan Sheridan (New York: W.W. Norton, 1977), p. 47.

7. WALLACE STEVENS, *The Necessary Angel: Essays on Beauty and the Imagination* (New York: Alfred Knopf, 1951), pp. 174–5.

8. See JAMES RIEGER, *The Mutiny Within: The Heresies of Percy Bysshe Shelley* (New York: George Braziller, 1967), pp. 181–2, where he writes that the *Ode* 'evokes memories of the birth of language itself, the "perpetual Orphic song", and of villages where music had the potency of magic and the lyrist and the shaman were a single person. Shelley's poem concerns the human voice, which sets stones dancing and echoes the spheres.'

9. See *Shelley's Poetry and Prose*, ed. Donald H. Reiman and Sharon B. Powers (New York: W.W. Norton, 1977), p. 223n. Admitting that the *Ode*'s 'analogy between the seasonal cycle and human affairs is not a perfect one' in *Percy Bysshe Shelley* (New York: Twayne, 1969), pp. 97–8, Reiman concludes that 'the conscious efforts of men of vision are required to turn the wheel past Winter to Spring'.

10. LOUIS ALTHUSSER, *For Marx*, p. 234.

11. PAUL de MAN, *Allegories of Reading* (New Haven: Yale University Press, 1979), p. 10.

# 10  Love's Universe: *Epipsychidion**

STUART M. SPERRY

Stuart Sperry's *Keats the Poet* (1973), widely regarded as one of the best books ever written on Keats, places close readings of the poems within a framework of concerns that are, in Sperry's words, 'ultimately philosophical' (p. ix). By contrast, his study of Shelley, *Shelley's Major Verse* (1988), hereafter *SMV*, sees philosophy as clipping an angel's wings, and takes issue with Earl Wasserman's 'philosophical reductiveness' (*SMV*, p. xiii). For Sperry, Wasserman's approach slights the affective and emotional workings of the poetry; he seeks to redress the balance by 'beginning to reintegrate the poetry with the life' (*SMV*, p. ix). *Shelley's Major Verse* is hospitable to a variety of critical approaches, but the dominant idiom of the book is a mixture of close reading and biographical-cum-psychoanalytical speculation. In particular, Sperry is influenced by Leon Waldoff's 'The Father–Son Conflict in *Prometheus Unbound*: The Psychology of a Vision', *The Psychoanalytic Review*, 62 (1975), which argues that the lyrical drama involves 'a passing of the Oedipus complex' (Waldoff, p. 92). Sperry's account of *Epipsychidion*, printed below, draws on Freudian ideas about the splitting of the ego, exploring Shelley's struggle to confront the darker implications of the idealising that was, as Sperry reads the poem, tragically necessary for his art. (See Introduction, pp. 15–16, 19–20.)

In December 1820 Shelley was introduced by Claire and Mary to Teresa Viviani, a girl of nineteen confined by her aristocratic father and stepmother to a Pisan convent until a suitable bridegroom could be chosen for her. The plight of the 'prisoner', beautiful, intelligent, and a

---

* Reprinted from Stuart M. Sperry, *Shelley's Major Verse: The Narrative and Dramatic Poetry* (Cambridge, Mass. and London: Harvard University Press, 1988), pp. 158–71, 176–82 (footnotes renumbered from the original).

youthful author, was bound to appeal to the knight-errantry of the poet who years earlier had rescued Harriet from the confines of her boarding-school. The stage was set for one more dramatic outpouring and coalescence of sympathies. During a series of repeated visits to Teresa, Shelley found himself again strongly drawn in an emotional attraction. Like *Adonais*, the elegy to Keats which he composed later the same year, the poetical effusion he addressed to Teresa early in 1821 has much more to say about Shelley himself than about the subject or circumstances that provide the occasion for the poem.

Following Shelley's own characterization of the work as 'an idealized history of my life and feelings',[1] some critics have read the poem as a chapter in the poet's spiritual autobiography. Others have insisted that it is really a treatise on poetry and the sources and processes of its creation.[2] The only reasonable view is that the poem is both, a work in which the emerging pattern of Shelley's life and the formulation of his verse are inextricably related. More specifically it is a revelation of the inveterate fatality dominating Shelley's life that is source of both his creativity and the particular character of his verse. It is a study in psychogenesis, an essay in the trials and difficulties of achieving poetic selfhood.

A deeply personal, indeed introverted, work, the poem is, as critics have pointed out, in many respects a redoing of *Alastor*. Like the earlier poem, it continues the search for the poet's psychological or spiritual antitype, 'this soul of my soul' (l. 238), the phrase in *Epipsychidion* that approximates the meaning of its title. Although it lacks the brilliant disorienting originality of *Alastor*'s psychological insights, it possesses, for all its hectic, febrile quality, a greater self-awareness, a defensiveness revealed in its construction. If it springs directly from the intensity of Shelley's involvement with Teresa, it also moves through a series of progressive disengagements. The lines are not addressed to Teresa Viviani but to an 'Unfortunate Lady, Emilia V——', or, more simply, the 'Emily' of the poem. They are written, as we learn from the prefatory 'Advertisement', by an unknown poet who has already died, somewhat ominously, while making preparations at Florence for the journey to 'one of the wildest of the Sporades',[3] a voyage imagined at the conclusion of the poem. The verses themselves, we are told at the very outset, are mere 'votive wreaths of withered memory' (l. 4), the tribute of a 'rose' whose 'petals pale / Are dead' (ll. 9–10).

The poem was published anonymously, at Shelley's request, and some time after its appearance in London he sought to have it suppressed. On few of his works has he commented in retrospect in terms so definitive and so estranging. When he sent the poem to Charles Ollier, his publisher, he wrote that it 'should not be considered as my own; indeed, in a certain sense, it is a production of a portion of me already dead; and in this sense the advertisement is no fiction' (II, pp. 262–3). The following year he wrote John Gisborne: 'The "Epipsychidion" I cannot look at; the person whom it celebrates was a cloud instead of a Juno; and poor Ixion starts from the centaur that was the offspring of his own embrace.' His words bring to mind his embracing his earlier soul sister, Elizabeth Hitchener, only to discover her a 'brown demon'.[4] 'I think one is always in love with something or other,' he went on to Gisborne. 'The error, and I confess it is not easy for spirits cased in flesh and blood to avoid it, consists in seeking in a mortal image the likeness of what is perhaps eternal' (II, pp. 434).

The history of the poem's composition and Shelley's immediate and deepening alienation from it suggests a curiously compulsive experience. It is as if he had seen the error of his compelling emotional involvement almost from the start of his affair with Teresa and yet found himself unable to resist it. The poem appears to record a pattern of experience he was condemned by fate to reenact periodically throughout his career, a form of experience with no apparent catharsis short of death – the demise of the anonymous poet which the 'Advertisement' of the poem reports. *Epipsychidion* is the record of a recurrent traumatic obsession, which reveals the workings of the poet's psyche and the demands of its creative energies. Once more we have a poem that demonstrates the inseparability of creativity and compulsion, of poetic vitality and spiritual disorder, a recognition for which the poem, like *Alastor*, ends by seeking justification and acceptance.

The first of the poem's three major formal divisions (ll. 1–189) is largely an invocation to Emily, a series of high lyrical flights in which Shelley repeatedly seeks to define both her and the nature of his attraction to her. The second part (ll. 190–387), his idealized autobiography, begins when Shelley gives over the attempt to characterize Emily directly and seeks rather to fix her within the enduring pattern of his life and feelings. The third (ll. 388–604) relates the author's imaginary voyage with Emily to the island paradise awaiting them in the Aegean. Each of the principal parts can be subdivided in various ways; more important is that the internal organization of the sections and their relationship to each other are throughout implicit rather than explicit. The logic of the sequence is tentative and exploratory rather than fixed. Indeed, one is led to wonder what the effect would be if the ordering of certain passages were altered or reversed, even to speculate if the poet – Shelley or the 'Writer' cited in the 'Advertisement' – was contemplating substantial changes, a speculation encouraged by the statement in the preface that 'The present poem appears to have been intended by the Writer as the dedication to some longer one.'[5] What we have is a work in which the trains of association connecting part with part are more than usually provisional and hypothetical but no less important, a work that makes exceptional demands on its readers.

The exordium begins on a high pitch, 'as though the poem,' as Harold Bloom writes, 'had already been in progress for some length.'[6] We proceed in a succession of brief verse paragraphs through a series of operatic leaps, each taking us higher into the empyrean: 'Poor captive bird!' (l. 5), 'High, spirit-winged Heart!' (l. 13), 'Seraph of Heaven!' (l. 21). The opening takes its cue from the poem's epigraph, a passage from Teresa's essay on love: 'L'anima amante si slancia fuori del creato, e si crea nel infinito un Mondo tutto per essa, diverso assai da questo oscuro e pauroso baratro' (The loving soul launches beyond creation, and creates for itself in the infinite a world all its own, far different from this dark and terrifying gulf).[7] We err, however, if, like many critics, we attempt to conform the poem to the partly Petrarchan, partly Platonic, idealism of Teresa's affirmation. The epigraph merely sets forth an initial premise against which the poem, as it continues, develops its own complex and ambivalent reaction.

There is from the first an evident strain as the poem proceeds from the image of Emily as the caged bird, shattered and stained with its own blood, to its ever more exorbitant claims for her:

> Sweet Benediction in the eternal Curse!
> Veiled Glory of this lampless Universe!
> Thou Moon beyond the clouds! Thou living Form
> Among the Dead! Thou Star above the Storm!
> Thou Wonder, and thou Beauty, and thou Terror!
>
> (ll. 25–9)

Emily evades the net of grand but empty abstractions the verse casts in its futile effort to contain her. In her sublimity she transcends the metaphoric power of the poetic imagination. Nor is it long before we are aware that we are witnessing a failure of the poetic process, a conclusion borne home by the verse itself: 'Aye, even the dim words which obscure thee now / Flash, lightning-like, with unaccustomed glow' (ll. 33–4). The process of association, with its flow of epithets, is working at full intensity; but paradoxically it serves only to obscure Emily, not to reveal her. Recognizing the 'mortality and wrong' (l. 36) of his attempt, the poet can only appeal to Emily to redeem his poem with her favor – 'Then smile on it' (l. 40) – the familiar benison of the feminine smile essential to Shelley's verse.

The failure of the opening paragraphs of *Epipsychidion* raises an interesting problem in critical evaluation. To what degree are we justified in condemning the opening verses as unsatisfactory (a host of critical pejoratives offer themselves: 'trite', 'undisciplined', 'vague', 'effusive')?

To what degree, on the other hand, is the failure to be seen as integral to the progress of the poem? *Epipsychidion* is highly uneven in quality. More than that, however, it is a work whose successful moments – its flights of sustained lyricism, its passages of epigrammatic wit – seem to arise directly out of failure and collapse. Like a number of Romantic works, it is a poem that can define its true direction only through a succession of false starts that involve disorder and uncertainty. Like much modern art, it is a work in which beauty and wonder are inseparable from boredom and horror. It makes special demands on our understanding and resourcefulness as readers. Whether we find the necessary patience to do justice to the work as a whole depends on whether we perceive that the poem's moments of lyrical intensity, its particular insights into the poetic psyche, could have been achieved (at least at this point in Shelley's career) in no other way.

*Epipsychidion* begins with the attempt to capture Emily and her significance for the poet through a series of abstract comparisons that derive their metaphoric power from the cosmos. We are not very far into the poem, however, before we begin to sense, if only indistinctly, a countermovement: 'I never thought before my death to see / Youth's vision thus made perfect' (ll. 41–2). The phrase 'Youth's vision' brings to mind the visionary maiden of *Alastor* and the quest for her which is really a process of inner investigation and discovery. The new countermovement is to find its full expression only with the rhapsodic flight of personal recollection of the second section. The point is, however, that the second, inner-directed movement is present from the outset and seeks to assert itself against the primary. For there are two major impulses that govern the work as a whole. One is centrifugal: the effort to externalize Emily, to see her as an influence governing nature and humankind, a power concentrated in the universe of sun, moon, and stars. The other is centripetal: the recognition that Emily and her power are constituents of the self. The first impulse attempts to project her, to discover her in the images and operations of the macrocosm. The second seeks to find her in the microcosm, the interior world of the self. The poem takes its initial momentum from the first impulse; it is, however, a momentum that cannot be maintained and that collapses. As it does so the second impulse begins to emerge and to provide a tension that polarizes the work and governs its development.

The identity of the narrator-poet now begins to grow in significance:

> Would we two had been twins of the same mother!
> Or, that the name my heart lent to another
> Could be a sister's bond for her and thee,
> Blending two beams of one eternity!

(ll. 45–8)

The problem is that of reconciling his love for Emily with his earlier emotional commitment to mother, sister, and spouse. The poet, of course, wants to see such names as interchangeable terms of a single relationship. Yet the verse goes on to acknowledge that this kind of interassimilation ('were one lawful and the other true', l. 49) is neither permissible nor faithful to his experience. The verse paragraph concludes with an exclamation that conveys a shock of recognition: 'How beyond refuge I am thine. Ah me! / I am not thine: I am a part of *thee*' (ll. 51–2). In his loss of self-possession, the poet feels altogether engrossed by Emily. Yet she remains a being whom he cannot identify except in terms of himself and those relationships that make up the most meaningful part of his past. Within the pattern of equivalences the verse has just offered, 'I am a part of thee' is only another way of saying, 'Thou art a part of me.'

The recognition of the pull into the self prompts by way of reaction another outburst of centrifugal energy. Like the spiraling moth or the 'dying swan who soars and sings' (l. 54), the poet attempts one more flight into the empyrean with a series of new comparisons. 'Art thou not', he asks,

> A Star
> Which moves not in the moving Heavens, alone?
> A smile amid dark frowns? a gentle tone
> Amid rude voices? a beloved light?
> A Solitude, a Refuge, a Delight?
>
> (ll. 56, 60–4)

The compiling of images recommences, the method employed in so much Romantic verse to start a flow of associations that will carry the verse forward to the coalescence of a theme or perception. Yet there is a new tone of doubt; the comparisons are phrased as questions, the interrogation mark has replaced the exclamation. Nor do the metaphors the verse heaps up lead anywhere except to a new collapse and a further realization of the poet's own limitation:

> I measure
> The world of fancies, seeking one like thee,
> And find – alas! mine own infirmity!
>
> (ll. 69–71)

No sooner is this recognition voiced than the verse shifts its direction yet again. The beginning of the paragraph that follows, 'She met me, Stranger, upon life's rough way' (l. 72), is the closest anticipation yet of the ecstatic outburst that opens the second major section of the work:

'There was a Being whom my spirit oft / Met' (ll. 190–1). It is as if, in the continuous war between the centrifugal and centripetal forces, the verse were struggling to break through a series of restraints to the recognition of its true object – the visionary maiden who haunts the recesses of the poet's interior consciousness. What kind of psychological resistance, one must wonder, accounts for a process of definition that can make its way only by overcoming repeated checks and diversions?

Already at the beginning of the new verse paragraph ('She met me, Stranger, upon life's rough way') Emily appears partly subsumed within a feminine archetype dominating the poet's psyche from his birth. The paragraph is particularly revealing because it contains the germ of primitive experience that is shortly to flower into the autobiographical recollections in the second section of the poem, rather like a leitmotif in Romantic music that appears before it is developed. Thus the verse describes the maiden and how

> from her lips, as from a hyacinth full
> Of honey-dew, a liquid murmur drops,
> Killing the sense with passion . . .

> (ll. 83–5)

The lines are an unmistakable premonition of the later baleful 'One' in the second section 'whose voice was venomed melody' (l. 256) and from whose 'living cheeks and bosom flew / A killing air, which pierced like honeydew' (ll. 261–2). These later lines depict a poisonous infatuation, which grows out of the earlier, more generalized attraction and the intensity that surrounds it. The central theme the paragraph expresses is the overwhelming longing generated by a kind of primitive knowledge beyond the senses and almost beyond expression – 'too deep / For the brief fathom-line of thought or sense' (ll. 89–90). Whereas the verse earlier sought to define the source of its attraction in terms of fixed abstractions, it now turns to the flowing, to shades 'of light and motion' (l. 94). The poet invokes the being he adores as a kind of power, an energy radiating from a single source,

> one intense
> Diffusion, one serene Omnipresence,
> Whose flowing outlines mingle in their flowing,
> Around her cheeks and utmost fingers glowing
> With the unintermitted blood, which there
> Quivers, (as in a fleece of snow-like air
> The crimson pulse of living morning quiver,)
> Continuously prolonged, and ending never,

Till they are lost, and in that Beauty furled
Which penetrates and clasps and fills the world.

(ll. 94–103)

The lines employ strongly erotic imagery to describe a feminine presence
that is curiously vague and intangible, known or remembered by the
power that radiates from her in endless reverberations. Perhaps the best
gloss for the lines is the passage from Tennyson's 'Tithonus' they
inspired, the description of the goddess of the dawn's diurnal revisitation
to her mortal lover and of how, as her 'cheek begins to redden through
the gloom', he watches

The lucid outline forming round thee; saw
The dim curls kindle into sunny rings;
Changed with thy mystic change, and felt my blood
Glow with the glow that slowly crimsoned all
Thy presence and thy portals.[8]

'Tithonus' is the most brilliant and moving of Tennyson's attempts to
define the wellsprings of his own poetic temperament, and the imagery
of its central section identifies it with Shelley's earlier endeavor. Like the
presence Tithonus would arrest, the power is fleeting and unfixable,
'Scarce visible' and sensed more by the 'fragrance [that] seems to fall
from her light dress, / And her loose hair' (ll. 104–6). As with the
visionary maiden in *Alastor*, her beauty is experienced more as a
sensation of past bliss, the recognition of a void that cannot be filled but
which for that very reason inspires the keenest longing, 'a wild odour
[that] is felt, / Beyond the sense, like fiery dews that melt / Into the
bosom of a frozen bud' (ll. 109–11). The power is frozen, dead, yet
paradoxically susceptible to eternal renovation, a 'motion which may
change but cannot die' (l. 114).

No sooner has the poet described the influence that haunts him as a
'motion' than he seeks once again to reify it as 'An image of some bright
Eternity' (l. 115), an effort that leads on to yet one more assemblage of
multiplying metaphors for Emily:

A shadow of some golden dream; a Splendour
Leaving the third sphere pilotless; a tender
Reflection of the eternal Moon of Love
Under whose motions life's dull billows move;
A Metaphor of Spring and Youth and Morning;
A Vision like incarnate April . . .

(ll. 116–21)

159

The failure of the attempt is by now almost predictable, and with it the consequent disintegration into despair: 'Ah, woe is me! / What have I dared? where am I lifted?' (ll. 123–4). One is struck by overtones of warning and prohibition.

In the effort to recover the forward momentum of his verse, the poet turns to reinvoke his inspiration yet again: 'Spouse! Sister! Angel! Pilot of the Fate / Whose course has been so starless!' (ll. 130–1). The three quite different relationships through which he seeks to express the nature of his love are each incomplete, and illustrate once again his need to reconcile them with a more dominant feminine archetype fundamental to his experience. Hence the renewed outburst of failure and frustration:

> O too late
> Beloved! O too soon adored, by me!
> For in the fields of immortality
> My spirit should at first have worshipped thine,
> A divine presence in a place divine;
> Or should have moved beside it on this earth,
> A shadow of that substance, from its birth;
> But not as now.

> (ll. 131–8)

Had they met 'in the fields of immortality', in the world of preexistence, he could have loved her entirely. But in the world of humankind, the terms 'spouse', 'sister', 'guardian angel' point to distinct relationships that must be kept divided; and he is already married to another. Yet the fact remains that if he has loved Emily 'too late', he has also loved her 'too soon' – not simply too quickly but too early. For he realizes that, whether he has recognized her before or not, he has known her as a part of his first and earliest adoration, an aspect of that greater presence that still animates and drives his existence.

The tantalizing play of paradox and insinuation is suddenly broken by the portentous lines that introduce the next verse paragraph: 'Thy wisdom speaks in me, and bids me dare / Beacon the rocks on which high hearts are wreckt' (ll. 147–8). The current of the poet's verse, for all its false starts and impediments, appears on the point of breaking through to some fresh clarification. What follows is a passage of verse written in a style precise, epigrammatic, fluent, which, although intimated earlier, is distinct from anything preceding it – a condensation in both the stylistic and the psychological sense:

> I never was attached to that great sect,
> Whose doctrine is, that each one should select
> Out of the crowd a mistress or a friend,

And all the rest, though fair and wise, commend
To cold oblivion, though it is in the code
Of modern morals, and the beaten road
Which those poor slaves with weary footsteps tread,
Who travel to their home among the dead
By the broad highway of the world, and so
With one chained friend, perhaps a jealous foe,
The dreariest and the longest journey go.

(ll. 149–59)

The lines are remembered by many readers, and known by heart by some, who have forgotten everything else in *Epipsychidion*, even the situation that occasioned them. The passage has always been described as Shelley's most forthright attack, at least in verse, upon the institution of marriage, his most fervent assertion of free love. However, the lines spring from a deeper, secret understanding. They convey a message that many find suspect, meretricious, even offensive, but one that Shelley represents in its most compelling light. It is a message writ large throughout Byron's poetry, which that poet was never able or willing to distill with such succinctness. It is the truth that no single woman can prove adequate to satisfy man's appetite for love or beauty (although it is wrong to define the principle along sexist lines). The limitlessness of human desire, the declaration of each individual's eternal birthright, the charter of his uniqueness and his independence constitutes equally his glory and his curse. For the very insatiability of longing that preserves the individuality of each being at the same time ensures its isolation, the realization that it will never meet its ideal mate or double of the Platonic fable, Yeats's 'yolk and white of the one shell'.[9] The journey remains the dreariest and the longest whether one undertakes it accompanied or alone.

Why are the two verse paragraphs that follow and conclude the first section of the poem, 'sermons', as Bloom characterizes them,[10] less memorable and satisfying? They have been often taken as one of Shelley's major paeans to the universality of love and the imagination, seen as correlative powers, a Dantean hymn to the ennobling effect of human aspiration for what is divine.[11] Yet the two paragraphs seem forced and stilted after the declaration that precedes them. They struggle to dispel the darker implications of the central insight through a series of metaphysical paradoxes ('to divide is not to take away', 'Each part exceeds the whole', ll. 161, 181) that in their condensation and rapidity seem mere scholastic platitudes. Once again one detects a strong centrifugal impulse, as the verse struggles to objectify and mediate its understanding if not within the imagery of nature and the macrocosm then through the eternal philosophical principles behind them. The verse becomes more involuted, more hyperbolic in its transcendental claims, then suddenly gives way to the autobiographical rhapsody that commences the second section of the poem.

It is unfortunate that Shelley's own phrase, 'an idealized history of my life and feelings',[12] has been adopted as a description of the middle section of his poem. The word 'idealized' in particular suggests a history ordered and set down as a pattern or a model. What we have in the narrator's account is rather the most revealing section of what Richard Holmes has called 'the most nakedly autobiographical poem [Shelley] ever wrote',[13] the record of a series of recurrent personal crises. The pattern of the history is 'idealized' primarily because it is struggling to condense and define itself and to emerge into conscious recognition. Inevitably the events it recounts invite, indeed demand, elucidation in light of what we know of Shelley's own life and psychological history. To be sure, he writes in his 'Advertisement' that 'The present Poem, like the *Vita Nuova* of Dante, is sufficiently intelligible to a certain class of readers without a matter-of-fact history of the circumstances to which it relates.' Yet he goes on to add: 'Not but that, *gran vergogna sarebbe a colui, che rimasse cosa sotto veste di figura, o di colore rettorico: e domandato non sapesse denudare le sue parole da cotal veste, in guisa che avessero verace intendimento'* (Great would be his shame who should rhyme anything under the garb of metaphor or rhetorical figure; and, being requested, could not strip his words of this dress so that they might have a true meaning).[14] The two statements, contradictory in their effect if not in their assertions, testify to the ambivalence that marks the work throughout, to a desire both to reveal and to conceal. Taken together the two statements constitute an invitation to read the narrator's account of his life history as a condensation of Shelley's own, a condensation, however, that reflects Shelley's effort to crystallize and comprehend it.

It has not been sufficiently observed that the autobiographical aura pervades the second section, albeit more suggestively than explicitly, from its very beginning:

> There was a Being whom my spirit oft
> Met on its visioned wanderings, far aloft,
> In the clear golden prime of my youth's dawn,
> Upon the fairy isles of sunny lawn,
> Amid the enchanted mountains, and the caves
> Of divine sleep, and on the air-like waves
> Of wonder-level dream, whose tremulous floor
> Paved her light steps; – on an imagined shore,
> Under the grey beak of some promontory
> She met me, robed in such exceeding glory,

That I beheld her not. In solitudes
Her voice came to me through the whispering woods,
And from the fountains, and the odours deep
Of flowers, which, like lips murmuring in their sleep
Of the sweet kisses which had lulled them there,
Breathed but of *her* to the enamoured air.

(ll. 190–205)

The lyrical exordium is in sharp contrast to the metaphysical conceits
preceding it. With its harmonic flow and power the verse transports us to
a range of sensibility we recognize at once as uniquely Shelley's. In a way
that is by now familiar, the lines revive the fragmentary impressions of
the child's expanding consciousness, a world pervaded by the imagery of
sleep and dreams in which lips murmur and kisses lull, a 'youth's dawn'
presided over by the dominant feminine presence, the supreme
expression of maternal love. The passage culminates in tribute to this
earliest remembered influence, a being who

Makes this cold common hell, our life, a doom
As glorious as a fiery martyrdom;
Her Spirit was the harmony of truth.

(ll. 214–16)

The dramatic assertion seeks to snatch victory from defeat. For the
fundamental truth the passage, like Wordsworth's 'Intimations Ode',
acknowledges is that the world of childhood rapture has forever faded.
The feminine presence at its center has vanished, leaving only the
memory of her being, a recollection more like a lack or thirst that never
can be satisfied and that drives the quester ever onward.

Like the Poet in *Alastor*, the autobiographical narrator in *Epipsychidion*
seeks to reunite himself with the spirit who has withdrawn from him,
abandoning him to the needs and longings she has aroused:

And as a man with mighty loss dismayed,
I would have followed, though the grave between
Yawned like a gulph.

(ll. 229–31)

The rift between them, however, is too great to overcome, and with the
failure comes the sense of separation and change intimated in 'And as a
man'. The phrase marks the first and only appearance of the principal
male noun within the poem. It is as if the experience of loss the passage
records were definitive, the initiation into adulthood, the mark of one's

humanity, perhaps even the crucial determinant of the male ego or identity.

The reassuring voice that whispers 'O thou of hearts the weakest, / The phantom is beside thee whom thou seekest' (ll. 232–3) provides the motive for the quest related in the remainder of the section. However, the brief exchange that ensues, 'Then I – "where?" – the world's echo answered "where!"' (l. 234), unmistakably recalls the story of Echo and Narcissus: 'dixerat: "ecquis adest?" et "adest" responderat Echo' ('He asked, "Is anyone here?" and "Here!" cried Echo back.')[15] The voice seems a mere repetition of the quester's own. Moreover, though he now begins his search to discover 'Whither 'twas fled, this soul out of my soul' (l. 238), the presence he seeks seems irrecoverably lost:

> neither prayer nor verse could dissipate
> The night which closed on her; nor uncreate
> That world within this Chaos, mine and me,
> Of which she was the veiled Divinity,
> The world I say of thoughts that worshipped her.
>
> (ll. 241–5)

The lines expose a paradox central to the poem. The 'veiled Divinity' may have vanished, but she remains crucial to the identity of her lover. Thus he insists on distinguishing between two parts of himself, a dark and engulfing 'Chaos' that is 'mine', and a central core of being, an immutable 'me', formed and indelibly marked by her spirit.[16] The division reflects an idealization that involves splitting of the ego into separate parts, one pure and harmonious, reflecting only her, the other evil and demonic and subject to the malign influences of the world.[17] The idealization is essentially the same as that in 'On Love', Shelley's earlier, fragmentary essay, which provides a valuable gloss for *Epipsychidion*. 'We dimly see within our intellectual nature,' Shelley had written, 'a miniature as it were of our entire self, yet deprived of all that we condemn or despise, the ideal prototype of every thing excellent or lovely that we are capable of conceiving as belonging to the nature of man.' This interior ideal, this 'soul within our soul', now provides the model to which 'we eagerly refer all sensations, thirsting that they should resemble or correspond with it', while life becomes the quest for the 'discovery of its antitype'.[18] The description epitomizes the process of idealization by which the narrator is driven, following his loss, to wander through 'the wintry forest of our life' seeking amid its various apparitions 'one form resembling hers' (ll. 249–54).

Understanding this idealization is crucial to interpreting the autobiographical reminiscences that follow, passages that from at least the time of Newman Ivey White have been recognized as the most astonishing and revealing of Shelley's self-disclosures in verse. As Richard Holmes has written, 'The shadows of Elizabeth Shelley, Harriet Grove, Harriet Westbrook, Elizabeth Hitchener, Cornelia Boinville, Sophia Stacey and perhaps others all fit along the margins of the verse.'[19] Yet the problem, intimated from the start in the poem's 'Advertisement', has been how to interpret the apparent allusions to the most intimate and important relationships in Shelley's life. Even before the major autobiographical revelation – the thinly veiled allegory of his changing ties with Mary, Claire, and others – we have the problem of interpreting the narrator's initiatory liaison with 'One, whose voice was venomed melody' (l. 256), a malignant and withering attraction:

> The breath of her false mouth was like faint flowers,
> Her touch was as electric poison, – flame
> Out of her looks into my vitals came,
> And from her living cheeks and bosom flew
> A killing air, which pierced like honey-dew
> Into the core of my green heart.
>
> (ll. 258–63)

Following Thornton Hunt's report of an indiscretion Shelley committed at Oxford, a number of scholars have accepted the notion that the passage refers to the poet's having contracted venereal disease from a prostitute while at university.[20] Whether the lines refer directly to an encounter during which Shelley became infected will never, in all probability, be proved. Yet the narrower reading obscures the deeper truth the passage conveys. For the imagery of mouth and touch, of melody and perfume, connects the mysterious beguiler with the larger prototype of the dream maiden who emerges at the outset of the second section. The enchantress of the later lines diverges from this primary model as her dark and evil antithesis. If the splitting of the ego leads to the projection of its idealized half in the form of the visionary dream maiden, it leads also to the personification of its other half as her wicked and deceiving opposite.[21]

Shelley throughout his life consistently tended to imagine women in terms of these extremes. He went on, moreover, to visualize his life and his career within governing relationships he constructed in imagination, which led to his conceiving those close to him in terms of the moral abstractions – either good or evil – he projected onto them. It is in this more exact sense that *Epipsychidion* is indeed, as he called it, 'an idealized history of my life and feelings'. The deeper truth the poem reveals is the difficulty of maintaining these abstract divisions, the fact that the changing pressures of life inevitably wrenched and ultimately collapsed the system of imaginative relations seemingly so essential to the preservation of his identity. As one system split up, another had to be created to replace it. As a personal history *Epipsychidion* reveals the psychological cost of creating these idealized relationships, the difficulty of maintaining them, and the extraordinary pain of their disintegration . . .

In its curious mixture of revelation and disguise, of apology and confession, *Epipsychidion* adumbrates the enduring fatalism of Shelley's career as poet. It brings almost to conscious recognition the pattern of repeated effort and failure that underlies both the poetry and the life. It reflects the poet's struggle to project and objectify within the macrocosm of the outer world those values dearest to the self in symbols and personifications that, under the pressure of reality, were forever collapsing back into the microcosm of the ego from which they originated. The poem demonstrates the difficulty, if not the impossibility, of reconciling the microcosm and the macrocosm, art and life. Yet the poem at the same time represents this desire as the ineradicable impulse of the true poetic soul; and it concludes by seeking understanding, tolerance, and even praise for the recurrent failure it brings to light.

The third major movement of the poem commences with the imaginary depiction of the lovers' union and flight: 'The day is come, and thou wilt fly with me' (l. 388). The pull of the verse is inexorable, reinforced by the emblems of a commanding necessity. 'The hour is come: – the destined Star has risen' (l. 394). The walls confining Emily are high but not sufficient to restrain true love. 'A ship is floating in the harbour now' (l. 408), and all the winds and portents are propitious. It is striking, as White has pointed out, that no sooner has Shelley imagined the reunification of his psychological and spiritual existence beneath the mutual sway of Emily, Mary, and Claire, a goal intimated from the poem's opening lines, than every trace of this design should vanish in the all-engrossing desire for union with Emily alone.[22] It is as if the power of the new attraction, like that of the star for the moth, overwhelmed every other remembrance or consideration. Mary drops from the poem until the concluding lines of the envoi, while every hope for the fulfillment of happiness is concentrated in Emily. For the third movement of the poem takes the form of an elopement, the withdrawal of the lovers to a lone Aegean island, 'Beautiful as a wreck of Paradise' (l. 423), which still reflects the harmony of a lost golden age and where the two are to consummate their union.

Like Asia's journey in *Prometheus Unbound*, the voyage is a regression backward to the sources of life, toward the recovery of a lost wholeness of primitive experience. Few poets have evoked the regressive impulse so powerfully as Shelley, as echoes in the poetry of a later age, from Tennyson's 'Lotos-Eaters' to the concluding stanzas of Arnold's 'Scholar-

Gipsy', testify. The island among the Aegean is inhabited by a few survivors of an earlier pastoral time, 'Simple and spirited; innocent and bold' (l. 429). The air is laden with the scent of flowers; strains of music 'fall upon the eye-lids like faint sleep' (l. 449). The tidal undulation rhythmically blends the various sense impressions synesthetically into one apprehension of an underlying source where

> every motion, odour, beam, and tone,
> With that deep music is in unison:
> Which is a soul within the soul – they seem
> Like echoes of an antenatal dream.
>
> (ll. 453–6)

Veil after veil of imagery falls away as the verse draws ever closer to the center of all sensory experience, the animating soul, the counterpart of the narrator's own,

> a Soul no less [which]
> Burns in the heart of this delicious isle,
> An atom of th' Eternal.
>
> (ll. 477–9)

If Emily is the projection of the narrator's 'me', that ideal part of himself, it is clear that the Edenic setting both harmonizes with and reflects the perfection of their love. As Wasserman has written, 'the union of the lovers with [the island] is of the same order as their union with each other. For the island is but the "internal" conceived of as "external", just as Emily is the finite self projected as perfect and infinite.'[23] There is no longer any division between macrocosm and microcosm; the two have been conflated.

The lovers will inhabit 'a lone dwelling', the architectural 'marvel of the wilderness' (ll. 483–4), which he has stocked with books and music for their pleasure. Yet their imaginary existence together recognizes no division between culture and nature.[24] Built no one knows 'by whom or how' (l. 484), the structure ready for their habitation seems to have taken its form within the heart of the earth, 'then grown / Out of the mountains, from the living stone' (ll. 495–6). Its decoration, 'all the antique and learned imagery' (l. 498) that once adorned it, has long since been replaced by ivy and wild vines. The substitution of art by nature is significant: a later form of development is replaced by one more primitive. So parasite flowers with their 'dewy gems' (l. 502) take the place of lamps to illuminate the halls. The dilapidations the building has suffered through the years have only rendered its galleries more airy and open to the lights of night or day, which provide a natural and ever-changing pattern of mosaic decoration. So perfectly is the building integrated with its setting that there seems no distinction between interior and exterior, the domestic and the out-of-doors. The view from the high terraces is of an all-subsuming harmony and dreamlike interassimilation, in which

> Earth and Ocean seem
> To sleep in one another's arms, and dream
> Of waves, flowers, clouds, woods, rocks, and all that we
> Read in their smiles, and call reality.

> (ll. 509–12)

Here the two lovers will dwell, like the ancient king and builder with his sister-spouse before them, where minutes are measured by the pant of sleeping deer and years by the silent accumulation of leaves, until their existence together merges inseparably with all that surrounds them:

> Let us become the over-hanging day,
> The living soul of this Elysian isle,
> Conscious, inseparable, one.

> (ll. 538–40)

They will become both the circumference and the vital center of the heavenly canopy enfolding them, united with each other and with all else (for 'conscious' here means chiefly 'thinking and feeling as one').

The scene represents the most extended and intense effort of imagination in Shelley's poetry to characterize that unity with the ideal of his own soul for which he longed. Yet the attempt is hardly unique. One is reminded of the harmony of the kingdom where Laon and Cythna are drawn into their incestuous relationship at the opening of the second canto of *The Revolt of Islam*. As in the earlier poem, the first destabilizing movement originates with the sexual impulse. Overtones of the erotic are present everywhere within the landscape, in the 'lightest winds [which] touch their paramour', the island, or the shore which 'Trembles and sparkles as with ecstacy' beneath 'the quick, faint kisses of the sea' (ll. 545, 547–8). Like Laon and Cythna before them, the two lovers are led to the embrasure of a cavern, throughout Shelley's verse the customary setting for consummation. Quiet words proceed to looks and looks to kisses while the rapture of their embrace leads on irresistibly to culminate in sexual orgasm:

> Our breath shall intermix, our bosoms bound,
> And our veins beat together; and our lips
> With other eloquence than words eclipse

The soul that burns between them, and the wells
Which boil under our being's inmost cells,
The fountains of our deepest life, shall be
Confused in passion's golden purity.

(ll. 565–71)

The desire for complete union can consummate itself in no other way
than through sexual fulfillment. Yet the rapture ends in the distressing
recognition of division: 'We shall become the same, we shall be one /
Spirit within two frames, oh! wherefore two?' (ll. 573–4). The ecstasy of
their imaginary union concludes in the recognition of a fundamental
division. It is as if the struggle to achieve identity (in the sense of
'sameness', 'oneness') led only to a fuller realization of identity as
'personal or individual existence'. The ambivalence of the concept
suggests the impossibility of its achievement:

One passion in twin-hearts, which grows and grew,
'Till like two meteors of expanding flame,
Those spheres instinct with it become the same,
Touch, mingle, are transfigured; ever still
Burning, yet ever inconsumable.

(ll. 575–9)

The planetary imagery here specifically recalls the scene at the
culmination of the first canto of *The Revolt of Islam* in which two lights roll
forward on the floor of the Temple of the Spirit, ascending 'Like meteors'
and 'commingling into one, / One clear and mighty planet' (ll. 625,
627–8) to reveal the majestic, bisexual figure who takes its seat beneath
it.[25] The figure emerges from the sphere, however, only to preside over
the appearance of Laon and Cythna and the account of their separation,
adventures, and reunion after death.

The larger prospect of repeated divisions and higher reintegrations
progressing steadily toward an ever-nearer ideal of human perfection
advanced in *The Revolt* is implicitly rejected in *Epipsychidion* in the quest
for total union. All else gives way to the burning desire to merge totally
with the ideal:

One hope within two wills, one will beneath
Two overshadowing minds, one life, one death,
One Heaven, one Hell, one immortality,
And one annihilation. Woe is me!

(ll. 584–7)

The more relentlessly 'one' struggles to assert itself over 'two', the more apparent it makes the underlying division.[26] The effort to compound two bodies, minds, and wills as one ends not in unification but annihilation. The current of the verse sinks back into the recognition of rhetorical failure and the limitations of its medium:

> The winged words on which my soul would pierce
> Into the height of love's rare Universe,
> Are chains of lead around its flight of fire. –
> I pant, I sink, I tremble, I expire!
>
> (ll. 588–91)

The fact is that language, even the symbolic language of verse, depends ultimately on nature, and can only approach those idealizations conceived within the self. At the same time the perpetuation of the sexual metaphor in the final line, the last in the poem proper, suggests that ecstasy can be achieved only at the cost of ultimate dissemination and collapse. As Wasserman has written, 'the poem closes with the same desperate and ecstatic confusion' we have noted from the beginning.[27] The rhetorical breakdown is symptomatic of the poem's alternating construction and deconstruction.

How is one to account for the analysis of recurrent failure in a love poem dedicated to Teresa Viviani, a failure that in various ways casts such a long shadow over Shelley's relationship with Mary? For if his attraction for Teresa, however intense and ecstatic, was virtually dead from the start of composition – actually more a catalyst for a deeper range of personal concerns – Mary was still a vital part of his existence. *Epipsychidion* is a hymn to love, an autobiography, a manifesto, a confession, an apology, a kind of prophecy, and, last, a prayer or entreaty. Above all it is the anatomy of a compulsion central to the poet's life and art. Unless we see the poem as all of these, we miss some element essential to its composition. The best clue we have for interrelating such different functions lies in the thirteen lines of irregularly rhymed verse Shelley appended by way of an envoi.

The envoi has often been passed over without comment. When considered at all, its burden has usually been summarized in one aphorism: love's 'reward is in the world divine / Which, if not here, it builds beyond the grave' (ll. 597–8). Ideal love can find its perfect consummation only in the world to come, not in this.[28] Yet one wonders if such a summation is adequate to the psychological depth and complexity of the completed work. Not surprisingly, Shelley begins his envoi by returning once more to the theme of his governing compulsion, bidding his verses kneel in farewell at their mistress's feet to reaffirm both her rule and their triumph over the poet: 'We are the masters of thy slave' (l. 593). Yet the ending of the envoi is less predictable, as Shelley goes on to task the verses to intercede for him with 'Marina, Vanna, Primus' and to appeal to them to 'love each other' and 'leave the troop which errs and which reproves, / And come and be my guest, – for I am Love's' (ll. 603–4). What is this Dantesque company of partly allegorized initiates? Why are they entreated to love each other, and what and why are they asked to cease reproving?

At the very end of his poem, Shelley turns to Mary (Marina) and to Jane and Edward Williams, shortly to become two of his closest friends. The Williamses, living together as husband and wife though actually unmarried, were to join the Shelleys in occupying Villa Magni, the forlorn little house on the Italian coast at Lerici in the summer of 1822, when Shelley's life came to an end. Jane (*Giovanna*) was to become the last of Shelley's passionate attachments, to whom he wrote his greatest love lyrics. Edward (*Primus*) was the inseparable companion of his last days, who drowned with him when their boat foundered during a squall in the gulf of La Spezia in July. It is curious to find a poem that lays bare the troubled history of Shelley's past idealizations ending with an appeal to Mary to take her place with the Williamses in what was ultimately to become one more constellation of idealized relationships. It is disconcerting to find prefigured a situation in which Shelley was to become deeply involved with Jane while at the same time pleading loyalty to both Edward and to his wife.[29]

In writing *Epipsychidion* Shelley laid to rest a brief but extraordinary episode of his life. Yet the work represents a very imperfect catharsis. At a deeper level the poem is the revelation of an enduring compulsion too strong to be checked or moderated, a desire that overrides all testimony and reasoning against it. In the words of the envoi, 'Love's very pain is sweet' (l. 596). It suited Shelley, in writing his apology, to adopt the high style of Dante in *La Vita Nuova*. Yet the enduring life the poem reveals is neither new nor, in Dante's sense, transformed. If the work is a manifesto, it is less metaphysical, less a Platonic testament of beauty than the admission of personal and psychological necessity. By invoking with remarkable clairvoyance the sympathy of Jane and Edward Williams, the figures who, along with Mary, were destined to play the principal roles in the next and last act in the idealized drama of his life, he was really entreating understanding and forgiveness. At the end of his remarkable self-revelation, he was soliciting the pardon of those few who could truly understand him; he was asking for the acceptance of a part of himself that could never change.

## Notes

1. *The Letters of Percy Bysshe Shelley*, ed. Frederick L. Jones, 2 vols (Oxford: Clarendon Press, 1964), II, p. 434.

2. Newman Ivey White and Kenneth Neill Cameron have been at the head of those for whom the primary interest and meaning of the work are the light it sheds on Shelley's life and its quality of autobiographical revelation. See White's *Shelley* (New York: Knopf, 1940), II, 259–69, and Cameron's 'The Planet-Tempest Passage in *Epipsychidion'*, *PMLA*, **63** (1948), 950–72, reprinted in slightly revised form in *Shelley's Poetry and Prose*, ed. Donald H. Reiman and Sharon B. Powers (New York: Norton, 1977), pp. 637–58, and incorporated in Cameron's *Shelley: The Golden Years* (Cambridge, Mass.: Harvard University Press, 1974), pp. 275–88. On the other hand, Earl R. Wasserman, in *Shelley: A Critical Reading* (Baltimore and London: Johns Hopkins University Press, 1971), pp. 417–61, takes the poem as an extended philosophical and aesthetic meditation whose ideas exist in an intellectual realm totally removed from Shelley's life. Harold Bloom, who resembles Wasserman in eschewing biographical elucidation, writes that the poem 'is a poem about poetry, and consciously so', *Shelley's Mythmaking* (New Haven: Yale University Press, 1959), p. 210. Likewise, Daniel J. Hughes declares that 'the poem is ultimately about poetry itself and the process by which it is created', 'Coherence and Collapse in Shelley, with Particular Reference to *Epipsychidion'*, *ELH*, **28** (1961): 265. Among readings that try to strike some balance, the brief account by Donald H. Reiman in *Percy Bysshe Shelley* (New York: Twayne, 1969), pp. 125–33, is especially notable.

3. *Shelley's Poetry and Prose*, eds. Donald H. Reiman and Sharon B. Powers, p. 373. [*Epipsychidion* is quoted from this edition.]

4. The comparison is made by White, II, p. 325.

5. Reiman and Powers, p. 373. See also the statement in one of the canceled prefaces to the work that the poem 'was evidently intended to be prefixed to a longer poem or series of poems – but among [the author's] papers there are no traces of such a collection', *Shelley: Poetical Works*, ed. Thomas Hutchinson, 2nd edn, corrected by G.M. Matthews (London: Oxford University Press, 1971), p. 426.

6. BLOOM, p. 209.

7. Reiman and Powers' translation, p. 373.

8. 'Tithonus', *The Poems of Tennyson*, ed. Christopher Ricks (London: Longman, 1969), pp. 1116–17.

9. 'Among School Children', *The Variorum Edition of the Poems of W.B. Yeats*, ed. Peter Allt and Russell K. Alspach (New York: Macmillan, 1957), p. 443.

10. BLOOM, p. 216.

11. See EARL SHULZE, 'The Dantean Quest of *Epipsychidion'*, *Studies in Romanticism*, **21** (1982): 191–216.

12. Shelley so characterized the work in his letter of 18 June 1822 to John Gisborne (*Letters*, II, 434).

13. RICHARD HOLMES, *Shelley: The Pursuit* (London: Weidenfeld and Nicolson, 1974), p. 635.

14. Reiman and Powers' translation, p. 373.

15. OVID, *Metamorphoses*, III, l. 380.

16. Carlos Baker calls attention to the distinction, which he analyzes in a somewhat different way, in his note glossing the passage in *Shelley's Major Poetry: The Fabric of a Vision* (Princeton: Princeton University Press, 1948), p. 229n. 28. See also DONALD H. REIMAN, *Percy Bysshe Shelley*, p. 129.

17. The splitting of the ego is a phenomenon discussed throughout Freud's work. See for example the discussion in 'The Neuro-Psychoses of Defence' and the later paper, 'Splitting of the Ego in the Process of Defence', in *The Standard Edition of the Complete Psychological Works of Sigmund Freud*, trans. James Strachey (London: Hogarth Press, 1964), III, pp. 45–7; XXIII, pp. 275–8. Among later analysts Melanie Klein has discussed 'the weakening and impoverishment of the ego resulting from excessive splitting and projective identification' in idealization and their relation to certain forms of schizophrenia, in a way that throws special light on Shelley, in 'Notes on Some Schizoid Mechanisms', in *Developments in Psycho-Analysis*, ed. Joan Riviere (London: Hogarth Press, 1952), esp. pp. 301–4, 306, 308–9, 315–16, 319–20. See also her essay 'On Identification', in *New Directions in Psycho-Analysis*, ed. Melanie Klein, Paula Heiman, et al. (London: Tavistock, 1955), esp. pp. 310–12. Throughout her *Contributions to Psycho-Analysis 1921–1945* (London: Hogarth Press, 1968), she discusses 'how a failure to maintain the identification with both internalized and real loved objects may result in psychotic disorders' (p. 309). See esp. pp. 290, 308–9, 317, 320, 321–2, 331, 337–8.

18. Reiman and Powers, pp. 473–4.

19. HOLMES, p. 632.

20. Cameron, for example, has written that 'The obvious meaning of this passage is that Shelley, early in life, encountered a prostitute and contracted a venereal disease' (*Shelley: The Golden Years*, p. 280; see also pp. 56–7). See further Cameron's fuller analysis of Hunt's account in *The Young Shelley: Genesis of a Radical* (New York: Macmillan, 1950), pp. 145–6, where he concludes that Hunt's 'deduction from the *Epipsychidion* passage is clearly justified'. In *Sexuality and Feminism in Shelley* (Cambridge, Mass., and London: Harvard University Press, 1979), Nathaniel Brown considers the evidence on both sides and writes that Hunt's 'explanation has much to recommend it . . . Without external corroboration, however, the lines stop far short of being conclusive. It is equally possible that the imagery conveys a strictly emotional experience' (pp. 209–10). In *Percy Bysshe Shelley*, pp. 129–30, Reiman argues for a more general interpretation of the passage. Very recently Nora Crook and Derek Guiton have reargued for the probability that Shelley was infected by venereal disease, in their elaborately researched *Shelley's Venomed Melody* (Cambridge: Cambridge University Press, 1986). Like others before them they take the passage as a piece of leading evidence (see pp. 147–55) in support of a contention they admit from the outset of their study they cannot prove.

21. It is notable that Crook and Guiton in good part perceive the underlying archetypal relationship even while pressing the case for their clinical diagnosis. Thus they write: 'However this does not mean that the One is a

173

particular prostitute. Thornton Hunt did not say that she was. She could be a personified abstraction' (p. 150); and again, 'Shelley presents Emily as Love, the elixir of True Life, who will redeem him from the consequences of encountering the poisonous One. She is described in terms that contrast almost point for point with the latter's baleful physical features. The honey-dew example has already been given; in addition, Emily's voice, cheeks, perfume and eyes are presented in the same way' (p. 154).

22. WHITE, II, 268.

23. EARL R. WASSERMAN, *Shelley: A Critical Reading* (Baltimore and London: Johns Hopkins University Press, 1971), p. 450. In *Shelley and Synesthesia* (Evanston, Ill.: Northwestern University Press, 1964), pp. 106–7, Glenn O'Malley discusses the way effects of synesthesia create the impression that 'the lovers merge with the island's soul'.

24. J. Hillis Miller elaborates this point in his brief but suggestive consideration of *Epipsychidion* in 'The Critic as Host', in Harold Bloom et al., *Deconstruction and Criticism* (New York: Seabury Press, 1979), pp. 238–47.

25. O'MALLEY, p. 111, calls attention to the resemblance between these two scenes. [*The Revolt of Islam* is quoted from *Shelley: Poetical Works*, ed. Thomas Hutchinson, rev. edn G.M. Matthews (London: Oxford University Press, 1970).]

26. The irony has been noted by Miller: 'The more the poet says they will be one the more he makes them two by reaffirming the ways they are separated' (p. 245).

27. WASSERMAN, p. 460. In his essay Daniel Hughes also studies the pattern of repeated collapse, tracing it in other poems and relating it to the *Defence* and to Shelley's conception of the poetical process. More recently Jean Hall takes a surprisingly optimistic view of this same pattern in reading *Epipsychidion*, in pointed contrast to Wasserman, 'as a radical and spectacularly successful enactment of the poet's power to create the worlds he wishes for'. 'He stops,' she writes of the poet at the conclusion of the poem, 'not because he has failed but because he has completely succeeded. The ideal of the poem has been so far attained that there is no more room for movement, and in the final rapture of universal fusion his world passes beyond existence . . . The Shelleyan poem simply dies of its own happiness.' *The Transforming Image: A Study of Shelley's Major Poetry* (Urbana: University of Illinois Press, 1980), pp. 104, 146, n. 19.

28. Such, for example, is Wasserman's conclusion: 'the poet is aspiring to an identity of the finite and the infinite that is not possible in life', an 'identity possible only in afterlife' (p. 460).

29. The nature of Shelley's relationship with Jane remains something of an issue. G.M. Matthews argues that Shelley conducted a highly passionate love affair with her during the weeks immediately preceding his death. 'Shelley and Jane Williams', *RES*, **12** (1961): 40–8; and 'On Shelley's "The Triumph of Life"', *Studia Neophilologica*, **34** (1962): 104–34. Cameron also concludes that 'by June [1822] Shelley's feelings for Jane had become deeply passionate' (*Shelley: The Golden Years*, p. 302; see also p. 310). Donald Reiman, after a thorough review of the evidence, asserts that there are no grounds for proving that their

intercourse was anything but chaste. 'Shelley's "The Triumph of Life": The Biographical Problem', *PMLA*, **78** (1963): 536–50. Whether or not the relationship was physical, the lyrics Shelley composed for her are sufficient evidence of the intensity of his emotional involvement.

# 11 Last Clouds: A Reading of 'Adonais'*

Peter Sacks

*Adonais* (1821), Shelley's elegy for Keats, asks to be read in relation to the poet's use of genre, which in turn demands that the critic considers how the poem handles the emotion of grief and the process of coming to terms with grief. Peter Sacks illustrates these matters by reading the poem with psychoanalytical considerations in mind; *Adonais* is read in Freudian terms as though it were a psyche as well as a text, working its way through the stages of grief by way of the ego-splitting which Freud discusses in 'Mourning and Melancholia'. A central idea here is that narcissism, as a defence against grief, has conflicting effects. Part of Shelley's ego, according to Sacks, experiences a sense of weakness and vulnerability, identifying with Keats, the lost object; part projects itself in the form of an idealised self, the seemingly transcendent Adonais of the final section. The consolation thus supplied is seen as fragile by Sacks, who draws on both Jacques Lacan and post-structuralist textual theory to support his position: Lacan is used to bring out how any notion of wholeness is a precarious fantasy, and post-structuralist textual theory underpins the essay's interest in the poem's deeply ambivalent and contradictory attitude to its existence as a text; in Sacks's view the poem seeks to propel itself beyond pastures new, almost to claim for itself at the end the self-subverting status of a poem that has got beyond the medium which allows it to exist. Sacks reminds us that though a text can be read as a psyche it does not cease to be a text. (See Introduction, p. 15.)

In what follows, I shall try to go beyond a description of the form of 'Adonais' to suggest how the pattern of its language relates to

---

* Reprinted from *Studies in Romanticism*, 23 (Fall 1984): 380–400 (footnotes renumbered from the original).

psychological and philosophical currents running deep within the poem. My questions include the following: What and how does Shelley mourn? How does he revise the inherited fictions of elegy? What is his relation to Urania? How does his narcissism affect the work of mourning? (This relation between narcissism and mourning, so carefully stressed by Freud, is noticeable in English elegies since the time of Spenser, and is of great importance to 'Adonais'.) What are the implications of the poem's extraordinary ending, and how does it relate to Shelley's ambivalence toward figurative language? Finally, how does this ambivalence, directed against the very fabric of the poem, relate specifically to the predicament of a mourner?

'Adonais' has two epigraphs. The first is a Greek couplet ascribed to Plato in the *Greek Anthology*. Following the common misattribution of the couplet to Plato the philosopher, Shelley translated these lines:

> Thou wert the morning star among the living,
>> Ere thy fair light had fled; –
> Now, having died, thou art as Hesperus, giving
>> New splendour to the dead.[1]

Besides drawing attention to the stellar imagery of consolation, Shelley's choice of the epigraph indicates his desire to believe in a poetry somehow compatible with Platonic thought.[2] The fact that Shelley misattributed the lines to the harsh judge of poetry underscores the problem, and it is interesting to see how thoroughly and with what personal urgency 'Adonais' reveals the contradictory nature of Shelley's aspiration.

The second epigraph quotes the lines in Moschus's elegy for Bion, referring to the poet's having been poisoned by some insensitive scorner of verse. Shelley will return to this in stanza 36, elaborating his theory about Keats's death. While stressing the accusation's relevance to the poem, the epigraph foregrounds Shelley's debt to the Alexandrian elegy at large.[3] The debt is immediately apparent in the opening line, which reads almost as a translation of Bion's lament for Adonais:

> I weep for Adonais – he is dead!
> O weep for Adonais! though our tears
> Thaw not the frost which binds so dear a head!
> And thou, sad Hour, selected from all years
> To mourn our loss, rouse thy obscure compeers,
> And teach them thine own sorrow, say: 'With me
> Died Adonais; till the Future dares

> Forget the Past, his fate and fame shall be
> An echo and a light unto eternity!'
>
> (ll. 1–9)

The first difference from Bion is of course the name Adonais, blending those of the vegetation deity, Adonis, and the Judaic Adonai. As historians of religion have shown, the originally physical significance of the fertility gods was allegorized and spiritualized by successive cults; and elegists, too, have continually revised the meaning of this most crucial figure of the genre. It is especially intriguing to note how Shelley has conserved the original figure within the new, for the poem itself unfolds the very *process* of resignification, moving from natural, sexual referents, towards their spiritualized successors. Shelley's act of renaming neatly suggests his intention to use and yet alter the inherited elegiac tradition: to use its essential strategy of assimilating the deceased to a figure of immortality, while redefining the meaning of that figure.

A second difference declares itself at once: unlike Bion, Shelley turns immediately to question the efficacy of weeping. By so doing, he begins a long interrogation of conventional gestures and figures of mourning. This oddly skeptical employment of convention marks this poem as a true heir of 'Lycidas' and 'Astrophel', whose obsessions with 'false surmise' and 'verses vaine' had driven them to carefully persuasive consolations. As our reference to the 'Plato' epigraph hinted, and as the poem will in fact show, Shelley's struggle with his legacy and with his very medium itself is particularly vexed. We can perhaps see this in the unusual prematurity with which he initiates the self-questioning or self-qualifying mode. Spenser had at least gathered momentum before examining the vanity of verse. And although Milton did begin with a self-doubting admission of sour immaturity, he at least did not suspect the 'meed of some melodious tear'.

Shelley's struggle to begin his work of mourning is further apparent in his deliberate *delegation* of such work to various figures throughout the opening sections of the poem. In fact it is not until quite far into the poem that Shelley moves beyond these delegate-mourners to assume a more personal voice. The delegates have at least two functions: they are all inadequate mourners, allowing Shelley to criticize them and to distance himself from various forms of unsuccessful grieving; and yet they keep his poem in motion, giving it the processional character of traditional elegies, allowing it to achieve the self-purifying and self-surpassing ceremonies so important to the work of mourning.

Already in the fourth line, therefore, Shelley turns to the first of these delegates, calling on the Hour to grieve, and asking her in turn to transfer her sorrow to her compeers. The Hour's utterance reaches forward to the traditional conclusion of elegy, with its eternizing assertion. But this is felt to be proleptic, for the grief has somehow been elided and the consolation unearned. It is too quick, with the kind of problematic sheerness of the opening line. We reread the statement and register a complication: 'With me / Died Adonais'. This Hour is past and dead. With its death died Adonais. Is it speaking from within death, speaking with the odd death-in-life intonation of a sepulchral inscription? And since this is a persona-voice for Shelley, does it not already suggest some troubling association between Keats's death and Shelley's sense of having died with him? It is precisely this double death that the poem must avoid, or at least postpone long enough for Shelley to have immortalized himself and Keats. How else will Adonais' fate and fame keep echoing and shining to eternity?

In the second stanza, Shelley moves further into the conventions of pastoral elegy by querying the absence of the attendant deity:

> Where were thou, mighty Mother, when he lay,
> When thy Son lay, pierced by the shaft which flies
> In darkness? Where was lorn Urania
> When Adonais died?
>
> (ll. 10–13)

The figure of Urania is of immediate interest. Just as he had compounded the sexual–spiritual identity of Adonais, so now Shelley merges Venus (mother of earthly life, and the incestuous lover of Adonis), with her intellectual and spiritual self (Urania, muse of astronomy, 'Heav'nly Muse' of Milton). More significantly, Shelley's turn to the 'mighty Mother' recalls Milton's anguished 'What could the Muse herself . . . for her enchanting son . . . ?'[4] We are at the core of loss, the elegist's bereavement not only of his friend or fellow, but of the maternal figure, the original loss of whom this new bereavement recapitulates. As was true for Milton, Shelley will have eventually to work free from his attachment to this unavailing figure of the mother-muse, submitting both her and himself to the ironic and repressive force of death. Only in the harsh light of that repression may an abiding object of consolation be found.

Shelley calls on Urania to mourn, but his address, like that in the first lines of the poem, turns to criticize its own futility:

> Oh, weep for Adonais – he is dead!
> Wake, melancholy Mother, wake and weep!
> Yet wherefore? Quench within their burning bed
> Thy fiery tears, and let thy loud heart keep
> Like his, a mute and uncomplaining sleep;
> For he is gone, where all things wise and fair

> Descend; – oh, dream not that the amorous deep
> Will yet restore him to the vital air;
> Death feeds on his mute voice, and laughs at our despair.
>
> (ll. 19–27)

The echo of 'Hyperion' is unmistakable, and Shelley had in fact been reading Keats's poem immediately before composing 'Adonais'. Here Shelley sounds like Thea, skeptical of her attempt to rouse the fallen Saturn:

> 'Saturn, look up – though wherefore, poor old King? . . .
>
> Saturn, sleep on – O thoughtless, why did I
> Thus violate thy slumbrous solitude?'[5]

Shelley, lacking Thea's sedate fatigue, moves quickly to a bitter ironizing of the grief, again somehow obstructing its release. It is an odd situation: Shelley attempting to awaken a sleeper to mourning, while at the same time checking that very attempt. And if the yet ungrieving Urania is the 'most musical of mourners', surely Shelley is still trying to rouse himself to fuller song. Shelley appeals to Urania as the mother of a line of poets – Homer, Dante, and Milton – and he calls on her to weep for her most recent loss. From this perspective, Shelley, like Thea, is trying to compel a certain recognition: while Thea would have Saturn recognize his own divinity, Shelley would have Urania recognize and admit the poet Keats to a grand genealogy, one that would perhaps include himself, if she should recognize and respond to his cry.

At first, however, Shelley seems to make little impression on Urania. She is presented 'with Veiled eyes', the first of many derogatory references to any form of interpositional texture or cloud. This very veiledness is somehow paradisal, a false Eden of blindness in which the deluded Muse fondly supposes her poets to be invulnerable, There is, too, a faint suggestion that a certain kind of poetry may itself share the blame for this delusional masking of mortality ('. . . the fading melodies, / With which, like flowers that mock the corse beneath, / He had adorned and hid the coming bulk of Death'). Perhaps Shelley seeks a more clear-eyed poetry that unveils and takes account of the coming bulk. The traditional association of flowers with rhetoric alerts us to how disconcertingly Shelley is already moving against the very properties of poetic language, linking them here with precisely the natural, vegetative, and material realm that the poem so forcefully attacks and so desperately seeks to transcend.

Pursuing this critical association of flowers, material fabrics, and mortality, Shelley describes the physical death of Adonais. The details are significant, for Adonais is presented as a sexually unfulfilled and indeed broken flower ('Like a pale flower by some sad maiden cherished, / And fed with true-love tears, instead of dew'). In line with this castrative imagery of deprivation and submission, Shelley introduces the repressive, patriarchal figure of 'kingly Death', in whose capital the shadow and the 'mortal curtain' are forever drawn.

The presence of these gathering fabrics of shadow and veil testifies to an elegist's acceptance not only of Death's castrative power (a power associated with the intervention of the Father, and with the mourner's original experience of loss), but also of that elegist's recapitulated entry into and submission to those very mediations of language that interpose between him and his object of loss and desire. The elegist's riposte to Death, his consoling counter-assertion, however displaced, of desire and of the trope for a surviving power must, therefore, come to terms with the enforced fabric of substitutions. This is where one of Shelley's most vexing problems comes to the fore. For while trying to rebut Death's power, Shelley also struggles to purge his counter-assertive language of its inherent association, as language, with all the interposing fabrics – of Death's curtain, or of life's erotic but mortal physicality, or of the traces of this latter physicality in the material flowers, however spiritualized, of rhetoric.

For the moment, Death governs, and Shelley's repeated urgings of Urania fall on silence. This increases his isolation, as though he were circling on the outside of a center of power, and on the edges of a grander stance of mourning. Certainly, he is still circling his own grief. Part of this circling, as already suggested, involves the delegation and criticism of mourners. The flocks of Keats's 'ministers of Thought' are therefore shown to droop, incapable of renovation, 'round the cold heart'. One such angelic figure believes that the tear she sheds is Keats's own. Another's gesture of symbolic substitution is undone or at least exposed by the poet's analysis:

> Another in her wilful grief would break
> Her bow and winged reeds, as if to stem
> A greater loss with one which was more weak;
>
> (ll. 96–8)

Yet another unavailingly seeks to revitalize the body with a caress that fades out like a meteor enwreathed in vapor.

All these ineffective mourners keep the poem in motion even though they are distanced by the yet withdrawn poet. As they multiply in a profusion of allegorical figures, they appear to interpose further between the poet and his own emotions. This interposition, apart from Shelley's sense of their inadequacy as mourners, seems to lie behind his description of their 'moving pomp' as a 'pageantry of mist on an autumnal stream'. They are useless *forms* of mourning, a decorative mist or texture that seems to absorb rather than provide energy. This, too, is why each stanza has a movement of subsidence, an attempted quickening that trails off in a dying ebb. Shelley's particularly skillful use here of the Spenserian stanza will be reversed in the last section of the poem, where the stanzas yield their potential for exploratory romance, for the progressive crossing of thresholds. There the alexandrines do not seal a falling cadence; rather, they mount beyond themselves.[6]

Shelley ends the first movement of the poem by extending the cast of mourners to include even the traditional figures of consolation, the regenerated Hyacinth and Narcissus. These flower-tropes themselves are now impotent, like the broken lily, Adonais ('wan they stand and sere . . . with dew all turned to tears . . .'), and as with Adonais, their seminal dew had yielded to salt. So, too, Shelley includes Spring herself in this general loss of vigor. Though beautiful, she is unaroused, finding no reason to awake the sullen year. The gathering association between a failure of mourning and a lack of natural or even figurative regeneration seems fatal, but there is a surprising development within the seventeenth stanza:

> Thy spirit's sister, the lorn nightingale
> Mourns not her mate with such melodious pain;
> Not so the eagle, who like thee could scale
> Heaven, and could nourish in the sun's domain
> Her mighty youth with morning, doth complain,
> Soaring and screaming round her empty nest,
> As Albion wails for thee: the curse of Cain
> Light on his head who pierced thy innocent breast,
> And scared the angel soul that was its earthly guest!
>
> (ll. 145–53)

By a remarkable turn in the seventh line, the elaborate comparison is suddenly followed by a curse, as though that curse had been gathering like another voice beneath the preceding language. Now, disjunctively, the curse breaks through, and it carries perhaps the first true ring of Shelley's voice. It cuts impatiently through the pageantry of mourners, disrupting the delicate melancholy of their poise.[7] And this is, after all, the first reference to Keats's alleged destroyer, the hostile reviewer in the *Quarterly Review*.

It is fair to say that Shelley's notion of the cause of Keats's death was a misinterpretation motivated by his own experience of malignment. In the first draft of his preface to 'Adonais' he has written, 'Persecution, contumely, and calumny had been heaped upon me in profuse measure;

and domestic conspiracy and legal oppression have violated in my person the most sacred rights of nature and humanity' (*Works*, p. 444). This passage, which Shelley omitted on the advice of John Taaffe, confirms the identification, and leaves us certain that the sudden direct utterance in the seventeenth stanza is a burst of anger by Shelley partly on his own behalf. At last, by moving closer to the self in this way, Shelley has released some of the energy for mourning, hitherto held in check.

Interestingly enough, the second movement of the poem begins immediately after this release of anger. Yet critics have only related the ensuing expression of woe to the juxtaposition of a still mourning poet over against a reviving world. This is not untrue, but surely that first note of personal grief – 'Ah, woe is me' – is the result of the breakthrough at the end of the previous stanza. By expressing anger Shelley has begun to undo the repression of his grief, and stanzas 17 through 20 contain repeated images of a distinctly erotic release:

The amorous birds now pair in every brake, . . .

And the green lizard, and the golden snake,
Like unimprisoned flames, out of their trance awake.

Through wood and stream and field, and hill and Ocean
A quickening life from the Earth's heart has burst . . .

All baser things pant with life's sacred thirst;
Diffuse themselves; and spend in love's delight,
The beauty and the joy of their renewed might.

(ll. 159–71)

The irony behind this release is that the elegist himself remains apparently unmoved. He is unable to endorse the erotic flow, and channels it into nature's rather than his own renovation. This is crucial, for like Spenser and Milton, and indeed like any true mourner, Shelley must submit the natural force of his desire to a repressive refinement. It is essential that these energies be released – but only so that they may be troped and spiritualized.

Hence Shelley focuses contrastingly on what he would like to see immortalized; not man's genetic power, but rather his intellectual faculty, 'that which knows'. And yet, this higher faculty is represented by imagery which reflects originally physical referents:

. . . Shall that alone which knows
Be as a sword consumed before the sheath

> By sightless lightning? – the intense atom glows
> A moment, then is quenched in a most cold repose.
>
> (ll. 177–80)

The cognitive being is thus represented by a sword, or by an atom whose glow is surely related in kind to the 'unimprisoned flames' of Nature, and to the forces which spend themselves 'in love's delight'. Nevertheless, it is with such residually erotic and material images of elevation, penetration and glowing radiance that Shelley will have to reach for consolation, trying to cut or burn through all material textures (present once again, here, in the form of the sheath).

Fearing the extinction of these purer powers, Shelley is now moved to a further expression of genuine grief, his second truly direct utterance. Now recognition of his own mortality brings on not anger but painful perplexity, the gnomic questioning that one associates with elegy:

> Alas! that all we loved of him should be,
> But for our grief, as if it had not been,
> And grief itself be mortal! Woe is me!
> Whence are we, and why are we? of what scene
> The actors or spectators?
>
> (ll. 181–5)

Shelley still cannot bear this burden alone, and again he transfers it to his chief alter mourner, Urania. The language becomes urgent, irresistible, and Urania wakes abruptly: 'Swift as a Thought by the snake Memory stung, / From her ambrosial rest the fading Splendour sprung' (ll. 197–8). She moves 'like an autumnal Night' (l. 199) 'out of her secret Paradise' (l. 208). This disparadising of Urania by a snake suggests that Shelley has finally been able to arouse her by curiously satanic means. It is a troubling suggestion, and it will return with Shelley's later self-images of sexual transgression ('Had gazed on Nature's naked loveliness, / Actaeon-like' (ll. 275–6), and damnation ('branded . . . like Cain's', ll. 305–6). Predictably, Shelley's success here brings on its own rebuke, as Urania moves directly into the dominion of her father-figure Death, under whose aegis her extravagantly sexual mourning will be mocked, and where the separation from her son will be most punitively enforced.

As Urania enters the death-chamber, her intensity momentarily cows even Death, and seems to send a 'pale light' through the body of the dead poet. But hers is an intensity only of bereavement. She has nothing with which to oppose or menace Death, and he recovers his sway with a magisterially ironic gesture: 'her distress / Roused Death: Death rose and smiled, and met her vain caress' (ll. 224–5). Like the jealous father,

Death exercises his prerogative, claiming the caress meant for the son. With this submission of the mother–son attachment to the male figure of Death, a crisis in the work of mourning is confronted. The primary experience of rupture is represented, here in the guise of a role reversal similar to that of the primitive vegetation rites, or of the child's *fort–da* game described by Freud.* The child's separation from its mother, or man's separation from a withering nature, is performed but psychologically reversed, so that the mother/nature becomes the victim or mourner. And with this presentation of Urania, Shelley reaches his most acute and no doubt exorcistic critique of inadequate modes of mourning.[8] The speech is Urania's:

> 'Stay yet awhile! speak to me once again;
> Kiss me, so long but as a kiss may live;
> And in my heartless breast and burning brain
> That word, that kiss, shall all thoughts else survive,
> With food of saddest memory kept alive,
> Now thou art dead, as if it were a part
> Of thee, my Adonais! I would give
> All that I am to be as thou now art!
> But I am chained to Time,and cannot thence depart!'

(ll. 226–34)

In his essay 'Mourning and Melancholia', Freud distinguished between the normal response to loss, what he calls the work of mourning, and the abnormal condition of melancholia, in which the subject cannot move beyond an unhealthy, often inert reaction to loss.[9] The work of mourning requires a gradual detachment from the lost object, followed by a transfer of the detached affections or libido onto a new love-object outside the self. The case of melancholia is complex, but it may occur either when the subject cannot renounce the lost object, or when the detached and released libido regresses to an earlier form of narcissism by reattaching itself to the ego instead of to a new, external object. The various responses may be related to rhetorical tropes. It would seem that a detachment would involve a figure of disconnection, most simply irony or a strongly substitutive metaphor, while a refusal to detach oneself would be associated with the more connective tropes of metonymy or

---

* [Ed. Freud observed a child throwing a toy out of its pram and exclaiming 'fort' (gone away), then pulling it in again with a cry of 'da' (here). He interpreted this game as the child's way of coming to terms with the absence of the mother.]

synecdoche.* In her melancholia, Urania cannot turn away from the dead poet. On the one hand she would take a last kiss-word from him to serve as a metonymic reminder of him. In fact, so tenacious is her attachment that it forces her to drive that metonymy to a synecdochic extreme ('a part of thee, my Adonais'). The lost object would thus be synecdochically internalized within Urania's 'heartless breast and burning brain'. On the other hand, yet again refusing to withdraw from Adonais, she would relinquish her own ego in order to be identified with the object of her attachment. She remains prostrate, unable to *do* either, and yet unable to renounce the dead Adonais.[10]

Having used Urania in a way that has allowed him to objectify one form of potential melancholia, and also to further his own necessary departure from this mother-figure, Shelley turns in the remainder of the poem to work his way through other forms and stages that Freud unquestionably regarded as symptoms of a griever's melancholia. Freud writes:

> First there existed an object-choice, the libido had attached itself to a certain person; then, owing to a real injury or disappointment concerned with the loved person, this object-relationship was undermined. The result was not the normal one of withdrawal of the libido from this object and transference of it to a new one, but something different for which various conditions seem to be necessary. The object-cathexis proved to have little power of resistance, and was abandoned; but the free libido was withdrawn into the ego and not directed to another object. It did not find application there, however, in any one of several possible ways, but served simply to establish an *identification* of the ego with the abandoned object. Thus the shadow of the object fell upon the ego, so that the latter could henceforth be criticized by a special mental faculty like an object, like the forsaken object. In this way the loss of the object became transformed into a loss in the ego, and the conflict between the ego and the loved person transformed into a cleavage between the criticizing faculty of the ego and the ego as altered by the identification.[11]

To this Freud adds the logical suggestion that in such a case, the original object choice was narcissistic, this being indeed a part of 'the disposition to succumb to melancholia'. Now, as has been suggested, Shelley's original view of Keats's death *was* narcissistic, seeing Keats not only as a

---

* [Ed. *Metonomy*: a figure of speech which stresses likeness or nearness between itself and that which it stands for. *Synecdoche*: a figure of speech by which a part stands for a whole or, less commonly, a whole for a part.]

brother poet but also as a reflection of Shelley's own sense of martyrdom.
Reacting to the death of Keats, Shelley withdrew from the dead youth,
but reattaching his affections only to himself, he identified his ego with
the abandoned object. Or rather, and this is crucial, he identified *a part* of
his ego with the lost object. For the kind of splitting that Freud describes
occurs within Shelley, setting a criticizing voice over against the weaker,
vulnerable aspects of himself, seen now with frightening clarity in the
light of their identification with the dead Keats. The splitting takes the
form of an elaborate self-objectification. Not only does Shelley use the
third person *he* in referring to himself, but he emphasizes the division by
retaining, in close juxtaposition, the *I* that makes this reference.[12] Here is
Shelley's portrait of himself among the procession of poet-mourners who
pay homage to Adonais:

### XXXI

Midst others of less note, came one frail Form
A phantom among men; companionless
As the last cloud of an expiring storm
Whose thunder is its knell; he, as I guess,
Had gazed on Nature's naked loveliness,
Actaeon-like, and now he fled astray
With feeble steps o'er the world's wilderness,
And his own thoughts, along that rugged way,
Pursued, like raging hounds, their father and their prey.

### XXXII

A pardlike Spirit beautiful and swift –
A Love in desolation masked – a Power
Girt round with weakness; – it can scarce uplift
The weight of the superincumbent hour;
It is a dying lamp, a falling shower,
A breaking billow; – even whilst we speak
Is it not broken? On the withering flower
The killing sun smiles brightly: on a cheek
The life can burn in blood, even while the heart may break.

### XXXIII

His head was bound with pansies overblown,
And faded violets, white, and pied, and blue;
And a light spear topped with a cypress cone,
Round whose rude shaft dark ivy-tresses grew
Yet dripping with the forest's noonday dew,
Vibrated, as the ever-beating heart
Shook the weak hand that grasped it; of that crew

187

He came the last, neglected and apart;
A herd-abandoned deer struck by the hunter's dart.

The passage is complicated, in typically Shelleyan fashion, by a
multiplication of images. Within the flux we make out versions of the
vegetation deities, Actaeon and Dionysus (the [leo]pardlike spirit with
the thyrsis wand). 'Nature's naked loveliness' associates Diana with
Aphrodite–Venus, hence with the mother–Urania. Actaeon's
transgression is, therefore, precisely the error a mourner must forego,
and it is interesting to note how Shelley is both identifying with and yet
objectifying and distancing himself from just this error. Actaeon is
punished by the enervation and eventual *sparagmos* that typifies
castrative martyrdom.

The Dionysus identification is a more unsettling complex of weakness
and assertion. More precisely, assertive strength struggles to issue from
an enveloping wreckage. The latter is marked once again by sexual
expense and fragmentation ('It is a dying lamp, a falling shower, / A
breaking billow; – even whilst we speak / Is it not broken? On the
withering flower / The killing sun shines brightly . . .'). Shelley is here
even identified with Adonais, the broken lily. But there is the contrastive
figure of Dionysus holding his vibrating and dewy, cone-tipped spear.
Juxtaposed with the preceding imagery of expense and devastation, this
phallic thyrsis does seem to hold out the consoling promise of recovery,
but it will remain for Shelley to re-establish its significance. For the
moment, the promise is still 'girt round with weakness', as Shelley
switches back momentarily to the more Actaeon-like figure of the
stricken deer.

Returning to our recognition of the self-divisive aspect of Shelley's
work of mourning, it is clear that this self-presentation in terms of
wounded, withered, and annihilated vegetation figures identifies the
mortal part of Shelley's ego with the slain Adonais. And this
melancholically narcissistic identification prepares the way for a different
identification, one that continues yet transforms the poet's narcissism.
For even as Shelley's ego has cleaved into critic and criticized, observer
and victim, this division corresponds to a division perceived in the
nature of Adonais: the immortal poetic genius, the 'angel soul', as
divided from the empirical man who had been its temporary home. And
it is this former genius-soul with whom Shelley will come to identify his
own purified, immortal self. In the remainder of the poem, therefore,
Shelley completes the work of mourning by a powerful detachment from
the natural man and the natural world, and a subsequent reattachment to
a transcendent ideal instead.

But first, Shelley has a second, more expansive outbreak against the
object of his anger. This outbreak is well situated. On the one hand it

allows Shelley to discharge his wrath in a burst of energy that will fuel his subsequent ascent. On the other hand his vitriolic contempt for the anonymous reviewer, Croker, conveniently supplies an extreme example of the lowest, worm-like or kite-like level of existence that Adonais is immediately shown to have transcended ('Nor let us weep that our delight is fled / Far from these carrion kites that scream below').

As I have already suggested, Shelley's transcendent ideal definitely draws on his narcissistic libido. Just as Shelley had distorted in his own image his version of Keats's death, so, too, his version of the immortal Keats is cast in his own ideal likeness. The process of narcissistic idealization has been analyzed in general by Heinz Kohut, one of the first theorists to explore the beneficial potential of narcissism. Kohut's essay, 'The Forms and Transformations of Narcissism', is particularly relevant here, for he stresses the important connection between narcissism and the acceptance of loss and death:

> More difficult still, however, than the acknowledgment of the impermanence of object cathexes is the unqualified intellectual and emotional acceptance of the fact that we ourselves are impermanent, that the self which is cathected with narcissistic libido is finite in time. I believe that this rare feat rests not simply on a victory of autonomous reason and supreme objectivity over the claims of narcissism but on the creation of a higher form of narcissism.[13]

The 'higher form of narcissism' involves the construction of an ego ideal that Kohut calls the 'grandiose self'. For Shelley, this is the transcendent human or more strictly, the poetic spirit. I think Kohut's addition to Freud's theory of narcissism (particularly in relation to melancholia) may thus apply closely to the case of Shelley as he works through to the end of 'Adonais'.

Kohut's view of the 'higher narcissism' may itself be too idealistic, however, and in the concluding section of this essay, I hope to suggest how fragile and how specular the 'grandiose' self-image remains. We should here recall Lacan's portrayal of the mirror-stage, for I believe the mourner may regress to a version of this stage – a regression that could be another potential factor of narcissistic melancholia.[14] During the mirror-stage, an infant between the ages of six and eighteen months locates an idealized image of itself either in mirror-images or in the forms of others – in each case imagining itself to possess the integrity and functional completeness of what remains nevertheless a merely specular self. The actual and as yet primarily unformed and incompetent self is thus alienated and displaced by a coherent but fictional image of an idealized self, an imaginary 'rough-cast', as Lacan calls it, of the ego.

The child's relation to this mirror-image is dyadic, but it occurs within a fantasy of identification. If the child is to establish a stable, socialized sense of itself or of the outside world, this dyadic fantasy must be disrupted and submitted to the triadic intervention of the positional codes of society – an intervention associated with the role of the Father during the later oedipal stage. After that stage, the child will develop attachments that are more clearly perceived as being outside the self; and the child's narcissism will have achieved what we might regard as a more sophisticated or realistic form. But the present menace of death may shatter one's narcissistic illusions of security; and the loss of a loved person whose presence had supported one's self-image may join the threat of death to drive the mourner back to the earlier form of narcissism, in which a state of helplessness and fragmentation was masked by fantasies of wholeness.

Shelley's work of mourning does appear to revert to elements of the mirror-stage; and 'Adonais' (particularly following the self-portrait beginning in stanza 31) is marked by that phase's unstable opposition between the condition of fragmentation on the one hand and idealized images of coherence on the other. Shelley's represented reversion to the mirror-stage is, admittedly, controlled by an exorcistic self-objectification, one that shatters and discards its imagings in order to reconstitute a higher version of the self. But this higher version, despite its apparently triadic inclusion of Death, may not entirely escape the dangers of the earlier mirror-stage. If the griever seeks literally to identify with the new image – to literalize what must remain specular and fictional, and to make immediate what must remain a mediated resemblance – he risks a delusional entrapment within another dyadic fantasy. By stressing, with Lacan, the degree of alienation and fictionalizing in any narcissistic self-imaging, we may recognize the vulnerability of Kohut's 'grandiose self', even as we see with particular urgency the problems besetting Shelley in the remainder of his poem.

We have still to ask what ingredients, in Shelley's case, compose the immortal ideal ego. Of what, exactly, does Shelley construct the alternative to his fragmented and rejected self imaged earlier as a broken billow or withered flower? Who is the immortal Adonais with whom Shelley's higher self may be identified? Continuing the dramatic, oppositional argument that began with his rejection of the reviewer, Shelley pursues this exaltation of the soul:

> Dust to the dust! but the pure spirit shall flow
> Back to the burning foundation whence it came,
> A portion of the Eternal, which must glow

Through time and change, unquenchably the same,
Whilst thy cold embers choke the sordid hearth of shame.

(ll. 338–42)

After its shattering demise in the 'falling shower' of an explicitly sexual
and mortal ruin, the earlier sexual imagery of fertile liquids and glowing
fires here returns, but in a spiritualized version of itself, as the soul flows
back to its origin and glows beyond extinction.

In order for this pure spirit to be an ideal self *for Shelley*, it must be
more specifically defined. Most crucially, it must represent the poetic
genius – not any generalized poetic genius, but the genius as Shelley
defines it. This means that Shelley must modify the immortal
Keats–Adonais so as to reflect and accommodate the immortal Shelley.
Necessarily, this requires a distortion of Keats.

Shelley declares that the disembodied spirit of Keats flows back in
purity to the 'burning fountain whence it came'. It is free 'from the
contagion of the world's slow stain'. Now this in fact controverts Keats's
own view of the soul and of the mundane world. For Keats there is
indeed a part of every human being, the 'intelligence', which is a spark
of the eternal. 'Intelligences', he wrote to George and Georgiana Keats on
28 April, 1819, 'are atoms of perception – they know and they see and
they are pure, in short they are God'.[15] But whereas Shelley rejects the
circumstantial world as contagious dross, Keats goes on to insist that an
'intelligence' should be immersed 'in the medium of a world like this' in
order that it may advance to take on an 'identity'. Only this 'identity' can
be called a soul. For Keats, this attainment of a soul adequately stained
by the world and by the heart constitutes salvation – a far different idea
from that of Shelley's celebration of the return of a disembodied purity to
its source.

A further misrepresentation of Keats in Shelley's adaptation of
Adonais to his own ideal likeness, is his implicit negation of Keats's
espousal of empathy, unobtrusiveness, and negative capability. In their
stead, Shelley associates Keats's poetic spirit with a shaping power more
like that of egotistical sublimity:

XLII

He is a presence to be felt and known
In darkness and in light, from herb and stone,
Spreading itself where'er that Power may move
Which wields the world with never-wearied love,
Sustains it from beneath, and kindles it above.

XLIII

He is a portion of the loveliness

> Which once he made more lovely: he doth bear
> His part, while the one Spirit's plastic stress
> Sweeps through the dull dense world, compelling there,
> All new successions to the forms they wear;
> Torturing th'unwilling dross that checks its flight
> To its own likeness, as each mass may bear;
> And bursting in its beauty and its might
>   From trees and beasts and men into the Heaven's light.

Within Shelley's declaration, we also note his revisionary employment of the vegetation deity. That figure's original infusion into mother nature has now become a reunification, not with a matrix to be fertilized, but rather with the shaping power of a narcissistic demiurge.

Greater yet than this need to see not Keats but himself as the beckoning star, was Shelley's need to ensure that his star's orbit was well clear of the 'lone star' he had once called Wordsworth. This is perfectly consonant with Shelley's need to celebrate an alternative to loss and death; and the early sonnet in which he described Wordsworth as a 'lone star' had in fact begun with the lines, 'Poet of Nature, thou has wept to know / That things depart which never may return' (*Works*, p. 526).[16] For Wordsworth, the disappearance of the visionary gleam was irrevocable, but it led to the compensatory colorations that the humanized mind's eye lends to what remains. Shelley sought to refuse the very need for such a consolation. The glory and freshness were always here, within a poet's vision of the world. Or, if that glory seemed to have 'fled', then the poet's spirit, rather than remaining in an impoverished world, however hued by sad maturity, should follow after the gleam, returning to its first radiance.

In order to controvert Wordsworth, Shelley has to use Wordsworth's language, and the last eighteen stanzas of 'Adonais' contain many echoes of the 'Immortality' ode. This is partly a matter of certain words (such as embers, fountain, light, splendour, glory, radiance). But there are more concerted passages in which Shelley echoes Wordsworth, only to depart from him:

> . . . Thou young Dawn.
> Turn all thy dew to splendour, for from thee
> The spirit thou lamentest is not gone;
> Ye caverns and ye forests, cease to moan.
> Cease ye faint flowers and fountains, and thou Air,
> Which like a mourning veil thy scarf hadst thrown
> O'er the abandoned Earth, now leave it bare
>   Even to the joyous stars which smile on its despair.

(ll. 362–9)

What at first sounds like the final stanza of Wordsworth's ode veers off
into an un-Wordsworthian and characteristically Shelleyan address to the
air. The address cuts specifically against Wordsworth's stanza, which, as
we recall, goes on to appreciate 'the clouds that gather round the setting
sun'. Wordsworth's resignation colors and hymns the very barriers that
gather between him and the clear sky, and it is to the 'meanest flower'
here below that he finally turns in the last lines of his poem.

For Shelley, on the other hand, the earth is deliberately 'abandoned',
left to its despair (not unlike the desolate Urania), and no veiling scarf
must intervene between it and the smiling (rather cruelly joyous) stars.
By such antithetical counter-pointing, both to the mundane world and to
what he regarded as the defeated poetry of that world, Shelley in effect
begins to approach the beckoning ideal poetic self towards which he
makes his final trajectory:

### LIII

The soft sky smiles, – the low wind whispers near:
'Tis Adonais calls! oh, hasten thither,
No more let Life divide what Death can join together.

### LIV

That Light whose smile kindles the Universe,
That Beauty in which all things work and move,
That Benediction which the eclipsing Curse
Of birth can quench not, that sustaining Love
Which through the web of being blindly wove
By man and beast and earth and air and sea,
Burns bright or dim, as each are mirrors of
The fire for which all thirst; now beams on me,
Consuming the last clouds of cold mortality.

### LV

The breath whose might I have invoked in song
Descends on me; my spirit's bark is driven,
Far from the shore, far from the trembling throng
Whose sails were never to the tempest given;
The massy earth and sphered skies are riven!
I am borne darkly, fearfully, afar;
Whilst, burning through the inmost veil of Heaven,
The soul of Adonais, like a star,
Beacons from the abode where the Eternal are.

This magnificent conclusion is profoundly disturbing, as many readers
have found. Shelley, as we know, perished a year later, precisely by

giving sail to the tempest (accounts relate that Shelley, who could not swim, refused to follow a passing crew's advice to strike his sail during the storm).[17] But even if we did not know this, 'Adonais' surely concludes on a suicidal note, and we may wonder what measure of success to accord the poet's work of mourning. Has Shelley not somehow burst beyond the elegy as a genre? The problem is deep-seated, for in many ways Shelley's poem has, since its first epigraph, worked against the possibility, the very form and texture, of poetry itself.

Several of these contradictions in 'Adonais' have come to a head in the concluding stanzas of the poem. Shelley's ideal self, endowed with Light, Beauty, and Benediction, is nonetheless an image upheld in a mirroring relationship with the aspiring self. Here the latter is felt to be the reflection, while the ideal is seen as the original ('as each are mirrors of / The fire for which all thirst'). When Shelley moves to consummate his love for that ideal (that fire 'now beams on me, / Consuming the last clouds of cold mortality'), we may think of Narcissus diving to the depths of what he had taken to be a substantial self. Shelley's course ('No more let Life divide what Death can join together') would necessarily rupture the specular *medium*, the dividing mirror, in which his very goal is imaged.

But if Shelley's figure of the star depends on an intervening medium, this suggests an unexpected connection between images of light and those of textured veils and clouds which the light would seem to oppose. The destruction of one must threaten the other. To make war on poetic language as an interpositional texture associated with a scarf, a veil, a pageantry of mist, a sheath, a dome of many-colored glass, a web of being – all of which are to be trampled or torn – is to assault the very means by which the counter-image of a radiant star can be posited.[18]

From this point of view, we may look back on Wordsworth's sunset clouds as the markers of a sad but saving wisdom. They indicate an elegist's sober sense, as at the end of Clorinda's lay in 'Astrophel', of what divides the 'there' of the deceased from the 'here' of a survivor. Similarly, they reveal the elegist's self-knowledge regarding his unavoidable dependence on the fabric of his poem.

Indeed, if we review the entire history of the elegy, we recall countless images of weaving that characterize the genre. It is perhaps with something of a relief that we turn from Shelley's anti-textual flight to such figures as the basket-plaiting elegist in Virgil's 'Eclogue X'. Whether it be by way of Camus' bonnet 'Inwrought with figures dim, and on the edge / Like to that sanguine flower inscrib'd with woe', or Milton's framing review of his own Doric lay, or Jonson's witty focus on his 'best piece of poetry', or Gray's attention to his own engraved epitaph, or Stevens's 'weaving round the wonder of . . . need', almost all elegists have found a way to suggest the very materiality of their poems. After all, that material not only allows the dead to be 'robed', as Shelley himself could not help writing, 'in dazzling immortality'; it also marks the saving distance between the dead and their survivors.

Shelley has successfully completed so much of the work of mourning. He has renarrated and accepted the fact of death. He has ironized and surpassed inadequate modes of grief. He has expressed and purged his anger. He has submitted to a chastening power that deflects his own attachment to the dead and to the mother-muse. By transforming his primary narcissism, he has created a consoling substitute for the mortal identities of both Keats and himself. And he has apparently accepted the fabric of language, not only to mediate his anger and desire, but also to represent the substitutive object of his affections. But having done all this, Shelley insists on what seems to be a literal rather than figurative identification with the consolatory image. Refusing to accept that such an image exists only by virtue of his own material figurations, he threatens to 'consume' the entire network of mediations so painfully woven in the poem. It is the very triumph of his mourning imagination, its apparently literal rather than literary thrust, that draws him on to what all mourners most need to avoid, their own drive beyond life, and beyond the language whose detours and saving distances keep them alive.

Toward the end of 'Lycidas', Milton has spoken of the perilous flood. And it was a protective 'Genius of the Shore' that he transformed Edward King. For Shelley, the perilous flood is shoreless, more vertical than horizontal. And the beacon does not so much protect as beckon. 'Burning through the inmost veil', the star would seem to carry Shelley beyond the possibilities of poetry, certainly beyond the assurance of pastures new. If we wondered how Shelley could have accepted this most conventional of forms, the pastoral elegy, we recognize now how thoroughly he has driven his version of the genre to the brink of its own ruin. Not surprisingly, 'Adonais' marks an extremity that no later elegy would reach.

## Notes

1. PERCY BYSSHE SHELLEY, *Poetical Works*, ed. Thomas Hutchinson, corrected by G.M. Matthews (Oxford: Oxford University Press, 1970), p. 720; henceforth referred to as *Works*.

2. See JAMES A. NOTOPOULOS, *The Platonism of Shelley* (Durham: University of North Carolina Press, 1949). Notopoulos discusses 'Adonais', regarding it as the purest example of Shelley's Platonism. But he does not take up the question of the problematic relation between Shelley's ideology and his dependence on poetic figures.

3. Shelley had in fact translated parts of Moschus's elegy, in addition to Bion's 'Lament for Adonis'. He had also translated part of Virgil's elegiac 'Eclogue X'. Pehaps no one since Milton and Spenser had so closely reengaged the origins of the genre.

4. JOHN MILTON, *The Complete Poems and Major Prose*, ed. Merritt Y. Hughes (Indianapolis: Odyssey Press, 1957; reprint edn., 1975), pp. 58–9.

5. JOHN KEATS, 'Hyperion', ll. 51–69, in *The Poetical Works of John Keats*, ed. H.W. Garrod, 2nd edn (Oxford: Oxford University Press, 1959), p. 278.

6. The relation between 'Adonais' and Spenser's poetry is of course far greater than one of a copied stanzaic form. Besides the Neo-Platonism, there is what one might call the romance of resignification, that of crossing thresholds by a process of redefining certain figures. While the form recalls *The Faerie Queene*, the practice of resignification (particularly within an elegy) closely resembles that of 'Astrophel'. That poem, too, worked from one inadequate delegate-mourner to a successor who rejected and redefined the meaning of the first mourner's tropes. 'Adonais', however, will not share 'Astrophel''s apparently achieved acceptance both of the figuration itself and of the attendant distance between the survivor and the ideal image of the dead.

7. Impatient with mere comparisons, the curse disrupts not only the 'pageantry of mist' but also the elaborate texture of similes itself, together with the conventionally elegiac comparisons to which those similes allude (cf. Moschus's 'Lament for Bion').

8. However compassionate, the ironic manner in which Shelley describes Urania's enforced separation from Adonais not only separates Shelley and her from Adonais and divides Shelley from his own potentially inadequate response, but also widens the distance between Urania and Shelley, thereby furthering his work of mourning.

9. SIGMUND FREUD, 'Mourning and Melancholia' (1917), trans. Joan Riviere, in *General Psychological Theory*, ed. Philip Rieff (New York: Collier Books, 1963), pp. 164–79.

10. Shelley again uses explicitly sexual images to show what must be rejected. If Adonais survives, it will not be as a fertility god bequeathing his procreative legacy to the erotic Mother. While the figure of the martyred deity *is* used, the terms of his divinity are yet to be redefined.

11. FREUD, p. 170.

12. This is Shelley's internalization of the conventional elegiac division of voices. The singing match is now against himself, in an even more radical way than had been the case in 'Lycidas'.

13. HEINZ KOHUT, 'The Forms and Transformations of Narcissism', *Journal of the American Psychoanalytical Association* (1966): 265.

14. For fuller accounts see JACQUES LACAN, 'The Mirror Stage as Formative of the Function of the I as Revealed in Psychoanalytic Experience', in *Ecrits: A Selection*, trans. Alan Sheridan (New York: Norton, 1977). See also LACAN, *The Language of the Self: The Function of Language in Psychoanalysis*, trans. with notes and commentary by Anthony Wilden (New York: Dell, 1968); JULIET MITCHELL, *Psychoanalysis and Feminism* (New York: Random House, Vintage Books, 1975); ROSALIND COWARD and JOHN ELLIS, *Language and Materialism:*

*Developments in Semiology and the Theory of the Subject* (London: Routledge & Kegan Paul, 1977); ANIKA RIFFLET-LEMAIRE, *Jacques Lacan*, trans. David Macey (London: Routledge & Kegan Paul, 1977); JULIET MITCHELL and JACQUELINE ROSE, *Feminine Sexuality* (New York: Norton, 1983); JOHN P. MULLER and WILLIAM RICHARDSON, 'Toward Reading Lacan: Pages for a Workbook', *Psychoanalysis and Contemporary Thought*, **1**, No. 3 (1978): 323–72.

15. From the edition of Keats's letters by Hyder E. Rollins, 2 vols (Cambridge, Mass.: Harvard University Press, 1958), II, p. 102.

16. This sonnet also prefigures the closing imagery of 'Adonais': 'Thou wert as a lone star, whose light did shine / On some frail bark in winter's midnight roar.'

17. See RICHARD HOLMES, *Shelley: The Pursuit* (London: Weidenfeld and Nicolson, 1974), p. 729.

18. Ironically, the word *beacons*, derived as it is from the Old English term for a sign (*beacen*), reinforces our recognition that even while the 'soul of Adonais' and its star appear to burn beyond or through the veils of nature or of signification, they nevertheless function precisely as signs. Similarly, the image of the spirit's bark not only depends on a metaphor but may be seen to present a traditional image for metaphor itself. Commenting on Aristotle's account of metaphor, Derrida has noted 'the traditional recourse to the boat, its movement, its oars and its sails, to represent figuratively the figure of metaphor – itself a means of "carrying over"' (JACQUES DERRIDA, 'White Mythology', *NLH*, **6**, No. 1, Autumn 1974: 42).

# 12 Shelley's Last Lyrics*

WILLIAM KEACH

William Keach's *Shelley's Style* (1984), hereafter *SS*, is informed by, but resists some of the more extreme implications of, post-structuralist readings of Shelley. The book, in its author's words, 'argues that while [Shelley] recognizes in his own terms the problems inherent in the relation of words to thoughts and things, his writing is shaped by his working as an artist against, as well as in knowing submission to, what he calls "the limitedness of the poetical faculty itself" [*Defence of Poetry*]' (*SS*, p. xi). The book contains a fine discussion of the *Defence of Poetry* as 'at once bravely confident and radically unstable' (*SS*, p. 2) about language as the medium of poetry. Keach describes his approach as 'formalist', an approach he defends on the grounds that 'Criticism of Shelley's poetry may be said to have gone beyond formalism without ever having been there' (*SS*, p. xvii). But his is a formalism that goes beyond New Criticism: his account of 'the antithetical impulses in Shelley's disposition towards language' (*SS*, p. xvi) allows for greater instability than the New Critic would be happy with, and he is aware that the language of poetry cannot be sealed off from historical and social realities. Accordingly, his final chapter, from which an extract is printed below, uses formalist techniques to undo formalist assumptions, bringing out the way Shelley's late lyrics to or about Jane Williams problematise their status as poems. For Keach the poems transgress any supposed separation between writing and living; they send us back to, and are forms of, biographical evidence (about, for instance, Shelley's marital problems and the difficulties of his relationship with Byron), even as their workmanship and art give them a life of their own. The mix of theoretical self-awareness, scholarship, sensi-

---

* Reprinted from William Keach, *Shelley's Style*, (Methuen: New York and London, 1984), pp. 216–34 (footnotes renumbered from the original).

tive close reading, and humanist empathy in this extract makes it, in my view, one of the finest pieces of Shelleyan criticism written in recent years. (See Introduction, p. 19.)

The lyrics of 1822 transgress the boundary separating words from deeds. It is a deed, an act which springs from but also might be expected to cause suffering, for Shelley to make Jane Williams fill in the missing name at the end of 'The Recollection' when he gave the poems to her (this is how the last two lines appear in the British library fair copy):

Less oft is peace in ——'s mind
  Than calm in water seen.[1]

Other lyrics too are deeds in that they were not only written for Jane but were shown or given to her as half-furtive, half-open acts of personal communication. Consider three poems also belonging to the early months of 1822. On 26 January, a week before the walk in the Cascine pine forest that occasioned 'The Invitation' and 'The Recollection', Shelley enclosed a seven-stanza poem entitled 'To ——' and beginning 'The serpent is shut out from Paradise' with the following note to 'My dear Williams':

Looking over the portfolio in which my friend used to keep verses, & in which those I sent you the other day were found, – I have lit upon these; which as they are too dismal for *me* to keep I send them you [who can afford *deleted*].
  If any of the stanzas should please you, you may read them to Jane, but to no one else, – and yet on second thoughts I had rather you would not [*some six words scratched out*].[2]

The blatantly transparent disguise ('my friend'), divided emotions, insinuatingly underscored pronoun and still legible deletions in this note are all gestures to be found in Shelley's poems of this period as well. 'The Magnetic Lady to Her Patient' can be dated to about the same time.[3] At the top of the first page of the holograph Shelley wrote 'For Jane & Williams alone to see', and on an outer wrapping for the poem, 'To Jane. Not to be opened unless you are alone, or with Williams'.[4] Like the titles of these poems, such inscriptions are hard to keep separate from the poetic texts to which they are attached. Somewhat later, probably in February or March,[5] Shelley gave Jane a guitar accompanied by a beautifully written copy of the 'frightful scrawl' that Trelawny had found him working on in the woods outside Pisa. He now gave this poem the title 'With a Guitar. To Jane.'

These three poems adopt very different lyrical postures and tones of voice. 'The Serpent is Shut Out from Paradise', although the least successful and inventive of the three, presents some revealing difficulties. Parts of it are openly self-pitying; there is little of what Davie would call urbanity in the almost Petrarchan sequence of images with which the poem opens:

> The serpent is shut out from Paradise –
>   The wounded deer must seek the herb no more
>     In which its heart's cure lies –
>   The widowed dove must cease to haunt a bower
> Like that from which its mate with feigned sighs
>     Fled in the April hour. –
> I, too, must seldom seek again
> Near happy friends a mitigated pain.
>
> (ll. 1–8)

In the second stanza self-pity takes on a defiant, bitter edge and confronts the limitations of pity – although not, it seems, of self-pity:

> But not to speak of love, Pity alone
> Can break a spirit already more than bent.
>
> (ll. 12–13)

What really makes this poem so disturbed and disturbing is the furtive ambiguity of the emotional claims it makes on its immediate audience. As in the note he sent with the poem, Shelley shifts the focus of his attention from both Williams and Jane to just one of them – but to which one?

> Therefore, if now I see you seldomer,
>   Dear friends, dear *friend*, know that I only fly
>   Your looks, because they stir
> Griefs that should sleep, and hopes that cannot die.
>
> (ll. 17–20)

Given Shelley's note, we would expect Williams to see himself as the singular 'dear *friend*', but the lines that follow hardly make sense unless the narrowed reference is to Jane.[6] For how long in the poem is this narrowed reference meant to apply? Does it still hold for the next stanza, where another added emphasis that looks like bold directness only heightens a sense of slippery indirection?

>   *You* spoil me for the task
>     Of acting a forced part in life's dull scene.
>   Of wearing on my brow the idle mask
>     Of author, great or mean,
>       In the world's carnival. I sought
>   Peace thus, and but in you I find it not.
>
>                                   (ll. 27–32)

The autobiographical reference to the role Shelley was forced to play in
Byron's presence is obvious ('serpent' in line 1 alludes to Byron's favorite
nickname for him).[7] 'Idle mask' and the wavering of 'great or mean' seem
to convey weary detachment from that role, but this itself may be a mask
for defensive anxiety ('I have been long idle', Shelley wrote to Peacock on
11 January 1822; *Letters*, II, p. 374). Byron's influence on the poem may
even be reflected in its ottava rima scheme, which Shelley complicates
and partly disguises by varying the line lengths. But what effect do Jane
and/or Williams have on Shelley's 'acting a forced part'? '*You* spoil me for
the task' suggests that they made it more difficult; 'I sought / Peace thus,
and but in you I found it not' suggests that they made it easier.

This poem dramatizes its own uncertainty in ways that complicate
rather than clarify what it asks of its readers – of Jane and Edward
Williams, but also of us. The flowers the speaker reads in stanza 5 yield
an indeterminate message, yet he 'dread[s] / To speak' and his friends
'may know too well' one of its possible meanings. Is it this unspoken
meaning or the indeterminacy itself that constitutes 'the truth in the sad
oracle'? In the final stanza the vocal manner suddenly does become
urbanely colloquial; the speaker raises the question of resolution and
confesses that he lacks it:

>   I asked her yesterday if she believed
>     That I had resolution. One who *had*
>       Would ne'er have thus relieved
>     His heart with words, but what his judgment bade
>   Would do, and leave the scorner unrelieved. –
>
>                                   (ll. 49–53)

Does 'thus' in line 51 refer to the speaker's having 'asked her yesterday if
she believed / That I had resolution'? Or does it refer to his present act of
confessing his feelings in the poem itself? Either way, these lines are an
act against 'her', against Mary: the third-person pronoun is no longer
distanced from its biographical referent by being quoted in a folk saying,
as in stanza 5. Perhaps it is this gesture, and not the hesitant allusion to
'Griefs that should sleep, and hopes that cannot die' (l. 20) or to truths 'I
dread / To speak' (ll. 38–9), that makes him feel that he has 'relieved /

His heart with words'. What the poem's words leave the reader with is a
sense of unrelieved, even unrelievable, frustration.

'The Magnetic Lady to Her Patient' stands between the consciously
indulgent yet constricted self-absorption of 'The Serpent is Shut Out' and
that elegant and ostensibly liberating 'ariette', 'With a Guitar. To Jane'. It
is the only one of the 1822 lyrics written for more than one voice. Jane
herself is made to speak the first four stanzas (she is named in stanza 5);
what she says is rhythmically incantatory and, even in its demurrals,
erotic:

> 'And from my fingers flow
> The powers of life, and like a sign
> Seal thee from thine hour of woe,
> And brood on thee, but may not blend
> With thine.'[8]

(ll. 5–9)

Judith Chernaik may be right to say that the biographical 'explicitness of
the poem . . . is part of its charm',[9] but the charm is not without its
painful equivocations:

> 'Sleep, sleep, sleep on, – I love thee not –
> Yet when I think that *he*
> Who made and makes my lot
> As full of flowers, as thine of weeds,
> Might have been lost like thee, –
> And that a hand which was not mine
> Might then have charmed his agony
> As I another's – my heart bleeds
> For thine.

(ll. 10–18)

Apparently Shelley could rely on Williams to take these words as the
loyal compliment they seem to be and not to feel blamed for making his
lot full of 'weeds', but the grammar is ambiguous and potentially makes
Williams responsible for Shelley's unhappiness as well as for Jane's
happiness. It is also troubling that while Jane's sympathy is made partly
to depend on her imagining her husband in Shelley's unhappy situation,
she stops short in the poem of imagining herself in Mary's, or of taking
her explicitly into account at all. Jane's performance is contradictory: at
the end of the third stanza she tells her patient to 'forget me, for I can
never be thine' (ll. 26–7), but at the end of the fourth she claims 'By mine
thy being is to its deep / Possest' (35–6). Much of this veiled tension is

momentarily released in the chatty dialogue at the beginning of the last
stanza:

> 'The spell is done – how feel you now?'
>   'Better, quite well,' replied
> The sleeper –
>
> (ll. 37–9)

But as the dialogue continues, the tone of relaxed intimacy takes on a
tenser inflection:

>           'What would do
> You good when suffering and awake,
>   What cure your head and side?'
> 'What would cure that would kill me, Jane,
> And as I must on earth abide
> Awhile yet, tempt me not to break
>   My chain.'
>
> (ll. 39–45)

Medwin's comment on these lines gives them a morbid medical gaiety:
'he made the same reply to an enquiry as to his disease, and its cure, as
he had done to me, – "What would cure me would kill me." – meaning
lithotomy' (the surgical removal of stones from the bladder – without
anaesthesia, of course, in Shelley's day).[10] What Medwin deliberately
ignores – it is inconceivable that even he did not get it – is the sexual
implication of these lines. 'The "chain" he must not break', Chernaik
remarks, 'is the chain of life; also, undoubtedly, it is the chain of his
marriage.'[11] Undoubtedly, Shelley gave the poem to Jane with
instructions 'Not to be opened unless you are alone, or with Williams'.
That Shelley could imagine, even desire, that Jane would read this poem
in Edward's presence is the most disturbingly equivocal thing about it.

In 'With a Guitar. To Jane' the frustrated desire, alienation and guilt of
those early months in 1822 for once seem to be brought under playfully
sophisticated control. The fragility and vulnerability of that control are,
however, the poem's most interesting features. 'With a Guitar. To Jane'
introduces itself as a lyrical dramatic monologue – 'Ariel to Miranda'
(l. 1). And in addition to casting himself, Jane and Williams in roles
borrowed from Shakespeare, Shelley also revives the courtly Renaissance
tradition, as Richard Cronin has recently pointed out, of writing a poem
to accompany and explain a gift presented to the poet's mistress (Herrick
is again a possible influence, along with Donne).[12] Yet pain and sadness
are not excluded from this archaizing artifice; they are instead suspended
within and by it:

> Take
> This slave of music for the sake
> Of him who is the slave of thee;
> And teach it all the harmony,
> In which thou can'st, and only thou,
> Make the delighted spirit glow,
> 'Till joy denies itself again
> And too intense is turned to pain . . .

(ll. 1–8)

Joy is inherently unstable and self-destroying by virtue of its very
intensity: the idea is certainly familiar in Shelley's writing, but in
extending it here to the joy inspired by Miranda's anticipated music,
Shelley indirectly links this compliment-*cum*-warning to the Patient's wry
reply to the Magnetic Lady: 'What would cure that would kill me, Jane.'
Death is a continuous motif in Ariel's song, even though here, as in *The
Tempest*, it is made to seem dreamily fictitious by an elegantly deployed
fantasy of reincarnation:

> When you die, the silent Moon
> In her interlunar swoon
> Is not sadder in her cell
> Than deserted Ariel;
> When you live again on Earth
> Like an unseen Star of birth
> Ariel guides you o'er the sea
> Of life from your nativity . . .

(ll. 23–30)

For a reader who recalls the figure of the 'cold chaste Moon' in
*Epipsychidion*, Ariel's comparing himself to the darkened and 'silent
Moon' may seem the only instance in the poem where the biographical
speaker recalls a time when he was dominated by the influence of this
'Moon':

> And there I lay, within a chaste cold bed:
> Alas, I then was nor alive nor dead: –
> For at her silver voice came Death and Life,
> Unmindful each of their accustomed strife . . .

(ll. 299–302)

Ariel is not entirely free of this lunar influence; the illusory
reconciliations of 'her silver voice' echo through his celebration of
Miranda's warm, intense 'harmony'.

As it turns out this Ariel, unlike Shakespeare's 'airy spirit', is 'Imprisoned for some fault of his / In a body like a grave' (ll. 38–9).[13] His transitory release from this living death must come from Miranda's smiles and from her music. It is this idea that provides the intricate link between the first part of the poem and the second, with its tender etiological account of the guitar's death as a tree and double rebirth through art:

> The artist who this idol wrought
> To echo all harmonious thought
> Felled a tree, while on the steep
> The woods were in their winter sleep . . .
>          – and so this tree –
> O that such our death may be –
> Died in sleep, and felt no pain,
> To live in happier form again,
> From which, beneath Heaven's fairest star,
> The artist wrought this loved guitar,
> And taught it justly to reply
> To all who question skilfully
> In language gentle as thine own . . .
>
>                               (ll. 43–61)

In so far as it speaks 'In language gentle', art – the guitar-maker's and then Miranda's – transfigures death into an illusion. But we already know that this language may provoke joy so extreme that it 'denies itself again / And too intense is turned to pain' (ll. 7–8). Miranda's guitar, like the poem that accompanies it to explain its genesis and potential, speaks a double language, for

> It talks according to the wit
> Of its companions, and no more
> Is heard than has been felt before
> By those who tempt it to betray
> These secrets of an elder day. –
>
>                               (ll. 82–6)

The graceful wit of Shelley's octosyllabic couplets is almost, but not quite, enough to fend off suspicions that 'tempt it to betray' may mean 'tempt it to prove false to' as well as 'tempt it to reveal'. Such suspicions will be particularly hard to banish for a reader with the conclusion of 'The Magnetic Lady to Her Patient' still in her or his mind: 'tempt me not to break / My chain'. Shelley insists that it is not just a question of what 'has been felt before' by the guitar in its antenatal dream of nature's 'harmonies' (ll. 62–78), but of what Ariel and Miranda, he and Jane, have felt of 'Our mortal nature's strife' ('The Recollection', l. 48). Without them the guitar is a 'silent token', even though its music may express 'more than ever can be spoken' (ll. 11–12); it can 'echo all harmonious thought' (l. 44), and presumably all dissonant thought as well. They both know that even 'its highest holiest tone' (l. 89) can never be impervious to the strains of desire and loss.

It may seem contrary to emphasize the pessimistic interpretive possibilities of a text which is so clearly crafted to tease its readers, imaginary and actual, out of thinking about them. But I think it essential to recognize that the most urbanely playful writing in Shelley's last lyrics is never proof against the kind of 'unwelcome thought' that blots that 'one dear image out' at the end of 'The Recollection', or that stains all the images in 'When the Lamp is Shattered' – another lyric (if G.M. Matthews is right) that belongs to these early months of 1822. One sequence of images in this latter poem bears particularly on the undertones of vulnerable mortality and death in 'With a Guitar':

> When the lute is broken
> Sweet tones are remembered not –
> When the lips have spoken
> Loved accents are soon forgot.
>
> As music and splendour
> Survive not the lamp and the lute,
> The heart's echoes render
> No song when the spirit is mute –
> No song – but sad dirges
> Like the wind through a ruined cell
> Or the mournful surges
> That ring the dead seaman's knell.

(ll. 5–16)

The last line of this passage somberly echoes the last line of Ariel's 'Full fathom five' song from *The Tempest*: 'Sea nymphs hourly ring his knell' (I, ii, 405). Jane's guitar, though fashioned 'To echo all harmonious thought', is as subject to silence and dissonance as are the hearts of those that question it, however 'skilfully' (l. 60). The same could be said of the poem itself: Cronin is right to argue that while 'The poem explains the history and qualities of the guitar . . . the guitar acts as a metaphor explaining the genesis and the distinctive qualities of poetry'.[14] These last lyrics suggest that although poems may acquire their own separate existence as verbal forms and fictions, they are never entirely free of the vicissitudes of those who write and read them. Matthews claims that

'When the Lamp is Shattered' 'was undoubtedly written for the "Unfinished Drama" of early 1822' and insists that 'it is ludicrous to treat a song written for private theatricals as if it were the cry of Shelley's own soul.'[15] But thinking of the poem as a piece of dramatic 'artifice, creative play',[16] need not preclude our also thinking of it as a deed, as an act inevitably if indirectly linked to personal motives and consequences. What *if* the poem were written to be performed in private theatricals, possibly (Matthews suggests) by Jane and Mary together? Acting is acting, as Hamlet discovers, despite the interventions of art. And since Shelley never finished the drama and apparently gave Jane a copy of the poem separately, it is difficult not to imagine how it would have been read by the recipient of 'With a Guitar. To Jane'.

'Unwelcome thought[s]' about living and writing continue to emerge in the lyrics Shelley wrote later in 1822, during the last two months of his life. Since early February Shelley and Williams had been planning to find a summer place on the coast above Pisa where they could sail whenever they wanted and be out from under the shadow of Byron and his entourage. They looked for a house in the fishing village of Lerici, but all they could find was a dilapidated building, originally a boat-house, right on the water about a mile from Lerici, near the tiny village of San Terenzo. They were eager to move, however, so on 27 April the four of them – with their children, two servants and, at Shelley's urging, Claire Clairmont – sailed up the coast and moved in.[17]

Being away from Byron was good for Shelley's writing: he may have begun work on *The Triumph of Life* fairly soon after settling in at Casa Magni.[18] But the spectacle of Byron's success continued to oppress him, even at long distance. In February he and Byron had both ordered boats for their summer sailing to be built at Genoa. Byron's was to be much the larger and would be called the *Bolivar*; Shelley, with the financial assistance of Williams and Trelawny, commissioned a sleek twenty-four-foot yacht. Trelawny suggested that the boat be called the *Don Juan*, and Shelley initially agreed. But he eventually decided to assume full ownership of the boat and intended to change its name to the *Ariel*. Yet when the boat finally arrived in Lerici harbor on 12 May, Shelley was appalled to see stenciled on the forward mainsail, in large black letters, the name *Don Juan*. Even if the boat was to have kept the name originally given to it, such a display would have been totally inappropriate.[19] Shelley knew whom to blame, of course, but as he said in a letter to Trelawny of 16 May, there was very little he could do about it:

> The Don Juan is arrived, & nothing can exceed the admiration *she* has excited, for we must suppose the name to have [been] given her during the equivocation of sex which her godfather suffered in the

Harem . . . [*Heavily scratched over*: I see Don Juan is written on the
mainsail. This was due to] my noble friend, carrying the joke rather
too far; much I suspect to the scandal of Roberts [the shipcaptain
charged with getting the boat built to specifications], & even of
yourself . . . though I must repeat that I think the joke was carried too
far; but do not mention this to Roberts, who of course could do
nothing else than acquiesce in Lord Byron's request. Does he mean to
write the Bolivar on his own mainsail?[20]

(*Letters*, II, pp. 421–2)

Shelley's allusion at the beginning of this letter to the fifth canto of *Don
Juan*, where Juan is threatened with castration unless he agrees to
disguise himself as a woman and become Juanna, is revealingly
suggestive of the kind of threat he jokingly attributes to Byron's joke. To
catch the full force of Shelley's indignant sarcasm, one needs to know
that less than a year before, having heard Byron read the fifth canto of
*Don Juan* to him on his visit to Ravenna, he wrote in a letter to Mary: 'It
sets him not above but far above all the poets of the day: every word has
the stamp of immortality. – I despair of rivalling Lord Byron, as well as I
may: and there is no other with whom it is worth contending' (8 August
1821; *Letters*, II, p. 323). Shelley's admiration – even his words ('the
stamp of immortality') – had once again come back to haunt him. Byron
had stamped the name of his finest achievement on Shelley's boat: so
much for 'Ariel'. The joke infuriated and frustrated him: he tried for
hours to remove the letters from the sail with turpentine and all sorts of
other substances, but it was no use. An entirely new section of sail had
to be carefully sewn in to disguise the disfigurement. And after all the
fuss, the name *Don Juan* stuck, and even came to be accepted by Shelley
himself.

Just how much Shelley's affection for Jane Williams intensified during
these two months is a matter of conjecture. But that matters had grown
considerably worse between Shelley and Mary is evident from their
letters and from Mary's and Edward Williams's journals. Mary was
pregnant again, probably since the end of March or the beginning of
April, and this in itself might have made her unhappy about living in a
run-down boat-house near a remote fishing village, in late spring
weather that was oppressively hot even for Italy. And as if the deaths of
three previous children were not enough to give her forebodings, she,
and Shelley too, had to contend with the fact that just two days before
they left Pisa, Allegra died of typhus in the convent where Byron had
taken her to live, away from her mother Claire. On many days in late
May and early June Mary stayed in the house unwell, while Shelley
worked on *The Triumph of Life* and sailed in the bay with Williams, and
sometimes with Jane.

On 16 June Mary Shelley had a serious miscarriage and almost bled to death. It was hours before a doctor could be found, and Shelley probably saved her life by getting hold of some ice and making her sit in a tub of it until the bleeding stopped. Two days later he wrote to John Gisborne about the incident with relief and confidence: 'I succeeded in checking the hemorrhage and the fainting fits, so that when the physician arrived all danger was over, and he had nothing to do but to applaud me for my boldness. She is now doing well, and the sea-baths will restore her' (*Letters*, II, p. 434). But in fact Mary was slow to recover, and so, in a different way, was Shelley – the miscarriage must have disturbed him in ways that the letter to Gisborne does not reveal. A week after the miscarriage, in the middle of the night, he ran screaming into Mary's room (they had slept apart since coming to San Terenzo) claiming that he had been visited by two terrifying 'visions' – he insisted that they were not dreams. Here is Mary's account of what he had told her, in a letter to Maria Gisborne written more than a month after Shelley's death:

> He dreamt that lying as he did in bed Edward & Jane came into him, they were in the most horrible condition, their bodies lacerated – their bones starting through their skin, the faces pale yet stained with blood, they could hardly walk, but Edward was the weakest & Jane was supporting him – Edward said – 'Get up, Shelley, the sea is flooding the house & it is all coming down'. S. got up, he thought, & went to the his [*sic*] window that looked on the terrace & the sea & thought he saw the sea rushing in. Suddenly his vision changed & he saw the figure of himself strangling me, that had made him rush into my room. . . . talking it over the next morning he told me that he had had many visions lately – he had seen the figure of himself which met him as he walked on the terrace & said to him – 'How long do you mean to be content.'[21]

Even allowing for the effect Shelley's drowning had on Mary's emotions, for the possibility that his death activated her own fictionalizing powers, she gives us a text or scenario that disturbingly reflects what we know of Shelley's life and writing at Casa Magni. I want to use her narrative as both biographical and figurative context for looking selectively at the short poems Shelley wrote at this time.

Of the four or five lyrics generally thought to have been written during the last two months of Shelley's life, two may be dated with relative certainty because they appear in the midst of *The Triumph of Life* manuscript. The three parts of the lyric beginning 'The keen stars were twinkling' were originally drafted out of final sequence on widely separated pages of this manuscript. We know their final sequence because we also have Shelley's fair copy of the poem, which he left in

Jane's room with a cryptic and apologetic note ending, 'I commit them to your secrecy and your mercy, and will try to do better another time' (*Letters*, II, p. 437).[22] The poem celebrates and rhythmically evokes Jane's singing on an evening when 'The keen stars were twinkling / And the fair moon was rising among them' (ll. 1–2). Clearly some new pattern of association has momentarily eclipsed the figure of the cold, sad moon in *Epipsychidion* and 'With a Guitar. To Jane'. Once again Shelley's lyric perspectives straddle and place out of immediate reach the actual moment being celebrated. The first stanza, in the past tense, indicates that this moment is being recollected; the second stanza is in the present and also the future tense because it asks Jane to

> Sing again, with your dear voice revealing
> > A tone
> > Of some world far from ours,
> Where music and moonlight and feeling
> > Are one.

(ll. 20–4)

The world of ideal lyric unity is explicitly recognized as being 'far from ours', even though Jane has previously evoked it and may do so again. The first draft of the last two lines reads 'Where moonlight & music & feeling / Are *won*' (my emphasis),[23] suggesting that Shelley may have been initially less concerned with a nocturnal version of the unifying ideal we find at the end of 'To Jane. The Invitation', than with the thought of fully possessing, through a performance or exertion of the interpretive will, experiences which here in our world are always 'arising unforeseen and departing unbidden', as he says in *The Defence*.

The other, longer lyric drafted in *The Triumph of Life* manuscript but left unfinished is also a nocturne; it has come to be called 'Lines Written in the Bay of Lerici'. Its position in the manuscript, together with certain correspondences between its imagery and external circumstances worked out in detail by Matthews, suggest that it was written about a week after Mary's miscarriage. (If Matthews' dating is correct, it may even be based on an experience that happened earlier on the very evening when Shelley had his gruesome nightmares).[24] The first part of the poem, through line 32, works to sustain the memory of an intensely beautiful encounter, presumably with Jane, against a pervasive awareness that the moment has vanished and left the speaker with divided feelings. Until Matthews' work on the poem appeared in 1961, published texts began where the manuscript draft seems to begin, at line 7:

> She left me at the silent time
> When the moon had ceased to climb

The azure dome of Heaven's steep,
And like an albatross asleep,
Balanced on her wings of light,
Hovered in the purple night . . .

(ll. 7–12)

What Matthews noticed was that a group of lines crammed into the space at the top of the manuscript page and obviously written later – lines which before had always been published as a separate fragment – were in fact a new opening to the poem:[25]

Bright wanderer, fair coquette of Heaven,
To whom alone it has been given
To change and be adored for ever. . . .
Envy not this dim world, for never
But once within its shadow grew
One fair as [thou], but far more true.

(ll. 1–6)

No one had previously taken these lines to be part of the poem because they address the moon directly and seem to be written in a different key. But Matthews and Reiman agree on the textual status of the lines, and it is only reasonable to accept them as a revised beginning. Yet it is difficult to avoid thinking that they spoil one of Shelley's finest openings. The abrupt simplicity of 'She left me', followed by the image of the moon balanced and hovering at its zenith just before starting its descent, set the tone and direction of the first part of the poem deftly and movingly. Then why did Shelley add the new opening? Matthews says he wanted to parallel 'the fair but changeable and vanishing moon' with 'the fair, unchanging but vanished Jane'.[26] This may be so, but a further effect of the new opening is to disturb or contaminate in advance the image of the moon momentarily hovering at its height. It is as if Shelley had become uncomfortable retrospectively with the suggestion that the moon's suspended balance could be anything other than the delusive display of a 'fair coquette'. Considering the way in which the poem ends, we may have here from a compositional point of view a revised and contrived beginning distorted by an initially unforeseen ending.

Shelley's speaker clings to the memory of Jane's presence by first 'Thinking over every tone' of what she said or sang, and then by extending those thoughts in a way that leaves totally ambiguous whether Jane touched him as well as her guitar:

And feeling ever – O too much –
The soft vibrations of her touch

As if her gentle hand even now
Lightly trembled on my brow;
And thus although she absent were
Memory gave me all of her
That even fancy dares to claim.

(ll. 21–7)

The difference between 'Memory' and 'fancy' is blurred here in a
distinctively Shelleyan, un-Wordsworthian, un-Coleridgean way. The
uncertainty continues in the next couplet: 'Her presence had made weak
and tame / All passions' (ll. 28–9) could mean that when he was with
Jane he felt no passion, or that having spent his passion in her presence
he no longer felt it. The uncertainty is not resolved, and may even be
compounded by, our knowing that Shelley first wrote 'Desire & fear' in
line 29, then cancelled it in favor of 'passions'.[27] The critical question to
ask is what to make of the ambiguity in this part of the poem. It might
simply be said that we are dealing with an unfinished, incompletely
revised text about which it is inappropriate to make decisive interpretive
judgments. But the reader may still wonder whether the ambiguity is not
there to disguise or veil the kind of intimacy Shelley's speaker
remembers having experienced, the kind of passion he thinks he felt.
One may even want to ask whether or not the poem is fundamentally
uncertain or confused in its representations of intimacy and passion. Are
the evasive insinuations of what 'even fancy dares to claim' and the
blurring of 'Memory' and 'fancy' gestures of discretion or of protective
self-deception, or of both?

Tentative answers to these questions begin to suggest themselves as
the poem turns, dramatically, at line 33:

But soon, the guardian angel gone,
The demon reassumed his throne
In my faint heart . . . I dare not speak
My thoughts; but thus disturbed and weak
I sate . . .

(ll. 33–7)

Those who always complain when Shelley's speakers say that they are
weak or faint rarely make clear whether they are objecting to these
emotions *per se*, or to Shelley's way of writing about them. Judith
Chernaik is on the right track when she compares this poem to the
'Stanzas Written in Dejection, December 1818 – Near Naples'.[28] But the
way in which self-pity is dramatized in that poem – 'I could lie down like
a tired child / And weep away the life of care / Which I have borne and
yet must bear' (ll. 30–2) – is essentially different from this turn in 'Lines

Written in the Bay of Lerici'. Here Shelley is 'disturbed' by emotional and imaginative exhaustion, not just 'weak' with it; 'I dare not speak / My thoughts' confesses an unwillingness, perhaps too an inability, to come fully to terms with the 'demon' in his heart.

In the midst of this critical moment of emotional and expressive failure – and also, the reader may feel, as a way of escaping from it – Shelley returns in mid-sentence to the natural scene, and we get another passage of arresting lyric serenity that throws into relief the agitation he has just confessed. He remembered the boats out in the bay and imagines them sailing 'to some Elysian star'

> for drink to medicine
> Such sweet and bitter pain as mine.
>
> (ll. 43–4)

'Sweet and bitter pain' sounds Petrarchan: could Shelley have been using sonnet 164 from Petrarch's *Rime*, a sonnet beautifully translated by Surrey, as a way of trying to formalize or stabilize the poem's emotional turmoil at this point?[29] The poem moves towards its close through yet another sequence of delicately rhymed idyllic images:

> And the wind that winged their flight
> From the land came fresh and light,
> And the scent of sleeping flowers
> And the coolness of the hours
> Of dew, and the sweet warmth of day
> Was scattered o'er the twinkling bay . . .
>
> (ll. 45–50)

The graceful swing of these couplets, with their repeating 'And' – clauses, may lull us into thinking that the 'demon' has again been banished, this time without Jane's presence or even an explicit memory of her. But then we turn one last corner on 'And' and find him waiting in ambush:

> And the fisher with his lamp
> And spear, about the low rocks damp
> Crept, and struck the fish who came
> To worship the delusive flame.
>
> (ll. 51–4)

The way in which the predatory violence of this image emerges so unexpectedly from the delicately observed seascape, and through the same syntactic pattern as that of the preceding lines, is like nothing else in Shelley, or in English Romantic poetry. Line 51 is syntactically extended and enjambed much like line 48 – 'And the coolness of the hours / Of dew' – only now the initial phrase after the line-ending, 'And spear', marks a lethal addition to the scene. Then the cadence of the octosyllabic line is disrupted and distorted in 'about the low rocks damp / Crept': notice how the first strongly stressed syllable has crept forward in each line from 'And the fisher' to 'And spear' to 'Crept'. One effect of the passage is to give the reader a sense of having been lured into a beautiful but deadly situation. To say that, however, is to see Shelley not as most commentators have seen him here, in the role of the helpless fish lured to destruction by the 'delusive flame' (a refiguring of the coquettish moon from the beginning of the poem, as well as a variation on the opening image from 'When the Lamp is Shattered'), but rather as the 'fisher with his lamp / And spear' – or perhaps as both fisher and fish – luring the reader, Jane and himself towards a grim ending.

The poem itself ends with a kind of moral – sardonic, obscure and unfinished:

> Too happy, they whose pleasure sought
> Extinguishes all sense and thought
> Of the regret that pleasure [ ]
> Destroying [*or* Seeking] life alone not peace.
>
> (ll. 55–8)

Shelley changed his mind about the first word of the last line, and editors disagree about how it ought to read. Matthews, who reads 'Seeking life alone not peace', says that '*Destroying* is firmly cancelled in MS., with a space before the next word, and probably had no connexion with the rest of the line as it stands.' He paraphrases the entire conclusion: 'They are enviably happy who, in exchanging mere placid existence ("peace") for active sensuous enjoyment ("life"), can remain blind to the price they must pay for it (the spear).'[30] Reiman reads 'Destroying life alone not peace', arguing that although 'It is true that the first seven letters of "Destroying" are firmly cancelled', 'Seeking' is written a good distance below 'Destroying' as if it were to have been the first word of a new line. But 'even if one accepts Matthews' reading "Seeking" for "Destroying",' Reiman concludes, 'the basic implications of the figure are not drastically altered'.[31] This seems an astonishing claim to make – and yet in the context of Shelley's deeply unsettled stylistic performance in this poem, I think that Reiman is right. On one reading ('Seeking'), those who die in the instinctive, unreflective pursuit of pleasure are interested only in living, not in living peacefully; on the other reading ('Destroying'), these same creatures, when they die, lose only their life and not a peacefulness of which they were never aware. In either case, the bitter contrast with what Shelley has to lose is clear. It is nevertheless a remarkable thing to be able to say about a poem that its ending is not 'drastically altered' by the difference between 'Seeking life' and 'Destroying life'. No wonder Shelley left this poem without being able to find the rhyme he wanted for its last word, 'peace'.

Like several of the 1822 lyrics but in a more radically self-questioning way, 'Lines Written in the Bay of Lerici' couples an agitated uncertainty about desire and personal relationships with an agitated uncertainty about writing, about verbal representation. The coupling is important to Shelley's entire career: his writing is often most compelling when it questions, explicitly and implicitly, its own empirical origins and linguistic resources. It is also important to his last great piece of writing, *The Triumph of Life*. The draft of 'Lines Written in the Bay of Lerici', along with a draft of lines 11–18 of 'The Keen Stars Were Twinkling' and other fragments, cancellations and notes, appears at that very point in the manuscript of the ongoing poem where Rousseau claims:

> 'I
> Have suffered what I wrote, or viler pain! –
> 'And so my words were seeds of misery – '

Here *The Triumph of Life* draft appears to break off in the midst of a tercet, the lyric drafts and other scraps of writing intervene, and then Rousseau's speech is completed nine manuscript-pages later:

> 'Even as the deeds of others.'
>
> (ll. 278–81)

Even if the order of materials in the manuscript does not reflect the exact order of their composition, it is strikingly suggestive that 'Lines Written in the Bay of Lerici' should be framed by Rousseau's arresting internal rhyme: words as 'seeds', words as 'deeds'.[32] Shelley uses Rousseau to make himself and his readers think about the mutual entanglements of writing and living. He might also have used Byron. But he did not dare.

If Shelley had somehow been able to seal off his last lyrics from sexual, domestic and personal literary perturbations, they would be less important demonstrations of his distinctive, unsettled brilliance. Their stylistic range and deftness, their often masterful inventions of voice and rhythm and stanzaic or couplet arrangement, are the workmanship of an artist instinctively wilful yet profoundly unresolved about writing, and about living.

215

## Notes

1. Quoted from *Shelley's Poetry and Prose*, eds Donald H. Reiman and Sharon B. Powers (New York and London: Norton, 1977). All quotations from Shelley's work are taken from this edition (hereafter *PP*), unless indicated otherwise.

2. *The Letters of Percy Bysshe Shelley*, ed. F.L. Jones, 2 vols (Oxford: Clarendon Press, 1964), II, p. 384.

3. See NEWMAN IVEY WHITE, *Shelley*, 2 vols (New York: Knopf, 1940), II, pp. 345–6, and RICHARD HOLMES, *Shelley: The Pursuit* (New York: E.P. Dutton, 1975), p. 627.

4. See JUDITH CHERNAIK, *The Lyrics of Shelley* (Cleveland: Case Western Reserve University Press, 1972), p. 257.

5. Shelley wrote to Horace Smith on 25 January 1822, asking him 'to buy a good pedal harp' in Paris (*Letters*, II, p. 378). On 24 March 1822, Shelley wrote to Claire: 'Horace Smith has lately declined to advance 6 or 7 napoleons for a musical instrument which I wished to buy for Jane at Paris' (*Letters*, II, p. 400). Then on 11 April 1822, he concluded a letter to Smith by saying, 'I have contrived to get my musical coals at Newcastle itself' (*Letters*, II, p. 412).

6. See the note by Reiman and Powers, *PP*, p. 448.

7. See CHARLES E. ROBINSON, *Shelley and Byron: The Snake and Eagle Wreathed in Fight* (Baltimore: Johns Hopkins University Press), pp. 210–11, and JOHN BUXTON, *Byron and Shelley: The History of a Friendship* (New York: Harcourt Brace, 1968), p. 196.

8. Quotations from 'The Magnetic Lady to Her Patient' and 'When the Lamp is Shattered', neither of which is included in *PP*, are taken from the texts in CHERNAIK, *The Lyrics of Shelley*, pp. 254–9.

9. *The Lyrics of Shelley*, p. 164.

10. *The Life of Percy Bysshe Shelley*, rev. text, ed. H. Buxton Forman (London: Oxford University Press, 1913), p. 270; see HOLMES, *Shelley: The Pursuit*, p. 627.

11. *The Lyrics of Shelley*, p. 165.

12. *Shelley's Poetic Thoughts* (New York: St Martin's Press, 1981), pp. 243–5.

13. Shakespeare's 'Ariel', as Prospero explains, had been confined by the 'foul witch Sycorax' 'Into a cloven pine; within which rift / Imprisoned thou didst painfully remain / A dozen years' (I, ii, 258, 278–80): 'It was mine art, / When I arrived and heard thee, that made gape / The pine, and let thee out' (I, ii, 292–4). Shelley adapts this idea to the genesis of the guitar but retains and transforms, in a characteristic way, the notion of Ariel's imprisonment.

14. *Shelley's Poetic Thoughts*, p. 245.

15. 'Shelley's lyrics', *The Morality of Art: Essays Presented to G. Wilson Knight*, ed. D.W. Jefferson (London: Routledge & Kegan Paul, 1969), pp. 206–7.

16. Ibid., p. 209.

17. HOLMES, *Shelley: The Pursuit*, pp. 709–13.

18. For evidence that Shelley was working on *The Triumph of Life* in May and June of 1822, see Reiman, *Shelley's 'The Triumph of Life'* (Urbana: University of Illinois Press, 1965), Appendix D, pp. 244–50, and, most recently, BETTY T.

BENNETT and ALICE GREEN FREDMAN, 'A note on the dating of Shelley's "The Triumph of Life"', *KSJ*, **31** (1982): 13–15.

19. On the naming of Shelley's boat, see WHITE, *Shelley*, II, p. 366, and HOLMES, *Shelley: The Pursuit*, pp. 716–17.

20. Jones's note on the scratched-over portions of this letter is significant:

   'The following reading is highly conjectural. It is based mainly upon what Shelley *must* have said, as judged by what Mary actually did say in her letter of 2 June 1822 to Maria Gisborne [*Letters of Mary Wollstonecraft Shelley*, I, 236]. Trelawny himself must have scratched the lines out. When he published the letter . . . he omitted the entire passage relating to the name on the mainsail. . . . One would therefore suspect that he as well as Byron had some responsibility for disfiguring Shelley's boat'.

   (*Letters*, II, p. 422 n. 2)

21. *The Letters of Mary Wollstonecraft Shelley*, ed. Betty T. Bennett (Baltimore: Johns Hopkins University Press, 1980), I, p. 215, 15 August 1822.

22. See Reiman's discussion of the drafts in relation to the fair copy in *Shelley's 'The Triumph of Life'*, pp. 245–6, and in *PP*, p. 451, n. 4.

23. For the variants between draft and fair copy, see CHERNAIK, *The Lyrics of Shelley*, pp. 260–1

24. 'Shelley and Jane Williams', *RES*, ns **12** (1961): 40–1, 44–6.

25. Ibid., pp. 40–1.

26. Ibid., p. 41.

27. Ibid., p. 43; see also this and other cancellations noted by Chernaik, *The Lyrics of Shelley*, pp. 273–6.

28. *The Lyrics of Shelley*, pp. 175–6.

29.   Or che 'l ciel et la terra e 'l vento tace
      et le fere e gli augelli il sonno affrena,
      notte il carro stellato in giro mena
      et nel suo letto il mar senz' onda giace,

      vegghio, penso, ardo, piango; et chi mi sface
      sempre m'è inanzi mia dolce pena . . .

      (ll. 1–6)

   The quotation is from *Petrarch's Lyric Poems*, trans. and ed. Robert M. Durling (Cambridge, Mass.: Harvard University Press, 1976). Cf. Surrey's 'Alas! So All Things Now Do Hold Their Peace'.

30. 'Shelley and Jane Williams', p. 44.

31. DONALD H. REIMAN, 'Shelley's "The Triumph of Life": the biographical problem', *PMLA*, 78 (1963): 538.

32. See REIMAN, *Shelley's 'The Triumph of Life'*, pp. 175, 247.

# 13 Shelley's 'The Triumph of Life'*

J. HILLIS MILLER

J. Hillis Miller touches on *The Triumph of Life* in his essay 'The Critic as Host' (included in *Deconstruction and Criticism*, 1979), where he argues that the poem 'contains within itself, jostling irreconcilably with one another, both logocentric metaphysics and nihilism' ('Critic as Host', p. 226). Miller operates in this essay at a high level of generality, producing a kind of deconstructive manifesto: 'The poem, *like all texts* [my italics], is "unreadable", if by "readable" one means a single, definitive interpretation' ('Critic as Host', p. 226). In *The Linguistic Moment* (1985), hereafter *LM*, Miller offers a more detailed reading of the poem, even though the book as a whole is 'neither a work of pure literary theory nor a work of pure praxis, a series of explications', but, rather, 'criticism in the fundamental sense of critique, or of critical philosophy, a testing of the medium from which the bridge between theory and practice is made' (*LM*, p. xviii).

The chapter on Shelley from which the following extract is taken concentrates on *The Triumph of Life*; the first half (not printed here) launches the essay's interest in the poetry's generation of oppositions that are not oppositions, differences that verge on an undifferentiated sameness and yet, never quite abolishing themselves, always leave what Miller calls a 'residue' (*LM*, p. 125) that begins a further cycle of opposites that are not opposites. The essay's analytic procedures simultaneously mirror and concede the impossibility of mirroring 'the extraordinary pace and verve' which the critic discerns in the poem's 'rapid formation and destruction' (*LM*, p. 125) of versions of the same pattern. As Miller tackles the question, 'What . . . are Shelley's figures, figures of?' (*LM*, p. 132), he develops the

---

* Reprinted from a chapter entitled 'Shelley' in J. HILLIS MILLER, *The Linguistic Moment: From Wordsworth to Stevens* (Princeton, New Jersey: Princeton University Press, 1985; paper 1987), pp. 150–79 (footnotes renumbered from the original).

position that Shelley the idealist and Shelley the sceptic are equally 'function[s] in a system of displacements' (*LM*, p. 133), each the host to and parasitic upon the other. The essay is thoroughly deconstructive in its denial of grounds or centres; nothing is known save through language and since language is a system of endless displacements and substitutions nothing can be known through language; rather we encounter in the poem 'an anonymous energy of troping' (*LM*, p. 142); the very 'I' of the poem is 'only a power of naming in figures and personifications' (*LM*, p. 146). Miller does not so much deconstruct *The Triumph of Life* as imply that the poem has already, with sombre intelligence and intensity, deconstructed itself. (See Introduction, pp. 13–14.)

Miller cites the text of *The Triumph of Life* from Donald H. Reiman's *Shelley's 'The Triumph of Life': A Critical Study, Illinois Studies in Language and Literature, 55* (Urbana: University of Illinois Press, 1965).

The chain pattern of 'The Triumph of Life' as a whole is not so much an alternation of light and shadow as it is the replacement of one light source by another light source that puts out the previous one. The previous one soon can no longer be remembered, or is only indistinctly remembered as though it were being seen through an almost opaque screen. One name for Life would therefore be the impossibility of remembering. 'The Triumph of Life' reverses the pattern of Platonic reminiscence, as it is apparently (but not in fact, as Shelley knew) present in Wordsworth's 'Intimations' ode. Shelley's poem presents the mirror image or, perhaps it would be better to say, something like a photographic negative, of the Platonic system of light and dark. Shelley's light is not a Platonic principle of seeing, of remembering, of unveiling, and of revelation, as when the prisoners in the cave come dazzled out into the sunlight, but just the reverse, a principle of covering over and of oblivion. Light for Shelley is the condition of human seeing and naming, which means it is the principle of substitution and forgetting. Each thing is seen as another thing and so forgotten. Each new light at once veils the old and affirms itself as a new source of illumination. This light is always a screen. It covers over as it illuminates, since it is a power of figuration that makes things be what they are not.

As the poet in the opening scene of the poem will not tell the thoughts of the starlit night, and as the sun puts out the stars, so his personifications put out the sun, as does the waking vision that draws a 'veil of light' (l. 32) over the Apennine scene. In the same way the 'Shape' of Life in the chariot puts out the sun with his cold glare.

Shelley's waking vision is in turn replaced by Rousseau's narrative of his own life, with its climactic vision of the shape all light, the beautiful female figure who offers the glass of Nepenthe, drug of forgetfulness. This new shape obliterates the sun and then is once more obliterated in her turn by the last vision of all in the poem as we have it. This is Rousseau's confrontation of the chariot of Life and of the play of shadows projected by all the human victims of Life. The last scene is the ultimate version of the potentially endless turning that makes the chain of scenes in the poem, each scene erasing the previous one, until the break in the fold of the last fragmentary sentence ends all we have.

'The Triumph of Life' enacts a process of life as continuous forgetting. Each scene does indeed deconstruct the previous one, but not in the sense of giving the reader mastery over it. Rather, each new scene gives the elements of the poem another twist, making him forget what had come before, masking it. The reader never learns what are those thoughts that must remain untold and that precede the poem. The poem's ending was cut off by death and must remain forever blank. The reader cannot even clearly hold in his mind all at once the intricate sequence of permutations making up the poem as we have it. However many times he has read the poem, he partly forgets where he has come from and where he is going when he concentrates on any part of it.

This experience of amnesia is repeated again and again throughout the poem, but two passages, that describing the new moon embracing the old and that describing the shape all light, give perhaps the fullest means of understanding it.

The logic of the first of these passages comes to seem more odd the more the reader attempts to untwist its figures and give the passage a single unequivocal meaning:

> And a cold glare, intenser than the moon
> > But icy cold, obscured with light [*sic*]
> The Sun as he the stars. Like the young moon
>
> > When on the sunlit limits of the night
> Her white shell trembles amid crimson air
> > And whilst the sleeping tempest gathers might
>
> Doth, as a herald of its coming, bear
> > The ghost of her dead Mother, whose dim form
> Bends in dark ether from her infant's chair,
>
> > So came a chariot on the silent storm
> Of its own rushing splendour, and a Shape
> > So sate within as one whom years deform

Beneath a dusky hood & double cape
  Crouching within the shadow of a tomb,
And o'er what seemed the head, a cloud like crape,

  Was bent a dun & faint etherial gloom
Tempering the light . . .

(ll. 77–93)

What, exactly, is Shelley saying here, or what is his poetic persona saying? The passage seems at first straightforward enough. As the sun obscured the stars in the opening scene, so now the cold glare of Life, intenser than the noon, obscures the sun. The three lights, in chain sequence, seem to be essentially different from one another as sources of illumination. There are, it appears, at least three different kinds of light. The figure of the moon, however, does strange things to this theoretically plausible differentiation of each source of light from the others. The problem begins, as always in such cases, with the shift from seeing to saying or to writing, even if this shift involves, as in this instance, no more than seeing something visible, the new moon, as a figure of speech for something else. The moon of course shines with light reflected from the sun. The fact is especially evident at that liminal moment when the new moon appears at dusk in a crimson air still half illuminated by a sun that has just set. The moon is the presence of the sun when it has disappeared below the horizon. This means that the moon is the sun's presence as non-presence, as trope, though, as the opening scene makes clear, even in broad daylight, even at high noon, the sun can only appear tropologically, veiled in a personification. If the sun seems at first the source of moonlight, it is in fact, as the reader knows, in any of its appearances, only another version of that universal light that appears always as figure, or as a figure, as a veil of light, or as light veiled in a figure, as a shape all light. This is the case whether the light in question is starlight, sunlight, or moonlight.

Moreover, the figure of the new moon with the old moon in its arms reverses metaleptically the temporal sequence of cause and effect. The figure makes the later the bearer or cause of the earlier, as the vehicle of a metaphor bears its tenor. The new moon carries the ghost of her dead mother. The child becomes the mother of her mother, but mother of a mother who persists as a ghost, as the dim white form of the full moon circled with a faint rim of bright new light. For the relation of sun to moon, apparently primary light to secondary reflected light, is substituted the relation of moon to moon. That it is an act of substitution is indicated by the fact that Shelley says '*like* the new moon' (my italics). The result of this figurative substitution is a reversal of normal causal and temporal sequence. Whatever source of light is present at this moment

221

before the spectator (in this case the cold glare of the chariot of Life) becomes apparently the generative source of what preceded it. This is so in the sense that whatever remains of the past exists now only as the dead ghost of itself carried by the present figure of light, as the new moon carries the ghost of her dead mother. This relation is generalized later in the poem as the paradoxical relation of remembering and forgetting that any present scene has to the previous ones that exist as ghosts or figures within it. They are present as non-presences. This reversal of causal and temporal sequence is, for Shelley, as for his remembered precursors, the presage of a storm. This storm is consistently defined in 'The Triumph of Life' as a deafening cacophonous co-presence, in illogical mixture, of warring elements appealing to all the senses at once. These elements refuse to be sorted out or to sort themselves out in logical or causal sequence. The new moon as the mother of her mother is the sign of this reversal and confusion of the order of generation.

The relation of the new moon to the old defines not only the connection of one scene to the next contiguous one in this poem. It also defines the mode of presence within the poem of all those precursor texts that are there as ghostly echoes or figures – passages from *Ezekiel*, *Revelation*, Dante, Milton, Rousseau, Wordsworth, Coleridge, Blake. Each of these becomes the caused of what it causes when it is simultaneously remembered and forgotten in the poem, at once resurrected and killed. Each previous passage exists as a white ghost of allusion within the new poem, as each earlier example had itself once been both mother and child, carrying its own precursors, remembering and forgetting them at once, bringing them to life and obliterating them, as the chariot of *Revelation* unveils and at the same time obscures the chariot of *Ezekiel*. One version of this kind of chain is the image of the moon here. It comes from Coleridge's 'Dejection: An Ode', which takes it from 'Sir Patrick Spens'. Coleridge's borrowing is already inserted by him in a context that has to do with the storm of synesthesia and with the dependence of the past on a present that may or may not have power to make that past live again. It may or may not have that power because whatever life that past has is the phantasmal life given to it by the shaping spirit of imagination in the present.

In 'The Triumph of Life' the image from Coleridge is transformed again to become a figure of dark light or of darkness visible. This figure is applied not only to the relation of the glare of the chariot of Life to the sunlight it both displaces and encloses, but also, within the cold glare itself, to the relation between the head of Life and the ghastly halo that surrounds it. The head is a 'cloud like crape'. Around the head is 'a dun & faint etherial gloom / Tempering the light', as the new moon surrounds the white shell of the old. The head of Life is a reversed parody of the new moon, its negative image: gloom as a halo around a black cloud. The differentiation that is necessary to make a visible figure out of undifferentiated light exists within any scene of light, whether of sunlight or of dark light (but they are 'the same'), as well as in the relation between any one scene and its predecessor. This is another version of the cleft, or fold, the divisions, and divisions within divisions, that organize this poem throughout. The chariot of Life, appropriately, is guided by a 'Janus-visaged Shadow', actually with four faces, a doubling redoubled. Without some form of doubling, nothing would be visible, but this making visible is at the same time a blinding, since it veils the pure light as such. As the poet says, 'All the four faces of that charioteer / Had their eyes banded' (ll. 99–100). The relation of seeing and blinded vision matches the relation of remembering and forgetting in the poem. What is remembered is remembered as image or ghost, just as what can be seen is always only a veiled figure for the light.

Rousseau's recollected vision of the shape all light walking on the waters of the forest stream both restates the complex figuration of the image of the new moon bearing the old, and at the same time undoes it. The new vision unties the lines that bound the previous one together and allowed it to function as a way of understanding the relation of one scene to another in the pageant of political, personal, or literary history, however alogical the model for that understanding was. The passage in question is initiated by the poet's command to Rousseau: 'Speak'. It runs from line 300 to line 432. This episode is surely the most beautiful and powerful in a poem of great beauty and power throughout. The episode constitutes a reading both of Wordsworth and of Rousseau.

This reading has sometimes been misunderstood by critics in the same way as Hardy's reading of Shelley has been misunderstood.[1] Shelley did not read Wordsworth and Rousseau in a characteristic nineteenth-century or even twentieth-century way, as straightforward transcendentalists, as writers who believed in a harmony between nature, self, language, and in a 'visionary gleam' from beyond nature but mediated by nature. Shelley, the poem indicates, penetrated into the actual skepticism of Wordsworth and Rousseau concerning those harmonies and liaisons, just as Hardy's poems and novels are evidence that Hardy was a far better reader of Shelley than late-Victorian critics like Edward Dowden. It is probably best to assume that a great poet is a better reader than most critics, better certainly than the standard misreading of his own age. Whatever powerful motives a strong poet may have for misinterpreting his predecessors, these misreadings do not necessarily repeat the most banal errors of interpretation current in his time. His blindness may be the distortion of a more genuine insight.

Rousseau's answer to the poet's 'Speak', the reader will remember, is ostensibly in response to those basic questions of the poem: 'Whence camest thou & whither goest thou? / How did thy course begin, . . . & why?' (ll. 296–7). Rousseau answers that he 'seems' 'partly' to know where he has come from and how he got where he is, but has no idea where he is going or why. His narrative demonstrates that the force of the 'partly I seem to know' is such as to remove any possibility of ever reaching, by a recollected moving backward against the stream of time, any but a figurative or illusory origin. First the shape all light appears, 'as if she were the Dawn' (l. 353). She is accompanied by the rainbow of Iris, an echo no doubt of the rainbow in the epigraph to Wordsworth's 'Intimations' ode, as well as of other rainbows in other texts back to the one in *Exodus*. The shape all light manifests herself in a natural scene that, in another echo of Wordsworth, still 'seem[s] to keep' in 'broad day, a gentle trace / Of light diviner than the common Sun / Sheds on the common Earth' (ll. 336–9). A similar natural scene had been presented earlier in the poem (ll. 66–72) as an escape from submission to life that is ignored by all Life's shadow-chasing captives, but this later scene shows how illusory this promise of release is. When the shape all light is replaced by the chariot of Life, the light of the chariot is accompanied by a new rainbow, 'the vermilion / And green & azure plumes of Iris' (ll. 439–40) built by this new light. The shape all light is now in her turn an indistinct figure moving along the stream. She becomes herself no more than a trace, seen 'More dimly than a day appearing dream, / The ghost of a forgotten form of sleep, / A light from Heaven whose half extinguished beam / Through the sick day in which we wake to weep / Glimmers, forever sought, forever lost' (ll. 427–31). The *than* here makes the dream, the ghost, and the light from heaven merely tropes. They are figurative names given to the half-recollected previous scene of light from the point of view of the present one. Those figures, it will be remembered, are originated by the witnessing self. That self projects the masks of various personifications that give a new shape to the light in scene after scene. The self itself, however, the reader will also remember, is another mask, an effect of the impersonal energy of troping that governs all these changes, both inside and outside the encompassing and encompassed consciousness of the poet. Inside, that power appears as the seeming self. Outside, it appears as the ubiquitous light, or rather, since the light as such is invisible, it appears in whatever projected shape the light happens to take at the moment. The process is a narcissistic reflection of shape by shape, inner mask meeting outer mask as its mirror image or sister echo.

In an analogous way, elements in the outer world of perception in this poem seem always to found themselves on a prior element that not only came first but operates as their transcendent ground. The 'Wordsworthian' visionary gleam is a projection backward of an origin that can never be experienced by the present because it is not there and was never there. The 'gentle trace / Of light diviner than the common Sun / Sheds on the common Earth' is just that, a trace, something in the present taken as a sign of something absent. It is a fiction generated by that working of signs which sustains meaning. This was the case for Wordsworth, too, as I have shown [in *LM*] . . . For Shelley as for Wordsworth, the visionary gleam is an element in those 'structures the excited spirit builds mainly for itself'.[2] Wherever the excited spectator is *now*, what he sees casts magically backward to create the apparition of a transcendent light *then* as its source, but this is merely a seeming. The shape all light 'seems' to come from 'the realm without a name' (l. 396), and the glare of the chariot of Life makes the dim ghost of the shape all light 'seem' as if she had been a light from Heaven. The rapid substitution, in the text, of one version after another of this structure, with exactly the same elements – double light source, one extinguishing the other, personification, rainbow, synesthesia, and so on – brings into the open, for a moment, before the juxtaposition fades from memory (for it cannot be held for long in the mind), the fact that the whole system is a reversal of cause and effect. The apparently originary gleam is an effect of 'present' light as trace or sign, as trope, as heliotrope with no *helos* in the sense of central and abiding light source. The trace creates the illusion of that to which it seems to refer. Shelley's light is phototropic, not heliotropic – phototropic in the sense of being the endless turning and substitution of one shape of light for another.

The beautiful female form walking the waters like Venus, appears, the poet says, 'as on the summer evening breeze / Up from the lake a shape of golden dew / Between two rocks, athwart the rising moon, / Moves up the east, where eagle never flew' (ll. 378–81). The odd final phrase here about the eagle, along with the image of the rising moon and the mention of the east, means that this ghostly figure is not 'oriented' by the sun but is a substitute for it. It rises in the east, like the sun, and it is contiguous to the rising moon, the figure in the poem for the borrowed or secondary quality of any light that can be seen. This shape of golden dew flies where eagle never flew because it is not drawn by the sun. The traditional image of the eagle who ascends into the eye of the sun, its 'native noon' (l. 131) appears earlier in the poem as a figure for the sacred few who could not tame their spirits to the conqueror, Life.

Any lingering conviction that the visionary gleam is the glimpse of a transcendent source is further undone by the poet's insistence that any light in the 'present' is above all a power of forgetting. It is a power obliterating the past and substituting for it a fictional past whose truth value can never be tested. The motif of forgetting also undoes whatever generative continuity seems implicit in the image of the new moon with the old moon, her mother, in her arms. Rousseau tells the poet that he remembers waking up in April in a scene that is one of the archetypal

Shelleyan or Romantic landscapes: a mountain with a cavern from which flows a stream down through a flowery forest. The scene is archetypal in the sense that it recurs and in the special sense that it always has something to do with the unsuccessful search for an archetype, the original form of which it is the repetition. In fact Rousseau's waking repeats the first scene of the poet's waking. As the reader may remember (in defiance of Shelley's theory of forgetting), the first scene was presented as itself a repetition, something already seen and felt: 'and I knew / That I had felt the freshness of that dawn . . .' (ll. 33–4). The poem, however, forgets, or at any rate does not explicitly note this repetition in Rousseau's experience of something experienced earlier by the poet as already a repetition. Or rather, since Rousseau's experience of waking, in historical time if not in its presentation in the poem, precedes the poet's experience of waking, the poem forgets to note that the poet's sense of *déjà vu* in the opening scene may have been a dimly remembered repetition of something that had happened to someone else, a strange species of metempsychosis. The writing and then the reading of the poem demonstrates that impossibility of remembering that the poem affirms.

I said above that Rousseau wakes in the springtime scene. In fact, he says, 'I found myself asleep' (l. 311). No doubt this literally means, 'I woke up', but it is an odd way to put it. What follows confirms the fact that, for Shelley or for the Rousseau of this poem, to be awake is to be asleep. It is to be asleep in the sense of forgetting all those things one usually assumes the waking mind remembers. To find oneself in the sense of becoming conscious of oneself and conscious of what is there immediately before one is to be asleep. To find oneself is to find oneself asleep. This is so in a double sense. The presence of the natural scene makes the spectator first forget all the past and become totally absorbed by the present. It then makes him even forget himself. His mind becomes a *tabula rasa* from which every thought has been erased. This is in fact what the historical Rousseau said of the relation between the self and nature, and of course it has many analogies in eighteenth-century English and French empiricism. Juliet Flower MacCannell has demonstrated this for Rousseau in a brilliant essay, and Paul de Man has argued the same thing as one facet of a more comprehensive reading of Rousseau.[3] Contrary to what is often said about Rousseau's theory of the relation of the self to nature, Rousseau saw nature as no ground for the self but rather as a danger to it in its multitudinous appeal to the senses. The self responds to this danger by an elaborate effort of metaphorical construction and substitution. Using these instruments the self creates a fictive world that is against nature, 'unnatural', a falsification of nature and a shield against its dangerous power. This effort, far from securing the self as a stable entity not in need of nature for its support, makes the self a principle of instability and insubstantiality. The self is itself a trope*, and it turns everything it encounters into more tropes.

Shelley wrote the word *Julie* in the margin of the manuscript of 'The Triumph of Life'.⁴ The section of the poem on Rousseau is in part an admirable interpretation of Rousseau's *Julie, or la Nouvelle Héloïse*. 'The Triumph of Life' is evidence that Shelley was a superb reader of Rousseau. He was a superb reader on just those points having to do with the nature of the self and with the relation of the self to nature. Shelley differs from Rousseau not in the elements that enter into his analysis of the relation between the self and nature, but in his greater emphasis on the fragility of the constructed self and on the fragility of the projected personifications of nature. He also puts even more emphasis on the suffering those ungrounded fabrications cause. Shelley's vision is even darker and more shadowed. For all its rapid pace and linguistic exuberance, 'The Triumph of Life' is surely one of the darkest and most shadowed of all major poems in English. Nevertheless, the conceptual and rhetorical systems of Rousseau and Shelley are similar. They are analogical, for example, in the way both see a negative power in a natural spectacle that has been metaphorically transformed by a self seen as itself an impersonal power to make such transformations – turning one thing into another thing. This negative energy projected on nature is expressed for both Rousseau and Shelley as its ability to make the spectator forget everything but itself. The self forgets everything, inside the self and outside, including the self itself. 'The spectacle', writes Saint Preux to Julie of his Alpine experience, 'has I know not what of the magical about it, something surnatural which ravishes the spirit and the senses; one forgets all, one forgets oneself, one no longer knows where one is.'⁵ *Surnatural* here, as the context makes clear, does not mean supernatural, in the sense of coming from a transcendent realm. It names that second nature imposed over nature by the figurative energy of the imagination, as the poets of a later generation were to speak of 'surrealism'.

A similar energy, an energy both creative and destructive, has confected the April scene in which Shelley's Rousseau finds himself asleep. The first effect, for Shelley as for the Rousseau of *La Nouvelle Héloïse*, of finding oneself asleep in nature is the obliteration of all memory of the past. The stream 'fill[s] the grove / With sound which all who hear must needs forget / All pleasure & all pains, all hate & love, / Which they had known before that hour of rest' (ll. 317–20). Pleasure and pain, hate and love, are additional examples of those nondialectical binary oppositions into which experience and the naming of experience divide as soon as there is naming and experience at all. They are also the

---

* [Ed. *Trope*: a figure of speech, a rhetorical device.]

passive and active names for the primary feelings that are for Shelley here, as for Rousseau, the chief motive power behind the projection of thoughts. Such thoughts make those figures on the bubble of life described earlier in the poem. Since pleasure and pain, hate and love make those figures, they make also the pageant of human life and of human history. The confrontation of nature leads to the forgetting of the thoughts born of all anterior passions and to the forgetting also of the ills to which those passions led. The sense-impressions of nature are indeed a kind of morphine, inducing sleep. 'I found myself asleep' is to be taken literally and does not mean 'I woke up.' 'Thou wouldst forget' says Rousseau of the sounds filling the April scene, 'thus vainly to deplore / Ills, which if ills, can find no cure from thee, / The thought of which no other sleep will quell / Nor other music blot from memory – / So sweet & deep is the oblivious spell' (ll. 327–31).

The effect of nature is to blot all memory of the past. One implication of this is that seeking origins or causal sequences is a quest doomed to failure. There is no way in which an answer to the poet's question about origin can be given except fictively, as an illusory projection backward from the present. Rousseau says he has no certain knowledge of what his life was like before he found himself asleep: 'Whether my life had been before that sleep / The Heaven which I imagine, or a Hell / Like this harsh world in which I wake to weep, / I know not' (ll. 332–5). He does not know whether he remembers or forgets. This is immediately followed by the passage, already cited, describing the way the scene 'seems' to keep the gentle trace of light diviner than the common sun sheds on the common earth. Any notion of an anterior heaven as source is an imagination, a seeming. It may be a valid notion. It may not. Whether or not it is valid is forever undecidable.

A generative link between past and present was affirmed, in however, complex a way, by the image of the new moon carrying the old in her arms. The breaking of this link in Rousseau's narrative is accomplished by two striking images, one personal, one political. These are images for the pains of memory nature makes us forget. The power of nature transfigured by the imagination is such that it would make a mother forget, even in her dreams, the child who has just died. It would even make a king just deposed forget to envy his deposer: 'A sleeping mother then would dream not of / The only child who died upon her breast / At eventide, a king would mourn no more / The crown of which his brow was dispossest / When the sun lingered o'er the Ocean floor / To gild his rival's new prosperity' (l. 321–6). The human situation, these images suggest, is to be cut off toward the future, without progeny, like a mother whose only child has died or like a king who has been deprived of the power to establish a dynastic succession. These images, in another case of metalepsis, stand for that process of constant forgetting which

forbids any access to the past as a possible origin of the present.
Detachment from the future goes along with detachment from the past.
Each is a figure for the other. Such radical forgetting forbids any
establishment of an authenticity for the present based on its succession
from the past. In place of such images of continuity as the relation of
mother to child, or of new moon to old, or of king to king in regular
succession, the poem puts a picture of human life as a discontinuous
series of presents. Each of these violently cuts itself off from the past. It
obliterates that past from memory, and at the same time, by that self-
destructive violence, forbids the present to have any future, any
progeny. Each present moment consumes itself through the efforts of its
own creative energy. The power of the light of the present natural scene
in which Rousseau finds himself is like a dreamless sleep in the darkness
which consigns all that happened during the previous day to oblivion. It
obliterates even what happened at the end of that day when the sun was
just sinking into the ocean, even the death of a child, the loss of a crown.

The paradox of Rousseau's narration, it will be seen, is that he
remembers and is able to tell in detail what at the same time he says he
has forgotten, both through the effect of the natural scene and through
the effect of the Nepenthe. He not only remembers he has forgotten, he
even remembers what it is he has forgotten. The effect of the natural
scene and of the lady who personifies it is to make Rousseau forget the
past. Their effect is even to make him forget himself and all the thoughts
of that self in the present. His mind loses all power of thinking and
becomes a vessel empty of thoughts, an extinguished fire, a blank slate
washed clean of any writing:

> And still her feet, no less than the sweet tune
> To which they moved, seemed as they moved, to blot
> The thoughts of him who gazed on them, & soon
>
> All that was seemed as if it had been not,
> As if the gazer's mind was strewn beneath
> Her feet like embers & she, thought by thought,
>
> Trampled its fires into the dust of death . . .

(ll. 382–8)[6]

In this utmost violence of object on subject, the reversible relation of
night and day is reversed again. The lady is said now to be not like night
obliterating day but like day obliterating night. The spectator is blinded
by light. The lady's feet extinguish Rousseau's thought 'As Day upon the
threshold of the east / Treads out the lamps of night, until the breath / Of
darkness reillumines even the least / Of heaven's living eyes – like day
she came, / Making the night a dream' (ll. 389–93).

In the 'light' of these lines the full functioning of the image of the effect of the Nepenthe on Rousseau as like a wave washing out marks on sand may be identified. Shelley has twice used the word *blot* to describe the 'disremembering, dismembering'[7] effect first of the April scene itself, then of the feet of the shape all light moving on the waters: 'blot from memory'; 'seemed as they moved to blot / The thoughts of him who gazed on them'. This figure describes the mind as a slate or writing tablet and light as something that effaces what had been written on that tablet. When Rousseau touches his lips to the cup of Nepenthe, his brain becomes as sand. This sand is not only something diffuse, heavy, and shapeless. It is also a flat surface on which marks may be made. The wave that more than half erases the deer's track must stand for the light and its power of obliteration, though the light, or rather the play of light and shadows that makes visible shapes of light, is also the power that writes on the sand. The light writes, and erases at once. The instrument of oblivion is not the vanishing of signs but the imposition of new signs over the old ones in palimpsest. Shelley's scene of writing anticipates Freud's scene of writing in 'The Magic Writing-Block', though apparently without Freud's structure of layers and of ineffaceable memory traces.[8] That Shelley too sees forgetting as never total is suggested by the qualification in 'more than half erased' (l. 406) as well as by the fact that Rousseau remembers what he says he forgot and by the fact that the poem itself, 'The Triumph of Life', remains as the traces of the thoughts it records. At least it remains as long as a copy of the poem survives.

For Shelley, as for Freud, thinking and perception are forms of writing. This means that the problems of life are always also problems of language. As a consequence, the linguistic moment, for Shelley, is not an intermittent feature in an interchange between mind and world involving primarily perception, thinking, and feeling, and language only secondarily. The linguistic moment in Shelley too, as in Wordsworth or in Arnold in different ways, has such momentum that it spreads out to occupy the whole poem or rolls up that whole so that there is no thinking, feeling, or perceiving that is not at the same time a process of inscription. This constant writing is performed by a light that is both inner and outer at once. To put this in another way, the light obliterates the membrane between inner and outer. The light is an energy constantly making marks or 'figures' on the screen as it abolishes that screen. The screen is there and not there, inner and outer at once, at the borderline between mind and 'Life'. As the light writes, it obliterates the figures that were there before. The light is a beam that writes and erases at once, as the stamp of the wolf's footprint replaces the deer's track when the wolf chases the deer, or as each successive ocean wave washes out the marks that were made on the sand by the previous wave, or as each successive vision, in Shelley's poem, makes a visible shape of light that in its visibility consigns the previous scene to oblivion, or at least to a vague half-visibility, as the shape all light is still barely visible in the glare of Life, like the ghost of a forgotten form of sleep, or as the deer's track is only half erased, or as Rousseau in fact remembers what he says he has forgotten, or at any rate can narrate it, tracing in that narration more figures on the bubble of Life, figures that repeat earlier figures, or as this sentence, in its shifting serial syntax, mimes the Shelleyan sequence that is not incoherent but cannot be held all in the mind at once and destroys its integrity in its own inexhaustible power of continuation.

If the 'shape of all light'(l. 352) is a visible oxymoron, since a shape all light has no shape, she is not a personification of nature, Wordworthian or simply 'Romantic', but just what she is said to be – light, that medium of seeing which pervades this poem as what is common to all of its scenes. Light is what generates spectacle, the theatrically visible, and also what generates concept, theory, or idea. Theatre and theory have of course the same Greek root (*theoria*, what can be seen), and *idea* in Greek means perceptible image, again what can be seen. The light can only be seen in theatrical personifications. It is never seen as itself. It must always be seen in image or in figure. To be seen it must be turned away from itself, masked. It is always seen veiled but revealed in its veiling, forgotten and remembered at once. The shape all light is the manifestation in Shelley's poem of the incompatibility between pure seeing or pure theory, and that instant interpretation of the light that names it, gives it a shape, makes it a sign, a figure, or an allegorical person.

The constant substitution of one such figure for another will indicate the meaning of that sense-confusing (in both senses of the word *sense*) synesthesia which is so conspicuous a feature of the poem. Synesthesia appears especially in the penultimate scene of the shape all light and in the last scene of the shadow-making glare of Life. Light, sound, smell, and feeling are all interchanged in these scenes. Music is the primary trope for this synesthesia. The mixture of appeals to the various senses makes a medley like the 'many sounds woven into one / Oblivious melody, confusing sense' (ll. 340–1) in the first of these scenes, or like the 'savage music, stunning music' of Rousseau's 'Vision' of the chariot of Life in the second (ll. 434–5). That music is not Apollonian, in spite of its association with the sun, but Dionysiac, irrational. Shelley's light, even his sunlight, is always the dark light of Life. The savage music of nature deprives its auditors of clear-headed reason, like that music, echo of Shelley's, in Yeats's 'News for the Delphic Oracle': 'Down the mountain walls / From where Pan's cavern is / Intolerable music falls'.[9] Rousseau's vision turns into audition, which destroys the integrity of clear seeing. For Shelley, whatever is seen, heard, smelled, or felt with one sense turns into something perceived by a different sense. The constant exchange of one sense for another is like stunning music that tramples out thought and memory as well as even the power of distinct perception itself.

Shelley's insistence on images of feet treading or trampling indicates the physical violence of this blotting from memory. As de Man has seen, the motif of treading joins the image of music to indicate that the instrument of oblivion is not undifferentiated sense experience, the appeal to all the senses of the natural scene, but the metrical, rhythmical ordering of sense data. As a mere sound becomes music when it is joined to other sounds at regular intervals and rhythmically ordered, so sounds become words and words become poetry when they are differentiated, modulated, and then divided into 'feet'. The patterning that makes order and beauty in music or poetry at the same time gives them a power to 'stun' their auditors, to obliterate the past and even to blot out clarity of mind in the present. For Shelley, as I have indicated, there is no pure perception as such. Whatever is seen, heard, or felt is seen, heard or felt as already turned into signs. For this reason, the linguistic moment for him is not intermittent but perpetual. This transformation of perception into interpretation, the projection and reading of signs, at once makes things intelligible and at the same time deprives them of intelligibility or deprives the victim of the power to read them. It is not so much signs as such that have this stunning power as the rhythmic patterning of these signs, the repeatable metrical or syntactical paradigms into which they are ordered and which is the condition of their beauty and of their intelligibility. An example would be the arrangement and rearrangement of the same figurative and conceptual elements that make up the sequence of scenes in 'The Triumph of Life'. The identification of this recurrent pattern is both the means by which the reader comprehends the poem, and at the same time it is a musical ordering that numbs his mind and deprives him of the powers to remember the specificity of previous scenes or even to see clearly what is going on in the present one just before his eyes. The effect of the poem on its reader re-enacts the effect of the savage music on Rousseau. The reader of the poem experiences again what Rousseau experienced when his brain became as sand.

The exchanges of figuration that take place under the aegis of the shape all light are, it can be 'seen', by no means viewed as a benign process by Shelley. This is indicated in the way all light displaces the sun. When the sun rises on the April morning in which Rousseau finds himself asleep, it is seen, as it was for the poet in the opening scene, as a radiant male figure narcissistically admiring himself reflected in his creation. As Rousseau says, the 'Sun's image radiantly intense / Burned on the waters of the well that glowed / Like gold, and threaded all the forest maze / With winding paths of emerald fire' (ll. 345–8). The sun

reflects himself to himself in masculine splendor (ll. 349–50), but the
female figure of the shape all light, mother, sister, mistress, muse,
'[stands] / Amid the sun, as he amid the blaze / Of his own glory' (ll.
348–50). She interferes with the self-enclosed circuit of the sun and image
of the sun, displacing it, blotting it out, unmanning the sun. Sexual
differentiation blocks the perfection of male self-admiration and induces
a wandering into figurative substitutions with no identifiable beginning,
end, or answer to the question, 'Why?' The shape all light stands amid
the sun *as* the sun stands in his own glory. In that *as*, the turning begins
again, and the light henceforth can never return to itself. The diverted
play of reflection forbids the light to return to the *heliologos*, its seeming
paternal source, just as Narcissus, in one version of his story, can never
join himself to himself by way of that twin sister he has loved, and just
as Shelley's heroes in his various quest-poems can never satisfy a desire
for unity with a counterpart of the other sex. That desire is consistently
dramatized by Shelley, from 'Laon and Cythna' on, as incestuous love.
Sexual desire appears in 'The Triumph of Life' not only in the early
sequence about erotic love but also in the relation of Rousseau to the lady
all light who offers him Nepenthe, so making him forget nature, which
had made him forget himself, and so making him one more of light's
victims. The female light as shape-changer stands between a man and
the masculine sun, unmanning that sun by making it appear no more
than one of the changing shapes of light. This revelation renders
powerless the man who seeks through the mediation of the female shape
all light to take possession of the sun's power or of the power behind the
sun.

This subversive feminine shifting of the light is figured in the
identification of the lady with that star which in the morning is called
Lucifer, in the evening Venus. The passage is of great beauty:

> ' – so on my sight
> Burst a new Vision never seen before, –
>
> 'And the fair shape waned in the coming light
> As veil by veil the silent splendour drops
> From Lucifer, amid the chrysolite
>
> 'Of sunrise ere it strike the mountain tops –
> And as the presence of that fairest planet
> Although unseen is felt by one who hopes
>
> 'That his day's path may end as he began it
> In that star's smile, whose light is like the scent
> Of a jonquil when evening breezes fan it,

'Or the soft note in which his dear lament
  The Brescian shepherd breathes, or the caress
That turned his weary slumber to content, –

'So I knew I in that light's severe excess
The presence of that shape which on the stream
  Moved . . .'

(ll. 410–26)

The process dramatized here is only by a chiasmic reversal called a removing of veils, a revelation or 'apocalypse' in the literal sense. What is revealed is invisibility. It is as if the light itself were a veil, a cover for the black light of Lucifer. As the sun rises, veil after veil of the silent splendor of the morning star drops not to reveal the star in all its naked glory but to darken it completely. To present the ubiquitous light in the allegorical figure of the lady and then to identify her with starlight distinguishes this light from sunlight or from any of sunlight's derivatives – for example, the secondary light of the moon. This presentation also identifies the light of the shape all light with the internal, sign-making, poetry-writing light of the human imagination. Starlight was, at the beginning of the poem, the reader will remember, used as a figure for the poet's night-time thoughts that must remain untold. Since the star in question is in the morning named Lucifer, the light must be diabolical, subversive, Satanic, a counterlight challenging the apparent originality of the sun. The name *Lucifer* means of course light-bearer, just as the word *metaphor* means, etymologically, bear across. Both words contain the same root, *fer* or *phor* – 'carry'. To call the shape all light Lucifer is to name her the principle of figurative transfer. She is the one who presides over that slipping of the universal principle of light from shape to shape in a constant substitution of one figure for another. 'The Triumph of Life' enacts this process from beginning to broken 'end'.

The feminine principle of slippage has power even over the sun. It has power to force the spectator to see the sun itself as only another shape of light. In the passage using the figure of the morning and evening star, the sun itself has become merely a figure. It is an image for the light of the chariot of Life. That light displaces the shape all light, 'as' the sun puts out the morning star. The light is borne here, there, elsewhere, by whatever shape happens for the moment to carry it as temporary 'Lucifer'. Lucifer proper, the morning star, becomes in the evening Venus, star of love. This is a further example of metaphorical slipping and of its connection with a naming that is never really 'proper' but always in one way or another figurative.

That the star of diabolical shape-changing is also the star of love

234

identifies the drama of figuration with a drama of sexual desire. The early passage about the dancing lovers has already shown this to be the case. To love is to become subject to the shifting of light and so to become a victim of Life and a captive of his triumphal car. This casts an ironic light on the claim sometimes made by critics that Love, for Shelley, is a transcendental principle free of the play of substitutions and governing it. One passage (ll. 471–80) describes the generation of legions of shadows by the victims of Life as a wonder worthy of Dante's rhyme. This passage might seem to authorize a universalizing of Love. It affirms that Dante showed 'how all things are transfigured, except Love', and it projects the sphere of Venus as a serene realm 'whose light is melody to lovers', far above the wrathful sea of Life. In the perspective of the identification of Lucifer and Venus with one another and with the shape all light made a little earlier in the poem, however, to say all things are transfigured, except Love, is to say no more than that the light persists through all its changes of figure. This includes those transfigurations motivated by erotic love and by its special power to cast shadows in the light. This is dramatized again in the final vision of the multitude of self-consuming shadows projected by the victims of Life. This process is a wonder worthy of Dante's rhyme because it is the same wonder as the one he dramatized, in Shelley's skeptical reinterpretation of what Dante meant by showing how all things are transfigured, except Love.

The passage about the double-named star makes explicit the identification of synesthesia with metaphorical substitution. The star that is both Lucifer and Venus is like a flower's scent, or like a song, or like a love caress, because it is the emblem of that principle of interfiguration among all things that may be seen, smelled, heard, or felt. These make a potentially endless chain: or . . . or . . . or. A final form of this interchange is that from one sex to another. In the passage describing the displacement of the female shape by the Vision of Life, Life is also apparently a woman. She is now figured as female sun or star. This is indicated by the pronoun *her* in line 438. The four-faced charioteer must be the locus of another interchange of the sexes, like that between Lucifer and Venus. The reader is at first inclined to assume that Life, as a conquering general celebrating his triumph in battle, must be unequivocally masculine, like the sun. This warrior must be also female, however, even in his/her first appearance to the poet, if the implications of the image of the moon are accepted. The charioteer is the mother moon held in the arms of her more luminous daughter, the halo around her head.

When the light of Lucifer–Venus is put out, or almost put out, by the sun that is no sun but another shape of light here troped as the sun, Rousseau, as he says, soon plunges into the 'thickest billows of the living storm' and bares his bosom to the clime of Life's cold light (ll. 466–8).

This gesture of plunging leads to the end of the poem as we have it. It will lead also to the last move in my zigzag course threading through 'The Triumph of Life'. I have moved back and forth across the surface of this text like an ant exploring the pattern of a quilt, tracing its warp and woof in mingled multicolored yarn. My last step returns to the issue of comprehension. Does the poem provide answers to the questions it so insistently asks about the origin, end, and why of Life? Does the poet find answers to these questions? Does Rousseau? Can I as critic formulate answers that the reader of this essay can comprehend rationally and take away as a total interpretation of the poem?

I do not think a positive answer can be given to any of these questions. The final impasse both of the poem and of the vision of life the poem proposes is that neither of these can be understood by either of the two strategies of comprehension the poem itself proposes. One of these is the spectator's detachment that sees all comprehensively and with cool rationality from the outside. 'The onlookers see most of the game.' The other is that actor's involvement which plunges into the storm and understands it from within, as experience proved on the pulses. Neither strategy of understanding works, for reasons that the poem specifies. The alternatives surface most explicitly in Rousseau's ironic invitation to the poet in answer to his questions about the whence, the whereto, and the why:

'But follow thou, & from spectator turn
  Actor or victim in this wretchedness,

'And what thou wouldst be taught I then may learn
  From thee. – '

(ll. 305–8)

What happens if this strategy is followed Rousseau's own example shows. It leads to obliteration, oblivion, the undoing of memory. One's brain becomes as sand. All hope of finding origin, end, or ground is lost. Neither involvement nor detachment finds an answer to the questions posed by the poem, though life forces each man and woman to try one or the other strategy, or both. The uninvolved spectator sees nothing but a confused spectacle, and so sees nothing. Life can only be explored from within. The involved actor, however, is always a victim of the light's perpetually renewed power of disremembering, and so he too sees nothing but a confused spectacle. He has no hope even of knowing what came just before or will come just after, so blinded is his vision. Much less can he hope to know the source, the goal, or the cause of the whole chain of visions that imprisons him. Thinking according to polar oppositions here breaks down once more. To be an actor is to be a victim, the victim is an actor, as the poem abundantly shows. It shows this both for the main protagonists, the poet and Rousseau, and in its historical portraits – for example, that of Napoleon. A spectator is already willy-nilly an actor, since even the most passive and detached seeing is always an activity of interpretation. Interpretation plunges the spectator into the thickest billows of the living storm and so obliterates for him the beginning and end of that storm.

This situation applies equally to human life as it is dramatized within Shelley's poem and to the situation of the reader or critic who would seek to understand the poem totally, to encompass and command it. A complete comprehension of either a single work by a writer or of his work as a whole would see all around that work and recapitulate it from some *point de départ*, perhaps in the author's *cogito* or act of self-consciousness, to some endpoint toward which that work moves in obedience to its own laws. Such comprehension is forbidden by the fact that to understand the work at all it is necessary to enter into it, to abandon oneself to the itinerary traced out by the text. To do so is to become lost in interminable wanderings within that text. These wanderings are only arbitrarily put in order and concluded by some *finis*. No critical essay does final justice to the poem in question. Each leaves the work of criticism to be done over again. The reader adds himself to the chain made by Shelley, by Rousseau, and by all those precursors fading back like ancestors in a genealogical tree: Milton, Dante, St John, Ezekiel. The reader's position is no different from theirs and no more capable of achieving mastery over life or over language. To attempt to see the game, the play of language in 'The Triumph of Life', the reader must enter into it. He must play the game himself. This means becoming himself a victim of Life and of language. This victimization, for the critic, takes the form of an experience of uncertainty about the meaning of the poem. This uncertainty is constituted by the fact that he cannot decide for sure whether or not the text is readable, in the sense of being open to a univocal reading. He cannot demonstrate whether or not the poem is open to a single definitive interpretation, and so he must continue his exploration of it.

To become a victim of the poem means experiencing the impossibility of ever unravelling all its threads. Instead of that final straightening out he seeks, the reader untwists one part of the poem while in that act he twists up again another part. The chain as a whole remains as knotted as ever. The critic's activity – for example, mine in this essay – is a moving back and forth across the text attempting to untangle it all, but tangling it up again in some other section when the one on which attention is centered is straightened out. This frustrating activity – Penelope performing the day's weaving and the night's unweaving in the same gesture – is, to vary the metaphor, a remembering that is at the same time a forgetting. It never succeeds in holding the whole text in an absolute clarity of understanding all in the mind at once. Since it never succeeds, it may never be completed. Reading too is an experience of an-anamnesis, the reverse of Platonic remembering.

This essay has proceeded through a sequence of sections focusing narrowly on one passage after another of the poem. The essay is at once too short and too long. It is too short because it by no means exhaustively interprets the whole poem. Much that could and should be said is left unsaid. On the other hand, it is too long to be seen through perspicuously (as Aristotle said should happen with a good work) or to be held all in the mind at once. In a critical essay too, the intense concentration on a given passage or topic necessitates the forgetting, or at least the partial forgetting, of what has already been said. The experience of reading the critical essay corresponds to the experience of reading the poem. This is so not because the essay foolishly attempts to be 'poetic', but because the critic too is caught in a double bind. If he writes something wholly logical and transparent, a shapely essay, he will falsify the poem. If he does even approximate justice to this admirably intricate poem, he will present again in his own essay the pattern of forgetting and remembering that the poem itself both exemplifies and is 'about'.

This simultaneous remembering and forgetting is described and enacted within the poem itself. The metaphors of the traces on the sand and of the figures on the bubble that fade as they are drawn are tropes of writing. They are tropes, that is, for the writing of the poem and for its reading. Rousseau answers the poet's questions with more speech, and I in my turn, or any other critic, must do the same. To do this is a way of turning from spectator to actor and so of becoming another victim of Life, that is, of language. My situation as reader of the poem is no different from that of Rousseau as seer, since reading and seeing are the same in the sense that both are acts of deciphering. This deciphering at the same time creates more cryptic signs to be decoded. It covers the signs to be read with more signs. The new signs cause the earlier ones to fade into oblivion, as Lucifer fades in the morning light.

The moment of reading is the moment of forgetting. It is the moment when one turns from spectator to actor and enters into the text in an attempt to answer those questions basic to literary criticism since Aristotle: whence, where, and why. Instead of an answer the reader gets Nepenthe, literature as the drug of forgetfulness. However hard the reader tries to stay awake, his brain becomes as sand. It is washed clean, or almost clean, by a great wave of light. The reader then gets the next vision, the next writing on the screen or shore or bubble of the next shadowy figure, the next sand-script replacing that just effaced. The new writing is inscribed in palimpsest over what has almost been effaced, as each episode replaces the last in 'The Triumph of Life', or as this essay is written over the text of the poem and repeats its serial structure. Each new writing both obliterates what came before and unwittingly prolongs it. This act is unwitting because its relation to what it replaces can never be wholly clear, neither to the commentator nor to his readers. It can never give, once and for all, an answer to the whence, the whither, and the why.

At the end of all my commentary, I find myself where I began. As a reader of 'The Triumph of Life' I am the next in a chain of repetitions without beginning or end. I find myself again enfolded in a fold, asleep under a caverned mountain beside a brook, watching a sequence of shapes all light, projecting in my turn figures over those shapes, figures that fade even as they are traced, to be replaced by others, in an unending production of signs over signs. . . .

## Notes

1.   [Ed. In a passage earlier in the chapter, not included in this extract, Miller argues that Hardy does not regard Shelley as a mystified idealist. Instead, Hardy reads Shelley as 'a Romantic skeptic', and his 'dialogue' with Shelley corresponds to a dialogue with himself, 'analogous . . . to the dialogues within Shelley's own work' – for instance, 'that between "Rousseau" and the primary "I" in "The Triumph of Life"' (p. 116).]

2.   William Wordsworth, *The Prelude*, ed. Ernest de Selincourt, 2nd ed. rev. Helen Darbishire (Oxford: Oxford University Press, 1959), 1850 text, VII. ll. 651–2.

3.   See JULIET FLOWER MACCANNELL, 'Nature and Self-Love: A Reinterpretation of Rousseau's "Passion primitive"', *PMLA*, XCII, 5 (October 1977): 890–902, and PAUL DE MAN, 'Part II, Rousseau', *Allegories of Reading* (New Haven and London: Yale University Press, 1979), pp. 133–301.

4.   Or at any rate Donald Reiman thinks he reads the word there. See his *Shelley's 'The Triumph of Life': A Critical Study*, p. 211: 'the word GM [G.M. Matthews] reads as "Jane" I believe to be "Julie" . . .' And see Reiman's extensive discussion of the presence of Rousseau in 'The Triumph of Life' (ibid., pp. 39–85).

5.   The passage is from the twenty-third letter of the first part of *La Nouvelle Héloïse* (J.-J. Rousseau, *Oeuvres complètes*, ed. B. Gagnebin and M. Raymond, II [Paris: Bibliothèque de la Pléiade, 1964], p. 79): '*le spectacle a je ne sais quoi de magique, de surnaturel qui ravit l'esprit et les sens; on oublie tout, on s'oublie soi-même, on ne sait plus où l'on est*'. See MACCANNELL, 'Nature and Self-Love', pp. 895–6 for a commentary on this letter.

6.   See Paul de Man's discussion of this image in 'Shelley Disfigured', *Deconstruction and Criticism*, pp. 50–66. My chapter here on 'The Triumph of Life' was written before de Man's admirable study, though of course his was published earlier. Our conversations about the poem before either essay was written nevertheless deeply influenced my thinking about it.

7.  GERARD MANLEY HOPKINS, 'Spelt from Sibyl's Leaves', l. 7, *Poems*, 4th edn. eds W.H. Gardner and N.H. MacKenzie (London, Oxford, New York: Oxford University Press, 1970), p. 97.

8.  See SIGMUND FREUD, '*Notiz über den "Wunderblock"*' (1925), *Gesammelten Werke*, XIV (London: Imago Publishing Co., Ltd., 1948), pp. 3–8, trans. James Strachey, 'A Note upon the "Mystic Writing Pad"', *The Complete Psychological Works*, std. edn, XIX (London: The Hogarth Press, 1953–66), pp. 225–32. For a commentary on Freud's essay, see JACQUES DERRIDA, '*Freud et la scène de l'écriture*', *L'écriture et la différence* (Paris: Éditions du Seuil, 1967), pp. 293–340, trans. Alan Bass, 'Freud and the Scene of Writing', *Writing and Difference* (Chicago: The University of Chicago Press, 1978), pp. 196–231.

9.  Lines 30–2, W.B. Yeats, *The Variorium Edition of the Poems*, ed. Peter Allt and Russell K. Alspach (New York: Macmillan Publishing Co., Inc., 1977), p. 612.

# 14 Idealism and Skepticism in Shelley's Poetry [*The Triumph of Life* and *Alastor*]*

TILOTTAMA RAJAN

Theoretically adroit and sensitised to the imaginative life of poetic texts, Tilottama Rajan has emerged over the last decade or so as a major critic of Romanticism. Her shifting positions are fascinating to track, and alert us to the amount of debate that exists between and within those influenced by Derrida and de Man. In an important article, 'Displacing Post-Structuralism: Romantic Studies After Paul de Man' (*Studies in Romanticism*, 24 (Winter 1985)), she describes her earlier book, *Dark Interpreter* (1980; hereafter *DI*), from which the following extract is taken, as 'deconstructive but phenomenological/ psychological rather than post-structuralist, in that it posits a subject who uses discourses as part of a drama of concealment and disclosure' (p. 451, n. 1). Rajan draws attention in 'Displacing Post-Structuralism' to the fact that de Man's own work is 'a series of conflictual sites' (p. 453), coupling different approaches, and argues for a deconstructive criticism of Romantic literature that is not 'monolithic' (p. 453). In this essay and her second book, *The Supplement of Reading* (1990), she focuses on 'the role of the reader in romantic theory and practice' (*Supplement of Reading*, p. 2), even though she disputes the claim of some reader-response critics that the reader gives meaning to the text; for Rajan, reading is to text as supplement to that which is supplemented; reading 'points to a gap in the written text even as it fills it' (*Supplement of Reading*, p. 2). This capacity for subtle theoretical refinement is already apparent in *Dark Interpreter* which is concerned both to deconstruct 'the official Romantic metaphysic of the imagination' (*DI*, p. 21) and to respect 'the Romantic poet's sense of the limits of demystification as an attitude to life' (*DI*, p. 22); hence Rajan's interest in the presence

---

* Reprinted from *Dark Interpreter: The Discourse of Romanticism* (Ithaca and London: Cornell University Press, 1980), pp. 58–83.

241

within Romantic poetry of the 'sentimental', that is, the 'displacement or repression of insights that are nevertheless acknowledged' (*DI*, p. 34), and her emphasis on the relevance of Sartre's theory of imagination to her view of the Romantics: Sartre, like the Romantics, is trapped by 'the problem of how to account for the fact that consciousness is "positioned in the world" and yet is free' (*DI*, p. 271).

Rajan's reading of Shelley in *Dark Interpreter* reviews his poetic career in the light of his last fragment, *The Triumph of Life*, which she sees as laying bare tensions (especially between text and sub-text) concealed within the earlier poetry. The extract printed here moves from an account of *The Triumph* to a consideration of the contradictions within his poetic theory (as articulated in *A Defence of Poetry*) and concludes with a discussion of *Alastor*. (See Introduction, pp. 12–13.)

>                            their lore
> Taught them not this – to know themselves; their might
> Could not repress the mutiny within,
> And for the morn of truth they feigned, deep night
> Caught them ere evening.
>
>                                (*The Triumph of Life*)

Martin Price writes of Blake that his critical remarks are a fierce attack on all doctrines that seem to undermine the authority of the imagination:

> In this respect, he differs greatly from writers of more skeptical temper or tentative attitudes. Perhaps the greatest threat to the visionary is the sense of self-division and doubt. . . . Doubt, as Blake puts it, 'is Self-Contradiction', the self divided into the visionary and the questioner.[1]

While no one would claim that Shelley possessed Blake's confidence in the power of the imagination to resist inner doubt or extend opposition, critics have tended to assume that given the choice he would have preferred the unmediated vision to the state of being in doubt and half-knowledge.[2] Such a view is based on the assumption that either *Prometheus Unbound* or *Adonais* is the central poem in the canon, and that *The Triumph of Life* is a postscript rather than a new plateau in Shelley's development, as T.S. Eliot long ago recognized it to be. Thus Bloom sees the pattern of Shelley's poetry as involving a moment of heightened relationship between the 'I' and its universe, and subsequent falling away into experience which does not, however, 'invalidate the apotheosis' of the moment of relationship. Daniel Hughes, following Bloom, sees the poetic process of Shelley as a kindling and dwindling, and reads *The Triumph of Life* as a defeat of the myth which nevertheless leaves intact as the core of affirmation in Shelley's work 'the continuous fire' achieved in *Prometheus Unbound*. Wasserman, for his part, does not even deal with *The Triumph of Life*.[3]

To a great extent Shelley himself encourages such views, because his encounter with skepticism leads him to postpone or relocate rather than revise his idealism, to respond to skepticism sentimentally rather than ironically or tragically. The seemingly pessimistic and platonic image of poetry as a fading coal preserves in the past the radical image of poetry as 'pregnant with a lightning which has yet found no conductor',[4] without giving up the idealistic view of art as vision and illumination implicit in both images. The radical, revolutionary image of poetry, which seems to claim the immanence of vision, is itself a way of rationalizing absence by converting it into hope. But the fact that Shelley's last poem, like Keats's last poem, is an interior dialogue between a visionary and the self-projected specter of his own doubt should lead us to ask whether *The Triumph of Life* does not revise Shelley's Promethean myth rather than confirm it in defeat, and whether it does not temper the nature of poetry to the imperfection of the self. Rousseau, the protagonist of Shelley's poem, himself wrote dialogues in which he split himself into judge and defender, for the purpose of defying criticism by perceiving it as misunderstanding. The different nature of the dialogue in Shelley's poem stands, among other things, as a reexamination of the Romantic tendency to use dialogue and drama in such a way that the very forms of self-doubt are converted into the forms of exculpation, and inner division is projected away from the self. It seems possible to say that *The Triumph of Life* moves away from idealism and, moreover, that it is the culmination of a debate between Shelley's skepticism and his idealism that is present as early as *Alastor*. The unconventional disposition of this chapter, which begins at the end of Shelley's career [. . .] may seem to prejudge the discussion by giving Shelley's final poem an initial authority within the canon. It reflects, however, my feeling that the tension between text and subtext in the earlier work is best understood retrospectively in the light of the poem which 'psychoanalyses' and finally subsumes and overcomes its predecessors. Because Shelley is, from the beginning, a sentimental and not a naive poet, the tragic understanding of the role of the visionary which becomes explicit in his final poem is latent even in his earlier work. It is first confronted as early as 'Mont Blanc', but in the mode of lyric which, as an abstraction from life, lacks the existential finality conferred by the more extensive and public mode of narrative. It is finally confronted in *The Triumph of Life*, which seems at first to continue

Shelley's sentimental commitment to a defeated idealism, but which proves to be a transitional poem involved in reformulating its own initial assumptions.

The very form of *The Triumph of Life*, which is dialogical and historical rather than annunciatory and mythic, points to a questioning of Shelley's earliest poetic stance not immediately apparent at the beginning of the poem. In the course of Shelley's dialogue with Rousseau a logocentric poem of the soul, which is predictable from *Adonais*, becomes a skeptical and existentialist poem of the self (to borrow a Yeatsian antithesis). This new poem is willing to put in jeopardy the fiction of a transcendental discourse to which Shelley had earlier aspired. It is only one of the many inconsistencies in *The Triumph of Life* that Rousseau, who begins by advising the poet to 'forbear / To join the dance' (ll. 188–9),[5] ends by telling him,

> 'But follow thou, and from spectator turn
> Actor or victim in this wretchedness,
>
> 'And what thou wouldst be taught I then may learn
> From thee.'
>
> (ll. 305–8)

Also of importance is the fact that Rousseau, who described himself as reluctantly and passively 'swept' into the procession of Life, goes on to speak of himself as having 'plunged' actively and voluntarily into a confrontation with the 'cold light' of the Car (ll. 461, 467–8). Similarly the ribald crew which follows the chariot, though it is first shown as physically loathsome in the manner of the denizens of Dante's Hell, is also shown as possessed of an energy that makes it the object of sublimity rather than pathos (ll. 138ff). The poem begins by insisting sentimentally on an idealist separation between the sacred few and the multitude, or as Bloom would have it, between imagination and the fallen nature where the myth must inevitably fail if it attempts to act itself out. But it ends by insisting on the Triumph as a vale of soul-making rather than a vale of tears, a tragic knowledge into which every human being must be initiated.

Of particular interest to the process of revision and reassessment at the heart of the poem are the lines on the bards of elder time:

> 'who truly quelled
>
> 'The passions which they sung, as by their strain
> May well be known: their living melody
> Tempers its own contagion to the vein

'Of those who are infected with it – I
Have suffered what I wrote, or viler pain! –
And so my words were seeds of misery – '

(ll. 274–80)

Syntactically the lines seem to insist on the contrast between the
Arnoldian poet whose suffering is transcended in creation, and the
Keatsian dreamer who vexes the world and prefigures Artaud's equation
of literature with pestilence.[6] In so doing, they suggest that Rousseau's
error can instruct one in how to bring about a catharsis of life. Yet even
as Rousseau speaks the lines, they seem to change their meaning. The
imagery of contagion and infection used of the great bards suggests that
they differ from the dreamers who sow seeds of misery in degree rather
than kind. Where the poem had previously praised the flight of the
sacred few to the realm of the ideal, it now identifies the great bards with
the suffering multitude in such a way as to prepare for the later
recognition that there is something essentially creative even in 'a world
of agony' (l. 295). The metaphor of inoculation replaces an aesthetics of
immunity by one which recognizes the purgative effect of submitting to
contamination. Moreover, the bards, who must *temper* their own
contagion in communicating it, are if anything depicted as suffering what
they write at a higher intensity. Between the initial rejection of life and
the final acceptance of it there is a complex process of revaluation. The
shifting and ambiguous meaning of key images is symptomatic not only
of this process, but also of the fact that the poem's central question
receives no unambiguous answer: Rousseau cannot tell the poet what life
is, for Rousseau is only an externalization of the poet's own self-doubt,
and it is Shelley who must learn through experience the knowledge that
will enable him to teach his specter, and still his doubt.

At the heart of the poem's ambiguity is the nature of the Shape all
light, with its accompanying landscape, and the relation of both to the
shape in the Car of Life. The extremes of interpretation include Allott's
view of the Shape as the Wordsworthian visionary gleam and Bloom's
view of it as fundamentally deceptive and evil.[7] That the same lines
legitimately support such varying interpretations is evidence that the
poem is more complex and undecided than either critic will allow. The
'light diviner than the common Sun' which suffuses the landscape in
which Rousseau has his vision (ll. 335ff.) seems to refer to what Allott
calls 'a Wordsworthian glory in infancy'. Yet the setting of the experience
is not infancy and innocence but rather 'broad day', a setting that seems
to preserve 'a gentle trace / Of light diviner than the common Sun', but
to preserve it only for a moment. Thus one hesitates to say whether the
light divine and the Shape all light are experiences of beauty and
innocence, or whether the landscape of Rousseau's encounter with the

245

Shape is already the landscape of 'this harsh world in which I wake to weep', suffused only by a lingering light. One also hesitates to say whether the light, both fresh and fading, testifies to the Shape as true or as illusory. In a sense there is no question of choosing between interpretations, for both are equally true. One of the points about the Shelleyan as opposed to the Wordsworthian epiphany is that, both in the case of the vision in *Alastor* and in that of the Shape all light, the visionary gleam lacks the transcendental and unequivocal purity that it possess in Wordsworth by virtue of being pushed back into infancy. It is already viewed with the skepticism that attends its being located in a state halfway to experience and yet close to innocence.

The ambiguity carries over into the Shape itself. Allott is true to convention in interpreting the light imagery that surrounds it as an indication of the natural goodness of the Shape. Bloom, following Yeats, insists that Shelley indulged in Blakean inversions of normal image values, preferring night to the unpurged images of day, and using light to signify a hostile if not malevolent force.[8] Again, the ambiguity of the imagery suggests that Shelley approached the mystery of light and life with no clear preconceptions, and the poem is above all a poem of questioning, doubting, and emergent knowledge, a poem in which imagistic ambivalences signal the poet's growing awareness of the fact that the 'valley of perpetual dream' in which the Car of Life is seen and the 'realm without a name' from which the Shape of all light issues (ll. 396–7) are inextricably mingled, and that man must learn to take the measure of good and evil in a world in which all good things are confused with ill. It seems perverse not to accept the naturally positive connotations of the Shape's light. Yet one must also observe the perplexing way in which the Shape anticipates the Car of Life. The powerful lines, 'the fierce splendour / Fell from her as she moved under the mass / Of the deep cavern' (ll. 359–61), make the Shape's dispensation of grace curiously similar to the withering of grace brought on by the Car:

'And the fair shape waned in the coming light
As veil by veil the silent splendour drops
From Lucifer, amid the chrysolite

'Of sunrise . . .'

(ll. 412–15)

The Shape all light remains 'a shape of golden dew' (l. 379) and possesses a beauty we should not ignore. Yet the description of her effect *prior* to the drinking of the Nepenthe contains many disturbing elements:

'As if the gazer's mind was strewn beneath
Her feet like embers, and she, thought by thought,

'Trampled its fires into the dust of death,
As Day upon the threshold of the east
Treads out the lamps of night . . .

'. . . like day she came,
Making the night a dream . . .'

(ll. 386–93)

It is difficult to deny some validity to Bloom's feeling that the image values of night and day are reversed here. Furthermore, the Shape's trampling of the sparks of the mind recalls the manner in which the Car of Life put out the sparks which heaven lit in the sacred few (ll. 207ff.), thus suggesting that the Shape embodies something demonic. But one is also aware, on the other side of the argument, that the trampling of the sparks may be a reminiscence of *Adonais* (l. 464), that if the lines are read in context 'day' and 'light' still carry some of the positive connotations they had in the earlier lines of the vision, and finally that the whole passage on the sun putting out the stars, which Bloom also cites (ll. 76–9),[9] is in fact a carry-over from the uncanceled C-opening printed by Matthews, which carries an unmistakably positive connotation: 'Whilst she, the fairest of the wandering seven / Laughed to behold how in their fiery mirth / The clearest stars were blotted out of heaven.'[10]

In fact, Shelley is deeply ambivalent in his use of night and day imagery, because he is deeply ambivalent about whether truth resides in the ideal or in the reality that desecrates it, and whether Rousseau's career is a victory of darkness over light or of knowledge over innocence and ignorance. As one reads the various uncanceled openings of the poem printed by Matthews, it is evident that, even as he was writing, Shelley's conception of the experience he was describing was undergoing changes. The value system of the B-version is relatively simple. At the beginning, the sun is described as coming out of the shade of night, as a spirit of glory and good which rouses the earth 'out of the gloom / Of daily life'. Presumably the poem, as Shelley here conceives it, is to consist of a contrast between the paradisal light of Wordsworthian nature and the inferno of the procession, between vital and daily life; and as the enthusiasm and length of the natural description indicate, the spirit of good is ultimately to triumph over the shade of night. 'Life' may still be what it is in the essay 'On Life'. The first half of the C-version of the opening more or less repeats the tone of optimistic celebration, but a darker note begins to impinge on the poetry with the strange lines that describe the world rising out of the death of daily life as bearing 'Its portion in the *ruin* of repose'. Shelley in fact goes on to suggest the deceptiveness of beauty in such phrases as 'false wind' and 'flattering wave'. But the note of doubt is quickly suppressed and Shelley returns to his initial image of the sun leaving behind the night, in the line 'Before me rose the day, behind the night.'

Yet the mingling of glory and doubt present in this version carries over into the final E-version which forms the present opening of the poem, where the line just quoted is curiously reversed: 'before me fled / The night; behind me rose the day' (ll. 26–7). It is now the day and not the night which is behind the speaker, and the night and not the day which lies ahead of him. Thus it would seem, if we accept the conventional connotations of night and day, that the positive direction of the poem has been reversed, and that the speaker is passing from the spirit of good into the empire of evil. Yet the matter is not so simple, because within the new line itself, there is a curious reversal of verbs. If the day is behind and the night is ahead, it is the day which should be described as fleeing and the night which should be rising. Yet it is the approaching night which flees and the receding day which rises. Thus within the new version, which has the dreamer moving from day to night, the old version, which has him moving from night to day, is still retained.

The verbal confusion indicates a deepening ambivalence on Shelley's part as to the truth-value of light and dark terms. It suggests that as he approaches his vision he is uncertain as to whether it has the status of a revelation of the way things are or a demonic parody of the way things should be. This ambivalence, as I shall argue, is the core of truth that Shelley discovers in his descent to the Hades of his career. He enters his vision as Keats enters his purgatory blind, unable to take the measure of light and dark. The heaven is above his head, but the deep is at his feet, and the truth that he will learn may lead him in either direction. Had he completed the poem, contradiction might have been translated into an ambivalent but coherent image of what life is: a skeptical but strong image which encompasses both the ideal and its possible negation, and one which sees both the epiphanic falling of the mask of darkness from the awakened earth and the stripping away of mask after mask of illusion by Life as simultaneous truths (ll. 3–4, 536–7).

Bloom's view of the poem as enacting a failure is dependent on making Rousseau embody a position to be rejected. Yet he is a complex figure whose self-awareness distinguishes him from Shelley's earlier visionaries, and his interpretation of the procession is a strange mixture of self-rejection in which he sees himself as defeated and condemned to the Inferno, and self-justification in which he distinguishes himself from other members of the procession and almost sees his suffering as redeemable. It is Rousseau who describes himself as corrupted and stained. But it is the same Rousseau who separates himself from Life's other victims when he says, 'I was overcome / By my own heart alone' (ll. 240–1), implying that the heart which has the power to be weak may have the power to be strong again through the force of its own self-knowledge. Rousseau's revision of his self-image within the poem is indicative of the fact that *The Triumph of Life* is a poem in the process of understanding and assessing the experience it describes. He may begin by seeing the capacity of his writing to infect as an emblem of the defeat of all that artistic creation should be: the best and happiest thoughts of the best minds. Yet only a few lines later he says almost the opposite in the triumphant words 'I / Am one of those who have created, even / If it be but a world of agony' (ll. 293-5). What Shelley seems to be doing here, in admitting a second kind of nonideal art, is to redeem Rousseau (and therefore himself) from the world of the procession to which he had earlier consigned him, and to suggest that he possess a purgatorial wisdom. The process is analogous to that by which Keats softens Moneta's hard distinction between poets who pour out a balm upon the world and dreamers who vex it, and suggests not only that dreamers can become poets, but that all poets must first be dreamers who submit to the giant agony of the world. The poem as it stands provides no explicit way of transcending a world which describes the defeat of imagination. But it is not difficult to see in what direction Shelley was moving. The encounter between Rousseau and his former self provides an implicit paradigm for the way in which the poet's encounter with his own defeated earlier self is meant to function. Rousseau's interior dialogue leads to a reappraisal of Romantic idealism that releases him from the punishment which attends overidealization, the 'deep night' that traps those who have feigned a 'morn of truth' (ll. 214–15). Shelley's encounter with Rousseau is likewise meant to provide him with a way of confronting his own myth of a Promethean art and revising it in such a way that it does not fall victim to the inevitable disillusion that follows the failure to attain the ideal.

The point of Rousseau's lines about the creation of a world of agony, and the point also of the description of the car's harsh light as its 'creative ray' (l. 533), is that the vision of the Inferno is a necessary initiation without which life is not complete. Unlike Irving Babbitt, who sees Rousseau as the victim of an untempered overidealization and feels that the sacred few like himself can escape the errors of Romanticism,[11] the author of *The Triumph of Life* argues that the appalling process by which the ideal Shape becomes the hideousness that it seeks to repress is an experience that strikes Plato and Rousseau alike. The Car of Life has the quality of a revelation, is described as 'the coming light' and as having majesty and 'rushing splendour' (ll. 412, 87), because it is inevitable and necessary, like Keats's awakening from the fair grove to the terrifying ancient sanctuary at the beginning of *The Fall of Hyperion*. The Car is driven by a blind charioteer, not because it represents anything as facile as the blindness of institutions, but because, like blind justice, it impartially compels everyone to submit to its revelation. It is not so much horrible as terrible, using the distinction as Heath-Stubbs uses it, to signify by the horrible, the uncomprehending stare into a disintegrating world, and by the terrible an intellectual comprehension of the dark elements in experience[12] such as Shelley himself found in Dante but not in Michelangelo.[13] Like De Quincey's terrible *Mater Tenebrarum*, the Car is sent to man 'to plague his heart' until it has 'unfolded the capacities of his spirit'[14] through an agony that is creative.

Yet the ambivalence of the light-dark imagery does not only confer a truth value upon the vision of darkness in the Car. It also asserts, by dividing the light imagery equally between the Wordsworthian sun of the opening and the Car of Life, that truth is on both sides, in the terrible and chaotic and also in the beautiful and harmonious, in Apollo as well as Dionysos. There is finally nothing in the poem which says that the 'new vision, never seen before' (l. 411) is truer than the old vision it replaces. If the language used to describe the Car is already present in the language used to describe the Shape all light, then the reverse is also true: 'So knew I in that light's severe excess / The presence of that shape which on the stream / Moved, as I moved along the wilderness' (ll. 424–6; cf. ll. 97–8).

If Shelley had in any sense planned to follow the usual pattern of dream-visions, the poem could not have been intended to end with the passing of the Car, but would have returned to the purgatorial landscape of the opening, with the deep below and the possibility of heaven above. It is not Shelley's life but Rousseau's which ends in the Inferno – although even he acquires a purgatorial status that sets him above the inhabitants of the 'obvious valley' (l. 539).[15] But Rousseau's life is contained within something larger, namely Shelley's vision, and whereas Rousseau in his life awakes from the heaven of the visionary gleam to the hell of the Car of Life, Shelley, one must assume, would have awakened from the harsh world of his dream to the sweeter landscape of the very opening lines.

In other words, the infernal vision should not be seen as the final image of the poem, but rather as something with which the dreamer must come to terms: something which he must recognize as a perpetual possibility behind the Apollonian world of order and harmony governed by 'the Sun their father' that the poet envisages in the opening (l. 18). Rousseau's life does indeed detail the defeat of the Promethean myth, but Shelley's poem is not about a defeat but rather about the inner process by which the dreamer inspects the image of that defeat and seeks to know why it is so. Rousseau, significantly, does not make a final judgment on the illusoriness of the good:

'Whether my life had been before that sleep
The Heaven which I imagine, or a Hell
Like the harsh world in which I wake to weep,

'I know not.'

(ll. 332–5)

The word 'imagine' is not in the past tense, and Rousseau seems to draw back from complete defeatism. Or to put it differently, the infernal vision is mediated by the maturer Rousseau whose tentative and yet uncertain reinterpretation of his life precedes his actual account of it, and the mediation converts the infernal into the purgatorial, the agony into creation. Through the use of two framing visions (Shelley's and Rousseau's), which move in opposite directions between surface and depth, the poem thematizes the representation of life through art, and suggests that the function of art is the reconstruction of appearances as well as the disclosure of the Dionysiac knowledge that lies behind them.

There is, therefore, a kind of logic in the fact that Rousseau introduces the most terrible part of his vision of the waning of beauty with a reference to Dante's ascent to Paradise (ll. 472–9). But the reader also recognizes that the Dantesque pattern of a steady ascent from darkness to light is inappropriate to a poem which is characterized by a constantly shifting use of light and dark values and by a constant oscillation between the moment of vision and the waning of beauty. For Dante, whose guides know the moral geography of their universe, the vision of darkness and the vision of love are successive moments in the history of a spirit that believes in ascent and transcendence. For Shelley, led by a guide whose own self-image changes in the course of his narration, the outcome of the journey inevitably remains more in doubt. That is as it must be in a world where the knowledge one has is not received from a steady source of light above, but generated through an internal dramaturgy which has the soul confront the specter of its own self-doubt. The image of Life as a kind of Janus-faced power, deeply ambivalent and turned toward death as well as life, toward Dionysos as well as Apollo, is an ultimately skeptical one and promises no progress toward secular or sacred perfection. It demands a faith which recognizes that at any moment the Shape all light may again become the infernal Shape, and that such reversals are not merely temporary arrests in the progress toward the far goal of time but part of the shape of truth. Holistic ideals such as the love associated with Dante and Prometheus cannot redeem a world so lacking in serenity, because they require a simplification of the Janus-faced image and a purgation of that which gives it its dynamism. The agent of redemption is rather something which might be called the purgatorial imagination, an imagination that derives its power from the very manner in which it finds itself containing the reality that is to deconstruct it. Shelley's final poem does not deny the possibility of an optimism in which we are our own gods. But to be our own gods is also to submit to the lasting misery and loneliness of the world, and as Rilke said of the artist, to have the courage to walk beside our devils as in a triumph.

In his letters Rilke speaks of our tendency to convert death and darkness into external devils, so as to exclude from our search for meaning that which is 'so close to us that the distance between it and the inner centre of our hearts cannot be registered'. Yet we end by internalizing these elements, because we know that life has no meaning without death and light no meaning without darkness:

> Since the dawn of time man has fashioned gods in whom the deadly, the threatening, the annihilating and the terrible elements of life were contained, its power, its fury, its daemonic possessiveness – all amassed in one dense, malevolent concentration – something alien to us, if you will, yet at the same time permitting us to recognise it, to suffer it, even to acknowledge it for the sake of a certain mysterious kinship and involvement with it: [for] this also was part of us, only we did not know how to cope with this side of our experience; it was too massive, too dangerous.[16]

In *The Triumph of Life* Shelley moves toward an internalization of the destructive, Dionysiac element in experience which is very far from those beautiful idealisms of moral excellence which his idealistic aesthetic theory claims it is the function of the poet to provide. Yet Shelley's final poem is to a certain extent an emancipation of his imagination, and Bostetter is not wholly wrong in his comment that the basic Shelleyan conception, as it emerges elsewhere, is 'of a flowing together. . . . All things are drawn together, whether human beings or elements of nature. . . . But only the good and beautiful parts are so drawn, pulled away from the evil, ugly, painful and violent.'[17] Shelley's theory of imagination in 'A Defence of Poetry', like his theory of the epipsyche in the essay 'On Love', is generally taken to be a naive, logocentric theory which emphasizes the unity of the poetic experience and its participation in 'the eternal, the infinite, and the one'.[18] Shelley's poetics, according to John Bayley, seeks to exclude those discords of the real world which damage his sense of primal unity, and thus cuts itself off from 'everything that might give sense and weight to such a unity'.[19] The definition of the epipsyche, linked in Shelley's mind with the activity of the poetic psyche, is of an impossibly selective mirror: 'a mirror whose surface reflects only the forms of purity and brightness; a soul within our soul that describes a circle around its proper paradise which pain, and sorrow, and evil dare not overleap'.[20]

More accurate, however, than this post-Victorian view of Shelley is the comment by D.G. James already cited,* that Shelley's tendency to argue for the exclusion or ultimate powerlessness of evil coexists oddly with a considerable honesty about the existence of evil in the world. In the course of a few lines in *Alastor* the narrator claims that the world is 'this so lovely world' (l. 686), that 'Heartless things / Are done and said i' the world' (ll. 690–1), that worms inherit the earth (ll. 691–2), and that the symphony of nature 'Lifts still its solemn voice' (ll. 694–5). James's point is that Shelley's poetry, which does not weave a circle around the poetic *logos* and yet acts as though it does, is constructed around a lacuna between rhetoric and content. Shelley, in other words, is never properly the naive spirit envisioned by Bayley and Bostetter. The unresolved contradiction between the theory of art and the poetry of experience leads to the presence, in the earlier poems, of repressed subtexts which challenge and interrupt the logic of the text, even as they contain in embryo the knowledge that will be made explicit in *The Triumph of Life*. *Alastor* is an appropriate poem to consider at this point because it includes the same narrative elements as *The Triumph of Life*: the visionary, the ambiguous female Shape, and a narrator who, as *spectator ab extra*, functions as an implied reader within the poem. It contains almost the same spectrum of imagery that is present in *The Triumph of Life*. The 'bright silver dream' is mixed with visions of charnels and coffins (ll. 67, 24), the calm sky with the dark ocean (ll, 340–4), and the moment of epiphany with the consciousness of a world that is ruled by a sightless and 'colossal Skeleton' (ll. 610–15). The poem moves beyond the naive, almost to the threshold of the tragic. What distinguishes it from *The Triumph of Life* is the sentimental manner in which its narrator relates the light and dark elements of his universe. He leaves the image of the Poet 'Gentle, and brave, and generous' (l. 58), somehow untouched by the dark and sometimes demonic uncertainties of his journey, and purports to present an exemplary life even as he deconstructs his own idealization.

James's observation goes to the heart of Shelley's view of literature, which is itself less naive than it seems, and which mirrors the problematics of the poetry prior to *The Triumph of Life* in conflating mimetic and expressive theories that tend to contradict each other. While Shelley's poetic theory is not self-conscious enough to provide us with an explicit terminology in which to discuss his poetry, its tensions and contradictions serve as a useful introduction to similar tensions which

---

* [Ed. Earlier in *Dark Interpreter*; work cited is *The Romantic Comedy* (London: Oxford University Press, 1948), p. 96.]

will emerge when we discuss the earlier poetry. On the one hand, poetry is described in terms of light and lightning imagery that makes it a transforming and renovating force: it is among other things 'a sword of lightning' and the 'light of life', an 'immortal god' which descends 'for the redemption of mortal passion'.[21] But on the other hand, it is a mirror 'in which the spectator beholds himself . . . it teaches . . . self-knowledge and self-respect'.[22] The immediate occasion for the insistence on poetry as mimesis is Peacock's ironic attempt to demystify poetry by identifying it with a maximum of self-mystification. Shelley can make no claim for the high seriousness of poetry without grounding it in the world of truth, by defining it as an imitation of the real world. Yet he has the prophetic artist's impatience with subservience to present fact, and must also argue that poetry is an expressive outward projection of the golden world within. The result is a view of poetry as a mirror which is somehow also a lamp, a mirror which is not mimetic because it eschews fact, and instead of reflecting, 'makes beautiful' what is distorted:[23] 'The drama, so long as it continues to express poetry, is as a prismatic and many-sided mirror, which collects the brightest rays of human nature.' The mirror is therefore not one in which the spectator 'beholds himself', but one in which he beholds the epipsyche that he 'would become': 'The tragedies of the Athenian poets are as mirrors in which the spectator beholds himself, under a thin disguise of circumstance, stript of all but that ideal perfection and energy which every one feels to be the internal type of all that he loves, admires, and would become.'[24]

The passive mirror, as Shelley uses it elsewhere, does not necessarily supply us with an image of 'our entire self, yet deprived of all that we condemn or despise'.[25] It can become indifferently the Tower of Famine absorbing the surrounding desolation, or the mind of the hero of 'Marenghi', which grows like the immeasurable heaven it contemplates (l. 135).[26] Yet what Shelley seems to insist on in the 'Defence of Poetry' is the impossible concept of a mirror that has the power actually to transform what it reflects into the ideal. The conflation of realistic and idealistic theories may be a semantic accident, but it also goes to the heart of a recurrent aesthetic dilemma. In the impossible identity of mirror and lamp we encounter yet another attempt to submerge Dionysos in Apollo, and to silence an inevitable dialogue between the veil of language and the knowledge of life.

The disjunctive presence of a realistic poetics alongside a visionary poetics marks 'A Defence of Poetry' as a sentimental text, which engages in strategies of self-avoidance to escape being consumed by its own contradictions. It suggests, in turn, that Shelley's visionary narratives (*Alastor, Adonais, Epipsychidion*)[27] also communicate disjunctively, as products of a poetic consciousness that exists on two different levels of awareness. Critics have noted a contradiction between the preface to

*Alastor*, which seems to condemn the Poet, and the poem itself, which seems to put him forward as a pattern of virtue.[28] Within *Alastor* itself, there is a curious dissociation of sensibility which causes the poem to move in two contradictory directions. The facts of the narrative lead toward the hero's death, the failure of his quest, perhaps even the recognition of it as misguided. But the poetic sentiment idealizes that 'surpassing Spirit' (l. 714) who is seen in death as the animating force in nature, even though his life had been an existence debarred from nature's living images. There is a troubled ambivalence in the poem which is symptomatic of the dialogue of Shelley's mind with itself. But the dialogue seems to stop well short of the sort of self-awareness that Wasserman envisages in his interpretation of the poem as a skeptical debate between an empirical narrator and an idealist poet. *Alastor* is not an ironic poem in which Shelley has two points of view disciplining each other, 'like the Yeatsian self and the anti-self to prevent deception and to load either position with risks.'[29] Although this characterization too is inadequate, the poem is closer to being a work in which Shelley seeks to push back the encroachments of sad reality onto his beautiful idealism of moral excellence, and perhaps recognizing the impossibility of doing so, retreats into the moral censures of the preface without being able to abandon completely his view of the Poet as an ideal being.[30]

The narrator and the Poet, far from representing contrary positions, are essentially similar beings, like Wordsworth and his younger sibling in 'Tintern Abbey'. The dialogical tendencies inherent in the form of frame-narration are thus diminished by the fact that dialogue is conceived on the sentimental model of kinship and affinity rather than dissent: the emotional kinship of an older survivor with his lost and defeated younger self. Just as the Poet has pursued 'Nature's most secret steps / . . . like her shadow', the narrator has sought to unveil the 'inmost sanctuary' of nature (ll. 81–2, 37–8). Just as the Poet is already 'alienated' (l. 76) even at the period when he is alleged to be in harmony with nature, the narrator is a 'desperate alchymist' (l. 31) who seems curiously ill at ease in his Wordsworthian environment. The conclusion suggests itself that the Poet is not the narrator's opposite but his epipsyche, that the relationship between the narrator and the Poet thus duplicates the relationship between the Poet and his epipsyche, and that both function as narrative paradigms for the relationship between poet and poem in the creative act. In the same way as the Poet's epipsyche fails to take him beyond himself into a higher, less ambiguous, perfected self, so the narrator's epipsyche fails to still his 'obstinate questionings' (l. 26) by taking him beyond his peculiarly mixed existence of 'awful talk' and 'innocent love' (ll. 33–4), into the pure unmixed innocence that he seeks through the Poet and images in the two swans (ll. 275ff.). The Poet continues trying to still his obstinate questionings by pursuing his epipsyche; and the narrator too tries to mask the central failure of *his* quest by idealizing a being whose frail power is no more than a 'decaying flame' (l. 247), a fading coal.

At the heart of the poem's failure is its inability to come to terms with the deeply ambivalent nature of the epipsyche and of life itself, because of a belief that poetry should avoid ambivalence and depict life in a more simple and perfect form: 'the image of life expressed in its eternal truth'.[31] Shelley was obviously sensitive to the ambivalence of life. Yet as Milton Wilson points out, the skepticism that characterizes him as a thinker tends to be minimized in his poetry.[32] The Poet of *Alastor* is seen as impossibly perfect:

> all of great
> Or good, or lovely, which the sacred past
> In truth or fable consecrates, he felt
> And knew.
>
> (ll. 72–5)

Yet the same Poet's vision of the epipsyche is a deeply ambiguous and troubling experience. It does not simply offer him 'Knowledge and truth and virtue . . . / . . . and poesy' (ll. 158–60). It seems to couple 'truth' with a terrible and convulsive experience, which points toward the abyss and toward a deep truth which the author of 'A Defence of Poetry' does not contemplate:

> Does the bright arch of rainbow clouds,
> And pendent mountain seen in the calm lake,
> Lead only to a black and watery depth?
>
> (ll. 213–15)

The ideal is grasped, as in 'Hymn to Intellectual Beauty', as a dark shadow and not as a bright substance ('Hymn', ll. 59–60); its effect is like that of the Shape in *The Triumph of Life*, who strews the gazer's mind 'beneath / Her feet like embers' (*Triumph*, ll. 386–7). Where the vision comes from and what it is are uncertain: whether it is a product of innocence or experience, a vision that comes from the platonic realm without a name, or a projection from within that must inevitably be haunted by the possibility of its own death because it is born of a mortal source. The epipsyche, which is intended as a more perfect form of an already perfect Poet, seems instead to show the Poet an ambivalence in himself, and to point him toward his own 'treacherous likeness' (*Alastor*, l. 474), his own soul and its doubts.

The peculiar and terrifying vacancy that descends on the Poet after this experience is a product of the need to blot out the content of his vision.

This need is imposed by the inherited association of vision with illusion. Yet the duality of the Shelleyan epipsyche externalizes as image what is recognized intellectually by theorists such as Sartre, who see in the act of imagination something profoundly destructive and self-annihilating. Because the need to imagine an ideal arises only from the fact that this ideal is not possessed, because the imagination thereby posits its object as absent or even nonexistent, the imagination must enter its own nothingness to disclose the very reality that it seeks to transform. Although elegy is a sentimental form, the existence of *Alastor* in the mode of elegy rather than prelude and manifesto (like *Epipsychidion*) tacitly concedes the nothingness and death at the heart of the vision. *The Triumph of Life*, in which Shelley has revised his concept of art to include suffering as well as joy, reveals how the doubleness of imagination can become a source of both triumph and limitation to the poet. But the Poet of *Alastor* can accept kinship only to the beautiful, and as a result the bright flowers depart from his steps (ll. 536–7), as the joy drops from the forms of the multitude in *The Triumph of Life*.

A troubling ambiguity about whether the source of vision is internal or external is of crucial importance here. The narrator seems to invoke an external source of inspiration, the 'Great Parent' (l. 45), so as to convince himself that his epipsyche (the Poet) is real, and that his exaltation of the Poet is not just

> the dream
> Of dark magician in his visioned cave,
> Raking the cinders of a crucible
> For life and power.
>
> (ll. 681–4)

Yet the source of his vision seems to be a phantasm that 'Has shone within me' (ll. 40–1). A similar ambiguity arises in the case of the Poet's epipsyche. It appears to be sent by 'The spirit of sweet human love' (l. 203). Yet as he follows it he obeys 'the light / That shone within his soul' (ll. 492–3). For the Poet as for the narrator, the external source seems reassuring, while the internal source opens up a world of doubts and ambiguities:

> Hither the Poet came. His eyes beheld
> Their own wan light through the reflected lines
> Of his thin hair, distinct in the dark depth
> Of that still fountain; as the human heart,

Gazing in dreams over the gloomy grave,
Sees its own treacherous likeness there.

(ll. 469–74)

Because the internalization of vision does not mark a belief in the self as a source of value, so much as a doubt as to the reality of the ideal, Poet and narrator constantly mistake inner vision (or imagination) for external vision (or perception). Wordsworth sought to argue that the imagination could bestow a light on external nature and yet received that light *from* nature, because the act of perception was a cooperation of inner and outer lights in which a value projected from within already existed outside. But Shelley's similar desire to hypostatize vision by transferring it to the external world relies on a confusion rather than a cooperation of epistemological theories. As we have seen in 'A Defence of Poetry', the active process of illuminating something is mistakenly felt as a passive mirroring of ideal forms, so that imagination can claim for itself the assurance that what it is illuminating is really there. Thus, when Shelley actually faces the possibility that the source of vision may be within, he seems to be struck with a sense that his dreams are *pure* projection, with no corresponding form in the external world. His characteristic image for inner vision is not the light which radiates outwards (an image which he feels compelled to use in conjunction with the mirror), but the magician groping in his cave,[33] an image that Plato has loaded with skeptical implications, and the related image of a dark well, which has narcissistic overtones (*Alastor*, ll. 457–74). From the doubt that the possibility of inner vision seems to raise, there arises the basic structure of the Shelleyan quest as an idealism which evades skepticism, a search for an external ideal which evades the intentionality and ambiguity of an image projected from within. But the fact that Shelley must rely on a logical sleight-of-hand to protect his vision from its own solipsism invites the reader to see through his strategy, and perhaps marks Shelley's incipient questioning of his own idealism.

Yeats, who depicted Shelley as governed by a desire for synthesis, and as seeking through the image of a visionary moving 'among yellowing corn or under overhanging grapes' a mask for what he was not, suggests that Shelley uses 'automatonism' or the evasion of inner conflict to 'hide' from himself and others the 'separation and disorder' that lie behind his representation of the ideal poet.[34] Automatonism is perhaps a useful characterization of the psychology of the sentimental text, which is oriented toward idealization, yet objectifies the total content of the psyche, and which must therefore replace censorship with blindness. *Alastor* evades its own recognition on two levels. The Poet, like Prince Athanase, seems not to know that he is being consumed by a strange suffering, for 'there was drawn an adamantine veil / Between his heart and mind' ('Athanase', ll. 87–8). The narrator seems to know, but not wholly to face, the mortality of his epipsyche. The veil, adamantine in resistance to its own transparency, marks the unenforceable psychological bifurcation by which conscious representation seeks to be innocent of what it contains.

The peculiar misprision of interior projection as external vision is one means which the poem uses to avoid the nothingness of its own idealism. The surface conformity of the poem to the pattern of quest narrative, which is oriented toward an external goal, seems to confirm this misprision. Again, the fact that the narrator must depict the Poet's boat as entering the whirlpool twice suggests an initial reluctance to confront the destructive force of the poem's imagery. Moreover the emphasis on the ascending movement of the whirlpool, which is described as rising 'Stair above stair' (l. 380), reveals a desperate (if unsuccessful) attempt to wrest from nothingness a kind of ascent toward epiphany which reaches its climax in the celebration of the Poet as a 'surpassing Spirit' (l. 714). Similar in spirit is the ending of *Epipsychidion*, where the elision of death in a Wagnerian *liebestod* conflates nihilism with ecstasy and reveals a view of poetry as the alchemical conversion of existence into its opposite, the narrative of particular facts into poetry. .

The rhetoric of *Epipsychidion* claims to transform death into life, and therefore the real into the ideal. Because the poem is written in the first person, there is, moreover, no *external* vantage point from which to take a bearing on the self-enclosed rhetoric of a visionary discourse. But *Alastor* differs from the later poem through the inclusion of a narrator who survives the visionary, and remains to perceive immortality as death, thus becoming the reference point for the reader's deconstruction of the literal meaning behind the narrator's sentimentalized and figurative representation of the Poet's career. In *Adonais*, similarly about the death of imagination, the skeptical distancing of questioner from visionary through the separation of the mourners from Adonais himself is finally annulled when the mourner (Shelley) sentimentally transcends his own perception of temporality to merge with the Poet. But in *Alastor* the Poet's death returns the narrator (despite himself) to those disturbing charnels and coffins that he had sought to evade by turning his attention to something outside himself. It thus internalizes the darkness of the epipsyche as a darkness which haunts the very act of representation, considered as a flight from the nothingness of consciousness to substance and immortality. Unlike the two swans – the psyche and epipsyche present to each other in the physical plenitude of nature – the narrator reaches the Poet only through an act of imagination, which sets the latter in the space of the unreal. Whether the Poet has a historical existence is unclear. The poem's overt form as biography and quest masks its real existence as meditation and dream (l. 682). Poet and narrator never meet, and the Poet's death is thus only the consolidation of a vacancy which from the beginning lies concealed in the narrator's elegiac attempt to represent an absent Poet as embodying the living presence of his vision. Significantly, although the narrator tries to evade the nothingness of his 'dream / Of youth' (ll. 669–70) by making a phantom of the actual world and postponing reality to some afterworld that the Poet is presumed to inhabit (ll. 696ff.), he perceives the Poet in the materialist, almost atheistic language of decomposition. This depiction of the Poet undermines the poem's concluding sentimental assertion of a higher transcendent realm with reference to which the fiction of a logocentric discourse can be preserved.

The climactic image in which the Poet's body is represented as a wind-harp (ll. 703–5) takes us to the point where the poem's idealization verges on its own deconstruction. We cannot but be aware that the 'divinest lineaments' of the Poet, through which the wind plays, are in fact the remains of his decaying corpse. Because the lute is a metaphor for poetry, and because the narrator had previously compared himself to a lyre (l. 42), the image seems to sum up and expose the relationship between figure and ground that has characterized the poem from its opening. In 'A Defence of Poetry' Shelley distinguishes between the narrative of actuality and poetic narrative: the one is 'a mirror which obscures and distorts that which *should* be beautiful', while the other is 'a mirror which makes beautiful that which *is* distorted'.[35] But here the attempted sublimation of reality through image and figure is grotesque, not 'poetic'. By a kind of downward transformation, it draws attention to the very reality it had intended to transmute and reveals 'the secrets of anatomy and corruption' behind the 'surface' of poetry.[36] The image, finally, becomes a focus for the inadequacy of the poetic process, as Shelley defines it, to cope with the world, as he envisages it.

What Yeats called automatonism perhaps enables Shelley to elide the deconstruction of idealism consequent upon including within a rhetorically single-minded text, a conflict of epistemological perspectives or an incompatibility of figure and meaning. But the term 'automatonism' also suggests the failure of the dialectical separation of mask from life, of epipsyche from psyche. By its very transparency, the sentimentality of this poem verges on irony and invites the reader to assume the role later assumed by Rousseau, who makes explicit the subtext of vision which is the knowledge within imagination. Whether a final deconstruction of its idealism is intended by Shelley to be part of the hermeneutics of his text is extraordinarily difficult to say.[37] The inclusion of a preface thematizes the act of reading, and may thus provoke in the reader a critical self-consciousness (similar to the alienation effect in drama) toward the poem's aesthetics and its sentimental depiction of its two central figures. But Shelley also seeks to make this critical distance impossible, through conventions of elegy which demand the reader's sympathy and assent, his emotional identification with the narrator in the communion of grief. This incipient but incomplete insight is what makes the sentimental text so problematical, and at the same time so pivotal, in the nineteenth century's reexamination of an idealist aesthetics.

## Notes

1. MARTIN PRICE, *To the Palace of Wisdom: Studies in Order and Energy from Dryden to Blake* (New York: Doubleday, 1965), p. 438.

2. C.E. PULOS, *The Deep Truth: A Study of Shelley's Scepticism* (Lincoln: University of Nebraska Press, 1954); Earl Wasserman, *Shelley: A Critical Reading* (Baltimore: Johns Hopkins University Press, 1971). While Wasserman discusses Shelley's skepticism at length, he seems to regard it as intermediate rather than terminal; a way of strengthening the idealism which is Shelley's final position.

3. HAROLD BLOOM, *Shelley's Mythmaking* (1959; repr. Ithaca: Cornell University Press, 1969), p. 93; DANIEL HUGHES, 'Kindling and Dwindling: The Poetic Process in Shelley', *Keats-Shelley Journal*, 13 (1964): 17. Ross Woodman, who sees *Adonais* rather than *Prometheus Unbound* as the poem which best sums up Shelley's vision, treats *The Triumph of Life* as a version of *Adonais*, which confirms rather than questions the logocentrism of Shelley's poetry hitherto (*The Apocalyptic Vision in the Poetry of Shelley*, Toronto: University of Toronto Press, 1964, pp. 180–98).

4. SHELLEY, 'A Defence of Poetry', *Shelley's Prose*, ed. D.L. Clark (1954; corrected edn Albuquerque: University of New Mexico Press, 1966), hereafter *Prose*, p. 291. I have borrowed the terms 'radical' and 'platonic' from Milton Wilson, who uses them to indicate respectively the belief in immediate attainment of the millennium and the postponement of this attainment to the afterlife (*Shelley's Later Poetry: A Study of His Prophetic Imagination*, New York: Columbia University Press, 1959; pp. 176–7).

5. References to *The Triumph of Life* are to the edition by DONALD REIMAN, in his *Shelley's 'Triumph of Life': A Critical Study* (Urbana: University of Illinois Press, 1965).

6. ANTONIN ARTAUD, *Le théâtre et son double*, (1938; repr. Paris: Gallimard, 1969), p. 42.

7. KENNETH ALLOTT, 'Bloom on "The Triumph of Life"', *Essays in Criticism*, **10** (1960): 224; BLOOM, *Shelley's Mythmaking*, pp. 265ff.

8. ALLOTT, 'Bloom on "The Triumph of Life"', p. 266; BLOOM, *Shelley's Mythmaking*, p. 270.

9. BLOOM, *Shelley's Mythmaking*, p. 270.

10. G.M. Matthews, 'The "Triumph of Life" Apocrypha', *Times Literary Supplement*, (5 August 1960): 503.

11. IRVING BABBITT, *Rousseau and Romanticism* (New York: Houghton Mifflin, 1919).

12. JOHN HEATH-STUBBS, *The Darkling Plain* (London: Eyre & Spottiswoode, 1950), pp. 58–9. The horrible is a 'spiritual cowardice' which shrinks from contemplating suffering, the distortion of the soul, and the perversion of beauty.

13. SHELLEY, *The Complete Works*, ed. Roger Ingpen and W.E. Peck (London: Ernest Benn, 1926–30), X, pp. 32–3.

14. DE QUINCEY, *Suspiria de Profundis*, *The Collected Writings of Thomas de Quincey*, ed. David Masson (London: A. and C. Black, 1897), XVI, p. 32.

15. Another indication of the way in which the figure of Rousseau undergoes revision in the course of the poem itself is seen in the fact that Rousseau speaks of not knowing 'Whither the conqueror hurries me' (l. 304), but in the end seems to have detached himself from the procession, which passes on without him: 'The cripple cast / His eye upon the car which now had rolled / Onward, as if that look must be the last' (ll. 544–6).

16. RILKE, *Selected Letters of Rainer Maria Rilke 1902–1926*, trans. R.F.C. Hull (London: Macmillan, 1947), p. 265.

17. EDWARD BOSTETTER, *The Romantic Ventriloquists* (Seattle: University of Washington Press, 1963, revised edn 1975), p. 216.

18. SHELLEY, 'A Defence of Poetry', p. 279.

19. JOHN BAYLEY, *The Romantic Survival: A Study of Poetic Evolution* (London: Constable, 1957), p. 43.

20. SHELLEY, 'On Love', *Prose*, p. 170.

21. SHELLEY, 'A Defence of Poetry', pp. 285, 286; 'Preface to *The Cenci*', *Poetical Works*, ed. Thomas Hutchinson (1905; rpt. Oxford: Clarendon Press, 1967), p. 277. Shelley's poems, other than *The Triumph of Life*, are cited from this edition.

22. SHELLEY, 'A Defence of Poetry', p. 285.

23. Ibid., p. 281.

24. Ibid., p. 285.

25. SHELLEY, 'On Love', p. 170.

26. The idea of growing like what one contemplates turns up repeatedly in Shelley. In 'Prince Athanase', as in 'Marenghi', it is used idealistically to mean reflection of bright creations ('Prince Athanase', ll. 139–41). But in *Prometheus Unbound* it is used in the opposite way, 'Whilst I behold such execrable shapes, / Methinks I grow like what I contemplate' (I, 449–50). Cf. also *The Cenci*, V, iv, 30–1.

27. Though I deal only with *Alastor*, my method of analysis can be applied to the other two works, which are also sentimental poems.

28. For instance R.D. HAVENS, 'Shelley's "Alastor"', *PMLA*, **44** (1930): 1098–115.

29. WASSERMAN, *Shelley*, p. 34.

30. Both Wasserman and Albert Gérard tend to see *Alastor* as a full-fledged

debate. Wasserman finds two opposing (and clarified) points of view within the poem. Gérard finds a similar debate between German idealism and English respect for nature, the latter point of view being found (presumably) in the preface, since the poem itself is a 'demonstration *a contrario* where the hero is made to follow the logic of idealism to its ultimate developments' ('Alastor, or the Spirit of Solipsism', *Philological Quarterly*, **33** (1954): 219). The preface does, it is true, reveal an incipient desire on Shelley's part to dissociate himself from his hero, a desire which counteracts the Shelley-narrator's concluding identification of himself with the Poet through the lyre image. But the central problem in the poem is surely not solved by saying that the Poet should have been a man speaking to men. And indeed so unsatisfactory is this way of condemning him that Shelley immediately goes on to condemn the multitude with whom the Poet should have associated himself as blind, torpid, and above all (like the Poet himself) selfish. In so doing he is compelled once again to exalt the Poet as one who was good and died young, and his impulse toward dissociation ends by reassociating him with what he nevertheless dimly perceives to be inadequate.

31. SHELLEY, 'A Defence of Poetry', p. 281.

32. WILSON, *Shelley's Later Poetry*, p. 219.

33. *Alastor*, ll. 681–4; 'Mont Blanc', ll. 44–8; 'Hymn to Intellectual Beauty', ll. 49–52.

34. W.B. YEATS, *A Vision* (London: Macmillan, 1936), pp. 108–9, 141–4, 95.

35. SHELLEY, 'A Defence of Poetry', p. 281. Italics mine.

36. Ibid., p. 293.

37. The problem here is not whether *Alastor can* be read as partly ironic, but whether its *intention* is sentimental or ironic: whether the irony is accessible to a formalist analysis, or whether it emerges only in a hermeneutic analysis, in which a rebellious reader supplies the irony that the text resists. In practice, though not in intention, sentimental texts usually contain ironic elements, and ironic texts retain sentimental, utopian elements. But these complicating elements are not conscious ones. I have tended to classify Shelley's poem as sentimental because its irony is not internalized within the poem, through a narrator who takes a consciously ironic attitude toward a visionary protagonist. In this it differs from a predominantly ironic poem such as Keats's *Isabella*, where the narrator attempts to see through his deluded protagonist. On the other hand, *Alastor* is somewhat more complicated than the normal sentimental text, because the inclusion of a preface raises the possibility of an author who is different from the narrator within the poem. As suggested, the preface induces in the reader a higher degree of self-consciousness about the process of interpretation, and perhaps invites us to resist the text because it does not completely complement the text. On the other hand it must be added that while the formal existence of a preface distances us from the text, the tone of the preface is probably more sentimental than ironic.

# Notes on Authors

IsOBEL ARMSTRONG is Professor of English Literature at Birkbeck College, University of London. Among her publications are *Language as Living Form in Nineteenth-Century Poetry* (1982) and (ed.) *New Feminist Discourses: Critical Essays on Theories and Texts* (1992).

STEPHEN C. BEHRENDT is Professor of English at the University of Nebraska. Among his publications are (ed.) *Percy Bysshe Shelley, Zastrozzi and St. Irvyne* (1985), *Shelley and His Audiences* (1989) and *Reading William Blake* (1992).

TIMOTHY CLARK is a lecturer in English at the University of Durham. He is the author of *Embodying Revolution: The Figure of the Poet in Shelley* (1989) and *Derrida, Heidegger, Blanchot: Sources of Derrida's Notion and Practice of Literature* (1992).

KELVIN EVEREST is Professor of English at the University of Liverpool. He is the author of *Coleridge's Secret Ministry: The Context of the Conversation Poems* (1979) and *English Romantic Poetry: An Introduction to the Historical Context and the Literary Scene* (1990), and the editor of *Shelley Revalued: Essays from the Gregynog Conference* (1983) and (with Geoffrey Matthews) of *The Poems of Shelley, vol. 1, 1804–1817* (1989).

FRANCES FERGUSON teaches at the Johns Hopkins University. She is the author of *Wordsworth: Language as Counter-Spirit* (1977).

JERROLD E. HOGLE is Professor of English at the University of Arizona, and the author of *Shelley's Process: Radical Transference and the Development of His Major Works* (1988).

WILLIAM KEACH teaches at Brown University; he is the author of *Shelley's Style* (1984).

J. HILLIS MILLER teaches at the University of California at Irvine. Among his publications are *The Disappearance of God: Five Nineteenth-Century Writers* (1963), *Fiction and Repetition* (1982), *The Linguistic Moment: From Wordsworth to Stevens* (1985), and *The Ethics of Reading* (1986).

TILOTTAMA RAJAN is Professor in the Department of English and the Centre for the Study of Criticism and Theory at the University of Western Ontario. She is the author of *Dark Interpreter: The Discourse of Romanticism* (1980) and *The Supplement of Reading: Figures of Understanding in Romantic Literature and Theory* (1990).

PETER SACKS teaches at the Johns Hopkins University. He is the author of *The English Elegy: Studies in the Genre from Spenser to Yeats* (1985).

STUART M. SPERRY is Professor of English at Indiana University, and the author of

*Keats the Poet* (1973) and *Shelley's Major Verse: The Narrative and Dramatic Poetry* (1988).

RONALD TETREAULT teaches at Dalhousie University. He is the author of *The Poetry of Life: Shelley and Literary Form* (1987).

WILLIAM A. ULMER is Associate Professor of English at the University of Alabama. He is the author of *Shelleyan Eros: The Rhetoric of Romantic Love* (1990).

# Further Reading

## Texts of Shelley's Work

The state of Shelley's texts is so fluid, complex and interesting at present (with various major editions appearing or about to appear) that it has implications for *any* criticism of Shelley's poetry and prose. Hence I list some editions of which readers should be aware.

CAMERON, KENNETH NEILL and REIMAN, DONALD H. (eds), *Shelley and his Circle 1773–1822*. Vols I–IV, ed. Kenneth Neill Cameron (Cambridge, Mass. and London, 1961–70); vols V–VIII, ed. Donald H. Reiman (Cambridge, Mass: Harvard University Press, 1973–86). (Four further volumes are projected. Rich in contextual information and judgements.)

CHERNAIK, JUDITH, *The Lyrics of Shelley* (Cleveland and London: The Press of Case Western Reserve University, 1972). (Reliable texts and good commentary.)

HUTCHINSON, THOMAS (ed.), MATTHEWS, G.M. (corr.), *Shelley: Poetical Works* (London: Oxford University Press, 1970). (Useful one-volume edition, but textually faulty.)

JONES, FREDERICK L. (ed.), *The Letters of Percy Bysshe Shelley* (2 vols, Oxford: Clarendon Press, 1964).

MATTHEWS, GEOFFREY and EVEREST, KELVIN (eds), *The Poems of Shelley* (London and New York: Longman). Volume One (1804–17) has appeared so far (in 1989); two further volumes are projected.

MURRAY, E.B. and WEBB, TIMOTHY (eds), *The Prose Works of Percy Bysshe Shelley*. The first volume of this major edition has recently appeared, edited by E.B. Murray (Oxford: Clarendon Press, 1992).

REIMAN, DONALD H. and POWERS, SHARON B. (eds), *Shelley's Poetry and Prose* (New York and London: Norton, 1977).

REIMAN, DONALD H. (general ed.), *The Bodleian Shelley Manuscripts* (23 vols planned; New York and London: Garland, 1986– ). See also the companion series from Garland, *Manuscripts of the Younger Romantics* (8 vols devoted to Shelley), general ed. Donald H. Reiman. (These two ventures not only provide readers of Shelley's work with essential materials, but could also be the focus of future debates about whether Shelley's poems have stabilised meanings.)

DONALD H. REIMAN and NEIL FRAISTAT are contracted by Johns Hopkins

University Press to edit *The Complete Poetry of Percy Bysshe Shelley* in four
volumes; the first volume is scheduled to appear soon.

WEBB, TIMOTHY (ed.), *Percy Bysshe Shelley: Selected Poems* (London: Dent, 1977).


## New Criticism and formalism

CRONIN, RICHARD, *Shelley's Poetic Thoughts* (London and Basingstoke: Macmillan,
1981). (Subtle interpretations of a range of poems, especially good on language
and structure; discussed in Introduction.)

KEACH, WILLIAM, *Shelley's Style* (New York and London: Methuen, 1984).
(Excerpted in this volume and discussed in Introduction.)

LEAVIS, F.R. *Revaluation: Tradition and Development in English Poetry* (First published
1936; Harmondsworth: Penguin, 1972). (Discussed in Introduction.)

LEIGHTON, ANGELA, *Shelley and the Sublime: An Interpretation of the Major Poems*
(Cambridge: Cambridge University Press, 1984). (Studies Shelley's handling of
the sublime; crosses acute formalist analysis with lightly worn deconstructive
preoccupations.)

O'NEILL, MICHAEL, *The Human Mind's Imaginings: Conflict and Achievement in
Shelley's Poetry* (Oxford: Clarendon Press, 1989). (Seeks to describe and evaluate
Shelley's 'achievement' in a range of poems.)

SWINDEN, PATRICK (ed.), *Shelley: Shorter Poems and Lyrics*, A Casebook (London
and Basingstoke: Macmillan, 1976). (See excerpts from Eliot, Tate, Pottle, all
discussed in Introduction, and others.)


## Beyond New Criticism

ARMSTRONG, ISOBEL, *Language as Living Form in Nineteenth-Century Poetry* (Brighton,
Sussex: Harvester Press; Totowa, New Jersey: Barnes and Noble, 1982).
(Excerpted in this volume and discussed in Introduction.)

BLOOM, HAROLD, *Shelley's Mythmaking* (First published 1959; Ithaca: Cornell
University Press, 1969). (Discussed in Introduction.)

WASSERMEN, EARL R., *The Subtler Language: Critical Readings of Neoclassic and
Romantic Poems* (First published 1959; Baltimore: The Johns Hopkins Press, 1968
paper). (Discussed in Introduction.)

—*Shelley: A Critical Reading* (Baltimore and London: The Johns Hopkins University
Press, 1971). (A major study that stresses Shelley's 'intellectual system' but is
alive to his scepticism; discussed in Introduction.)


## Ideology, history, politics, contexts

ABRAMS, M.H., *Natural Supernaturalism: Tradition and Revolution in Romantic
Literature* (New York and London: Norton, 1971). (Discussed in Introduction.)

BUTLER, MARILYN, *Romantics, Rebels and Reactionaries: English Literature and its Background 1760–1830* (Oxford: Oxford University Press, 1981). (Discussed in Introduction.)

CLARK, TIMOTHY, *Embodying Revolution: The Figure of the Poet in Shelley* (Oxford: Clarendon Press, 1989). (Excerpted in this volume and discussed in Introduction.)

CURRAN, STUART, *Shelley's Annus Mirabilis: The Maturing of an Epic Vision* (San Marino, California: Huntington Library, 1975).

DAWSON, P.M.S., *The Unacknowledged Legislator: Shelley and Politics* (Oxford: Clarendon Press, 1980). (Very useful account of Shelley's political ideas.)

EVEREST, KELVIN, 'Shelley's Doubles: An Approach to *Julian and Maddalo*', in *Shelley Revalued: Essays from the Gregynog Conference*, ed. Kelvin Everest (Leicester: Leicester University Press, 1983). (Excerpted in this volume and discussed in Introduction.)

FRAISTAT, NEIL, *The Poem and the Book: Interpreting Collections of Romantic Poetry* (Chapel Hill and London: The University of North Carolina Press, 1985). (Contains a fine chapter on the interrelations between the poems in the *Prometheus Unbound* volume.)

HOAGWOOD, TERENCE ALLAN, *Skepticism and Ideology: Shelley's Political Prose and Its Philosophical Context from Bacon to Marx* (Iowa City: University of Iowa Press, 1988). (Focuses on prose, and sees Shelley as reaching outward 'toward engagement as well as inward toward reflexivity', p. xix.)

KIPPERMAN, MARK, 'History and Ideality: The Politics of Shelley's *Hellas*', *Studies in Romanticism*, vol. 30 (1991): 147-68. (Seeks to embed the poem's idealism 'within its historical horizons' without wishing to condemn it as 'escapist', p. 150.)

LEVINSON, MARJORIE, *The Romantic Fragment Poem: A Critique of a Form* (Chapel Hill and London: The University of North Carolina Press, 1986). (Discussed in Introduction.)

McGANN, JEROME J., *The Romantic Ideology: A Critical Investigation* (Chicago and London: The University of Chicago Press, 1983). (Contentious and influential; discussed in Introduction.)

O'NEILL, MICHAEL, *Percy Bysshe Shelley: A Literary Life* (Basingstoke and London: Macmillan, 1989). (Discusses Shelley's literary career; suitable for undergraduates.)

QUINT, DAVID, 'Representation and Ideology in *The Triumph of Life*', *Studies in English Literature*, vol. 18 (1978): 639–57. (Reads the poem as treating the 'deformation' of 'imaginative experience into ideology', p. 639; though aware of deconstruction, a corrective to deconstruction's sometimes ahistorical bias.)

REIMAN, DONALD H., 'Shelley as Agrarian Reactionary', *Keats–Shelley Memorial Bulletin*, vol. XXX (1979): 5–15.

—*Percy Bysshe Shelley: Updated Edition* (Boston: G.K. Hall, 1990). (Updated version of Reiman's 1969 book; incisive and well-informed.)

SCRIVENER, MICHAEL HENRY, *Radical Shelley: The Philosophical Anarchism and Utopian Thought of Percy Bysshe Shelley* (Princeton: Princeton University Press, 1982).

WEBB, TIMOTHY, *Shelley: A Voice Not Understood* (Manchester: Manchester University Press, 1977). (A distinguished account of Shelley's thought and art, at home with the poetry's wide-ranging allusions, whether to Pindar, Humphry Davy or the Bible.)

## Deconstruction/post-structuralism

ARAC, JONATHAN, 'Shelley, Deconstruction, History', in *Critical Genealogies: Historical Situations for Postmodern Literary Studies* (New York: Columbia University Press, 1987), pp. 97–113.

DE MAN, PAUL, 'Shelley Disfigured', in Harold Bloom and others, *Deconstruction and Criticism* (London and Henley: Routledge & Kegan Paul, 1979), pp. 39–73. (*The* deconstructive account of *The Triumph of Life*; discussed in Introduction.)

FERGUSON, FRANCES, 'Shelley's *Mont Blanc*: What the Mountain Said', in *Romanticism and Language*, ed. Arden Reed (London: Methuen, 1984), pp. 202–14. (Reprinted in this volume and discussed in Introduction.)

HOGLE, JERROLD E., *Shelley's Process: Radical Transference and the Development of His Major Works* (New York and Oxford: Oxford University Press, 1988). (Excerpted in this volume and discussed in Introduction.)

MILLER, J. HILLIS, 'The Critic as Host', in *Deconstruction and Criticism*, pp. 217–53.

—*The Linguistic Moment: From Wordsworth to Stevens* (Princeton, New Jersey: Princeton University Press, 1985). (Excerpted in this volume and discussed in Introduction.)

RAJAN, TILOTTAMA, *Dark Interpreter: The Discourse of Romanticism* (Ithaca and London: Cornell University Press, 1980). (Excerpted in this volume and discussed in Introduction.)

—'Displacing Post-Structuralism: Romantic Studies after Paul de Man', *Studies in Romanticism*, vol. 24 (1985): 451–74.

TETREAULT, RONALD, *The Poetry of Life: Shelley and Literary Form* (Toronto: University of Toronto Press, 1987). (Excerpted in this volume and discussed in Introduction.)

ULMER, WILLIAM A. *Shelleyan Eros: The Rhetoric of Romantic Love* (Princeton, New Jersey: Princeton University Press, 1990). (Excerpted in this volume and discussed in Introduction.)

## Psychoanalysis

CALDWELL, RICHARD S., ' "The Sensitive Plant" as Original Fantasy', *Studies in Romanticism*, vol. 15 (1976): 221–52. (Lucid psychoanalytical study that reads the poem as 'a fantasy of origins, i.e., the origin of desire and of the subject as a result of desire', p. 227.)

GALLANT, CHRISTINE, *Shelley's Ambivalence* (Basingstoke and London: Macmillan, 1989). (Discussed in Introduction.)

SACKS, PETER, 'Last Clouds: A Reading of "Adonais"', *Studies in Romanticism*, vol. 23 (1984): 379–400. (Excerpted in this volume and discussed in Introduction.)

SPERRY, STUART M., *Shelley's Major Verse: The Narrative and Dramatic Poetry* (Cambridge, Mass. and London: Harvard University Press, 1988). (Excerpted in this volume and discussed in Introduction.)

WALDOFF, LEON, 'The Father–Son Conflict in *Prometheus Unbound*: The Psychology of a Vision', *Psychoanalytic Review*, vol. 62 (1975): 79–96.

## Reader-based criticism

BEHRENDT, STEPHEN C., *Shelley and His Audiences* (Lincoln and London: University of Nebraska Press, 1989). (Excerpted in this volume and discussed in Introduction.)

RAJAN, TILOTTAMA, *The Supplement of Reading: Figures of Understanding in Romantic Theory and Practice* (Ithaca and London: Cornell University Press, 1990). (Negotiates a space for itself between deconstruction and reader-response criticism; good but intricate. Discussed in Introduction.)

ROSS, MARLON B., 'Shelley's Wayward Dream-Poem: The Apprehending Reader in *Prometheus Unbound*', *Keats–Shelley Journal*, vol. 36 (1987): 110–33. (Fine reading of the poem as evoking and involving its audience's 'capacity for communal dreaming', p. 112.)

## Influence/intertextuality

BLANK, G. KIM, *Wordsworth's Influence on Shelley: A Study of Poetic Authority* (London: Macmillan, 1988). (Concentrates on what Shelley's response to and reworking of Wordsworth reveals about the younger poet's 'creative reflexiveness', p. x.)

BLOOM HAROLD, *A Map of Misreading* (Oxford: Oxford University Press, 1975).

—*Poetry and Repression: Revisionism from Blake to Stevens* (New Haven: Yale University Press, 1976). (Discusses Shelley's *Triumph of Life* in relation to Wordsworth's 'Ode: Intimations of Immortality', reading figures of speech as though they were expressions of a text's psychic defences. Touched on in Introduction.)

## Feminism

BROWN, NATHANIEL, *Sexuality and Feminism in Shelley* (Cambridge, Mass.: Harvard University Press, 1979). (Makes out a case for Shelley as 'seminal' (p. 3) for the development of feminist and androgynous ideals.)

GELPI, BARBARA CHARLESWORTH, *Shelley's Goddess: Maternity, Language, Subjectivity* (New York: Oxford University Press, 1992).

WOODMAN, ROSS, 'The Androgyne in *Prometheus Unbound*', *Studies in Romanticism*, vol. 20 (1981): 225–47.

See also books, listed elswhere, by Hogle and Ulmer (in whose work – in different ways – feminism meets post-structuralism) and by Sperry.

## Collections of essays

ALLOTT, MIRIAM (ed.), *Essays on Shelley* (Liverpool: Liverpool University Press, 1982).

BLANK. G. KIM (ed.), *The New Shelley: Later Twentieth-Century Views* (Basingstoke and London: Macmillan, 1991). (An important collection, 'our own scene of critical practice' (p. 11) well to the fore.)

EVEREST, KELVIN (ed.), *Shelley Revalued: Essays from the Gregynog Conference* (Leicester: Leicester University Press, 1983).

—(ed.), *Essays and Studies*, vol. 45 (1992). (This volume is devoted to essays on Shelley's poetry.)

HALL, SPENCER (ed.), *Approaches to Teaching Shelley's Poetry* (New York: The Modern Language Association of America, 1990). Stimulating short essays by many critics, most of which address issues raised by contemporary theory.

See also a forthcoming Special Issue of the *Durham University Journal*, guest-edited by MICHAEL O'NEILL, which will contain articles and review-articles on Shelley and Shelley studies.

# Index